Real Estate Exchange
and Acquisition Techniques
Second Edition

William T. Tappan, Jr.

PRENTICE HALL
Englewood Cliffs, New Jersey 07632

Prentice-Hall International (UK) Limited, *London*
Prentice-Hall of Australia Pty. Limited, *Sydney*
Prentice-Hall Canada, Inc., *Toronto*
Prentice-Hall Hispanoamericana, S.A., *Mexico*
Prentice-Hall of India Private Limited, *New Delhi*
Prentice-Hall of Japan, Inc., *Tokyo*
Simon & Schuster Asia Pte. Ltd., *Singapore*
Editora Prentice-Hall do Brasil, Ltda., *Rio de Janeiro*

10 9 8 7 6 5 4 3 2 1

Library of Congress Cataloging in Publication Data

Tappan, William T.
    Real estate exchange and acquisition techniques.

    Bibliography: p.
    Includes index.
    1. Real property, Exchange of--United States.
I. Title.
HD1395.T36   333.3'33   77-25395

        ISBN 0-13-762642-8

        ISBN 0-13-762618-5 PBK

PRENTICE HALL
BUSINESS & PROFESSIONAL DIVISION
A division of Simon & Schuster
Englewood Cliffs, New Jersey 07632

Printed in the United States of America

PENDING CHANGES IN THE LAW

As we go to press, there are three changes under consideration which will affect the exchange of real estate. It is possible that these changes will be enacted into law.

Consequently, it is essential for anyone who is planning an exchange to be alert to the effect of these proposed modifications in the law. These potential changes again illustrate the importance of using a qualified attorney to structure your exchange. As currently proposed the changes will "apply to transfers after July 10, 1989 (other than transfers pursuant to a written binding contract in effect on that date)."

The law changes under consideration would:

1. Replace the like kind requirement with the "similar or related in service or use" requirement applied in cases of a condemnation of real estate under section 1033. (See Rev. Rul. 68-394 for the current relationship between section 1031 and 1033—section 1031 now is used to define like kind for purposes of section 1033.) Also, the exchange of foreign real estate for U.S. real estate would be eliminated (declared not "similar in use").
2. Restrict the basis shifting techniques between related parties as defined for purposes of section 267. When a property is acquired by exchange with a related party (as defined by section 267) and disposed of within two years, the original exchange would not qualify under section 1031 except in cases of death or involuntary conversion of the property. (See Rev. Rul. 72-15 for the current application of section 267 to exchanges under section 1031.)
3. Require that the property transferred and received in an exchange be held for one year prior to and one year after the transfer.

The most far reaching of these proposals relates to the restriction of the like kind requirement. Of course we must wait for the final law, if it is passed, to see the specific effect on the exchange of real estate. Nevertheless, as proposed the change would prevent the exchange of real property for real property unless it is "similar or related in service of use."

Under current application of the similar use requirement this implies that you could not exchange improved real estate for vacant land and, therefore, by logical extension much of the flexibility of the nontaxable exchange would be restricted. (See Regulation section 1.1033(a)(2)(A); *Lakritz v. U.S.*, 418 F.Supp. 210; Rev. Rul. 76-84 for current application of "similar use.")

Also see *Liant Records, Inc.*, 303 F.2d 326, for types of similarities and *Capitol Motor Cab Co.*, 314 F.2d 469, where a building leased to a paint shop was replaced by a motel.

Be advised that these proposed changes would apply to transactions "after July 10, 1989 (other than transfers pursuant to a written binding contract in effect on that date)."

In Memory of
Gary Butler

ABOUT THE AUTHOR

William T. Tappan, Jr. is a Realtor specializing in commercial and investment real estate. He has served as a Director of the Albuquerque Board of Realtors and as Chairman of that Board's Exchange Division. He has taught a course on "Real Estate for the Investor" at the University of New Mexico and has conducted numerous in-depth seminars on real estate exchanging.

Foreword

Since the late 1950's, tax-deferred exchanging of real property has become increasingly synonymous with creative real estate brokerage. Nowhere, in my opinion, will the real estate licensee find an area of activity that will provide him or her with a greater sense of satisfaction and accomplishment over a job well done. Nowhere in real estate is the continued relevance of the licensee more assured.

Yet, while the interest of both the licensee and the property owner in tax-deferred exchanges has uninterruptedly increased with each passing year, the availability of good, *understandable* source material about the subject has simply not kept pace. Until now, the communication of this material has been accomplished primarily through seminars at which it is "passed on" in a way reminiscent of that by which folklore was transmitted to future generations before the advent of the printing press.

William Tappan's book changes all of that. We now at last have a single, comprehensive, authoritative reference to which we can resort, a book that combines the practical and the technical aspects of the subject in such a way as to make it a remarkably readable source of knowledge and authority. It will no doubt provide the needed springboard for an acceleration in the popularity and employment of tax-deferred exchanges as a key tool in the preservation of capital appreciation of real property, and will provide the wellspring of information necessary to improve the quality of the state of the art. I have no doubt that Mr. Tappan's book will soon become, and long remain, the "bible" of the industry, and I welcome its appearance on the scene.

Marvin B. Starr, Esq.

Foreword

Ignorance of the law is no excuse. It's also not a good idea. Especially for real estate investors who can pay tens of thousands of dollars in unnecessary taxes . . . or more . . . if they don't know exchange law.

Bill Tappan knows the law of tax-free exchanges. And when you finish this book, you will, too. As a result, you'll be better able to take advantage of the exchange provisions of the Internal Revenue Code, better able to find a tax advisor who really knows exchanges, and better able to work with that advisor.

As far as I know, Bill is the first author who put legal citations and brief descriptions of court decisions, regulations, and rulings in a book for laymen. Hooray for him. By doing that, he demystified the law . . . a critical prerequisite to taking advantage of it. The citations also greatly help the accountants and attorneys whose clients expect them to understand what they read in various tax books.

Virtually all other tax books for laymen treat legal citations as something beyond our poor ability to uderstand . . . something we shouldn't bother our pretty little heads about. Bill Tappan does not engage in that sort of patronizing and his readers and their advisors are better for it.

Depending on your situation, this book can save you tens of thousands, hundreds of thousands, or even millions of tax dollars. By that standard, its price represents one of the greatest bargains of all time.

Read it. Study it. Follow it. And get a competent accountant or attorney to help you when you exchange. I am confident that you will find that this book was one of the best "investments" you ever made in your real estate investment career.

John T. Reed
Editor, "Real Estate Investor's Monthly"
Danville, CA

What This Book Will Do
for You

This book has one purpose—to help you make money. Real estate exchanging has too long been an area of mystery for most of the people actively involved in real estate practice and investment. Often misunderstood and viewed as overly complicated, exchanging has not received the recognition it deserves among the techniques of applied real estate. This has been true over the years except in certain geographic areas in which local brokers have spread the word through exchange clubs and private seminars. Even in these instances, however, understanding and acceptance have depended on word-of-mouth and personal contact.

Although this knowledge has been limited to relatively few people, it has contributed toward defining the important areas that constitute real estate exchanging. These are:

1. The specific tax benefits of applying Section 1031 of the Internal Revenue Code to real estate.

2. The use of acquisition, financing and negotiation techniques to overcome the inevitable barriers that are part of all real estate transactions.

3. The legal foundation of exchanging, which contains a wealth of opportunities hidden in legal cases and revenue rulings.

This book brings together these three areas in one comprehensive volume designed for continued daily use.

Part I deals exclusively with the detailed mechanics of applying the nontaxable exchange, including everything you need to know to take an idea, get it to a legally binding agreement and close it safely and profitably. Emphasis throughout this section has been placed on use of techniques in actual practice. Part I also presents a complete explanation of the tax treatment of exchanging contained in the Internal Revenue Regulations. This is a process that can be applied in your planning with surprising ease. Forms designed specifically for this book reduce often confusing tax calculation to simple routine. Blank forms for your use are in Appendix B.

Chapter 1 covers the many opportunities for exchanging. Chapters 2 and 3 present the mechanics of structuring two-party, multiparty and multiple exchanges. Chapter 4 covers the tax aspects of exchanging, and Chapters 5 and 6 present the agreements needed to legally bind an exchange. Chapters 7 and 8 cover listing property for exchange and the mechanics of closing various types of exchanges. Chapters 9, 10, 11, 12 and 13 contain techniques for structuring profitable exchanges.

Few real estate transactions close without problems along the way, and exchanging is no exception. The techniques that are discussed in Part II are essential to the practical demands of holding an exchange together. But they are each self-contained, money-making methods as well. These techniques have been organized into categories according to application. Included are methods of acquiring real estate without cash, financing techniques and negotiation methods that are not commonly known but have often made the difference between a successful closing and a wasted effort.

Part III is a summary presentation of the case law and revenue rulings concerning exchanging, which are an important part of the authority for many of the techniques of exchanging. When read in full, they are a source of ideas and opportunity as well as dangers to avoid. The legal foundation is important to proper application of exchanging. Without a solid basis that conforms to accepted legal practice, any real estate transaction can lead to failure. In exchanging, a lack of legal knowledge can also lead to unexpected tax liability—a concern that has diminished as the broad application of Section 1031 to real estate has been more widely understood.

Chapters 12 and 13 have been added to cover the detailed application of the two most widely used methods of applying the multiparty exchange. Chapter 12 provides the agreements and procedural sequence for converting a written offer from a sale and purchase to a nontaxable exchange. It is well-established that a purchase and sale agreement can be amended to provide for a Section 1031 exchange. Chapter 12 shows you exactly how to do it.

Chapter 13 presents the procedure for completing a delayed exchange under the 45-day designation and 180 days to close provision of revised Section 1031 of the Internal Revenue Code. Complete agreements and escrow instructions are included as guidelines, as well as an explanation of the procedure allowing you to take a delayed exchange from start to finish.

In addition, Part II has been expanded as Chapters 14 through 20, providing a more complete explanation of the acquisition techniques that are so much a part of the world of exchanging.

Chapter 14, How to Use Cycles in a Real Estate Acquisition Strategy, adds a new dimension, which may help put the tumultuous real estate market of the last ten years in perspective. Real estate experienced a great inflation during the late seventies and into the early eighties, forming what now appears to be a major speculative market top.

As we complete the 1980s, real estate seems to be undergoing a failing struggle to maintain values that at best were overdone in many regions of the country. The gradual debt liquidation that this process requires is now rapidly changing public perception of real estate from a foolproof investment, which it isn't, into the management-intensive reality that it is.

The expansion of the acquisition techniques in Part Two is provided for those who want more of an explanation than appeared in the first edition. It is hoped that they will be of help to you in one book for reference in your continuing efforts to put deals together.

The new exchange cases since publication of the first edition have been added to Part Three. Summaries of these new legal cases are presented with citations for those who would like to read further and review the full texts.

Appendix A contains the new Section 1031 of the Internal Revenue Code of 1986. This is where you will find the changes that established the time limits on a delayed exchange. It is also where you will find the new exclusion of partnership interests from the provisions of Section 1031.

Appendix C has been added to provide the tax forms for reporting an exchange to the Internal Revenue Service. As with the blank forms, in Appendix B they are provided for your convenience.

The numerical notations appearing throughout the text refer to the bibliography. They are presented so that you can go directly to the source material for further reading if you wish.

The use of the masculine and feminine pronouns "he" and "she" that appear in this work are used to ease the flow of the text and without intent to offend either the male or female reader.

Case examples have been used extensively in an attempt to clearly illustrate the techniques and benefits involved in each type of transaction. Many of the examples have been adapted from exchanges, which were simplified to emphasize a certain point. They are merely examples offered as guides. Any resemblance to actual transactions and people is unintentional and entirely coincidental. The purpose of these examples is to help you by illustrating structures you can generalize to your own situation.

The objective of each part of this book is to provide "dirt on the boots" value in the form of techniques that you can include as part of your general real estate knowledge and apply with results measurable by money in your pocket.

Introduction

Applying the Nontaxable Exchange
in Light of Recent Tax Law Changes

The nontaxable exchange of real estate under Section 1031 of the Internal Revenue Code is probably the last great tax deferral and estate building technique still available to small investors and businesses. It allows you to preserve your estate and keeps capital in the private sector, preventing its loss through taxation. This technique continues to survive the unpredictability of our tax laws. In fact, exchanging has been strengthened.

The Tax Reform Act of 1984 (TRA '84) limited the time that can pass between conveyance of property by the taxpayer and receipt of replacement property. With this change Congress ushered the standard multiparty exchange into legislated law, removing the last vestige of objection that could possibly be raised to this well-established tax-saving technique.

The Two Basic Structures of a Multiparty Exchange

The multiparty exchange under the provisions of Section 1031 of the Internal Revenue Code is a pragmatic application of tax law that grew out of the business demands of the marketplace. For example, you want to exchange in order to avoid a large tax liability, but you realize that it's unreasonable to expect to find property you want that is owned by someone who coincidently wants to own your property.

Obviously, coming to this realization can stop an exchange cold for those unaware of the multiparty structure and its numerous variations. In fact, this objection is often the knee-jerk dismissal voiced by many old-timers in real estate at the mention of an exchange. One exception is the western ranch broker who has been putting "trades" together for years as a matter of everyday business.

Fortunately, the multiparty exchange solves the problem of finding property you want that just happens to be owned by someone who wants your property.

There are two standard ways to structure a multiparty exchange. Each grew out of the requirements imposed on the abstract tax law by the concrete realities of getting the job done in normal business practice.

The first alternative is for use when someone wants to buy your property, but you have not yet located property you would like to receive in exchange. You enter into an agreement that obligates the buyer to purchase property and exchange it for your property.

The second alternative is for use when you have located the exchange property you want but the owner does not want your property. You enter into an agreement that obligates the owner to accept your property in exchange, contingent on its sale out of escrow.

In the first alternative, you have a buyer and must find the exchange property. In the second alternative, you have the exchange property and must find a buyer.

The Requirements of a Section 1031 Exchange

The requirements of Section 1031 of the Internal Revenue Code are simple. You must receive property in exchange for the property you transfer in an interdependent transaction. You *cannot* sell your property and reinvest the proceeds.

The property you transfer and the property you receive must be held for use in trade or business or for investment. This requirement determines whether the property "qualifies." For example, property held for sale and your personal residence do not qualify, but land held for investment and income property do.

Also, the property you receive must be the same "kind" as the property you transfer. This is the *like-kind* requirement, which is broadly interpreted to refer to the distinction between real and personal property. For example, the full bundle of fee rights as determined by state law are viewed under Section 1031 as like-kind property. Consequently, all real property, such as apartments, offices, shopping centers, land, mineral rights, water rights, and leasehold interests with 30 years or more to run, can be exchanged with each other under Section 1031.

Furthermore, an exchange can be partially taxable to the extent that you realize gain and receive boot, but still qualify under Section 1031.

Surprises to Watch Out for in a Multiparty Exchange

As is true in many areas of tax law, the unexpected can become routine without careful planning. Here are some dangers to watch out for when structuring a multiparty real estate exchange:

(1) The actual or constructive (contractual) right to receive the cash used to purchase exchange property will trigger recognition of gain;

(2) Sale of the property received in the exchange without first holding it for use in trade or business or for investment will disqualify the exchange;

(3) Taxable boot in the form of liability relief is treated the same as receipt of cash;

(4) Recapture of depreciation is triggered by an exchange and is treated as ordinary income (this will increase your tax liability if ordinary income rates are higher than capital gain rates at the time you complete the transaction);

(5) Receipt or transfer of property that is excluded from nontaxable treatment (stocks, bonds, notes, real estate contracts, and partnership interests) is treated the same as receiving cash, or a sale for cash.

The Changes Imposed by the New Tax Laws

The Tax Reform Acts of 1984 and 1986 and The Revenue Act of 1987 are the latest in a long line of politically inspired attempts to control an increasingly out-of-control problem—insufficient income to pay the national debt. Defining the problem is itself part of the problem, but the political nature of the attempt is not hard to see. Just look at the titles of the early tax legislation of the 1980s: Economic Recovery Act of 1981; The Tax Equity and Fiscal Responsibility Act of 1982; The Tax Reform Act of 1984; The Tax Reform Act of 1986.

Congress is big on "tax reform" and seems oblivious to the logical implication inherent in the need to constantly reform our tax laws: The previous tax legislation passed by the same Congress is now in need of reform because it is corrupt or at best, no doubt, a mistake.

Each new tax law seems to be more complex and far-reaching in its impact—a fact that is in sharp contrast to the political rhetoric embodied in the titles.

It is especially important to note that the Tax Reform Act of 1986 had a major impact on real estate. It "reformed" the beneficial depreciation guidelines passed by the Economic Recovery Act of 1981 at a time when many segments of the real estate market were overbuilt, triggering a major cyclical contraction (see Chapter 14).

Now we are anticipating significant tax legislation every year. The Revenue Act of 1987 has now been followed by new legislation. Early in the morning of its last day the 100th Congress hurriedly passed a 3-foot stack of paper that started out as the Technical Corrections Act, but was euphemistically renamed the Miscellaneous Revenue Act (MRA) of 1988. Apparently, the word miscellaneous is intended to play down the significance of this very lengthy bill.

The message of this continuing comedy is clear. Stick to the economics of specific real estate deals—the ancillary tax benefits are as fickle as the politicians who control them.

Through all of this tax upheaval, the basic structure and requirements of the multiparty exchange have remained unchanged. In fact, they have been affirmed. But, TRA '84 did put to rest two issues that have been a source of conflict with the IRS.

First, the time between disposition and receipt of exchange property is now limited. An exchange must be completed within 180 days from transfer of the taxpayer's property, but not later than the due date, including extensions, of the taxpayer's return. In other words, if the tax return due date plus extensions is fewer than 180 days from the transfer of the taxpayer's property, that's the date by which the taxpayer must receive exchange property.

Furthermore, the property to be received must be designated within 45 days of the transfer of the taxpayer's property. Prior to TRA '84 no time limit was stated for the period between disposition and receipt of property in a Section 1031 exchange.

Second, partnership interests are now clearly excluded from nontaxable treatment under Section 1031. The exchange of partnership interests was an area of considerable debate and conflict in case law prior to TRA '84, but now it is settled.

The Subtle Trap of TRA '84

The important thing to remember is that TRA '84 changed nothing in the procedural requirement for making a nontaxable exchange: You must receive qualifying "like kind" property in exchange for qualifying like kind property without the actual or contractual right to the cash used to acquire the exchange property.

If you sell your property and put the money in a regular escrow account and subsequently purchase property, you will not meet the test of a nontaxable exchange. Properly written and executed exchange agreements and escrow instructions are essential to avoiding this trap. These agreements must legally restrict your right to receive the cash used to purchase exchange property.

The time limit placed on receipt of exchange property does not mean that the requirements of 1031 have been relaxed. The money designated for purchase of exchange property cannot be placed in an unrestricted escrow account until you find suitable exchange property. You must still be contractually limited from access to the funds used to purchase exchange property.

Consequently, the exchange agreement for a transaction involving a delay between transfer and receipt of property should be carefully drafted by a competent tax lawyer to avoid constructive receipt of the money used to purchase exchange property.

Points to Keep in Mind
When Reading
Real Estate Exchange and Acquisition Techniques

Obviously, any book that even remotely touches on tax matters is subject to the winds of change. Fortunately, though, the changes in federal tax law during the past few years have strengthened Section 1031 and consequently affirmed the content of *Real Estate Exchange and Acquisition Techniques*. The exclusion of partnership interests from Section 1031 and the time limit established between the transfer and receipt of property by the taxpayer are the only two direct changes.

The tax calculations which appear in certain parts of the book are intended to clarify the benefits of exchanging and are not intended to explain the current method of computing capital gains tax. They are examples of *how* you benefit by exchanging. These tax calculations are not explanations of tax law. Their use in illustrations is necessitated by the indirect effect on the benefits of an exchange and the tax liability you would incur by not making an exchange.

The taxation of real estate is historically the plaything of government and tends to change somewhat every year or two on the average. For example, there have been five useful life designations for depreciation of real estate since 1980—the old method we started the decade with, then down to 15 years in 1981 and up to 18 years in 1984. In September of 1985 Congress reached a compromise on imputed interest rules, and as part of the deal raised the useful life of real estate to 19 years. The Tax Reform Act of 1986 established the cost recovery system, setting the useful life for residential property at $27\frac{1}{2}$ years and $31\frac{1}{2}$ for nonresidential property, giving us five depreciation schedules in about five years.

Those attempts to raise revenue that are enacted and reversed from time to time do not directly affect Section 1031. But, they do have an indirect effect on the primary benefit of exchanging (the lower your basis, the more money you save by exchanging) and therefore have an impact on the intensity of desire to complete an exchange—the larger the tax liability, the greater the motivation to complete a nontaxable exchange.

As with the adjusted basis, capital gain liability and depreciation schedule, the overall tax impact of a specific transaction is an individual calculation that is best arrived at with the help of your accountant under the tax laws that happen to be in effect at the time you make an exchange.

William T. Tappan, Jr.

Acknowledgments

There are many persons who contributed in significant and varied ways to this book.

Realtor Michael C. Haley, J.D., C.C.I.M. read the first draft as well as the entire final manuscript and contributed many helpful suggestions which were incorporated in the organization and content of the finished work. His support and encouragement through the years had a direct effect on completion of this volume.

John S. Campbell, J.D., L.L.M. (in Taxation) served as a legal sounding board and devil's advocate as my understanding of exchanging and the underlying tax principles were put in writing. His counsel has always been a constructive force in getting transactions through closing. He was also most generous in contributing many of the sample multiparty exchange agreements and related documents that appear in the book.

Realtor G. Thomas Harris III, J.D., L.L.M. (in Taxation), C.C.I.M. was virtually a partner in structuring the Tax Treatment and Basis Computation forms that we designed especially for this book. His help with the tax calculations and concepts was an invaluable contribution. He is also directly responsible for several of the techniques discussed in Part II.

Realtor Chase Magnuson, C.C.I.M. was a great help to me in the market place, contributing his accomplished skill in putting together exchanges that would baffle most people. His friendship and encouragement during the years this book was in preparation provided support that only one who has been through the mill can understand.

Professor Albert Utton of the University of New Mexico Law School actually launched this book. He generously supplied me with copies of the case law and revenue rulings which formed the basis of my GRI exchange seminar many years ago. It was his timely help that made me realize the need for the current volume.

George Pulakos, C.P.A. was most helpful in his review of the initial draft and keeping me up to date on new developments in the tax law. His sardonic criticism helped keep the details in perspective.

Realtor James O'Leary provided many constructive suggestions after reading the first draft. His broad view was an encouragement to expand the coverage to include everything that needed to be said.

Marvin Starr, who graciously consented to write the foreword, was himself the original source of many of the concepts that have furthered the general understanding of exchanging. It is his insight that contributed the pot theory, the two part test of a multiparty exchange and much more. His enthusiastic counsel helped solidify my understanding of exchanging and get me through some rather difficult transactions.

P. C. Templeton, Mary Trujillo and Betty Murphy of First American Title Company provided the efficient help I needed to get the deals closed. Their contributions to Chapter 8 are greatly appreciated.

Lesley Williams, Cindy Yonushonis, Harriett North and Sandy Zimmerman were energetic typists during the several rough drafts and preparatory research. Their encouragement helped the book stay in motion more than once.

I would like to express my deep gratitude to Pauline Blossom, who edited and typed every word of the final manuscript. Her cheerful and steady work contributed to the completion of what sometimes seemed like a never-ending project.

Finally, I would like to thank four people who in their own unique ways made a significant contribution to the work that resulted in a second edition of this book:

Steven T. Erickson, CPA of Albuquerque, was most helpful in working with clients. His clear and authoritative explanations of the more obscure details of exchange accounting are appreciated.

John T. Reed of Danville, California has been instrumental in keeping me informed of the latest developments in real estate tax law and exchanging through the years. His intelligent perspective has been refreshing as well as helpful.

Ramon Sanchez of Albuquerque Title Co. has provided continued professional support in closings, and always with a smile.

And, in closing, I again would like to especially thank attorney John S. Campbell of Albuquerque for his efficient and speedy help in closing the exchanges and providing the documents that made this second edition possible.

William T. Tappan, Jr.

The following organizations kindly granted permission for reproduction of their preprinted forms:

Arizona Association of Real Estate Exchangors; "Agreement for the Exchange of Property" approved by Arizona Association of Real Estate Exchangors

California Association of Realtors; "Exchange Agreement" copyright 1972 by California Association of Realtors

Colorado Real Estate Commission; "Contract to Exchange Real Estate" approved by the Colorado Real Estate Commission

Professional Publishing Corporation; "Exchange Agreement" and "Exclusive Authorization to Exchange" copyright 1968 and 1969 by Professional Publishing Corporation

TABLE OF CONTENTS

FOREWORDS... v, vi

WHAT THIS BOOK WILL DO FOR YOU vii

INTRODUCTION xi

PART I—REAL ESTATE EXCHANGE TECHNIQUES

**1. Profitable Opportunities for the Nontaxable Real
Estate Exchange 3**

Conserve Equity Profit by Requiring an Exchange (3)
Fear of an Exchange Is Not a Valid Reason to Sell (4)
Exchanging Must Be a Mutual Effort (5)
Benefits of the Nontaxable Exchange (6)
Using the Nontaxable Exchange to Preserve Equity (7)
Sound Economics Sometimes Require an Exchange (8)
The Logic of Nontaxable Exchange (9)
General Requirements of Section 1031 of the Internal Revenue
Code (10)
Exchange Property Must Be "Held for Productive Use in Trade or Business or for Investment" (10)
The "Held Primarily for Sale" Trap (12)
Only "Property of Like Kind" Can Be Exchanged Tax-Free (12)
Boot Is the Opposite of Like Kind Property (13)
Structuring a Completely Tax-Free Exchange (13)
Exchanging Is an Opportunity to Improve Most Real Estate Transactions (15)

2. How to Apply the Two-Party Exchange 17

Considerations for a Complete Definition of Exchange Value (18)
Transaction Models for Two-Party Exchanges (18)
A Two-Party Exchange with Free and Clear Property of Equal
Value (19)

An Exchange with Unequal Values Balanced with Boot (20)
Pyramiding into a Higher Value and Loan (20)
Flexibility Can Help Balance Unequal Equities (21)
Balancing Equities in Multiple Asset Exchanges Involving Two
Parties (22)
Exchanging Multiple Parcels of Real Estate in One Transaction (24)
The Key to Exchanging: Restructuring Circumstances (25)
Refinancing a Two-Party Exchange Through Escrow (26)
Hidden Opportunities for Two-Way Exchanges (27)

3. Multiparty Exchanges Increase Transactions..................... **29**

The Two Standard Methods of Structuring a Multiparty Exchange (29)
Foundation Principles of the Multiparty Exchange (30)
To Understand the Multiparty Exchange, Look at It from the Taxpayer's
Point of View (31)
Structuring an Exchange When There's a Buyer for the Taxpayer's
Property (32)
Solving the Problems of Offers and Counters in a Multiparty Ex-
change (32)
Transferring Title in a Multiparty Exchange (33)
The Taxpayer Must Avoid the Right to Receive Cash (33)
Balancing Equities in a Multiparty Exchange (34)
How to Avoid Liability in a Multiparty Exchange (36)
The Taxpayer Can Qualify for Assumption and Receive Title Insurance
Without Reference to the Buyer (36)
Refinancing Property in a Multiparty Exchange (37)
Refinancing to Balance Equities (37)
Using the Multiparty Exchange to Arrange a Purchase Out of
Escrow (39)
Structuring Multiple Exchanges (41)
The CBA Multiple Exchange (42)
Using Refinancing to Balance Equities in a Multiple Exchange (42)
Applying the Essentials of the Nontaxable Exchange (45)

4. Calculating Tax Treatment Under Section 1031 .... **47**

Consistent Terminology Is a Must for Accurate Communication (47)
Applying Tax Concepts in an Exchange (48)
Computing Recognized Gain When Cash Is Received (51)
Calculating Recognized Gain When Boot Property Is Received (51)
Determining Basis Allocation (54)
Calculating Tax Treatment When There Is a Loss on the Boot Property
Transferred (54)
How Computing Tax Treatment in Advance Can Prevent Unexpected
Relief from Liabilities (57)

Liabilities Received Offset Liabilities Transferred (57)
The Benefits of Offsetting Go Beyond Loan Relief (59)
Determining the Basis of Property Acquired by Exchange (59)
Calculating Tax Treatment in a Multiparty Exchange (62)
Avoiding Recapture in an Exchange (65)
The Holding Period Stays with the Taxpayer (68)
The Tax Treatment of Brokerage Fees and Commissions in an Exchange (68)
How Transaction Costs Affect an Exchange (69)
Avoiding Hidden Disqualification Traps (69)
Tax Calculations Should Be Used as a Method of Maximizing
Benefits (71)

5. How to Write Two-Party and Multiple Exchange Agreements ... 73

Exchange Agreements Can Be Very Flexible (73)
Define the Exchange with a Written Agreement (74)
Three Primary Purposes of the Exchange Agreement (74)
What Counts Is What Actually Happened Not What Was Intended (74)
A Sale Can Be Viewed as an Exchange (75)
Writing a Two-Way Exchange Agreement (75)
Model General Phrases for Use in Exchange Agreements (76)
How to Change a Purchase Offer to an Exchange Agreement (76)
How to Make an Exchange More Attractive to a Purchaser by Including
an Obligation to Sell (79)
Writing an Offer to Exchange with a Cash Take-Out (82)
How to Tie Two-Party Exchanges into One Multiple Transaction
Escrow (82)
Map an Exchange by Using the Owners' Names (85)
Flexibility Is the Key to Successful Exchanging (97)

**6. Writing Multiparty Agreements That Will Make the
Exchange Work 99**

A Multiparty Agreement Should Conform to the Facts of the Transaction (99)
Adapting Multiparty Exchange Agreements to the Circumstances of the
Transaction (100)
Writing a Standard Multiparty Exchange Agreement (101)
How to Modify an Exchange Agreement So the Taxpayer Can Act as
Agent for the Buyer (103)
Using an Option to Tie Up the Exchange Property (104)
Using an Agent Other than the Taxpayer to Acquire Exchange
Property (104)
Designating the Exchange Property and Writing the Offer (106)

How to Provide for a Sale if Exchange Property Is Not Located (106)
Extending an Exchange Agreement (108)
Writing a Multiparty Exchange Agreement That Combines Three Alternatives in One Document and the Contingency of Refinance (109)

7. How to Write Listing and Commission Agreements That Will Protect You in an Exchange **113**

Guidelines to Getting Paid (114)
Writing an Exchange Listing Agreement (114)
Model Preprinted Listing Agreement (116)
Using a Fee Instead of a Percentage Commission (116)
Splitting Fees Between Brokers (119)

8. The Mechanics of Closing an Exchange **123**

Closing a Two-Party Exchange (124)
Closing Statements Account for Values and Costs (124)
Closing a Multiple Exchange (125)
Documenting a Multiparty Exchange Closing (125)
Closing an Exchange from the Title Company's Point of View (133)

9. How to Use the Nontaxable Exchange to Improve Investment Performance **139**

Exchanges Designed to Preserve Equity from Tax (140)
Exchanging to Increase Return on Equity (143)
Exchanging to Solve Problems and Secure Benefits That Go Beyond Tax and Business Considerations (147)
A Combination of Acquisition Techniques Is Often What Makes an Exchange Work (151)

10. Using Formulas to Make Exchanges Work **153**

Saving the Exchange with a Note Takeout (153)
Eliminating Mortgage Relief by Paying Down the Loan (154)
Offsetting Mortgage Relief with Boot (154)
Eliminating Mortgage Relief by Increasing the Loan on the Acquired Property (155)
Balancing Equities with Like Kind Property (156)
Offsetting Negative Cash Flow in an Exchange (156)
The Real Estate Owned Exchange (157)
Exchange with a Buy-Back Option (158)
Exchange Leaseback (158)
Making Free and Clear Land Easier to Exchange (159)
BLM and Forest Service Exchanges (159)

General Services Administration Exchange (160)
Flight Capital Exchange (160)
Eliminating Recapture in an Exchange (160)
Converting an Exchange to a Sale (161)

11. Advanced Exchange Techniques **163**

Formulating the Multiparty Exchange (163)
The Mineral Rights Exchange (164)
The Nontaxable Exchange of Water Rights (165)
The Exchange of Leasehold Interests (165)
Saving a Two-Way Exchange by Creating a Multiple Exchange (166)
The Equal Partnership Exchange (166)
The Exchange of Partial Interests (167)
The Business Exchange (167)
Exchanging Property You Don't Own (168)
Acquiring Exchange Property by Loan (169)
Using a Lease to Provide Possession Before Closing an Exchange (169)
Building a Building Solely for Exchange (170)

12. How to Change a Sale into a Multiparty Exchange **171**

How to Make the Transition from a Purchase to an Exchange (171)
A Simple Purchase Agreement Addendum That Protects an Exchange (172)
A Longer-Form Addendum for Converting a Purchase to an Exchange (173)
Protecting the Right to Assign the Purchase Agreement (174)
Documenting the Assignment of the Purchase Agreement (175)
Converting a Sale to an Exchange Is a Step-by-Step Process (175)
Guideline Escrow Instructions for Converting a Sale to an Exchange (176)
The Buyer Has No Liability When Cooperating in an Exchange (178)

13. Documenting and Closing a Delayed Exchange **179**

The Subtle Trap of the New Delayed Exchange Guidelines (179)
Applying the New Guidelines for a Delayed Exchange (180)
How to Establish the Structure for a Delayed Exchange (180)
Documenting a Delayed Exchange (181)
How to Set Up an Escrow to Protect a Delayed Exchange (183)
Designating the Exchange Property (185)
Notifying the Escrow Agent of the Designated Property (186)
Acquiring Exchange Property in a Delayed Exchange (187)
The Essential Documents of a Delayed Exchange (189)
How to Amend a Purchase Offer to Establish a Delayed Exchange (189)

How to Apply the Reverse Delayed Exchange (191)
How to Overcome the Problems of a Reverse Delayed Exchange (191)

PART II—REAL ESTATE ACQUISITION TECHNIQUES

14. How to Use Cycles in a Real Estate Acquisition Strategy........ 197

The Great Inflation Cycle of the 1970s (198)
The Role of Debt Expansion in the Real Estate Cycle (198)
The Great Debt Liquidation of the 1980s (199)
The Impact of Economic Cycles on Real Estate (200)
Four Ways to Make the Most of Economic Cycles (201)
How Investor Expectations Affect Real Estate Activity (201)
How to Recognize and Profit from Speculative Patterns (201)
How to Time Acquisitions to Take Advantage of Real Estate Cycles (202)

15. Techniques for Acquiring Real Estate Without Cash............. 205

Mortgage Out (205)
Refinance with the Seller Carrying Back a Second (206)
Create Paper (207)
Refinance Your Home (207)
Professional Services as Down Payment (208)
Effort Equity (208)
Borrow Against Paper (209)
Seller Pays Buyer (209)
Acquire with Future Profits (210)
Acquire with Closing Credits (210)
Assign the Rents (211)
Acquire with a Repair Partnership (211)
The Note Partnership (212)
Advertise for a Private Loan (212)
Commission as Down Payment (213)
Credit Union Loan (213)
Real Estate Equity as Down Payment (214)
Family Loan (214)
Acquisition with Soft Paper (215)
Acquire with a First and Second—Then Sell the First for Cash (215)
Collateral Security Agreement (216)
Borrow Against Your Trust (216)
Land Sale Lease-Back (217)
The Lease Down Payment (217)
The Installment Down Payment (217)

Assume the Mortgage—Seller Keeps the Land (218)
The Executive Incentive Plan (218)
The 100 Percent Solution (219)
The Performance Second (219)
Broker as Lender (220)
The Hidden Co-Signer (220)
The Insurance Policy Loan (220)
Issue Stock (221)
Trade Stock at Purchase Price (221)
Signature Loan (221)
Employer Advance (221)
Credit for Services Certificate (221)
Secured Corporate Note (222)
Multiple Notes—One Mortgage (222)
Pledge Future Income as Down Payment (222)

16. Institutional Financing Techniques **223**

Wraparound Mortgage (224)
Open End Mortgage (224)
Sale Buy-Back (224)
Equity-Kicker (225)
R.E.O. as Incentive to Finance (225)
Certificate of Deposit Delivery (225)
Collateral Assignment (226)
Negative Pledge (226)
Letter of Credit (226)
Compensating Balances (227)
Advance Payments Deposit (227)
Have Seller Move His Account to Your Bank (228)
Savings Account Transfer (228)
Blanket Mortgage (228)
Participation (229)
Employer Influence (229)
Joint Venture (229)
Long-Term Amortization—Halfway Due Date (230)
You Buy Our Stock—We'll Make Your Loan (230)
Standby Commitment (230)
Three Years with a Balloon (231)
Less than Five Years Secured (230)
18 Months Unsecured (231)
The Bridge Loan (232)
Finance Company Second (232)
Commitment Letter (232)

17. Private Financing and Negotiation Techniques **233**

Builder's Bailout (233)
Overpay (234)
Contingent Price Sale (234)
Private Wraparound (235)
Seller as Short-Term Lender (235)
Vary the Loan Payments Based on Occupancy (235)
Improvement Costs as Return of Down Payment (236)
Moratorium on Debt Service (236)
Automatic Discount (236)
Interest Only Until the First is Paid (237)
Balloon Payments (237)
Sell with Option to Buy Back (238)
Reduce the Interest but Increase the Constant (238)
Reduce the Constant but Increase the Interest (239)
Sale Lease-back (239)
Add the Interest to Principal (239)
Three-Year Interest Only Balloon (240)
Subordination to Construction Financing (240)
Subordination for Cash (240)
Purchase Money Mortgage (241)
Real Estate Contract (241)
Second Mortgage or Second Trust Deed (242)
Pledge, Collaterize, or Hypothecate (242)
Private Insurance Annuity (242)
Purchase a Remainder Interest (243)
Walk the Mortgage (243)
Reversing the Interest (244)
This Year's Interest as Down Payment (244)
The Bargain Sale (244)
Diamonds Pledge or Cutting the Down Payment in Half (245)
Lower the Interest and Increase the Price (245)
Reduce the Price and Pay Points (246)
Management Fee for Specific Services (246)
Acquiring Property from a Real Estate Corporation (246)
Applying the Multiparty Exchange as an Acquisition Technique (247)

18. Using a Lease to Acquire and Finance Real Estate **249**

Bond Lease (249)
Lease-Condo (250)
Sandwich Lease (250)
Master Lease as Security for Development (251)
Management Leaseback (251)

Lease Back the Vacancies (252)
Lease Cash-out (252)
Land Sale Lease-back for Development (252)
Package the Leases and Sell Out (253)
Lease When You Can't Buy (253)
Lender Land Lease (254)
Leased Land Pyramid (254)
Sale Lease-back as an Investment Opportunity (254)
Sell at a Loss and Lease the Land (255)
Using a Lease to Gain Possession Before Closing (255)

19. Acquisition with Options **257**

Interest Option (258)
Effort Option (258)
Letter of Credit Option (258)
An Automatic Rolling Option with First Right of Refusal (259)
Continuing Option (259)
Increased Payment Option (259)
Land Cost Option (260)
Real Estate as Option Consideration (260)

20. Acquisition Techniques for Special Deals **261**

Pledge Additional Real Estate as Security (261)
Financing Company Second (261)
Discount Buy-Back: For When You Need Cash Immediately (262)
Protect Level of Rental Income by Decreasing the Interest Rate as Vacancies Occur (262)
Lower Risk and Increase Profits by Subordinating Debt Service to Cash Flow (262)
When Money Is a Problem, Buy with Paper but Cash Out the Seller (262)
Make an Installment Purchase (262)
Minimize Your Risk by Making Price Contingent on Resale (263)
Protect Your Partnership Investment with a Buy-Sell Agreement (263)
When You're Uncertain, Set Up a Buy-Back Agreement (263)
Avoid Foreclosure by Entering into a Joint Venture with Notes (263)
Obtain a Discount in Exchange for a Large Cash Payment (263)
What to Do When a Note Is Due and There Is No Cash (263)
Maximize Leverage with Subordination to Construction Financing (264)
Reduce the Down Payment with a Broker Loan (264)
Refinance Property During Acquisition by Substituting Collateral While Preserving Installment Reporting (264)
Use an Inheritance Pledge to Facilitate Acquisition (264)

Use an Irrevocable Trust as Security (264)
Put Off Making Large Payments by Reversing the Interest (264)
When Mortgage Rate Is Too High, Escrow the Down Payment and Lease
the Property (265)
Protect Your Investment with a Noncompetition Agreement (265)
Use Anxious Seller as Co-signor (265)
Lower the Loan Amount by Increasing the Interest (265)
Buy Paper at a Discount and Trade at Face Value (265)
Assign the Payments—Don't Trade the Paper (266)
Always Try for a Release Clause to Lower Your Risk (266)

PART III—THE CASE LAW AND REVENUE RULINGS OF EXCHANGING

Recent Case Law (269)
Foundation Cases in Exchange Law (273)
Business and Partnership Interests in Nontaxable Exchanges (274)
Cases in Which the IRS Argued for an Exchange (274)
The Foundation of Multiparty Exchanging (275)
Successful Variations on Multiparty Exchanges (275)
Multiparty Exchanges That Failed (276)
Revenue Rulings (277)

APPENDIX A—INTERNAL REVENUE CODE, SECTION 1031 .... **283**

APPENDIX B—SAMPLE FORMS **287**

APPENDIX C—IRS FORMS FOR REPORTING AN EXCHANGE **293**

BIBLIOGRAPHY **297**

INDEX **299**

I

REAL ESTATE
EXCHANGE TECHNIQUES

1

Profitable Opportunities
for the Nontaxable
Real Estate Exchange

The nontaxable real estate exchange provides a variety of profitable opportunities that are not available through an ordinary sale and purchase. In fact, the dollar value gained in a nontaxable exchange makes it the only intelligent business action in many situations.

An investor who owned one acre of commercial land had this point emphasized to him. He purchased the land for $500, and during the 15 years of his ownership it had appreciated to $85,000. A development company wanted the acre and offered to purchase it for cash. Unfortunately, if he sold the land for cash, $24,575 in capital gains tax would be due based on the tax rates in effect at the time. The investor had planned to purchase an apartment complex with the proceeds of the land sale before he discovered the tax due. A sale would leave only $60,425 for the apartment complex down payment—and $80,000 was required. As if saving over $24,000 wasn't reason enough, it was absolutely essential to the acquisition of the apartment complex that a nontaxable exchange be structured.

Conserve Equity Profit by Requiring an Exchange

The investor had no choice. He had to exchange the acre for the apartments. Even though the apartment owner didn't want the land, the solution was still simple.

The development company agreed to purchase the apartment complex and exchange it for the acre. Instead of $85,000 in cash, the investor received $80,000 in apartment equity and $5,000 in cash. The development company received the land, and the apartment owner received an $80,000 down payment. The exchange saved the investor thousands

3

of dollars in equity appreciation and made it possible for him to acquire the apartments. Here's what would have happened in a sale:

Sale Analysis

Price	$85,000
Basis	– 500
Gain	$84,500

First $50,000 at 25% = Tax of $12,500
Balance of $34,500 at 35% =

Tax of......................................	12,075
Total Tax	$24,575

By requiring an exchange, the investor saved $24,575 of his $85,000 equity. This represented 29% of the total property value, which was, in effect, a significant part of his acquisition (purchasing) power. The land equity of $85,000 was virtually a perfect balance for the apartment down payment.

Exchange Analysis

	Land		Apartments
Value	$85,000	Value	$320,000
Loans	–0–	Loans	240,000
Equity	$85,000	Equity	$ 80,000

The $5,000 in equity difference was paid to the investor by the development company as boot. The investor then paid a commission of $5,000, which offset the boot and resulted in no tax due whatsoever. (55)

Fear of an Exchange Is Not a Valid Reason to Sell

Unfortunately, the benefits of a nontaxable exchange have all too often been bypassed due to fear that the procedures are too complicated or that the danger of "being taken" is too great. Fortunately, neither fear is justified.

The requirements of Section 1031 of the Internal Revenue Code are, in most applications, clearly defined and easy to meet. Furthermore, the rules relating to value which underlie any business transaction apply equally to property in an exchange. There is not one price for a sale and a higher price for an exchange. Fair market value is the same figure in a sale and in an exchange.

For example, in the following exchange, which again required the acquisition of property to exchange, each step was planned, agreed to in writing, and carried out in sequence.

Rapid Development Corp. wanted to purchase the Butler Farm for subdivision. Butler homesteaded the farm years ago and as a result had a very low basis. He wanted to retire and planned to purchase income-producing property with the proceeds of the farm sale. Although Butler was suspicious of exchanging—having been prejudiced by horse trades through the years—when he understood the tax savings and the sequence of steps, he was convinced that an exchange was the only way to go. In fact, the end result of the exchange was the same as his original objective, without the tax consequences.

To meet Butler's objective, Rapid Development purchased the Golf Shopping Center and exchanged it at fair market value for the farm. The exchange value of the shopping center was the same as the purchase price, and the steps of the exchange were clearly defined, as follows:

Step One: Rapid Development entered into an agreement with Butler that obligated Rapid to purchase property designated by Butler and exchange it for the farm. The value of the farm was established at $975,000 in the agreement.

Step Two: Butler located (through his broker) and designated (by letter to Rapid) the Golf Shopping Center, valued at $1,250,000.

Step Three: Rapid signed an agreement to purchase the Golf Shopping Center for $975,000, subject to a note and first mortgage of $275,000.

Step Four: At closing, Butler conveyed the farm to Rapid and received the Shopping Center, subject to the existing mortgage of $275,000.

This is how the equities balanced:

	Butler Farm	Golf Shopping Center
Market Value	$975,000	$1,250,000
Loans	–0–	275,000
Equity	$975,000	$ 975,000

Both Butler and Rapid received equity based on the actual market value of the property conveyed. Neither value was increased or decreased because the transaction was an exchange. Property in an exchange should always be valued in accordance with real market demand; that is, the fair market value of the property exchanged.

Exchanging Must Be a Mutual Effort

The process of exchanging real estate is often complicated and demanding. Consequently, all participants must work together toward the same end. The more complicated the exchange is, the more important it is that each participant contribute his efforts in a constructive direction, toward solving the inevitable problems that must be overcome before the exchange will close.

The following participants must combine their efforts for an exchange to succeed:

1. *The Exchangor*: The real estate broker or salesman who puts the transaction together and holds it together until it's closed. The exchangor is a catalyst who makes the elements of a transaction fit together and produce an exchange.

2. *The Taxpayer*: The investor or business who owns the property to be exchanged and wants a nontaxable transaction. Although "taxpayer" in this context may seem to be somewhat of a misnomer, it clearly describes what you would pay without the opportunity to exchange. The taxpayer is sometimes referred to as the exchanger.

3. *The Buyer*: A participant who has cash to acquire property for exchange purposes or to purchase property out of escrow; the party who will ultimately acquire the taxpayer's property.

4. *The Seller*: The party who owns the exchange property that the taxpayer will receive as the net result of a multiparty exchange.

5. *The Service Group*: The escrow or title company, lawyer and accountant who help the exchangor and the taxpayer meet the objectives of the exchange and close it in a way that protects the tax benefits.

No exchange would be possible without the cooperative effort of all participants. The unexpected complexities that occur in any real estate transaction are often magnified in an exchange. The difficulty many people have in conceptualizing the mechanics and, furthermore, understanding the tax aspects, contribute to this problem.

Consequently, it is essential that all participants pull together toward the ultimate objective of closing the exchange. The benefits of a successful exchange are in most cases too significant for one participant to stand in the way. The nontaxable exchange is a unique opportunity. By using it properly, you can meet any number of specific investment and business objectives.

Benefits of the Nontaxable Exchange

Exchanges are equally important for the Realtor who wants to create business and for the taxpayer who wants maximum investment or business performance. By taking advantage of the exchange, you can:

1. Conserve equity by not paying tax on realized gain.

2. Increase depreciable basis by acquiring property encumbered with a larger debt.

3. Acquire sheltered income by exchanging unimproved land for improved rental property.

4. Reallocate basis by acquiring property with a higher building-to-land ratio.

5. Acquire property without cash by structuring a transaction requiring only property and notes to balance values.

6. Increase sheltered income by acquiring property with a shorter economic life, allowing more rapid depreciation.

7. Increase sheltered income by exchanging for new property that qualifies for first-user depreciation (depending on the tax laws in effect at the time).

8. Receive nontaxable cash by exchanging for mortgageable property, which is then refinanced after, and independently of, the exchange.

9. Acquire property that is appreciating faster than the property transferred.

10. Increase net cash flow and equity build-up by acquiring property with a lower debt service payment and interest rate.

11. Consolidate assets by exchanging many properties for one equal to their combined values.

12. Pyramid holdings by exchanging up, acquiring properties with larger total value by using the profit realized through appreciation and loan amortization as nontaxable acquisition power.

13. Relocate or expand business facilities or investment holdings to a different geographic area without depleting the equity by paying tax.

14. Conserve an individual's estate by exchanging throughout life without loss of appreciated value to tax.

15. Complete a transaction not otherwise possible due to the tax consequences.

16. Automatically solve the problem of where to invest profit by arranging an acquisition by exchange, rather than a one-sided sale.

17. Diversify holdings and spread of investment risk among several smaller properties.

18. Create a multiparty exchange by arranging a sale concurrently with the exchange to meet the objective of an owner desiring cash.

19. Reduce property management problems by exchanging for property that is management-free or capable of supporting professional management.

20. Increase company value due to the accounting requirement that gain realized on an exchange be reported for financial statement purposes even though it is not recognized for tax purposes.

Of course, the opportunities for profitable transactions using the nontaxable exchange vary with the circumstances involved. In fact, knowledge of the benefits can provide the initial tools to create an exchange where no transaction would otherwise have occurred.

Using the Nontaxable Exchange to Preserve Equity

Of all the objectives that can be met by using an exchange, the primary one is to preserve equity. By not losing equity as a result of the tax due on a sale, you can acquire property with a larger value and receive a return on the equity you retained. If you were planning to sell land and buy apartments, for example, it would simply make good business sense to arrange an exchange and not literally give away *your* equity (which is in fact purchasing power) by paying tax.

This reasoning was put to good use by a doctor who owned an acre of land zoned for apartments when he exchanged this property for an eight-unit complex. Had he attempted to sell the land and then buy the apartments, he would have unnecessarily lost equity to taxes, and, as a result, he would not have had enough cash left to purchase the apartments. Here's what would have happened if he sold the land:

Land Value	$50,000
Adjusted Basis	10,000
Recognized Gain	$40,000
	× 25%
Tax Payable	$10,000

	Net Cash
Land Value	$50,000
Loan Secured by the Land	25,000
Equity	$25,000
Less Tax Payable	− 10,000
Cash Remaining for Purchase	$15,000

By exchanging, the doctor was able to preserve the 40% of his land equity that he would have paid in taxes. The equity saved by exchanging provided the value ($25,000) necessary to acquire the apartments—an acquisition he would not have made if he had lost $10,000 to taxes.

In another transaction, an investor-broker was able to acquire an apartment complex by using a rental house that provided the $20,000 in equity needed to close a multiple exchange. Again, the acquisition was made possible by use of a nontaxable exchange, not only because too much equity would have been lost to taxes by a sale, but also because he had no cash or other equities with which to acquire the apartments.

This exchange opportunity occurred when a participant in the multiple exchange needed $20,000 in some form of value to balance equities. The investor-broker satisfied this requirement by exchanging the rental for a 16-unit apartment complex as part of the transaction. The rental provided the $20,000 value needed to balance equities and was ultimately taken out as partial commissions. The apartment complex was a major step up in value for the new owner—a step that he couldn't have made without the exchange.

If he had sold the rental house and used the proceeds to buy the apartments, the $20,000 in equity would decrease by the tax paid, leaving insufficient funds to acquire the apartments. For example:

Rental House Sale

Rental Value	$25,000
Adjusted Basis	− 7,000
Gain	$18,000
	× 25%
Tax Payable	$ 4,500

Equity Analysis

Rental Value	$25,000
Loan	− 5,000
Equity	$20,000
Less Tax Payable	− 4,500
Cash Remaining	$15,500

If the taxpayer had sold the house outright, over 22% of his equity would have gone to pay taxes. By exchanging, he was able to keep all of his equity and use it to acquire additional investment property—a factor made more significant when the compounding effect of the appreciation on the 16 apartments is considered. Why make a donation to the government when you can exchange tax-free?

Sound Economics Sometimes Require an Exchange

In some situations, a nontaxable exchange is the only sound business decision. This fact was illustrated when ABC Manufacturing Corporation discovered that business was expanding beyond the capacity of its present location. Since the company's primary responsibility was to maximize after-tax profit for its shareholders, an exchange was used to acquire a new location. Exchanging was the only responsible method of acquisition— a fact often overlooked by corporations and businesses in general. Here's how the values compared:

	Present Location	*New Location*
Value	$100,000	$400,000
Loans	−0−	300,000
Equity	$100,000	$100,000

If ABC Corporation had sold its present location and bought the new one, the results would not have been in the best interests of the shareholders. In fact, a sale of the old site and purchase of the new site would have added $24,000 to the cost of the transaction. One way to fully understand the advisability of exchanging is to calculate the tax payable on a sale and add it to the purchase price of the new property. Looked at in this light, the new site would cost $424,000—a considerable penalty for not structuring an exchange. Another way of looking at it is that the tax on a sale of the old location adds almost 25% to the equity requirement for acquisition of the new site; that is $24,000 in tax on the sale (based on the tax rates in effect at the time) plus $100,000 in down payment on the new location. Disposition of one property to acquire another takes on a new financial perspective when they are viewed as one transaction, as in the following example.

Present Location Sale

Tax Analysis

Value	$100,000
Adjusted Basis	− 20,000
Recognized Gain	$ 80,000
	× 30%
Approximate Tax Payable	$ 24,000

Equity Analysis

Value	$100,000
Loan	–0–
Equity	$100,000
Less Tax Payable	− 24,000
Net Cash	$ 76,000

As you can see in the above example, the greatest benefit is the percentage of equity (24%) saved by exchanging. ABC Corporation would have made a poor business decision if it had sold outright and repurchased. But by arranging an exchange, they could apply $24,000 in equity, which would have gone to taxes, to acquisition of the new location. This tax savings represents capital asset value that remained with the Company. There is no argument in favor of unnecessarily paying out capital assets in tax—this is the logic behind exchanging.

The Logic of Nontaxable Exchange

The reasoning behind the nontaxable exchange reflects the wisdom of not dissipating capital assets by paying tax when the nature of the property owned is not changed (i.e., converted to cash) but, instead, ownership is simply transferred from one asset to another of like kind. The nontaxable exchange of property used in business or held for investment is not a loophole in the tax laws. It is a method open to all taxpayers, with the objective of conserving capital assets that yield taxable earnings, profit and income-producing jobs. Its benefits are available without distinction to all investors and business, whether they are large or small.

All too often the opportunity to exchange is overlooked by both businesses and investors. Missing a chance to exchange is particularly unfortunate when you consider the benefits that go beyond the transaction at hand. The tax savings in an exchange extend throughout the entire ownership period of the acquired property. The equity that was not lost in payment of taxes remains with the investor, contributing to compounded equity appreciation.

From the standpoint of a business, increased effectiveness of after-tax dollars automatically results from an exchange. Cash that otherwise would have been paid in taxes stays with the company and contributes to the business operation. Furthermore, the profit realized by the transaction, although not taxed, is reflected in the financial statement of the company. Consequently, the capital value of the company increases by the full amount of the gain realized, which can greatly improve a company's financial picture. (see APB Opinion #29.)

General Requirements of Section 1031 of the Internal Revenue Code

Section 1031 of the Internal Revenue Code of 1986 provides an exception to the general rule requiring the recognition of gain or loss upon the sale of property. Under Section 1031, no gain or loss is recognized "if property held for productive use in trade or business or for investment is exchanged solely for property of a like kind to be held either for productive use in trade or business or for investment." This concept is the foundation of the nontaxable exchange under Section 1031. The detailed requirements that must be met to protect the tax benefits of an exchange stem from the continuing need to define and interpret a growing number of transactions that come within the provisions of Section 1031.

Exchange Property Must Be "Held for Productive Use in Trade or Business or for Investment"

The requirement that exchange property be held for productive use in trade or business or for investment refers to the use of the asset by the taxpayer and includes both the property transferred and the property acquired. They must be used by the taxpayer for business or investment purposes to qualify for nontaxable exchange under Section 1031. To illustrate this requirement, real estate can be divided into four usage categories:

1. Primary residence of the taxpayer
2. Property held primarily for sale
3. Investment property
4. Property held for productive use

Numbers 1 and 2 do not qualify under Section 1031. Numbers 3 and 4 may be exchanged and qualify in any combination—investment for investment, investment for business, business for business. The tax-free sale of a residence is permitted under the very beneficial provisions of Section 1034.

The application of this requirement was clearly defined by the Court in Regals Realty Co. v. Commissioner:

Congress . . . said, "If the property received is of a like kind, it is immaterial whether it is to be held for investment or for productive use." Under the amended provision, so long as the purpose is one or the other or both, the exchange is tax-free. But, the taxpayer must still acquire the property for investment or productive use, rather than for inventory, sale, or similar purposes. The intention to hold for a sufficient time to reduce taxes, and no longer, does not satisfy the statutory test. (34)

Generally, the distinction between investment property and productive property is the same as the distinction between holding property for the increase in incremental value (land) and holding it for the production of income (apartments). "Investment" tends to refer to passive appreciation, "productive use" refers to the generation of income as a result of active use of the property. This distinction is not crucial since both classifications refer to property that the owner intends to hold. What must be guarded against is property ownership with intent to sell. (34)

Inventory held primarily for sale (for example, a house built by a contractor or a dealer in real estate) does not qualify for nontaxable treatment under Section 1031. This prohibition often forms a trap for the taxpayer who acquires property by exchange and sells it soon after. (5) Although there are no specific time guidelines, in one case the I.R.S. stipulated that the exchange property was held for use in business even though it was sold about six months after acquisition. (8)

The other general classification of real estate that does not qualify for nontaxable exchange under Section 1031 is the taxpayer's primary residence. But there are two approaches available to achieve tax-free treatment of a residence: 1) sell or exchange it under the provisions of Section 1034 (essentially residence for residence), or 2) convert the residence to income property by renting it.

After a reasonable period of time (possibly one year), the residence may meet the requirements for nontaxable exchange for other investment or income-producing real estate. The reason this approach is sometimes safe is that the taxpayer establishes a new primary residence while converting the old to a rental.

It is the use the taxpayer establishes that determines qualification of the property for him in an exchange. This stipulation applies to both properties—the property conveyed and the property acquired. The use of the property by the prior owner is of no consequence in determining the use by the new owner.

This difference is illustrated by the investor who owned a 16-unit apartment complex, which he exchanged for a 36-unit apartment complex built for sale by a builder-dealer. The transaction qualifies as a nontaxable exchange under Section 1031 for the investor, but it does not qualify as a nontaxable exchange for the builder-dealer.

The dealer built the 36 units for sale. The investor held the 16 units for productive use. Assuming the investor holds the 36 units for productive use, the transaction will be nontaxable from his standpoint.

The requirement that property be held for productive use in trade or business or for investment applies individually and separately to the parties involved in the transaction. It is not in any way influenced by the tax status or the use the property was put to by prior owners.

An investor may complete a qualifying nontaxable exchange even though the property acquired was held for sale or was used as a primary residence by the former owner. Consequently, an exchange may be tax-free for one party and yet fully taxable for the other party.

This does not necessarily mean that a builder-dealer may not own real estate for investment or business purposes that will qualify for exchange under Section 1031. (28)

The "Held Primarily for Sale" Trap

Special note should be taken that after the exchange the acquired property must be held for use in trade or business or for investment. It must not be acquired with intent to sell.

In one case, the taxpayer entered into an agreement to exchange and signed a separate agreement to sell the property acquired in the exchange. The court held that although the properties conveyed and acquired were like kind (real estate), the taxpayer did not hold the property acquired in the exchange for productive use or investment. In fact, he sold the acquired property on the same day of the exchange.

The court stated;

> It is a fact, however, that the Missouri Farm was not to be held and could not have been held for productive use in petitioners' trade or business or by them for investment. Prior to the exchange . . . they had a binding contract and obligation . . . to sell the property . . . for $110,550 no more than eight days from their acquisition of the land, and the facts show that the sale of the Missouri Farmland was actually made on the same day that they acquired it. . . . (22)

The danger in selling property acquired by exchange without establishing its use, and therefore the qualification of the exchange, is twofold: 1) The exchange may be disallowed for the selling taxpayer (not other parties in the transaction), resulting in full recognition of all realized gain in the year the exchange occurred, and as a result, 2) the benefits of an installment sale may be lost. Fortunately, there is a way to sell property acquired through exchange without falling into a trap.

If a participant in an exchange does not want the acquired property and plans to sell and elect installment reporting, he can do so provided the sale is a contingency of closing the exchange. This approach avoids the trap by never claiming an exchange. In fact, a sale out of the exchange escrow may protect the taxpayer's installment reporting election, but a sale after the close of the exchange will not.

Only "Property of Like Kind" Can Be Exchanged Tax-Free

The second requirement to consider under Section 1031 involves the difference between real and personal property. Only property of like kind may be exchanged under Section 1031. "Like kind" simply refers to the distinction between real and personal property. Real property may be exchanged for real property, and personal property may be exchanged for personal property. That is the like kind requirement. Real estate is like (kind) other real estate. Personal property is like (kind) other personal property.

Therefore, provided that the taxpayer's property is held for productive use in trade or business or for investment:

1. Real property may be exchanged for real property (like kind).
2. Personal property may be exchanged for personal property (like kind).

The exchange of real property for personal property does not qualify under Section 1031 for nontaxable treatment.

The definition of real property is very broad in this context, yet very specific. It is specific in that all fee interests qualify where they are considered real property under state law. It is broad in that all real estate qualifies regardless of the "grade or quality."

This simply means that like kind refers to the "nature or character" of the property (realty vs. personalty), not the improvements or the name of the improvements (such as motel, apartments, office building).

In Commissioner of Internal Revenue v. Chrichton the court emphasized the broad interpretation of "like kind."

> For the regulation and the interpretation under it, leave in no doubt that no gain or loss is realized by one, other than a dealer, from an exchange of real estate for other real estate, and that the distinction intended and made by the statute is the broad one between classes and characters of properties, for instance, between real and personal property. It was not intended to draw any distinction between parcels of real property however dissimilar they may be in location, in attributes and in capacities for profitable use. (17)

The Chrichton case involved the exchange of mineral interests and improved real estate. The mineral interests were held to be like kind property because under state law they were considered real property. Consequently, the exchange fell within the provisions of Section 1031. In a subsequent revenue ruling, the IRS indicated that water rights also meet the like kind test. (42)

Boot Is the Opposite of Like Kind Property

Few exchanges are completely nontaxable for all participants. The reality of property value differences usually requires balancing of equity with boot. Boot can take several forms and, by definition, is not qualifying like kind property. For example, stocks, bonds, cash, notes or personal property received in a real estate exchange do not qualify and, as a general rule, would result in a tax liability to the extent that there is gain realized.

Boot can also be received in the form of relief from indebtedness; that is, loan relief or mortgage relief, both of which are sometimes referred to as mortgage boot. Relief from debt secured by the property transferred, whether the loan is assumed or the property is transferred subject to the loan, is treated as receipt of cash. Mortgage boot is received automatically when the loans on the property acquired in an exchange are less than the loans on the property transferred. Mortgage boot is the result of circumstances, not something paid to the taxpayer by one of the other participants in the exchange.

Boot is generally thought of as value given to entice the other party to trade. But its meaning has greater impact when it is considered in light of the tax consequences to the party who receives it. In fact, in one case two businesses were exchanged under Section 1031 and the assets were viewed in the composite as like kind property. But one participant received additional real estate, which was considered boot. (32)

Structuring a Completely Tax-Free Exchange

To structure a completely tax-free exchange you must acquire property with an equal or greater equity and larger fair market value than the property you transfer; that is, you must exchange up in value and equity. This general rule assumes that there is gain realized and implies that the taxpayer will probably pay boot and assume a larger loan. For example, Brown owns a strip retail center valued at $72,000 with a loan of $51,000. His basis is $55,000. He exchanges for Moore's apartment complex, which is valued at $120,000, subject to a first mortgage of $81,000. Moore's basis is $92,000.

Step One: Balancing Equities

	Brown	Moore
Market Value	$71,000	$120,000
Loans	−51,000	−81,000
Equity	$21,000	$ 39,000
Boot Paid	+18,000	−0−
Balance	$39,000	$ 39,000

Note: To balance equities Brown must pay Moore $18,000 in some form of value.

Step Two: Computation of Realized Gain

	Brown	Moore
Real Estate Recd.	$120,000	$ 72,000
Boot Received	−0−	18,000
Loans on Property Transferred	51,000	81,000
Total Consideration	$171,000	$171,000
Less Adjusted Basis of Prop. Transfrd.	55,000	92,000
Less Loans on Property Received	81,000	51,000
Realized Gain	$ 35,000	$ 28,000

Step Three: Computation of Recognized Gain

	Brown	Moore
Loans on Property Transferred	$51,000	$81,000
Less Loans on Property Recd.	−81,000	−51,000
Equals Mtg. Boot (Loan Relief)	$ −0−	$30,000
Plus Cash Boot Recd.	−0−	+18,000
Equals Total Boot Received	$ −0−	$48,000
Recognized Gain	$ −0−	$28,000

Note: Recognized gain (the amount that must be reported as capital gain) is either the realized gain or the boot received, whichever is the smaller amount.

Brown is not liable for tax on the exchange because he is exchanging up in value and equity. Moore is liable for the tax because he has realized gain and is receiving boot in the form of cash and loan relief.

The requirements for a completely tax-free exchange can be summarized as follows:

1. The real estate transferred and received in the exchange must be held by the taxpayer for use in trade or business or for investment.

2. The property received by the taxpayer must be like kind property, as defined under Section 1031 of the Internal Revenue Code.

3. The taxpayer must be restricted from actual or constructive receipt of boot in any form: whether cash, loan relief, other property, notes, stocks or bonds.

Exchanging Is an Opportunity to Improve Most Real Estate Transactions

The nontaxable exchange is an extremely beneficial technique for the disposition and acquisition of real estate. It is available for use in virtually every real estate transaction as an alternative to the loss of equity by payment of tax. It is so flexible and universally applicable that you can use it even though you think you've made a sale and it's too late. With proper planning you can build an exchange around almost any circumstance.

If you are planning to sell, analyze the added benefits of an exchange. There are scores of ways to structure an exchange, and one might meet your objectives better than a sale.

2

How to Apply the Two-Party
Exchange

The first step in any real estate transaction is to specify the objectives of the owner. Objectives should be stated in dollars and cents and in terms of the less easily measured personal goals of the owner. Although personal objectives are often the deciding factor, they are difficult to establish and tend to change.

The most important question to answer in setting up an exchange is: "What do you want to accomplish?" The ease and success of the transaction will depend on how specifically this question is answered and understood as the transaction evolves. The answer may simply be "to get out." Those are the easy transactions. But more often, the reason will center on a specific problem or something about the property that's not in tune with the owner's objectives. Maybe there is a management problem, low cash flow, or the property is just too far away to control. Whatever the reason, you can bet it's a good one or the owner wouldn't let go of the property.

Matching an owner who probably doesn't really want to dispose of his real estate with a buyer who wants a steal is the normal challenge of daily real estate practice— and in an exchange it is often twice the challenge. In fact, the real skill involved in exchanging is the broker's ability to work with all of the participants to structure an improved investment or business position. This requires a knowledge of the legal requirements and tax planning opportunities, as well as a sensitivity to the people involved in the transaction.

This chapter deals with economic value considerations and practical uses of the two-party nontaxable exchange. Emphasis is placed on the financial aspects of a transaction in the expectation that each reader will be able to adapt the mechanics to his own style of working with people.

Considerations for a Complete Definition of Exchange Value

The underlying requirement of any exchange is that all participants get the same in value as they give. If this rule is followed, there can and should be as many winners as there are participants.

There are several methods that can be used to balance equities in an exchange. The methods used should be selected according to their possible contribution to meeting the objectives of the parties in the transaction. When equities are balanced in a way that meets the requirements of the owners, by definition, economic feasibility has been determined. Feasibility in a practical sense is certainly not limited to balancing equities, but sound economics requires it as part of the total process of establishing that equal value was received and given.

Occasionally, exchanges are completed with unequal dollar equities. A successful transaction involving equities that are not balanced is an indication that another form of value was received that was not measurable in dollars. This type of exchange is not particularly surprising in view of the fact that, unlike those of many investment forms, the benefits of real estate ownership can go far beyond a dollar measure. In one exchange, for example, an investor accepted a property with a lower equity so he could move from Hawaii to his home town in California. He reasoned that the California property would appreciate faster, and over the years he would be ahead in equity without management problems. For him, direct control over the variables that affect the performance of his property was more important than equity balance. (The benefit of direct control possible with real estate can be appreciated by anyone who has suffered through the ups and downs of the stock market.)

Realizing the extent to which variables can be controlled is essential to understanding that structuring a transaction is a process of changing the circumstances surrounding property ownership. This controlled structuring is effective because of the large number of techniques and formulas available for use in an exchange. Techniques which can be used to customize an exchange increase the chance of success. They provide the tools for flexible action and allow you to choose and create circumstances using real estate as the supporting structure. When an awareness of alternatives is combined with a flexible attitude, real estate becomes a vehicle for moving from one position or investment circumstance to another.

Value calculation in a real estate exchange is incomplete without consideration of the improvement the transaction will make in the owner's life. No exchange can be completely analyzed out of the context of the participant's unique personal circumstances. Relying on a mathematical analysis alone is inadequate.

Transaction Models for Two-Party Exchanges

The following exchanges were chosen to illustrate the various circumstances confronting the exchangor and taxpayer. These models start with the free and clear exchange of real estate and run through the exchange of multiple assets involving two taxpayers. Emphasis is placed on the economic structure of the transactions and how two taxpayers mutually accomplished what they intended.

The first step in establishing a transaction model is to balance equities. This process is easily accomplished using the following format:

	Property	*Property*
Market Value		
Loans (−)		
Equity (=)		
Difference (+)		
Balance (=)		

Market Value = The price a willing buyer would pay in a reasonable time period.
Loans = All encumbrances on the real estate.
Equity = Market value less loans.
Difference = The amount to be paid in value to balance equities.

Use of the above model can be a great help in conceptualizing the elements of an exchange. It is especially useful when the transaction involves more than two properties.

A Two-Party Exchange with Free and Clear Property of Equal Value

Here's an example of how two owners met their objectives in a two-party exchange with free and clear property. In an unusual situation, both wanted the other's property and the market values were equal. It's an example of a straight-forward exchange of like kind property.

On March 12, 1954, Jason Kelly purchased ten acres of irrigated land. In June of 1973, he was approached by the adjoining landowner, Ben Hoover, who offered to exchange a triplex rental for the ten acres. Land near Kelly's was currently selling in the range of $3,500 per acre. The triplex was free and clear and netted $3,500 a year in income after all expenses. Kelly expressed an interest in the exchange offer because the rentals would contribute to his income—a 10% return on equity was more appealing than no income at all from the land.

The net operating income of the triplex was capitalized at 10% to establish a fair market value of $35,000. The ten acres was valued at $35,000, based on recent sales in the area.

On July 1, 1973, Jason Kelly and Ben Hoover exchanged property by warranty deed. No cash consideration was received by either party. Here's how the properties fit together.

	Kelly *10 acres*	*Hoover* *Triplex*
Market Value	$35,000	$35,000
Loans (−)	–0–	–0–
Equity (=)	$35,000	$35,000

Hoover met his objective of acquiring land adjacent to his current holdings by exchanging a triplex he had purchased in 1968 for $28,000. Kelly met a much-needed requirement for supplemental retirement income by moving from a frozen equity to an income-producing equity. There was no tax effect on either party.

Both Kelly and Hoover received only like kind property. No cash (boot) consideration changed hands. Consequently, Kelly's basis in the land moved with his change in ownership and became his basis in the triplex. And Hoover's adjusted basis in the triplex became his new basis in the land. This particular exchange was a tax-free transaction for both parties. If at some time in the future either one sold his new property, the tax treatment would be calculated based on the adjusted basis of the property at the time of the sale. Gain on a subsequent sale by either party would be computed without reference to the exchange, which was completely tax-free under the provisions of Section 1031.

An Exchange with Unequal Values Balanced with Boot

Rarely is there a situation where there are two people willing to exchange properties which coincidentally have equal values. More often, one of the participants must add value in some form to meet the requirement that all parties give the same in equity as received. The following exchange is an example of how equities were balanced with cash.

Real estate with unequal total value was exchanged by Tom Persell and Joe Ricardo, who both wanted to consolidate their respective land ownership. Here's how the transaction looked in the model:

	Ricardo	Persell
Market Value	$150,000	$100,000
Loans	–0–	–0–
Equity	150,000	100,000
Difference	–0–	50,000
Balance	$150,000	$150,000

To acquire the land he needed, Persell paid Ricardo $50,000 in cash boot. Although not routinely required, both properties were appraised for the exchange. The cash boot payment best met the objectives of both Ricardo and Persell. Ricardo needed the cash, and Persell had it. Persell wanted Ricardo's land, which was adjacent to other property Persell had developed with apartments. By exchanging the property Ricardo wanted plus cash, Persell was able to continue his rental property development.

But Ricardo was subject to partial tax because he received cash boot. This didn't bother him a bit—the cash was used to pay off an overdue loan. Furthermore, he wanted Persell's property.

Pyramiding into a Higher Value and Loan

One of the best opportunities for estate-building investors is an exchange up in value and equity. This is essentially what Persell did in the example above.

But when the advantages of leverage are added, the benefits really begin to stack up. Used as a pyramiding device, the nontaxable exchange can be a more effective estate-building technique than any other approach available to the beginning or experienced investor.

In the following example, I was able to make a major acquisition that would not have been possible without the benefits of a nontaxable exchange.

In 1968, I purchased a duplex for $11,500 and exchanged it in 1973 for a 12-unit apartment complex. The 12 units owned by Jeb Scott was valued at $140,000. Not only was I able to take advantage of the appreciation of the duplex without income tax on the transfer, I also acquired property with a much higher total value.

	Tappan Duplex	Scott 12 Units
Market Value	$19,500	$140,000
Loans	9,500	100,000
Equity	10,000	40,000
Difference	30,000	–0–
Balance	$40,000	$ 40,000

In this transaction, I balanced the equity difference of $30,000 by executing a carry-back loan secured by the 12-unit complex.

As a result of the exchange, Scott moved out of the management problem he had with the 12 units—the motivating factor for him. And I was able to gain control of a much larger asset with all the accompanying benefits of greater dollar appreciation, loan amortization, tax shelter and income. The management problem was eventually solved as demand for apartments increased over the following two years.

Flexibility Can Help Balance Unequal Equities

The key to success in an exchange is the willingness to deal with alternatives and the flexibility to accept them. There's no right way. There's no wrong way. There are only exchanges that close and exchanges that don't. A detailed consideration of alternative methods of structuring an exchange to meet an owner's objectives is essential.

In the following exchange, there is a $25,000 difference between equities. Walker owes Alexander $25,000 in some form of value.

	Alexander Apartments	Walker Offices
Market Value	$100,000	$75,000
Loans	50,000	50,000
Equity	50,000	25,000
Difference		25,000
Balance	$ 50,000	$50,000

These are some of the alternatives for balancing equities that are available to Alexander and Walker:

1. Walker could add $25,000 in cash.

2. Walker could add paper (note and mortgage, trust deed, real estate contract) of $25,000.

3. Alexander could increase the loan on his apartments by $25,000 through the bank.

4. Alexander could carry back $25,000 on a note and mortgage.
5. Walker could buy and add additional real estate worth $25,000.
6. Walker could give Alexander $25,000 in personal property.
7. A reappraisal may indicate that Alexander has valued his property too high.
8. A reappraisal may indicate that Walker valued his property too low.
9. Walker could pay down his loans by $25,000.
10. Alexander and Walker could agree to any combination of the above that was feasible and met their objectives.

Obviously, there are many alternatives available for balancing equities in a given transaction and many more yet to be discovered. The one chosen should fit the circumstances and objectives of the parties involved in the exchange. That is, if one wants cash, fine; if one wants no tax at all, fine—that can be arranged also. The important thing is that action be taken that mutually benefits all of the participants to the maximum extent. If the decision makers are flexible, there's no lack of methods.

Too many good transactions are lost because one or more of the participants said, "That won't work." And maybe more are lost when there is simply a lack of exploratory thought and problem-solving effort. There's no one answer to meeting a real estate owner's objective. In any given transaction there are probably methods that no one has thought of that would be more beneficial to the owner than what he thinks he wants to do. That is, a more nearly complete knowledge of alternatives can change the objectives—and why not? If an exchange evolves into a more beneficial transaction for the participants, all the better.

In the Alexander-Walker exchange, for example, both participants agreed that the best approach would be for Alexander to increase the amount of the loan on the apartments by $25,000. Walker then assumed the new loan.

After this restructuring, the transaction balanced:

	Alexander Apartments	Walker Offices
Market Value	$100,000	$75,000
Loans	75,000	50,000
Equity	25,000	25,000
Difference	–0–	–0–
Balance	$ 25,000	$25,000

Balancing Equities in Multiple Asset Exchanges Involving Two Parties

The importance of flexibility can be readily seen when multiple assets are transferred in a real estate exchange. This relatively complicated situation usually arises in farm or business exchanges when a substantial part of the property used in the business is not real estate.

In a multiple asset exchange, values are established for each parcel of real estate and each item of personal property. In the case of farm exchanges, the value of the real estate must be allocated between: 1) property used in trade or business or held for investment (Section 1031), and 2) principle residence (Section 1034). That is, the value of the farmer's residence must be separated from the other real estate used in the farm business. (36)

The value of personal property should be separately calculated. In fact, when both real and personal property are exchanged, it is best to view them as two transactions even though they are written on the same agreement.

In the following exchange of two farms, both owners wanted various personal property needed in the operation. In this case, it was not only a matter of balancing equities. There were actually two exchanges: one involving the farming equipment (personalty) and the other involving realty. Furthermore, the value of the real estate had to be allocated between the farmers' residences and the realty used for farming. Preliminary analysis of the real estate indicated the following:

	Richardson Farm	Clark Farm
Market Value	$800,000	$650,000
Loans	–0–	–0–
Equity	800,000	650,000
Difference	–0–	150,000
Balance	$800,000	$800,000

Clark owed the difference of $150,000 in value to Richardson. But Richardson owned milking equipment that Clark needed. And Richardson wanted mowing equipment that Clark owned. Furthermore, both farmers needed cash to pay commissions on the transaction and start-up costs on the farm operations.

Consequently, the exchange value can be added to summarize the total values involved:

	Richardson	Clark
Farm	$800,000	$650,000
Milking Equipment	50,000	
Mowing Equipment		45,000
Total	$850,000	$695,000

Clark owes Richardson a total of $155,000

The economics of the exchange require Clark to pay Richardson $155,000 in additional consideration. Clark arranged a loan on his new farm for $225,000, and the proceeds were disbursed at closing. With this, Richardson received $155,000, $40,000 went to commissions and closing costs and Clark retained $30,000 for operating capital.

Here's how the allocation between real and personal property looked from a tax standpoint:

Exchange of Realty	Clark	Richardson
Residence Value	$ 25,000	$ 40,000
Farm Value	625,000	760,000
Total	$650,000	$800,000
Diff. paid in cash by Clark:	$150,000	
Total	$800,000	$800,000
Exchange of Personalty		
Mowing Equipment	$ 45,000	
Milking Equipment		$ 50,000
Total	$ 45,000	50,000
Diff. paid in cash by Clark:	5,000	
Total	$ 50,000	$ 50,000

Clark accomplished a tax-free exchange. The farm and equipment constituted a non-taxable exchange under Section 1031. The residence exchange was tax free as provided for in Section 1034. The fact that Clark retained $30,000 in loan proceeds does not affect his tax-free treatment.

Richardson also received the benefits of a nontaxable exchange, but only partially. He was subject to capital gains tax to the extent that he received $155,000 in cash. A portion of his gain was allocated to his residence under Section 1034, and the balance was allocated to the gain on the farm property per Section 1031. (36)

Richardson paid out $60,000 in commissions and transaction costs, which in part offset the boot received. (55)

Exchanging Multiple Parcels of Real Estate in One Transaction

In exchanges involving a consolidation of properties, the exchanging parties often convey and receive several separate parcels in the same transaction. This type of two-party exchange with multiple properties can be easily organized provided values of the different properties are clearly established in the exchange agreement.

A transaction of this sort occurred when the Southeastern Investment Corporation exchanged an existing shopping center for two parcels of vacant land in two separate states.

The land was owned by a dentist named James Pargin. He had owned the two parcels for over ten years and, consequently, had a very low basis. His objective was to receive a return on appreciated land value without touching his equity or losing any portion of it in the payment of tax.

Southeastern Investment Corporation was interested only in acquiring the land for future shopping center locations. The shopping center Southeastern proposed to exchange was valued at $2,720,000 and was encumbered with a first mortgage of $1,510,000. The two parcels of land owned by Pargin were valued at one dollar per square foot. One parcel contained 10 acres; the other contained 12 acres. Both were free and clear.

	Pargin	Southeastern
Market Value (10 ac.)	$ 435,600	$2,720,000
Market Value (12 ac.)	522,720	
Loans	–0–	1,510,000
Equity	958,320	1,210,000
Difference	251,680	
Balance	$1,210,000	$1,210,000

To balance equities, the circumstances surrounding the property were restructured to provide the value due Southeastern Investment Corporation.

The Key to Exchanging: Restructuring Circumstances

The key to putting together apparently difficult transactions is the willingness to look beyond the property as it is now and take action to meet the objectives of the participants. The techniques used—and there is no shortage of techniques—are chosen by matching the taxpayer's objective with the consequences of a given action.

In the Pargin-Southeastern exchange, the objective of each taxpayer was clear. Pargin wanted to preserve the appreciation in his land and receive a cash return on his equity. To sell outright and reinvest would leave him with an unbearable (and unnecessary) tax liability. Southeastern wanted to acquire Pargin's land to build additional shopping centers and was willing to accept any gain realized as an increase in profits for the year.

With this understanding of the objectives of each taxpayer, a wraparound mortgage was arranged with a small insurance company, which provided $251,680 in cash to Southeastern and increased the loan on the center to $1,761,680, which Pargin assumed.

Southeastern obtained the loan through its sources and arranged for its transfer to Pargin at close of escrow. Here's the way the values looked after restructuring:

	Pargin	Southeastern
Market Value (10 ac.)	$435,600	$2,720,000
Market Value (12 ac.)	522,720	
Loans	–0–	1,761,680
Equity	$958,320	$ 958,320

It made no difference whatsoever that Pargin's property was located in two different states. The values were simply added, and equities were balanced by increasing the loan on the shopping center. Pargin's basis in the two parcels was added to the debt on the shopping center to establish his basis in the center.

Refinancing a Two-Party Exchange Through Escrow

In the Southeastern exchange, the loan was established by Southeastern before closing and then assumed by Pargin.

In the Leland and Johnson exchange, it was necessary to refinance Johnson's motel through escrow to balance equities.

The flexibility available in an exchange becomes apparent when it is necessary to refinance one or more of the properties in the transaction. In this particular case, Johnson was tired of running the motel and solving the daily management problems. The chance to change his ownership position to the passive responsibilities of a professionally managed office building had great appeal.

On the other hand, Leland was looking for a move up in value and welcomed a chance to try his management skills. Acquiring a motel fit the bill—especially since it was a tax-free move for him. Here's how the transaction looked initially:

	Leland Offices	Johnson Motel
Market Value	$290,000	$425,000
Loans	125,000	100,000
Equity	165,000	325,000
Difference	160,000	
Balance	$325,000	$325,000

The difference in equity values presented a real problem for Leland since he didn't have $160,000 to pay Johnson as boot.

The problem was solved by arranging for Leland to obtain a new loan on the motel in the amount of $260,000. The loan closed through escrow concurrently with the close of the exchange. Part of the proceeds paid the existing note on the motel ($100,000), and the balance went to Johnson. Consequently, Johnson received $160,000 in cash and $165,000 in equity. This is how the exchange looked *after closing*:

	Leland Motel	Johnson Offices
Market Value	$425,000	$290,000
Loans	260,000	125,000
Equity	165,000	165,000
Cash Received		160,000

Both Leland and Johnson gave and received equal value. Leland gave $165,000 in office building equity and received $165,000 in motel equity; Johnson gave $325,000 in motel equity and received $165,000 in office building equity plus $160,000 in cash from the loan proceeds on the motel, for a total of $325,000.

Leland paid no tax. He moved up in market value and debt and received no boot. Johnson was subject to tax on realized gain to the extent that he received cash.

Refinancing can be a practical approach to balancing equities. In the above example, Leland qualified for the new loan with all the accompanying liability. It would have been equally possible for Johnson to apply for the loan and for Leland to assume it at closing.

Hidden Opportunities for Two-Way Exchanges

The opportunity to participate in the benefits of a nontaxable exchange under Section 1031 is often hidden in little-known law. In fact, each year, as new cases are decided and new revenue rulings come out, the possible benefits increase.

"Real estate" has a broad meaning in many states. It often includes mineral, water, leasehold and other rights. In general, where a state law has defined a right as a real interest it will fall within the provisions of Section 1031, but usually there will be certain conditions that must be met.

In one such application, the exchange of perpetual water rights for a fee interest in land was ruled to constitute a nontaxable exchange. (42) In a similar situation, mineral rights were exchanged for improved real estate. (17)

Section 1031 was also ruled to apply when a leasehold interest in a producing oil lease extending to the exhaustion of the deposit was exchanged for the fee interest in an improved ranch. (52) It is also a little-known fact that partition proceedings fall within the nontaxable provisions. (41)

In one very important ruling, the government permitted the use of a sale and purchase agreement in a two-party exchange because state law did not allow a guardian to exchange a ward's property—the form of the agreements did not change the substance of the transaction. (45)

In a similar case, a taxpayer sold old equipment used in his business and bought new business equipment from the same dealer. The circumstances of the transaction indicated that the sale and purchase were reciprocal and mutually dependent. Consequently, it was ruled that an exchange occurred under Section 1031 even though the sale and purchase were accomplished by separately executed contracts and were treated as unrelated transactions by both parties on their books. (47)

Flexibilty in an exchange extends to the location of the properties. In one ruling, it was specifically held that location of the property was immaterial to application of Section 1031. (53)

If you are creating what to some may seem an unusual exchange, don't be surprised if it has been done before and is part of "hidden law."

3

Multiparty Exchanges
Increase Transactions

The multiparty exchange is probably the most widely used method of transferring real estate under Section 1031. The reason for this is that it offers greater flexibility and ease of application than practically any other technique for disposing of and acquiring real estate.

In this chapter, we will see how the multiparty exchange permits the taxpayer with a ready buyer to accomplish a tax-free exchange and how it allows an owner who doesn't want an exchange to participate with the taxpayer and end up with a sale. We will also cover the tax principles that underlie the methods of applying the multiparty exchange; that is, conceptualizing and structuring the transaction so that the barriers to understanding and application are easily overcome in a manner that leaves no doubt as to the protection of the taxpayer.

The Two Standard Methods of Structuring a Multiparty Exchange

There are two standard methods of structuring a nontaxable multiparty exchange under Section 1031:

1. The taxpayer and the buyer enter into an exchange agreement that obligates the buyer to purchase property designated by the taxpayer and exchange it for the taxpayer's property. (1), (7)

2. The taxpayer and the owner of the exchange property enter into an agreement to exchange properties provided that a buyer is found who will purchase the taxpayer's property (from the other property owner, not the taxpayer) out of escrow. (23), (29)

There is potential for a multiparty exchange when you have a buyer and the taxpayer doesn't want cash and when you have an offer to exchange and the owner of the other property doesn't want the taxpayer's property. Structuring an exchange under these circumstances is often easier than closing a two-way transaction. In fact, because of the preliminary documentation that legally binds the parties, a properly structured multiparty exchange is more likely to begin with a higher probability of success than many conventional attempts to sell or purchase that never progress to written agreements. For example, a multiparty exchange will often take form only after a buyer is at least verbally committed to acquire the taxpayer's property, and when the exchange agreement is signed, the buyer is legally bound—a rare event in general real estate practice. Usually there is no method of contractually binding a buyer to purchase, but it is routine in a multiparty exchange.

Foundation Principles of the Multiparty Exchange

There are two principles founded in tax law that underlie application of the multiparty exchange:

1. Exchanges are viewed as a whole and are not to be broken down into their components. (12), (30), (45), (47) "Where a series of closely related steps are taken pursuant to a plan to achieve an intended result, the transaction must be viewed as an integrated whole for tax purposes." (Redwing Carriers, Inc. v. Tomlinson, (C. A. 5) 399 F.2d 652 (22 ARTR 2d 5448))

2. In an exchange, the important thing is what actually happens (substance), not what the parties intend (form). (1), (2), (11), (45), (47) "Questions of taxation must be determined by what was actually done, rather than the declared purpose of the participants; and where applying the provisions of the sixteenth amendment and income laws enacted thereunder, we must regard matters of substance and not mere form." (Harry H. Weiss v. Louis Stearn, et al., 262 U. S. 242, T. D. 3609, C. B. III-2, 51, at 53 (1924)) "The economic substance of a transaction must govern for tax purposes rather than the time sequence or form in which such transaction is cast." (Gregory v. Helvering, 293 U. S. 465 (14 AFTR 1191))

In a multiparty exchange, the steps taken to get to a given point are considered as part of one transaction—provided they are the correct steps; the economic substance of the exchange decides its qualification—not the form the transaction followed; that is, what the participants actually did, not what they intended to do places a transaction within the provisions of Section 1031. It is a mandatory section that must apply if the facts so require. These principles and their interpretation in case law and revenue rulings have established the methods that today make the multiparty exchange one of the most practical real estate techniques available.*

The first principle is referred to legally as the *step transaction doctrine*; the second is an ongoing interpretation of whether the substance or form of an action should determine its legal consequences. Together they form a solid legal foundation for the multiparty exchange.

The step transaction doctrine applies when a binding contract requires a series of contingent steps, the net result of which places the taxpayer within certain provisions of the tax code. Form is the appearance of the transaction structure, which is usually reflected by the agreements. Substance is what actually happened to the taxpayer, usually

---

* For an excellent presentation of the Court's position see Franklin B. Biggs v. Commissioner 69TC78 (1978).

determined by viewing his rights and obligations during the transaction. Since these rights and obligations are often limited by the agreements, it is safest to make sure form and substance conform.

In application, a method of looking at the multiparty exchange has developed which brings together these two principles and combines them with exchange case law and revenue rulings to form a practical conceptual framework for understanding a multiparty exchange.

To Understand the Multiparty Exchange, Look at It from the Taxpayer's Point of View

The best way to look at a multiparty exchange is as if the agreements between the parties form a big pot. The taxpayer is allowed by the construction of the pot to put in and take out only certain things. His tax consequences are determined by what he puts in and takes out, not by what goes on in the pot. This is the essence of the two underlying principles. The taxpayer will be taxed according to what happened to him as the net result of the exchange—what he owned at the beginning and what he owned at the end "when the smoke has cleared." (15)

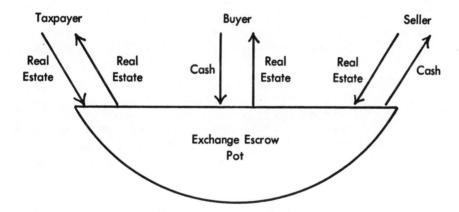

To understand the multiparty exchange, the transaction must be viewed separately for each participant. If the taxpayer puts in like kind property and receives like kind property, he has an exchange. If the buyer puts in cash and receives property, he has a purchase. If the seller puts in property and receives cash, he has a sale.

It is part of the nature of the multiparty exchange for each participant to have a different and independently calculated tax result. In the standard multiparty structure, the taxpayer has an exchange, the buyer has a purchase and the seller of the property acquired for exchange has a sale. The tax consequences are calculated separately for each participant without regard to the others. The interlocking, mutually dependent and reciprocal relation that establishes the protection of the taxpayer comes from the exchange agreement, which establishes the limits of the exchange—the pot—and not from the closing statements or the basis for calculating the tax treatment of each party.

Structuring an Exchange When There's a Buyer for the Taxpayer's Property

The vast majority of multiparty exchanges arise when a buyer wants the taxpayer's property and the taxpayer-owner is consequently faced with reasonable motivation to sell, but he is restricted by the often large tax that would be due if he did. A multiparty exchange solves the problem, but what are the steps that must be followed to guard the owner from the unknown interpretations of Section 1031?

The first requirement for completing a multiparty exchange is to fully understand the conceptual structure—how the pieces fit together and what goes in and comes out of the pot. The second is to get the game plan in writing and signed by all of the parties. The key to ease in an exchange is the way in which the agreements are written.

The exchange agreement must contain certain items which, in effect, describe the rights and obligations of the participants. The buyer agrees to purchase property, designated by the taxpayer, that has an equity value equal to that of the taxpayer's property solely for purposes of exchange and without incurring liability. A time limit is usually placed on finding suitable exchange property, after which the taxpayer must sell for cash. The agreement must clearly restrict the taxpayer's right to the cash used to purchase the exchange property—most multiparty exchange failures can be traced to constructive receipt of cash by the taxpayer because the original structure (form) was not conformed to in fact (substance). (11), (24)

There is really no use in pursuing a multiparty exchange until an agreement between the taxpayer and buyer is signed. Then the real work begins.

Sifting through available properties in an attempt to find the best possible acquisition within the time limit of the agreement, usually six months or more, is a partnership effort between the Realtor and the taxpayer. For all practical purposes, the buyer stays out of it. But if the buyer is not directly involved in the search and acquisition process, who will make offers and counteroffers on the exchange property?

Once you locate potential exchange property, as in all real estate deals, offers and counters must be negotiated in writing before a transaction is accepted and legally binding. There are several methods of accomplishing this in a multiparty exchange which can be adapted to the practical requirements of the transaction and circumstances of the participants.

Solving the Problems of Offers and Counters in a Multiparty Exchange

As any Realtor knows, unless a transaction is in writing, it doesn't exist. And even then it falls through more often than we like to think about. Consequently, for a multiparty exchange to be practical, there must be freedom to negotiate acquisition of the exchange property in writing without having to run back and forth to the buyer and his lawyer for approval and signatures. Furthermore, if the buyer lived halfway across the country or was a large corporation that makes decisions by committee, how could you ever get the job done?

There are two practical approaches to solving the problem.

1. Have the buyer appoint an agent with limited power of attorney to sign purchase agreements within the restrictions of the initial exchange agreement. In practice, the taxpayer would sign a letter designating the property and present it with a purchase agreement ready for signature to the buyer's agent. The process of countering would follow without the necessity of a new designation letter from the taxpayer.

The other method of dealing with this problem is less conservative than the first but much more practical. In the past, it was thought that the taxpayer had to "walk on eggs" to avoid possible disallowance of a multiparty exchange. The following approach reflects a more complete understanding of what the taxpayer can and can't do.

2. In this approach, the buyer and taxpayer agree in the initial agreement that the taxpayer may make offers to acquire the exchange property as agent of the buyer with the right to then assign all *rights* and *obligations* under the purchase agreement to the buyer. Consequently, the taxpayer actually signs the offers to purchase the exchange property. Written in the offer is a clause which states that he will assign the purchase agreement to the buyer for acquisition, subject to the initial exchange agreement.

The first approach is more conservative, the second more practical. As an alternative, both approaches can be used with options if the seller agrees, but this method reduces the power of negotiating with a firm offer.

As a practical matter, the cash deposit for the purchase offer is provided by reference to the buyer's cash deposit paid in escrow at the time he signed the initial exchange agreement.

The second method described above resulted from two cases. In one, the daughter of the taxpayer signed the buyer's escrow instructions (unwittingly), and in the other, the taxpayer acquired options on the exchange property and then assigned the options to the buyer. (1), (13) In any event, the way you acquire exchange property will probably be decided by weighing practical considerations against risk—a decision that should only be made with the help of informed legal counsel.

Transferring Title in a Multiparty Exchange

What if the buyer not only refuses to make offers on exchange property, but he won't even talk about going into title on a property that has a two-million-dollar debt? Good news: He doesn't have to. Keeping in mind the step transaction doctrine and the subordinance of form to substance which combine in the "pot theory," we can easily solve this problem. If the taxpayer receives property for property, there is an exchange. If he receives cash for property (even the right to unilaterally receive cash), there is no exchange. The exchange occurs when property is conveyed by and to the taxpayer.

Assuming the agreements are correctly written, if the taxpayer puts a deed into the exchange escrow and receives a deed, for that taxpayer an exchange has occurred. It is irrelevant from whom the deed comes, and it is irrelevant to whom the taxpayer writes his deed. Consequently, the taxpayer may deed directly to the buyer, and the seller of the exchange property may deed directly to the taxpayer without first deeding to the buyer. (23) (43) The essential requirement is that the executed agreements bind all parties in one cohesive transaction.

But if the taxpayer's lawyer wants the buyer to go through title and it doesn't kill the deal, there is no harm done. If the buyer simply refuses, at least there is a strong authority to support the alternative. So much of what can be done is the decision of the taxpayer's counsel, and rightly so, but not at the expense of a sound exchange.

The Taxpayer Must Avoid the Right to Receive Cash

One warning cannot be over-emphasized: At no time may the taxpayer have the right, as defined by the agreement, to unilaterally call the exchange off and take cash.

It is customary to provide for a sale if suitable exchange property is not found by a certain date, and this is perfectly acceptable. (7) But in practice it can be a source of liability if sound tax planning is not followed.

For example, if the buyer assigns the purchase agreement acquiring the exchange property to the taxpayer and gives him the cash to buy it, the tax-free benefits will be lost. (11) And if the buyer neglects to sign the initial exchange agreement that restricts the taxpayer's right to cash, the transaction will be taxable. (35) The most blatant example of this danger occurs when the exchange agreement just doesn't legally restrain the taxpayer from contact with the cash. (24) In most multiparty exchanges, there are several opportunities to stumble into constructive receipt of cash. And it is up to the taxpayer's lawyer to insure that this ever-present danger is avoided.

The agreements must specifically restrict the taxpayer's right and control over the cash used by the buyer to purchase the exchange property. This, of course, does not prevent the buyer from requiring a clause in the agreement that forces the taxpayer to accept a cash sale after a certain date if exchange property is not found, but don't let that date pass and expect to have a nontaxable exchange. If you haven't found suitable property by the date, extend it by written agreement or by modification and initialing of the original before the date occurs.

Virtually all of the challenges to multiparty exchanges by the IRS—and there have been very few—occur in transactions in which the taxpayer has the right to accept cash in lieu of property after a certain date. If you want to "play it safe" in an exchange, don't worry about who's going to make offers on the exchange property or how the deeds should be conveyed; worry about how the exchange agreement limits the taxpayer's right to cash.

Balancing Equities in a Multiparty Exchange

When the conceptual blocks that seem to characterize initial contact with multiparty exchanges are overcome, the mechanics quickly fall into place.

The multiparty exchange is based on the same economic principle as a two-party transaction. Everyone must receive the same in value as he gives, regardless of the form of the consideration.

In the Sherman-Reinhart exchange, for example, the taxpayer was able to meet a long-standing objective and secure the full benefits of Section 1031. Sherman had wanted to acquire an apartment complex near his home for years. He got his chance in the form of a verbal purchase offer on some land he owned. Instead of accepting the offer, he negotiated an exchange wherein the potential purchaser, Reinhart, agreed to buy the apartments and exchange them for the land. Since the apartment complex equity was less than Sherman's land value, he also received cash out of the deal. After the smoke cleared . . .

- Sherman exchanged his land for apartments and received $20,000.
- Trenton sold his apartments for $105,000 cash to loan.
- Reinhart acquired Sherman's land at market value of $125,000.

As the worksheet in Figure 3–1 illustrates, each participant received the same in value as he gave. Sherman transferred $125,000 in land equity and received $105,000 in apartment equity, plus $20,000 in cash. Trenton received $105,000 in cash for his apartment complex equity. Reinhart received land for $125,000.

WILLIAM T. TAPPAN JR., INC.

COMMERCIAL INVESTMENT REAL ESTATE
6400 UPTOWN BOULEVARD, N.E., SUITE 366 WEST
ALBUQUERQUE, NEW MEXICO 87110

—

505 - 299-1031

EXCHANGE WORK SHEET

BALANCING EQUITIES

	Sherman		Trenton		Reinhart	
	Transferred	Received	Transferred	Received	Transferred	Received
	Land	Apts	Apts	Cash	Cash	Land
1. Market Value	$125,000	$200,000	$200,000			$125,000
2. Existing Loans		95,000	95,000			-0-
3. New Loans						
4. Equity (L.1 less L.2 & 3)	125,000	105,000	105,000			125,000
5. Cash Boot		20,000		$105,000	$125,000	
6. Other (Boot) Property						
7. Loan Proceeds						
8. Balance	$125,000	$125,000	$105,000	$105,000	$125,000	$125,000

NETTING CASH

9. Cash Received (L.5 + L.7) Or (Paid) (L.5)	$20,000	$105,000	($125,000)
10. Commissions	$10,425	$11,990	
11. Transaction Costs	725	930	
12. Total Capitalized Costs (L.10 + L.11)	(11,150)	(12,920)	( )
13. Net Cash Received Or (Paid) (L.9 less L.12)	$8850	$92,080	($125,000)

Figure 3–1

How to Avoid Liability in a Multiparty Exchange

One question never fails to come up: "What is the extent of the buyer's liability?" In fact, in some situations if the answer to this question is not correctly understood, it can kill the whole exchange.

In one exchange, for example, an advisor for the taxpayer couldn't understand how you could transfer real estate from the seller to the buyer and then to the taxpayer without the buyer qualifying for assumption of the loan and the subsequent qualification of the taxpayer. Fortunately, this is a non-problem.

It is now well established that "one need not assume the benefits and burdens of ownership in property before exchanging it but may properly acquire title solely for the purpose of exchange." (1), (30) Therefore, if in the above example Reinhart (the buyer) was required to pass through title to the apartments and then deed them to Sherman (the taxpayer), he could do so subject to the existing loan without assumption or implied liability.

If Sherman's lawyer did not require Reinhart to go into title to the apartments, then the question of Reinhart's liability on the exchange property loan never arises. But what about his liability on the purchase agreement—to what extent can he be held liable for nonperformance if the exchange for some unforeseen reason does not close? This can be a real problem.

There are two steps that should be taken to protect the buyer from liability during offers on the acquisition of the exchange property.

1. In the offers to purchase exchange property, state that the offer is subject to and contingent on the terms of the initial exchange agreement.
2. Also state that, in the event of default, the seller will look only to the buyer's good faith deposit for damages.

The question of whether or not the buyer will assume liability should never stand in the way of an exchange, and neither should a question of liability during attempts to acquire exchange property. Liability can be avoided on the acquired property loans by not going into title (23), (43) or by going into title as a formality, subject to the loans and without assumption. Liability in the event of default on a purchase offer can be guarded against by provisions in the initial exchange agreement and the purchase offers.

The Taxpayer Can Qualify for Assumption and Receive Title Insurance Without Reference to the Buyer

Another common question is: "Will we have to pay for two title policies on the exchange property—one from the seller to the buyer and another from the buyer to the taxpayer, both of which cover the same property?" As with the question of deeding and liability, the "pot theory" provides the framework for the answer.

The tax advantages in an exchange are in no way jeopardized by the steps taken to reach a planned objective—provided these two questions are answered correctly:

1. Did the taxpayer give and receive qualifying like kind property?
2. Did the taxpayer at any time during the exchange have the right to unilaterally call off the exchange and accept the cash that was to be used to acquire exchange property?

If the answer to question one is "yes" and the answer to question two is "no," then the exchange is in good shape. Questions of loan assumption and title insurance liability, regardless of the answer, will have no effect on the tax benefits of Section 1031.

Applying this principle to the questions at hand, it is clear that the title company can issue a policy directly to the taxpayer and the taxpayer can qualify for direct assumption of the loans on the exchange property without in any way endangering his tax benefits.

Refinancing Property in a Multiparty Exchange

A major stumbling block in understanding the mechanics of a multiparty exchange often arises when it is necessary to refinance the taxpayer's property to generate the cash to acquire the exchange property or when it's necessary to refinance the exchange property to balance equities. The "pot theory" can again be relied upon to clear up this question of mechanics.

It's the role of the initial exchange agreement to spell out clearly what the taxpayer is putting into the exchange and what he will receive out of the exchange—what goes in and comes out of the pot—keeping in mind that what happens while the pot is cooking will not destroy the ultimate outcome.

Therefore, if you are faced with a situation which requires that the buyer secure a new loan on the taxpayer's property to get the cash to buy the exchange property, there is no problem if the taxpayer has no right to the refinance proceeds. In fact, if the buyer could not qualify for the loan, the taxpayer could apply for it during escrow with the protection that he would have no right to or control over the cash. The cash would simply go to acquisition of the exchange property. The buyer could then acquire the taxpayer's property subject to the new loan.

For purposes of calculating tax consequences, look only to the loans on the property prior to refinance and the loans on the property at close of the exchange. The step involved wherein the taxpayer qualified for a new loan during escrow would have no effect on the tax treatment provided that he had no right to the loan proceeds. His loan application would be a contingent part of the whole transaction as specified in the exchange agreements or escrow instructions.

By the same reasoning, the taxpayer could arrange a loan on the exchange property he is to acquire if necessary to balance equities; that is, the cash from the new loan on the acquired property would go directly to the seller. The taxpayer would have the liability of paying the loan but would receive no cash—only like kind property. In fact, refinancing is often the only way to generate the cash needed to balance equities and pay commissions and transaction costs in an exchange.

Refinancing to Balance Equities

Refinancing will often solve the problem when the buyer doesn't have enough cash to buy the exchange property.

In the Griego-Hedrick exchange, it was necessary for Wells (the buyer) to arrange a new loan on Griego's apartment complex to generate the cash needed to buy the exchange property from Hedrick. (See Figure 3–2.)

Wells had about $112,500 to use as down payment on Griego's apartments. Griego didn't want the cash but did want Hedrick's apartments. To generate the additional

WILLIAM T. TAPPAN JR., INC.
COMMERCIAL INVESTMENT REAL ESTATE
6400 UPTOWN BOULEVARD, N.E., SUITE 366 WEST
ALBUQUERQUE, NEW MEXICO 87110

505 · 299 · 1031

EXCHANGE WORK SHEET

BALANCING EQUITIES

	Griego Transferred	Griego Received	Hedrick Transferred	Hedrick Received	Wells Transferred	Wells Received
	Apts.	Apts.	Apts.	Cash	Cash	Apts.
1. Market Value	$375,000	$800,000	$800,000			$375,000
2. Existing Loans		425,000	425,000			
3. New Loans						262,500
4. Equity (L.1 less L.2 & 3)	375,000	375,000	375,000			112,500
5. Cash Boot				112,500	112,500	
6. Other (Boot) Property						
7. Loan Proceeds				262,500		
8. Balance	$375,000	$375,000	$375,000	$375,000	$112,500	$112,500

NETTING CASH

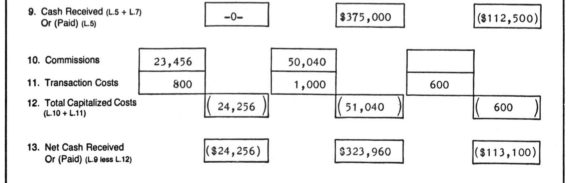

	Griego	Hedrick	Wells
9. Cash Received (L.5 + L.7) Or (Paid) (L.5)	-0-	$375,000	($112,500)
10. Commissions	23,456	50,040	
11. Transaction Costs	800	1,000	600
12. Total Capitalized Costs (L.10 + L.11)	(24,256)	(51,040)	(600)
13. Net Cash Received Or (Paid) (L.9 less L.12)	($24,256)	$323,960	($113,100)

Figure 3–2

$262,500 necessary to purchase Hedrick's property, Wells qualified for a new loan secured by Griego's apartments. Here's how the initial situation looked:

	Griego	Hedrick	Wells
Value	$375,000	$800,000	
Loans	–0–	425,000	
Equity	375,000	375,000	$112,500

In order to match Griego's equity, Wells had to obtain a loan at 70% of the apartment value. The loan proceeds combined with the $112,500 cash he had in hand to buy Hedrick's apartments for exchange to Griego. Wells simply used the loan proceeds and his cash to buy Hedrick's apartments, which he then exchanged with Griego:

1. Griego put in $375,000 in equity and received $375,000 in equity subject to a loan of $425,000.
2. Hedrick put in $375,000 in equity and received $375,000 cash to loan for a total sale price of $800,000.
3. Wells put in cash and borrowed cash for a total consideration of $375,000, which went directly to Hedrick without contact with Griego.

Did the exchange meet the test of the "pot theory"? Griego put in like kind property and received like kind property. At no time during the transaction did he have the right to the cash used to purchase the exchange property. Therefore, he accomplished a non-taxable exchange under Section 1031.

Using the Multiparty Exchange to Arrange Purchase Out of Escrow

The multiparty exchange can take other forms when the circumstances require. The other standard approach occurs when the property the taxpayer wants is located but the owner doesn't want the taxpayer's property. This scenario presents the problem of locating a buyer for the unwanted property.

The same principles that apply to the transferring of deeds, refinancing (if necessary) and assumption of liabilities apply here. In fact, the only change here is one that involves sequence and strategy. The substance of the transaction remains unchanged: like property for like property and no right to cash by the taxpayer.

The first approach is referred to as the ABC exchange; the second is an ACB exchange. In the ABC exchange, the taxpayer (A) refuses the buyer's (B) purchase offer, so the buyer (B) buys the seller's (C) property and exchanges with the taxpayer (A).

In the ACB exchange, the taxpayer (A) attempts to exchange with the seller (C), who agrees provided that a buyer (B) is located to purchase the taxpayer's property from the seller (C) out of the exchange escrow—not from the taxpayer. This interrelationship is established by the agreements, which must be signed by all participants to form a mutually contingent transaction.

An ACB exchange occurred when Anderson approached Balduini with an exchange. (See Figure 3–3.) Balduini wanted to sell and wouldn't accept an exchange unless a sale was involved.

Therefore, Anderson wrote an offer to exchange his office building for Balduini's apartments contingent on a sale of Anderson's property out of escrow. The transaction

WILLIAM T. TAPPAN JR., INC.
COMMERCIAL INVESTMENT REAL ESTATE
6400 UPTOWN BOULEVARD, N.E., SUITE 366 WEST
ALBUQUERQUE, NEW MEXICO 87110
505 - 299-1031

EXCHANGE WORK SHEET

BALANCING EQUITIES

	Anderson		Balduini		Cortez	
	Transferred	Received	Transferred	Received	Transferred	Received
	Offices	Apts.	Apts.	Cash	Cash	Offices
1. Market Value	$200,000	$350,000	$350,000			$200,000
2. Existing Loans	125,000	275,000	275,000			125,000
3. New Loans						
4. Equity (L.1 less L.2 & 3)	75,000	75,000	75,000			75,000
5. Cash Boot				75,000	75,000	
6. Other (Boot) Property						
7. Loan Proceeds						
8. Balance	$75,000	$75,000	$75,000	$75,000	$75,000	$75,000

NETTING CASH

	Anderson	Balduini	Cortez
9. Cash Received (L.5 + L.7) Or (Paid) (L.5)	-0-	$75,000	($75,000)
10. Commissions	12,510	21,893	
11. Transaction Costs	750	1,000	400
12. Total Capitalized Costs (L.10 + L.11)	(13,260)	(22,893)	(400)
13. Net Cash Received Or (Paid) (L.9 less L.12)	($13,260)	$52,107	($75,400)

Figure 3–3

was one unified exchange with all parts mutually contingent. Balduini accepted Anderson's offer contingent on the sale to an as yet unlocated buyer. Then the work began—finding a buyer. This contrasts with the ABC exchange, which requires location of exchange property when the buyer is ready and waiting.

Fortunately, a purchaser was found and the exchange closed. Cortez signed an agreement with Balduini in which he agreed to purchase Anderson's property from Balduini contingent on a concurrent closing of the exchange between Anderson and Balduini. Here's how the equities compared:

	Anderson	Balduini	Cortez
Market Value	$200,000	$350,000	$ Cash
Loans (−)	125,000	275,000	
Equity (=)	75,000	75,000	$75,000
Boot (+)	–0–	–0–	–0–
Balance (=)	$ 75,000	$ 75,000	$75,000

When the exchange closed, Anderson had an exchange; Balduini had a sale and Cortez had a purchase. The question is: How do you calculate the seller's (Balduini's) tax consequences? We know that Anderson has an exchange and that the rules for transferring basis are reasonably clear. We know that Cortez has a purchase and that his basis will be the cost of the property acquired. But Balduini went into title (probably unnecessarily). Do you report an exchange and a subsequent sale?

Look to the "pot theory" without regard to the steps. What was Balduini's position at the beginning of the exchange and after closing? At the beginning, he had property, and after closing, he had cash. For tax purposes, he reports a sale of his original property, using its basis and market value to establish the recognized gain. The fact that he may or may not have gone into title to Anderson's property to satisfy an unnecessary requirement of form is of no consequence in calculating the consequences.

The tax consequences for each party to an exchange are calculated based on the position of the participant before signing of the exchange agreement and after closing of the transaction. (15), (30)

Structuring Multiple Exchanges

The requirements for a properly structured exchange are the same regardless of the number of people and properties in the transaction. The exchange must be tied together legally by agreement, and the tax treatment must be calculated separately for each participant. Nowhere is this more clearly illustrated than in a multiple exchange.

A multiple exchange, a multiparty exchange and a two-party exchange are different in quantity only. A multiple exchange consists of three or more properties and three or more taxpayer-owners; a multiparty exchange involves two properties, cash and three parties; a two-way exchange consists of two properties and two owners. The procedures for multiple exchanges can help eliminate any misunderstanding of the rationale behind direct deeding and the other aspects of a multiparty exchange.

Multiple exchanges are virtually never challenged by the IRS. This is no doubt due to the fact that they rarely involve the right to sell one of the properties after a certain date for cash in lieu of like kind property. Consequently, there is simply no opportunity to stumble into constructive receipt of cash. The only danger relating to cash in a multiple exchange occurs when one of the properties is refinanced. In such a case, the agreements must clearly specify the parties who will receive the proceeds and those who have no legal right or control over the cash.

The CBA Multiple Exchange

The common nontaxable CBA multiple exchange occurs when three parties exchange property in such a way that each receives property from someone other than the party to whom they convey property. That is, A conveys to B but receives from C; B conveys to C but receives from A; C conveys to A but receives from B.

In one such exchange, three taxpayers, Alderson, Bernard and Carlton, had acquired acreage that they held for investment. About three years after acquisition, they decided to exchange. The parcels varied in size, so an arrangement was made to balance equities with cash, based on a value of $1,000.00 per acre.

At closing, Carlton received the land owned by Bernard, Bernard received the land owned by Alderson and Alderson received the land owned by Carlton. In addition, Carlton and Bernard each received $500, which was subject to capital gains tax to the extent that they realized gain on the exchange. Here's how the market values of the three properties compared:

	Alderson	Bernard	Carlton
Market Value	$6,500	$7,000	$7,500
Loans	–0–	–0–	–0–
Equity	$6,500	$7,000	$7,500

In a multiple exchange, it is helpful, and often essential, to set up a side-by-side comparison of the properties transferred and received. The entire economic picture of this CBA exchange can be seen at a glance in Figure 3–4.

In this exchange, you can readily see how meaningless it is for Bernard to deed to Alderson and then Alderson to deed Bernard's land to Carlton. Fortunately, that type of exercise, although often practiced, is not required to qualify as a nontaxable exchange. (43) In summary:

- Carlton received a deed (signed by Bernard) and $500 from the pot.
- Bernard received a deed (signed by Alderson) and $500 from the pot.
- Alderson received a deed (signed by Carlton) and paid $1,000 into the pot.

"After the smoke cleared," each participant received the same in total consideration as he gave. Although the transaction involved three people, it was still interlocked by agreement so that the steps taken to get from the beginning to the end of the exchange were viewed as mutually contingent and, therefore, as one integrated transaction.

Using Refinancing to Balance Equities in a Multiple Exchange

Combining refinancing with an exchange can be an excellent method of making an exchange succeed. Not only can a new loan provide the cash for commissions and other costs, it also is often the only feasible way to balance equities.

WILLIAM T. TAPPAN JR., INC.
COMMERCIAL INVESTMENT REAL ESTATE
6400 UPTOWN BOULEVARD, N.E., SUITE 366 WEST
ALBUQUERQUE, NEW MEXICO 87110

505 - 299-1031

EXCHANGE WORK SHEET

BALANCING EQUITIES

	Alderson Transferred	Alderson Received	Bernard Transferred	Bernard Received	Carlton Transferred	Carlton Received
	Land	C's Land	Land	A's Land	Land	B's Land
1. Market Value	$6,500	$7,500	$7,000	$6,500	$7,500	$7,000
2. Existing Loans						
3. New Loans						
4. Equity (L.1 less L.2 & 3)	6,500	7,500	7,000	6,500	7,500	7,000
5. Cash Boot	1,000			500		500
6. Other (Boot) Property						
7. Loan Proceeds						
8. Balance	$7,500	$7,500	$7,000	$7,000	$7,500	$7,500

NETTING CASH

	Alderson	Bernard	Carlton
9. Cash Received (L.5 + L.7) Or (Paid) (L.5)	($1,000)	$500	$500
10. Commissions	406	438	469
11. Transaction Costs	50	50	50
12. Total Capitalized Costs (L.10 + L.11)	(456)	(488)	(519)
13. Net Cash Received Or (Paid) (L.9 less L.12)	($1,456)	$12	($19)

Figure 3–4

WILLIAM T. TAPPAN JR., INC.
COMMERCIAL INVESTMENT REAL ESTATE
6400 UPTOWN BOULEVARD, N.E., SUITE 366 WEST
ALBUQUERQUE, NEW MEXICO 87110

505 - 299-1031

EXCHANGE WORK SHEET

BALANCING EQUITIES

	Chang		Levi		McMann	
	Transferred	Received	Transferred	Received	Transferred	Received
	12-Unit	Land	Land	Offices	Offices	12-Unit
1. Market Value	$150,000	$150,000	$150,000	$320,000	$320,000	$150,000
2. Existing Loans				225,000	225,000	
3. New Loans						100,000
4. Equity (L.1 less L.2 & 3)	150,000	150,000	150,000	95,000	95,000	50,000
5. Cash Boot						
6. Other (Boot) Property						
7. Loan Proceeds				55,000		45,000
8. Balance	$150,000	$150,000	$150,000	$150,000	$95,000	$95,000

NETTING CASH

	Chang	Levi	McMann
9. Cash Received (L.5 + L.7) Or (Paid) (L.5)	-0-	$55,000	$45,000
10. Commissions	9383	15,638	20,016
11. Transaction Costs	800	800	1,000
12. Total Capitalized Costs (L.10 + L.11)	(10,183)	(16,438)	(21,016)
13. Net Cash Received Or (Paid) (L.9 less L.12)	($10,183)	$38,562	$23,984

Figure 3–5

The taxpayer who wants a completely tax-free transaction can get it even if his property is refinanced through escrow by the acquiring party—provided the taxpayer has no right to the refinance proceeds.

The Chang-Levi-McMann exchange is an excellent example of how financing can make a multiple exchange work without loss of tax benefits.

Chang owned a 12-unit apartment complex that had been fully depreciated using the straight line method. His objective was to acquire land to build a larger complex and, consequently, increase his tax shelter and income. Levi owned the land Chang wanted but would not sell, although he was interested in exchanging for an office building owned by McMann. McMann didn't want Levi's land but was interested in Chang's 12-unit complex if he could end up with at least $20,000 cash to pay a bank note that was coming due.

During a meeting of the minds, an agreement was drawn outlining the terms of the exchange: Chang was to exchange his apartments for land; Levi was to exchange his land for offices; McMann was to exchange his offices for the apartments, provided that he could obtain a new loan of $100,000 secured by the apartments.

At closing, Chang completed the tax-free acquisition of land for apartment construction, Levi moved his dormant land equity into income-producing offices and McMann received a 12-unit apartment complex and the cash he needed to pay the bank.

The entire exchange and the important role played by refinancing is illustrated by the exchange worksheet in Figure 3–5. Notice that Chang received only like kind property, the proceeds from the loan McMann obtained were paid out of the pot to both McMann and Levi to balance equities and, although McMann arranged the loan, his tax liability is limited to the amount of net cash proceeds he received. (30), (55)

Applying the Essentials of the Nontaxable Exchange

The multiparty and multiple nontaxable exchanges are so filled with varied opportunities (and therefore seemingly complex) and far-reaching benefits (and therefore seemingly too good to be true) that it is no wonder that they are so often misunderstood. But if the underlying rationale and principles are kept clearly in mind, adaptation to the unique characteristics of each exchange will naturally follow.

The principles of the step transaction doctrine and the dominance of substance over form provide the basic structure and can be distilled into one concise question: What did the taxpayer start with and what did he end with?

With that question in mind, we can apply the ultimate test of the "pot theory" to determine the safety of the tax benefits for the taxpayer. The test has two parts. If the facts of the transaction pass the test, the exchange qualifies whether it is a two-party, multiparty or multiple transaction. The two parts are:

1. Did the taxpayer transfer and receive qualifying like kind property?
2. Did the taxpayer have the right to unilaterally accept cash instead of qualifying like kind property?

If the answer to question one is "yes" and the answer to question two is "no," then the taxpayer has an exchange that qualifies under Section 1031 of the Internal Revenue Code.

4

Calculating Tax Treatment
Under Section 1031

The primary reason to exchange is to secure the nontaxable benefits of Section 1031; and the only way to find out what these benefits are is to calculate the tax treatment in detail. Furthermore, it is essential in planning the outcome of a transaction to correctly calculate the end result prior to acting on a given game plan. This is especially important when a number of alternative courses are available to the taxpayer.

This chapter presents the procedures for calculating the tax effects of exchanging, including techniques that can be used before the exchange to maximize tax savings and the concepts used by the accounting profession to form the framework for calculating exchange tax treatment; for example, how to determine gain realized, boot received, gain recognized and potential tax liability before it's too late to act.

The procedure for transferring basis from the property conveyed to the property acquired will be covered also, including the adjustments that must be made in each unique exchange. Finally, we will see how the treatment for tax purposes is the same whether an exchange is a two-party, multiparty or multiple exchange and the traps that must be watched for to prevent an unexpected loss of tax benefits regardless of the size of the transaction.

Consistent Terminology Is a Must for Accurate Communication

Understanding the unique tax consequences of real estate exchanging in a way that allows effective communication among Realtors, accountants and attorneys is only possible when they all use the same terms and the same methods to calculate the tax treatment of an exchange. Daily contact with accountants and attorneys on behalf of a taxpayer can be an exercise in frustration if they don't all "speak the same language." For this reason, only accepted accounting practice and language have been used in this chapter, as well as throughout the book. For a Realtor, this consistency is essential to establishing practical communication and a team relationship with your client's (the taxpayer) accountant and attorney—and that is the objective of this chapter.

It is only when the broker and taxpayer communicate clearly with accountants and attorneys that the full range of benefits available through the nontaxable exchange can be achieved. This necessary level of communication comes with the confidence of a thorough understanding of the tax consequences of a transaction. All too often a legally sound and profitable transaction is killed by one of the taxpayer's advisor's uncertainty about the results of a given course of action. This uncertainty falls both within the legal requirements discussed earlier and the calculation of the tax consequences that follow.

I had the importance of consistent terminology—and therefore communication—emphasized to me in a rather sudden way. After completing an exchange of a duplex for a 12-unit apartment complex (which was fortunately for my own account), I ran a quick form calculation of the tax consequences and my basis in the acquired property. When I presented the form to my accountant, he took one look at it and with an "expletive deleted" threw it in the wastebasket. It wasn't until two years later that I fully appreciated the lesson of that encounter.

As a result of this CPA's confident reaction to my calculations, I took the time to learn the accepted accounting procedures for tax treatment of an exchange and how they differed from what I thought was correct. Later, I was able to apply what I had learned to communicating on an accurate and equal footing with a client's accounting firm in order to successfully close an exchange which had a value of over two million dollars.

Applying Tax Concepts in an Exchange

Section 1031 of the Internal Revenue Code of 1986 provides an exception to the usual requirement that capital gains or losses be included in the taxpayer's gross income for the year in which property is transferred. This is not an elective provision; it is mandatory and has been applied by the IRS in certain cases in which the taxpayer attempted to claim a sale at a loss.

The mandatory nature of Section 1031 requires the taxpayer who receives like kind property as consideration for like kind property given in "mutually dependent transactions" to treat the transfer as an exchange and not a sale. (47) Although the taxpayer may prefer to argue that a sale at a loss occurred, he must treat the transaction as an exchange and not report either gain or loss. (2)

Basis

The first step in determining the specific tax treatment in an exchange is to establish the adjusted basis of the property the taxpayer is transferring. *Basis* is the starting point for computing gain or loss in any transaction. It is increased by all capitalized costs attached to the property and reduced by any partial divestiture and depreciation. These adjustments are made during the time of ownership—holding period—up to the day the transaction closes to establish the "adjusted basis" of the property transferred. Therefore:

Adjusted Basis = Original property cost plus all capitalized costs less depreciation and partial divestitures.

Gain

There are two types of gain: 1. Realized gain is generally the difference between the total consideration received and the basis of the property transferred. 2. Recognized gain is that portion of the realized gain which is subject to tax. Realized gain can be thought of as an economic concept analogous to profit. Recognized gain is a tax concept which specifies the degree to which the gain realized is subject to taxation. In an exchange that qualifies under Section 1031, realized gain is recognized in part or in total to the extent that nonqualifying consideration (boot) is received.

Gain recognized (subject to tax) can never be more than gain realized. Consequently, the amount of gain recognized is always limited to the gain realized or the nonqualifying consideration received, whichever is the smaller amount. Therefore, for a transaction that results in realized gain to be completely tax-free (no recognition of gain) the taxpayer must receive property with an equal or greater market value and debt and receive no boot.

To summarize, in an exchange, the *recognition* of any gain *realized* is limited to the smaller of:

1. The amount of gain realized
2. The amount of boot received

Under no circumstances is an exchange subject to tax in excess of realized gain. For example, if the realized gain in an exchange is $40,000 and the total boot received is $80,000, the amount taxable is limited to $40,000. Conversely, if the realized gain is $80,000 and the boot is $40,000, the recognized gain will be limited to $40,000.

Consequently, an exchange can be partially tax-free and partially taxable, that is, part of the economic profit of an exchange—realized gain—will be taxed if it is received in the form of boot rather than like kind property.

In 1968, John Barker bought a $10,000 lot for a new business location. Due to the economy, he was unable to build. During 1973, he exchanged the lot for a commercial building. The value of the lot was $15,000 at the time of the exchange. The equity in the building was $12,000, and he received $3,000 in cash.

	Lot	Building
Market Value	$15,000	$55,000
Loans	–0–	43,000
Equity	15,000	12,000
Difference		3,000
Balance	$15,000	$15,000

The tax consequences to Barker are calculated as follows (Regs. Section 1.1031 (b)-1 (a) example (1):

Value of prop. recd.	$55,000
Cash received	3,000
Total consideration recd.	$58,000
—loans on prop. recd.	− 43,000
—adjusted basis of property transferred	− 10,000
Gain realized on exchange	$ 5,000
Gain recognized	$3,000

In the above example, Barker realized a gain of $5,000 but was subject to capital gains tax only on the nonqualifying consideration (boot) received. If Barker had exchanged his lot worth $15,000 for a building with an equity of $15,000 and, therefore, not received any boot, the gain recognized would have been zero.

Boot

Traditionally, boot is thought of as anything of value given or received in an exchange as additional incentive to trade; that is, an almost nonquantifiable thing which equalizes values. For tax purposes, the meaning can be expanded to cover anything given or received in an exchange that is not qualifying like kind property.

Boot can be in the form of cash, securities, loan relief, personal property, nonqualifying real estate (inventory or residence) or "other property," which is described in Section 1031 as property received "in addition to property permitted to be received without recognition of gain." (Regs. Section 1.1031 (b)-1 (2))

Under Section 1031, when property subject to liabilities is transferred, the amount of the liabilities that the taxpayer is no longer obligated to pay is treated the same as receipt of money. This rule applies whether loans on the property are assumed or the property is transferred subject to the loans. There is logic to this rule, and there is a trap that goes with it, too.

The rule is designed to prevent the situation that occurs if the taxpayer obtains a loan on his property and then exchanges it for a free and clear property, pocketing the loan proceeds without the financial requirement of paying off the loan. The trap occurs when the taxpayer expects a tax-free exchange, is relieved of loans, has realized gain on the exchange and, therefore, must pay an unexpected tax. Loan relief is sometimes called "mortgage boot"—and correctly so since it is treated as money.

Offsetting and Netting

Fortunately, certain consideration received in a nontaxable exchange may be offset by or netted against certain consideration given. In computing realized gain, you may offset the liabilities on the property transferred against the liabilities on the property acquired. (Regs. 1.1031 (b)-1 (c))

It is also permitted to net loan relief by subtracting the cash and fair market value of the boot property given from the liabilities on the property transferred. "Consideration given in the form of cash or other property is offset against consideration received in the form of an assumption of liabilities or a transfer of property subject to a liability." (Regs. 1.1031 (d)-2 example (2) (c))

Cash that is, in general, paid into an exchange is netted against cash received from an exchange escrow. Consequently, the taxpayer is subject to tax only on the net cash received. This rule also covers commissions and transaction costs. The specific treatment of brokerage commissions was presented in a 1972 revenue ruling, which also clarified the general rule that permits netting of all cash. "Section 1.1031 (d)-2 of the regulations, example (2), indicates that money paid out in connection with an exchange under Section 1031 of the Code is offset against money received in computing gain realized and gain recognized and is also added in determining the basis of the acquired property." (55)

In determining the net boot received, there is currently no authority for netting the fair market value of the other (boot) property received by subtracting the fair market value of the other (boot) property given or for subtracting cash paid from the value of boot received. In view of the general application of netting, it would seem logical, but until specific authority is established we can only offset boot property in the permitted manner. Currently, only the adjusted basis of boot property transferred may be subtracted from the total consideration received in arriving at realized gain. (Regs. 1.1031 (d)-1 (e))

The importance of the rules governing offsetting and netting lies in the opportunity to reduce both the nonqualifying consideration received and realized gain, thus reducing any potential tax liability.

Computing Recognized Gain When Cash Is Received

The first step in determining the tax consequences of an exchange is to calculate the gain realized by the taxpayer. Because of the unique nature of Section 1031, gain realized in an exchange is calculated differently than gain realized in a sale.

In a sale, the price of the property disposed of usually correctly represents the consideration received by the former owner. However, this is not necessarily true in an exchange. The value of the property transferred by the taxpayer does not represent the consideration he received; it is the consideration he transferred. The consideration received in an exchange is the value of the like kind property acquired plus cash, relief from loans and other (boot) property—all of which must be totaled to establish total consideration received. After this is done, the consideration transferred and basis of the property given can be subtracted to arrive at the gain realized by the taxpayer, and even then we are a long way from determining his tax liability.

Since taxable gain in an exchange is determined only by the boot (nonqualifying consideration) received by the taxpayer, an accurate analysis (which involves extensive netting) of the boot must be made. When this is accomplished, we have the two elements that determine the extent of any tax liability: gain realized and net boot received.

Due to the somewhat complicated procedure for calculating tax treatment in an exchange, we have developed a form that presents the sequence necessary to arrive at recognized gain. The following example is a transaction in which the taxpayer exchanged free and clear property and received $2,000 in cash. (Regs. 1.1031 (b)-1 example (1)) Although the taxpayer in this example realized a $3,000 gain, he was taxed only on the cash received, which was $2,000.

In 1984, Vern Atwood, who is not a dealer in real estate, exchanges real estate held for investment, which he purchased in 1980 for $5,000, for other real estate (to be held for productive use in trade or business), which has a fair market value of $6,000 and $2,000 in cash. The gain from the transaction is $3,000, but it is recognized only to the extent of the cash received, which is $2,000.

As Figure 4–1 illustrates, the taxpayer realized a gain of $3,000 but was required to include only $2,000 in his income for the year as long-term capital gain.

Calculating Recognized Gain When Boot Property Is Received

The following example adds the element of boot property to the gain calculation. In this case, the taxpayer realized a gain that was smaller than the amount of boot received. Therefore, as can be seen in Figure 4–2, his taxable gain is the entire amount of the gain realized because it is smaller than the boot received. (Regs. 1.1031 (d)-1 (c) example)

In 1954, Sam Aranjo, who is not a dealer in real estate, transfers real estate held for investment, which he purchased in 1940 for $10,000, in exchange for other real estate

VERN ATWOOD
EXCHANGE TAX TREATMENT
(Regs. 1.1031 (b)-1 example (1).)

COMPUTING REALIZED GAIN

1. Market Value Of Qualifying Property Received	$ 6,000	
2. Market Value Of Other (Boot) Property Received		
3. Cash Received	2,000	
4. Liabilities on Property Transferred		
5. Total Consideration Received (L.1+2+3+4)		$ 8,000
6. Adjusted Basis Of Qualifying Property Transferred	5,000	
7. Adjusted Basis Of Other (Boot) Property Transferred		
8. Cash Paid		
9. Liabilities on Property Received		
10. Total (L.6+7+8+9)		5,000
11. Gain Or (Loss) Realized (L.5 less L.10)		$ 3,000

DETERMINING BOOT RECEIVED

12. Liabilities on Property Transferred	$ -0-	
13. Liabilities on Property Received	-0-	
14. Relief From Liabilities (L.12 less L.13)		$ -0-
15. Market Value of Other (Boot) Property Transferred		-0-
16. Difference (L.14 less L.15)		-0-
17. Cash Received		2,000
18. Total (L.16+L.17)		2,000
19. Cash Paid		-0-
20. Difference (L.18 less L.19)		2,000
21. Market Value of Other (Boot) Property Received		-0-
22. Total Boot Received (L.20+L.21)		$ 2,000

RECOGNIZED GAIN (L.11 or L.22 whichever is smaller) | $ 2,000 |

Loss attributable to boot property transferred only (L.15 less L.7) ( )

Figure 4–1

SAM ARANJO

EXCHANGE TAX TREATMENT
(Regs. 1.1031 (d)-1 (c))

COMPUTING REALIZED GAIN

1. Market Value Of Qualifying Property Received	$ 9,000	
2. Market Value Of Other (Boot) Property Received	2,000	
3. Cash Received	1,500	
4. Liabilities on Property Transferred		
5. Total Consideration Received (L.1+2+3+4)		$12,500
6. Adjusted Basis Of Qualifying Property Transferred	$10,000	
7. Adjusted Basis Of Other (Boot) Property Transferred		
8. Cash Paid		
9. Liabilities on Property Received		
10. Total (L.6+7+8+9)		10,000
11. Gain Or (Loss) Realized (L.5 less L.10)		$ 2,500

DETERMINING BOOT RECEIVED

12. Liabilities on Property Transferred	$ -0-	
13. Liabilities on Property Received	-0-	
14. Relief From Liabilities (L.12 less L.13)		$ -0-
15. Market Value of Other (Boot) Property Transferred		-0-
16. Difference (L.14 less L.15)		-0-
17. Cash Received		1,500
18. Total (L.16+L.17)		1,500
19. Cash Paid		-0-
20. Difference (L.18 less L.19)		1,500
21. Market Value of Other (Boot) Property Received		2,000
22. Total Boot Received (L.20+L.21)		$ 3,500

RECOGNIZED GAIN (L.11 or L.22 whichever is smaller) $ 2,500

Loss attributable to boot property transferred only (L.15 less L.7) ( )

Figure 4–2

(to be held for investment), which has a fair market value of $9,000, an automobile, which has a fair market value of $2,000, and $1,500 in cash. He realizes a gain of $2,500, all of which is recognized under Section 1031 (b).

Determining Basis Allocation

The taxpayer's basis in the property received is the same as his basis in the property transferred, adjusted for money received and gain recognized:

Basis in the Property Transferred	$10,000
Decreased by the Money Received	− 1,500
	$ 8,500
And Increased by the Gain Recognized	2,500
Equals Basis in the Property Received	$11,000

Furthermore, the basis of the total properties received must be allocated between the car and realty acquired—first to the car in the amount of its fair market value on the date of the exchange, $2,000, and then the balance, $9,000, to the realty.

This procedure for allocating basis between like kind and boot property received specifically requires that the fair market value of the boot property ("other property") be established and used as the basis of the acquired boot property (see Figure 4–3).

> . . . the basis (adjusted to the date of the exchange) of the property transferred by the taxpayer, decreased by the amount of any money received and increased by the amount of gain recognized, must be allocated to and is the basis of the properties (other than money) received on the exchange. For the purpose of the allocation of the basis of the properties received, there must be assigned to such "other property" an amount equivalent to its fair market value at the date of the exchange. (Regs. 1.1031 (d)-1 (c))

Calculating Tax Treatment When There Is a Loss on the Boot Property Transferred

In the event the taxpayer transfers boot property at a loss that is recognized under Section 1002, he may deduct the loss from his income for the year. The basis of the property received is calculated by adding the adjusted basis of the like kind property to the adjusted basis of the boot property, increasing the total by the amount of the gain recognized on exchange of the like kind property and decreasing it by the amount of the loss on the boot property. This rule assumes that the taxpayer received an amount equal to the fair market value of the boot property as of the date of the exchange. (Regs. 1.1031 (d)-1 (e))

Bill James exchanges real estate held for investment plus stock for real estate to be held for investment. (See Figure 4–4). The real estate transferred has an adjusted basis of $10,000 and a fair market value of $11,000. The stock transferred has an adjusted basis of $4,000 and a fair market value of $2,000. The real estate acquired has a fair market value of $13,000. He is deemed to have received a $2,000 portion of the required real estate in exchange for the stock since $2,000 is the fair market value of the stock at the time of the exchange. A $2,000 loss is recognized under Section 1002 on the exchange of the stock for real estate. No gain or loss is recognized on the exchange of the real estate

EXCHANGE BASIS COMPUTATION
(Regs. 1.1031 (d)-1 (c))

TRANSFERRING BASIS

1. Adjusted Basis of Qualifying Property Transferred $10,000

2. Adjusted Basis of Other (Boot) Property Transferred

3. Cash Paid

4. Liabilities On All Property Received

5. Total (L1+2+3+4) $10,000

6. Cash Received   1,500

7. Liabilities on All Property Transferred

8. Total (L.6+L.7)   1,500

9. Difference (L.5 less L.8)   8,500

10. Gain Recognized   2,500

11. Total (L.9+L.10)

12. Loss Recognized on Other (Boot) Property Transferred

13. Basis of All Property Received (L.11 less L12) $11,000

ALLOCATING BASIS

14. Basis of All Property Received (L.13) $11,000

15. Market Value of Other (Boot) Property Received*   2,000

16. Basis Allocated to Qualifying Property (L.14 less L.15) $ 9,000

17. Market Value of Improvements on Qualifying Property

18. Market Value of Qualifying Property Received

19. Percentage Allocated to Improvements (L.17÷L.18)

20. Basis Allocated to Improvements on Qualifying Property (L.19×L.16)

*The basis of the boot property received is the same as its market
value as indicated on line 15.

Figure 4–3

BILL JAMES
EXCHANGE TAX TREATMENT
(Regs. 1.1031 (d)-1 (e))

COMPUTING REALIZED GAIN

1. Market Value Of Qualifying Property Received	$13,000
2. Market Value Of Other (Boot) Property Received	-0-
3. Cash Received	-0-
4. Liabilities on Property Transferred	-0-
5. Total Consideration Received (L.1+2+3+4)	$13,000
6. Adjusted Basis Of Qualifying Property Transferred	10,000
7. Adjusted Basis Of Other (Boot) Property Transferred	4,000
8. Cash Paid	-0-
9. Liabilities on Property Received	-0-
10. Total (L.6+7+8+9)	14,000
11. Gain Or (Loss) Realized (L.5 less L.10)	($ 1,000)

DETERMINING BOOT RECEIVED

12. Liabilities on Property Transferred	$ -0-
13. Liabilities on Property Received	-0-
14. Relief From Liabilities (L.12 less L.13)	$ -0-
15. Market Value of Other (Boot) Property Transferred	2,000
16. Difference (L.14 less L.15)	-0-
17. Cash Received	-0-
18. Total (L.16+L.17)	-0-
19. Cash Paid	-0-
20. Difference (L.18 less L.19)	-0-
21. Market Value of Other (Boot) Property Received	-0-
22. Total Boot Received (L.20+L.21)	-0-

RECOGNIZED GAIN (L.11 or L.22 whichever is smaller)   -0-

Loss attributable to boot property transferred only (L.15 less L.7)   ($2,000)

Figure 4—4

since the property received is of the type permitted to be received without recognition of gain or loss. The basis of the real estate acquired by him is determined as follows:

Adjusted Basis of Real Estate Transferred	$10,000
Adjusted Basis of Stock Transferred	4,000
	$14,000
Less Loss Recognized on Transfer of Stock	− 2,000
Basis of Real Estate Acquired Upon the Exchange	$12,000

How Computing Tax Treatment in Advance Can Prevent Unexpected Relief from Liabilities

Relief from liabilities can be one of the most costly and surprising results of incomplete tax planning. But it is a problem that can be planned for and, therefore, avoided.

The rule governing relief from liabilities required the taxpayer to treat the liabilities on the property he transfers as money: "Consideration received in the form of an assumption of liabilities (or a transfer subject to a liability) is to be treated as other property or money." (Regs. 1.1031 (b)-1 (c))

As Figure 4–5 illustrates, Hank Barlow was liable for tax on a gain of $200,000—$150,000 of which resulted from loan (liability) relief. If he had acquired property with a loan of at least $150,000, tax would have been due only on the $50,000 cash received.

Hank Barlow, an individual, owns an apartment house that has an adjusted basis in his hands of $500,000 but is subject to a mortgage of $150,000. On September 1, 1984, he transfers the apartment house to Richard Crenshaw, receiving in exchange therefor $50,000 in cash and another apartment house with a fair market value on the date of $600,000. The transfer to Crenshaw is made subject to the $150,000 mortgage. (1.1031 (d)-2 example (1))

Liabilities Received Offset Liabilities Transferred

The regulations that explain Section 1031 require that: "The amount of *any* liabilities of the taxpayer assumed by the other party to the exchange (or of any liabilities to which the property exchanged by the taxpayer is subject) is to be treated as money received by the taxpayer upon exchange. . . ." (Regs. 1.1031 (d)-2). Special care should be taken because the word covering this rule is "*any*," which in certain exchanges could include liabilities not attached to the property that were assumed as a condition of the exchange. Furthermore, the word "liabilities" refers not only to loans secured by the property but also water, sewer, paving and other liens that the taxpayer escapes when the property is transferred.

Fortunately, the effect of "liability" relief is offset by liabilities on the property received. The beneficial result of this provision allows you to acquire exchange property with total liabilities equal to or larger than the loans on the property transferred and thus avoid the loan relief trap.

HANK BARLOW
EXCHANGE TAX TREATMENT
(Regs. 1.1031 (d)-2 example (1))

COMPUTING REALIZED GAIN

1. Market Value Of Qualifying Property Received	$600,000	
2. Market Value Of Other (Boot) Property Received	-0-	
3. Cash Received	50,000	
4. Liabilities on Property Transferred	150,000	
5. Total Consideration Received (L.1+2+3+4)		$800,000
6. Adjusted Basis Of Qualifying Property Transferred	500,000	
7. Adjusted Basis Of Other (Boot) Property Transferred	-0-	
8. Cash Paid	-0-	
9. Liabilities on Property Received	-0-	
10. Total (L.6+7+8+9)		500,000
11. Gain Or (Loss) Realized (L.5 less L.10)		$300,000

DETERMINING BOOT RECEIVED

12. Liabilities on Property Transferred	$150,000	
13. Liabilities on Property Received	-0-	
14. Relief From Liabilities (L.12 less L.13)		$150,000
15. Market Value of Other (Boot) Property Transferred		-0-
16. Difference (L.14 less L.15)		150,000
17. Cash Received		50,000
18. Total (L.16+L.17)		200,000
19. Cash Paid		-0-
20. Difference (L.18 less L.19)		200,000
21. Market Value of Other (Boot) Property Received		-0-
22. Total Boot Received (L.20+L.21)		$200,000

RECOGNIZED GAIN (L.11 or L.22 whichever is smaller) $200,000

Loss attributable to boot property transferred only (L.15 less L.7) ( )

Figure 4–5

There are three ways to directly prevent loan relief:

1. Acquire property with equal or larger loans.
2. Pay off the loans on the property transferred prior to the exchange.
3. Increase the loans on the property received prior to the exchange.

In the following example, Darwin is relieved of an $80,000 mortgage but assumes a mortgage of $150,000 and, as a result, has no liability relief. His recognized gain was limited to the cash received ($40,000), as illustrated by Figure 4–6. Elan's gain was limited to $30,000—the difference between the cash paid and loans he was relieved of, as indicated by Figure 4–7.

John Darwin, an individual, owns an apartment house. On December 1, 1980, the apartment house owned by Darwin has an adjusted basis in his hands of $100,000 and a fair market value of $220,000 but is subject to a mortgage of $80,000. Tom Elan, an individual, also owns an apartment house. On December 1, 1980, the apartment house owned by Elan has an adjusted basis of $175,000 and a fair market value of $250,000 but is subject to a mortgage of $150,000. On December 1, 1980, Darwin transfers his apartment house to Elan, receiving in exchange therefor $40,000 in cash and the apartment house owned by Elan. Each apartment house is transferred subject to the mortgage on it. (Regs. 1.1031 (d)-2 example 2 (a))

The Benefits of Offsetting Go Beyond Loan Relief

Generally, there are two calculations that employ offsetting or netting: (1) Computing realized gain and (2) determining boot received. The first calculation establishes the economic profit of the exchange (gain realized) by essentially subtracting the consideration transferred from the consideration received. The second calculation involves more specific netting restrictions in determining the net nonqualifying consideration (boot) received.

In determining boot received:

1. Liabilities received offset liabilities transferred. (1.1031 (b)-1 (c))
2. Boot property transferred offsets liabilities transferred. (1.1031 (d)-2 example (2) (c))
3. Cash paid offsets cash received and liabilities transferred. (1.1031 (d)-example (2)(c)); (Rev. Rul. 72–456)

But there are certain items that can't be offset in arriving at net boot received:

1. Cash or boot property received is not offset by liabilities assumed. (1.1031 (d)-2 example (2) (c))
2. Currently no authority specifically permits offsetting the market value of boot property received in arriving at net boot received.

Determining the Basis of Property Acquired by Exchange

In general, the basis of the property transferred becomes the basis of the property received from the exchange. This rule is, of course, subject to certain adjustments, based on the details of the exchange.

The rules that must be followed in transferring basis from the property transferred to the property received are:

JOHN DARWIN
EXCHANGE TAX TREATMENT
(Regs. 1.1031 (d)-2 example (2)(b))

COMPUTING REALIZED GAIN

1. Market Value Of Qualifying Property Received	$250,000	
2. Market Value Of Other (Boot) Property Received	-0-	
3. Cash Received	40,000	
4. Liabilities on Property Transferred	80,000	
5. Total Consideration Received (L.1+2+3+4)		$370,000
6. Adjusted Basis Of Qualifying Property Transferred	100,000	
7. Adjusted Basis Of Other (Boot) Property Transferred	-0-	
8. Cash Paid	-0-	
9. Liabilities on Property Received	150,000	
10. Total (L.6+7+8+9)		250,000
11. Gain Or (Loss) Realized (L.5 less L.10)		$120,000

DETERMINING BOOT RECEIVED

12. Liabilities on Property Transferred	$ 80,000	
13. Liabilities on Property Received	150,000	
14. Relief From Liabilities (L.12 less L.13)		$ -0-
15. Market Value of Other (Boot) Property Transferred		-0-
16. Difference (L.14 less L.15)		-0-
17. Cash Received		40,000
18. Total (L.16+L.17)		40,000
19. Cash Paid		-0-
20. Difference (L.18 less L.19)		-0-
21. Market Value of Other (Boot) Property Received		-0-
22. Total Boot Received (L.20+L.21)		40,000

RECOGNIZED GAIN (L.11 or L.22 whichever is smaller)　　$ 40,000

Loss attributable to boot property transferred only (L.15 less L.7)　( )

Figure 4–6

TOM ELAN
EXCHANGE TAX TREATMENT
(Regs. 1.1031 (d)-2 example (2)(c))

COMPUTING REALIZED GAIN

1. Market Value Of Qualifying Property Received	$220,000	
2. Market Value Of Other (Boot) Property Received	-0-	
3. Cash Received	-0-	
4. Liabilities on Property Transferred	150,000	
5. Total Consideration Received (L.1+2+3+4)		$370,000
6. Adjusted Basis Of Qualifying Property Transferred	175,000	
7. Adjusted Basis Of Other (Boot) Property Transferred	-0-	
8. Cash Paid	40,000	
9. Liabilities on Property Received	80,000	
10. Total (L.6+7+8+9)		295,000
11. Gain Or (Loss) Realized (L.5 less L.10)		$ 75,000

DETERMINING BOOT RECEIVED

12. Liabilities on Property Transferred	$150,000	
13. Liabilities on Property Received	80,000	
14. Relief From Liabilities (L.12 less L.13)		$ 70,000
15. Market Value of Other (Boot) Property Transferred		-0-
16. Difference (L.14 less L.15)		70,000
17. Cash Received		-0-
18. Total (L.16+L.17)		70,000
19. Cash Paid		40,000
20. Difference (L.18 less L.19)		30,000
21. Market Value of Other (Boot) Property Received		-0-
22. Total Boot Received (L.20+L.21)		$ 30,000

RECOGNIZED GAIN (L.11 or L.22 whichever is smaller) $ 30,000

Loss attributable to boot property transferred only (L.15 less L.7)   (   )

Figure 4–7

1. In an exchange where no gain or loss was recognized, the basis of the property acquired is the same as the basis of the property transferred by the taxpayer with proper adjustments to the date of the exchange. (1.1031 (d)-1 (a))

2. If additional consideration is given by the taxpayer in the exchange, the basis of the property acquired shall be the same as the property transferred increased by the amount of additional consideration given. (1.1031 (d)-1 (a))

3. The basis of the property acquired is the basis of the property transferred decreased by the amount of money received and increased by the amount of gain recognized on the exchange. (1.1031 (d)-1 (b))

4. If the taxpayer received other (boot) property and gain was recognized, the basis of the property transferred, decreased by the amount of any money received and increased by the amount of gain recognized, must be allocated to and is the basis of the properties received on the exchange. (1.1031 (d)-1 (c))

5. The basis of the property received must be allocated to such other (boot) property in an amount equivalent to the fair market value of the boot property at the date of the exchange. (1.1031 (d)-1 (d))

6. If the taxpayer exchanged other (boot) property and gain or loss is recognized under Section 1002, the basis of the property acquired is the total basis of the properties transferred increased by the gain and decreased by the loss recognized on the other (boot) property. (1.1031 (d)-1 (e))

7. Liabilities on the property transferred are subtracted from the liabilities on the property received in transferring basis. (1.1031 (d)-2 ex (2) (b))

These seven rules, which are taken directly from the Internal Revenue Regulations, have been translated into a practical preprinted form: Figure 4–8 illustrates the calculation of John Darwin's basis; Figure 4–9 illustrates the calculation of Tom Elan's basis. The sequence of the calculations in the "Exchange Basis" form reduce a difficult procedure to a logical, easy-to-follow mathematical calculation.

Calculating Tax Treatment in a Multiparty Exchange

The major problem to avoid when you are calculating the tax treatment of a multiparty exchange in mixing legal and tax requirements. Although to some degree the participants in an exchange have contractually established rights and obligations, they should not be intermixed conceptually in computing individual tax consequences.

The tax consequences of a multiparty exchange are easily calculated if the essential points are kept in mind. In the Sherman-Reinhart exchange, for example, Sherman is the only party to the transaction who attempted a tax-free exchange, Reinhart, although a party to the exchange, made a purchase; Trenton made a sale. The parties to the exchange are interdependent legally, but the tax computations for each taxpayer must be arrived at independently of what may have happened to the other parties.

In the Sherman-Reinhart exchange, Reinhart wanted to purchase Sherman's property for $125,000 cash. Sherman wanted Trenton's property by exchange. Trenton wanted cash. For tax purposes, Reinhart paid $125,000 cash into escrow and received Sherman's property out of escrow and has a basis of approximately $125,000. Legally he was a party to an exchange, but from a tax stand-point, his basis is the price of the property he received out of the exchange escrow.

Trenton contributed property valued at $200,000 with loans of $95,000 to the exchange escrow and received cash of approximately $105,000. He also was legally part of the

JOHN DARWIN

EXCHANGE BASIS COMPUTATION

(Regs. 1.1031 (d)-2 example (2)(b))

TRANSFERRING BASIS

1. Adjusted Basis of Qualifying Property Transferred $100,000

2. Adjusted Basis of Other (Boot) Property Transferred

3. Cash Paid

4. Liabilities On All Property Received   150,000

5. Total (L1+2+3+4) $250,000

6. Cash Received   40,000

7. Liabilities on All Property Transferred   80,000

8. Total (L.6+L.7)   120,000

9. Difference (L.5 less L.8)   130,000

10. Gain Recognized   40,000

11. Total (L.9+L.10)   170,000

12. Loss Recognized on Other (Boot) Property Transferred   -0-

13. Basis of All Property Received (L.11 less L12) $170,000

ALLOCATING BASIS

14. Basis of All Property Received (L.13)

15. Market Value of Other (Boot) Property Received*

16. Basis Allocated to Qualifying Property (L.14 less L.15)

17. Market Value of Improvements on Qualifying Property

18. Market Value of Qualifying Property Received

19. Percentage Allocated to Improvements (L.17÷L.18)

20. Basis Allocated to Improvements on Qualifying Property (L.19×L.16)

*The basis of the boot property received is the same as its market value as indicated on line 15.

Figure 4–8

TOM ELAN

EXCHANGE BASIS COMPUTATION
(Regs. 1.1031 (d)-2 example (2)(c))

TRANSFERRING BASIS

1. Adjusted Basis of Qualifying Property Transferred	$175,000	
2. Adjusted Basis of Other (Boot) Property Transferred		
3. Cash Paid	40,000	
4. Liabilities On All Property Received	80,000	
5. Total (L1+2+3+4)		$295,000
6. Cash Received		
7. Liabilities on All Property Transferred	150,000	
8. Total (L.6+L.7)		150,000
9. Difference (L.5 less L.8)		145,000
10. Gain Recognized		30,000
11. Total (L.9+L.10)		175,000
12. Loss Recognized on Other (Boot) Property Transferred		
13. Basis of All Property Received (L.11 less L12)		$175,000

ALLOCATING BASIS

14. Basis of All Property Received (L.13)

15. Market Value of Other (Boot) Property Received*

16. Basis Allocated to Qualifying Property (L.14 less L.15)

17. Market Value of Improvements on Qualifying Property

18. Market Value of Qualifying Property Received

19. Percentage Allocated to Improvements (L.17+L.18)

20. Basis Allocated to Improvements on Qualifying Property (L.19×L.16)

*The basis of the boot property received is the same as its market value as indicated on line 15.

Figure 4–9

exchange, but for tax reporting purposes, he sold property for $200,000, and the tax is computed as long-term capital gain.

Sherman is the only taxpayer who falls within the bounds of Section 1031 both legally and for tax purposes. He is the only party who put property into the exchange escrow and received property out of the escrow. He has a nontaxable exchange, and his gain and basis are computed accordingly, as illustrated in Figures 4–10 and 4–11.

Avoiding Recapture in an Exchange

There are several situations that may result in the recapture of depreciation in an exchange. Fortunately, an exchange can usually be structured to avoid recapture and the subsequent increase in ordinary income for the taxpayer.

The danger of recapture as the result of an exchange under Section 1031 can be classified in two categories:

1. Recapture under Section 1250 when real property is transferred.
2. Recapture under Section 1245 when personal property is transferred.

Recapture liability is created under Section 1250 when you transfer real estate depreciated in excess of straight line or held less than one year. If you are transferring real property in an exchange that is subject to recapture, you can avoid the problem by acquiring depreciable real estate with a market value equal to or greater than the recapture liability and making the exchange completely tax-free.

Conversely, if the recapture liability exceeds the market value of the depreciable real estate (not land) received, you are required to report the excess as ordinary income in the year of the exchange. If there is a gain recognized on the exchange, it must be reported as ordinary income to the extent of recaptured depreciation. In the event there is both recapture in excess of the market value of the depreciable real estate received and recognized gain, you must report the larger amount.

If you are able to avoid recapture, the liability avoided must be deducted from the portion of the total basis of the property received that was allocated to depreciable real estate. Furthermore, the liability stays with the property received and may be recaptured in the event of disposition.

In an exchange, the holding period of the property transferred carries over to the property received. This is not the case for computing the reduction of recapture carried over in an exchange. When a recapture liability is attached to the property received in an exchange, it is reduced based on a new holding period beginning with the new acquisition. When the acquired property is sold, the excess depreciation that carried over on the exchange may be in part recaptured as ordinary income.

If depreciation is recaptured as ordinary income, it is added to the basis of the property received, as is recognized gain.

There may be an even greater problem with recapture in an exchange when personal property is involved. Under Section 1245, when you transfer personalty at a gain, the full amount of depreciation taken is immediately recaptured as ordinary income. Therefore, in an exchange of real estate involving the transfer of furniture, allocation must be made between the market value of the furniture and the market value of the real estate. In the event the market value of the furniture is larger than the taxpayer's basis, recapture will automatically occur. This sometimes unexpected by-product of an exchange can be avoided in two ways:

RICHARD SHERMAN
EXCHANGE TAX TREATMENT

COMPUTING REALIZED GAIN

1. Market Value Of Qualifying Property Received	$200,000
2. Market Value Of Other (Boot) Property Received	-0-
3. Cash Received	20,000
4. Liabilities on Property Transferred	-0-
5. Total Consideration Received (L.1+2+3+4)	$220,000
6. Adjusted Basis Of Qualifying Property Transferred	90,000
7. Adjusted Basis Of Other (Boot) Property Transferred	-0-
8. Cash Paid	11,150
9. Liabilities on Property Received	95,000
10. Total (L.6+7+8+9)	196,150
11. Gain Or (Loss) Realized (L.5 less L.10)	$23,850

DETERMINING BOOT RECEIVED

12. Liabilities on Property Transferred	$ -0-
13. Liabilities on Property Received	95,000
14. Relief From Liabilities (L.12 less L.13)	$ -0-
15. Market Value of Other (Boot) Property Transferred	-0-
16. Difference (L.14 less L.15)	-0-
17. Cash Received	20,000
18. Total (L.16+L.17)	20,000
19. Cash Paid	11,150
20. Difference (L.18 less L.19)	8,850
21. Market Value of Other (Boot) Property Received	-0-
22. Total Boot Received (L.20+L.21)	8,850

RECOGNIZED GAIN (L.11 or L.22 whichever is smaller) $8,850

Loss attributable to boot property transferred only (L.15 less L.7)   ( )

Figure 4–10

RICHARD SHERMAN

EXCHANGE BASIS COMPUTATION

TRANSFERRING BASIS

1. Adjusted Basis of Qualifying Property Transferred	$ 90,000	
2. Adjusted Basis of Other (Boot) Property Transferred	-0-	
3. Cash Paid	11,150	
4. Liabilities On All Property Received	95,000	
5. Total (L1+2+3+4)		$196,150
6. Cash Received	20,000	
7. Liabilities on All Property Transferred	-0-	
8. Total (L.6+L.7)		20,000
9. Difference (L.5 less L.8)		176,150
10. Gain Recognized		8,850
11. Total (L.9+L.10)		185,000
12. Loss Recognized on Other (Boot) Property Transferred		-0-
13. Basis of All Property Received (L.11 less L12)		$185,000

ALLOCATING BASIS

14. Basis of All Property Received (L.13)	$185,000	
15. Market Value of Other (Boot) Property Received*	-0-	
16. Basis Allocated to Qualifying Property (L.14 less L.15)		$185,000
17. Market Value of Improvements on Qualifying Property	170,000	
18. Market Value of Qualifying Property Received	200,000	
19. Percentage Allocated to Improvements (L.17+L.18)		85%
20. Basis Allocated to Improvements on Qualifying Property (L.19×L.16)		$157,250

*The basis of the boot property received is the same as its market
value as indicated on line 15.

Figure 4–11

(1) Make sure that personal property is not transferred when the market value is in excess of its adjusted basis; or

(2) acquire in exchange other qualifying personal property with a value in excess of the recapture liability of that transferred. The effect of the second solution would be to divide the exchange into two separate transactions under Section 1031—one being an exchange of real property and the other being an exchange of personal property—both nontaxable.

In an exchange that has more than one kind of like asset on each side of the transaction, the structure should be allocated to maximize the benefits of Section 1031 by setting up an exchange of the real property and a separate exchange of the personal property. This type of planning not only can prevent recapture but also can enable the taxpayer to take full advantage of the tax-free benefits in a situation that might at first appear to be an exchange with receipt of boot.

The Holding Period Stays with the Taxpayer

Holding period in an exchange moves with the owner. That is, the period the taxpayer owned the property transferred is attached to the property received. For example, if the taxpayer bought a lot for construction of a new building July 1, 1977, was unable to build but exchanged for a completed building in November and subsequently sold the building September 30, 1978, due to bankruptcy, his holding period would be 15 months, computed as follows:

$$
\begin{array}{lll}
\text{Lot: July–November 1977} & = & \text{5 mos.} \\
\text{Building: December–September 1978} & = & \underline{10} \text{ mos.} \\
\text{TOTAL} & & \text{15 mos.}
\end{array}
$$

In this example, the continuation of the holding period allowed capital gains treatment for profit realized on the sale of the building—a benefit that could be significant in similar emergency dispositions. This rule relating to holding period is like the one governing basis—it doesn't stay with the property as mortgages do; it moves with the taxpayer from one property to the next.

The Tax Treatment of Brokerage Fees and Commissions in an Exchange

The question of how to handle brokerage fees in a nontaxable exchange was clarified by Revenue Ruling 72–456. Realized gain is reduced by the amount of the brokerage commission on the property transferred; the basis of the property acquired is increased by the amount of the brokerage commission paid on the property transfer. In other words, the commission reduces realized gain and increases the basis of the property acquired. Three situations are illustrated below:

Received:	*1*	*2*	*3*
Land-F.M.V.	$20,000	$20,000	$20,000
Cash	10,000	10,000	–0–
TOTAL	$30,000	$30,000	$20,000

Less: Brokerage Commission	2,000	2,000	2,000
Amount Realized	$28,000	$28,000	$18,000
Given Up: Land-Basis	12,000	29,500	10,000
Realized Gain (loss)	$16,000	$(1,500)	$ 8,000
Recognized Gain: (Lesser of realized gain or net cash received)	$ 8,000	$ –0–	$ –0–
Basis: Land Given Up	$12,000	$29,500	$10,000
Less Cash Received	(10,000)	(10,000)	–0–
Plus Rec. Gain	8,000	–0–	–0–
Plus Brkg. Commission	2,000	2,000	2,000
Basis of Land Received	$12,000	$21,500	$12,000

How Transaction Costs Affect an Exchange

Transaction costs other than brokerage commissions must be handled in a manner consistent with the guideline indicated in Revenue Ruling 72–456. That is, capitalized costs of an exchange, such as title, closing fees, title insurance, must properly reduce realized gain on the exchange while increasing the basis of the property received.

Therefore, in calculating capitalized transaction costs other than brokerage fees, the computation should be carried out exactly as the computation of the brokerage was above. There is no specific example for the treatment of general transaction costs, so we must rely on the rule governing payment of money in an exchange as expressed in Revenue Ruling 72–456:

> Section 1.1031 (d)-2 of the regulations, example (2), indicates that money paid out in connection with an exchange under Section 1031 of the Code is offset against money received in computing gain realized and gain recognized and is also added in determining the basis of the acquired property.

Avoiding Hidden Disqualification Traps

The Allocation Trap

Although it is now well established that "like kind" refers only to the nature of the property, such as the distinction between real and personal property, there are precautions that must be taken when an exchange involves both real and personal property. For example, an exchange of two apartment complexes, one furnished and one unfurnished, requires an allocation of the value between the furniture and the real property based on the fair market value of each at the time of the transaction. If this is not done in the initial exchange agreement, it is possible that both parties might experience unexpected tax liability. For example:

1. The taxpayer transferring the furnished apartment complex might be subject to recapture of the difference between his basis in the furniture and its fair market value as of the date of transfer. This amount, to the extent of the depreciation taken, would be included in his ordinary income for the year. The recapture provisions relating to personal property under Section 1245 present one of the most often overlooked problem areas in real estate transfers.

2. The taxpayer transferring the unfurnished apartments is receiving personal property that must be reported as boot in an amount equal to its fair market value as of the date of the exchange.

Another trap related to qualification of property in an exchange is the allocation between Section 1031 and Section 1034. This problem occurs in an exchange of farms and ranches in which the owners live on the properties. To avoid the trap, values must be established for the residences, the exchange of which must be treated as a separate exchange under Section 1034. (36) (46)

To avoid the allocation trap, make sure the kind of property is defined and the values are specified in the initial exchange agreement. Allocation of values between different assets is often overlooked in normal purchase agreements. This oversight can be a real problem in an exchange.

Avoiding Disqualification Requires Caution After the Exchange

There is a serious trap that relates to "qualification" of property in an exchange. Property held for investment or use in trade or business qualifies for nontaxable exchange under Section 1031, but property held for resale and a taxpayer's residence do not.

The problem occurs when the taxpayer acquires property by exchange and does not hold it for investment or business use; i.e., he sells it or uses it for his residence. For example, acquiring land by exchange, dividing it into lots and selling the lots would open the possibility that the taxpayer acquired the land for resale.

A similar situation may arise if a taxpayer acquires a rental house by exchange but subsequently moves into it and establishes it as his primary residence. There are no firm time guidelines for holding property acquired by exchange for investment or for use in business before you do something else with it. It's a judgment based on what you intended when the exchange property was acquired and how you went about demonstrating that intent. (8)

Not Signing the Agreements Forms a Subtle Trap

Who would ever think that one party to an exchange could go through the entire transaction and close without signing the initial exchange agreement? It happened in Rogers v. Commissioner of Internal Revenue (377 F 2nd 534). One of the parties to the transaction did not sign the agreements to restrict the taxpayer's right to cash and establish a multiparty exchange rather than a sale and purchase. The end result was the loss of benefits for the taxpayer.

The Constructive Receipt of Cash Trap

In a multiparty exchange in which the taxpayer agrees to sell for cash after a certain date, if suitable exchange property has not been acquired, the date on which the taxpayer has a right to sell must be carefully watched. If the exchange hasn't closed, play it safe and extend the agreement. If the extension is not made before the date on which the taxpayer has a legal right to sell, the tax benefits may be lost.

Restriction of the right to cash is the one element in a multiparty exchange which must be adhered to in order for the exchange to remain safe for the taxpayer. This trap has repeatedly been a cause of the failure of nontaxable exchanges. Conversely, when the right to cash is clearly restricted, the courts have pointed to its absence as evidence of a Section 1031 transaction.

Informal Exchanges Warrant Documentation

Many casual exchanges occur each year without formal written agreements. This can lead to difficulty in reconstructing circumstances to support the facts in the event of audit. A one-page "Memorandum of Exchange" (see model) signed by all parties can save a lot of time and money. Inadequate documentation is an easy, but unnecessary, trap to fall into in a fast-moving exchange consisting of verbal agreements.

MEMORANDUM OF EXCHANGE

On February 16, 1973, John Overstreet, owner of Lot 2, Block 5, Yucca Addition, and Barry Ely, owner of Lot 10, Block 5, Yucca Addition, exchanged the above-described lots.

Both Lots were free of all liens and encumbrances. The only consideration received by each party was the above-described real property.

_____	_____
John Overstreet	Barry Ely
_____	_____
Date	Date

The Loan Relief Trap

Relief from liabilities has probably caused as much surprise and unexpected tax liability as any danger area in an exchange. It usually stems from planning a transaction without first seeking proper legal and accounting advice. The trap is formed, for example, when encumbered property is exchanged for property that has a smaller loan or is free and clear. If the taxpayer realized a gain and is relieved of loan obligations, tax liability will occur. Solving this problem takes nothing more than a little calculation to avoid surprise and plan for the tax liability that may be there.

Tax Calculations Should Be Used as a Method of Maximizing Benefits

Tax calculations in an exchange are just one more tool to help in constructing a transaction that will benefit the taxpayer. Not using this aid, or using it incorrectly or after the exchange is closed, is to invite unknown surprises.

The purpose of doing a complete tax analysis prior to commitment by the taxpayer is to assure that the benefits expected are those that are received. It is not practical to expect review of the regulations and calculation of the unique tax treatment of each possible exchange. And this is the problem that the two tax forms designed for this book correct. The "Exchange Tax Treatment" and "Exchange Basis Computation" forms, which are used throughout this chapter, reduce an otherwise complicated calculation to a one-minute exercise. Use of these forms can help protect the planned benefits of an exchange. Blank forms for your use are located in Appendix B. The one thing that must be kept in mind though is that there is no substitute for competent tax counsel and no exchange should be pursued without it.

5

How to Write Two-Party and Multiple Exchange Agreements

Without a doubt, the most important tool of the real estate exchangor is the written exchange agreement. It defines the economics of the exchange and establishes the legal protection of the taxpayer. A correctly written agreement will make the deal; an incorrect agreement will destroy it.

The written exchange agreement is simply a description of the transaction in terms of its legal and economic requirements. When it is legally correct and carried out as written, the agreement is the transaction. In many transactions, the exchange agreement is the only complete record of what has occurred and is absolutely necessary to verify the facts of the transaction and protect the taxpayers. Consequently, written agreements not only define the terms between the participants, they also substantiate the exchange, thus protecting the tax-free consequences to the taxpayer. The courts look to the agreements and the manner in which they are carried out to establish the legal correctness of an exchange. (11), (19), (35)

Exchange Agreements Can Be Very Flexible

In this chapter, we will cover the use of the two-party exchange agreement. Preprinted two-party exchange agreements are easily available, and with the necessary phrases and clauses to draw from, they can be a very flexible tool for all Realtors because:

1. A two-way exchange can be linked together into a multiple transaction.
2. An exchange can be set up for one party and a sale can be established for another.
3. An offer to purchase can be changed to an exchange.
4. Any amendment can be made if it is done before the agreement is carried out.

Define the Exchange with a Written Agreement

Anyone who has sold real estate would agree that the most important step in putting a deal together is to get the terms written down and signed by the principals. This fact of real estate life applies to an exchange, whether it is a two-party transaction where both participants really want the other's property or the beginning of a multiple exchange where no one wants anything.

The purpose of the exchange agreement is to define what the parties to the transaction will do; that is, what they will transfer and what they will receive and their legal rights and obligations. The agreement must cover all property in the exchange, including qualifying like kind property, cash and other (boot) property. Nothing should be left out.

Three Primary Purposes of the Exchange Agreement

The agreement in an exchange is often the only documentation that can be referred to at a later date. Therefore, it must be written to serve several purposes. These are:

1. It should accurately present the economics of the exchange.
2. It must serve as a guide for the title company closing the transaction.
3. It must establish the intent and legally restrict certain actions of the taxpayer in order to clearly document a nontaxable exchange in the event the transaction is questioned at a later date by the Internal Revenue Service.

As we will see, this can be done very naturally by simply stating the various facts of the exchange and how they specifically apply to each participant in the exchange.

Consequently, an agreement should define the exchange process in terms of each taxpayer involved. The definition must be stated in terms that will be understandable to the people who will refer to it for an explanation of the transaction:

1. The principals in understanding the benefits of the transaction.
2. The escrow agent in closing the transaction.
3. The Internal Revenue Service agent in the event of audit.

The agreement, then, is a definition of the exchange process, and it must be written to meet the needs of the people who will use it. Although the terms of an agreement may change and, of necessity, require a written amendment, it is what actually happened "after the smoke clears" that counts legally. (1), (15)

What Counts Is What Actually Happened Not What Was Intended

In an exchange and matters of taxation in general, what actually occurs must be considered, even if what happens is not what the parties intended. (11) This legal requirement applies to the nontaxable exchange as it does to all other tax matters. (45) In the final analysis, what was intended doesn't matter if it doesn't conform to what happened. (34) Intent may have value in explaining the actions of the taxpayers, and it may be important in preventing a misunderstanding by the Internal Revenue Service during an audit, but in court the facts of the transaction govern the outcome. (2), (11)

If the taxpayer intended to make a nontaxable exchange but had the unilateral right to receive cash rather than qualifying property, the transaction becomes taxable. (11), (24) Although an exchange is planned, if the agreement allows legal right by the taxpayer to the cash that is to be used to purchase exchange property in a multiparty transaction, the exchange is a sale and purchase in the eyes of the Internal Revenue Service. The taxpayer is viewed as receiving cash for property, not property for property. This is a major danger which must be avoided when you are writing a two-party agreement that later evolves into a multiparty exchange. The converse is equally possible. Although the parties intend to make a sale and purchase, they may, in fact, accomplish a mutually contingent and reciprocal transfer of property—a nontaxable exchange. (2), (47)

A Sale Can Be Viewed as an Exchange

When a loss results from a reciprocal transfer by sale and purchase of property by the taxpayer, it is possible that the Internal Service will declare an intended sale to be an exchange and disallow the loss. This actually happened when two taxpayers sold each other property and one tried to claim a loss on the transfer.

Since the nontaxable provisions of Section 1031 are mandatory, thus preventing recognition of either gain or loss, the court found that although the taxpayers intended to make a purchase and sale and declare a loss, they had, in fact, by their actions, completed a nontaxable exchange, and the loss was disallowed. (2)

The importance of what happens as opposed to what was intended was further emphasized in a situation in which a sale and purchase in "form" was allowed as an exchange in "substance" where state law prohibited an exchange by the guardian of a ward's property. In this revenue ruling, a purchase agreement was used to acquire and transfer farms because state law prevented use of the form of an exchange. (45)

Writing an exchange agreement and intending to make an exchange do not necessarily qualify a transaction under the nontaxable provisions of Section 1031. Likewise, writing a purchase agreement does not necessarily avoid a nontaxable exchange. Although intent to complete a nontaxable exchange should be clear or, in some cases, even stated in the document in order to set the stage for action, what actually occurred will determine the tax consequences. The individual elements of each exchange must conform to the basic requirement of Section 1031. Qualifying like kind property must be received for qualifying like kind property transferred.

Writing a Two-Way Exchange Agreement

The procedure used in writing a two-way exchange agreement is fundamentally the same as the procedure used in writing a purchase agreement. The difference is that at closing the consideration received by the taxpayer is qualifying like kind property instead of money. The agreement normally contains five distinct elements which should be stated as accurately and completely as possible. These are:

1. *The Parties* to the exchange as they hold and are to take title to the property.
2. *The Legal Description* of the property and its location or address.
3. *The Loans* and other encumbrances on the property, such as water, paving and sewer liens, and standby and pro rata charges that are attached to the property.
4. *The Restrictions* and reservations on the property.
5. *The Terms* of the exchange, including assumption of loans, refinancing, payment of transaction costs and the transfer and receipt of boot.

The exchange agreement in Figure 5–1 illustrates the completed sections. The back of the form contains the standard items characteristic of real estate transfers in general. This particular form is one of several used throughout the United States.

Model General Phrases for Use in Exchange Agreements

There are certain areas that should be covered by standard exchange agreements. The requirements vary from state to state, and the wording used should follow your lawyer's guidelines. The following model general phrasing is designed to be adapted to your individual needs.

Each party to this exchange agrees to:

1. Assume and pay the loans herein specified on the property acquired current as of the date of transfer
2. Pay the cost of title insurance due on the property conveyed
3. Pay the escrow closing fees allocated to the property conveyed
4. Pay the recording fees due on the property acquired
5. Pay the mortgage transfer fees on the property acquired
6. Pay the transaction costs due at closing in cash

This agreement is subject to:

1. First/second party furnishing a rental statement showing tenants' names, rent amounts, due dates and amount of security deposits for each unit
2. Inspection and approval of the property to be acquired
3. Verification and approval of the income, expense and occupancy history of the property to be acquired
4. Inspection and acceptance of the condition of the roof, walls and foundation of the property to be acquried
5. Inspection and acceptance of the condition of the heating, cooling, plumbing and electrical systems of the property to be acquired

How to Change a Purchase Offer to an Exchange Agreement

One of the practical requirements of completing an exchange is dealing with an offer to purchase property that the owner will only exchange. This necessitates a method of converting a sale offer to an exchange. As you might expect, it is usually easier to complete an exchange when you have a standing offer to purchase.

An example of this situation occurred when an investor named Ed Baily received an offer to purchase his five-store strip center from one of the tenants. Although Baily had a relatively low return on equity, he could not bring himself to sell outright and reinvest the proceeds because of the large tax due. Furthermore, he needed the monthly income from the property.

Finally, the tenant made a very attractive cash offer. Baily was able to take advantage of this once-in-a-lifetime opportunity, avoid the income taxes and increase his monthly income by accepting the purchase offer on one condition: that the purchaser, Starline Cleaners, Inc., acquire other property and exchange it to Baily instead of giving the cash

EXCHANGE AGREEMENT

Victor and Marie Leonardo HEREINAFTER CALLED FIRST

PARTY, HEREBY OFFERS TO EXCHANGE THE FOLLOWING DESCRIBED PROPERTY:

ADDRESS: _1694 West Harvard Street_

CITY OF _Tucson_, COUNTY OF _Pima_, STATE OF _Arizona_,

LEGAL DESCRIPTION: _Lots 5 and 6 Block 10 College addition_

SUBJECT, TO: _A first mortgage in the approximate amount $26,250_

payable at $200 per month including interest of 8% per

year to be assumed by second party.

FOR THE FOLLOWING DESCRIBED PROPERTY OF _Richard Blackman_

_____, HEREINAFTER CALLED SECOND PARTY.

ADDRESS: _2130 North 2nd Street_

CITY OF _Tucson_, COUNTY OF _Pima_, STATE OF _Arizona_,

LEGAL DESCRIPTION: _Lot 3 Block 7 Terrace Addition_

SUBJECT TO: _A first mortgage in the approximate amount of $32,000_

payable at $300 per month including 8% interest per year to be

assumed by second party.

TERMS AND CONDITIONS OF EXCHANGE

Both parties agree that the value of 1694 West Harvard Street

is $42,000 and the value of 2130 North 2nd Street is $48,500.

First party agrees to pay second party $750 in cash at closing

to balance equities.

Figure 5-1

The parties hereto shall execute and deliver within __30__ days from this date of acceptance, all instruments, in writing, necessary to transfer title to said properties and complete this exchange. Certificate of Title shall be furnished by the owners showing their titles to be insurable and free of all liens and encumbrances, except taxes to be assumed by grantee, and those liens and encumbrances as otherwise set forth herein. Each party has investigated the property to be acquired, and has placed his own valuation thereon without relying upon any representation by agent. Each premises is conveyed subject to existing easements not inconsistent with purchaser's intended use, convenants, conditions, restrictions, and rights of way, if any, whether imposed in the title or by government regulation. Title shall be conveyed by Warranty Deed free of encumbrances or defects except those noted herein.

If either party is unable to convey an insurable title, except as herein provided, within six months after acceptance hereof by second party, or if the improvements on any of the herein named properties be destroyed or materially damaged prior to transfer of title or delivery of agreement of sale, then this agreement shall be of no further effect, except as to payment of broker's fees, and expenses incurred in connection with examination of title, unless the party acquiring the property so affected elects to accept the title the other party can convey or subject to the conditions of the improvements.

Taxes, insurance premiums (if policies be satisfactory to party acquiring the property affected thereby), rents, interest and other expenses of said properties shall be pro-rated as of the date of transfer of title, unless otherwise provided herein. Security deposits, advance rentals or considerations involving future lease credits shall be credited to the party acquiring title. Each party agrees to pay to closing agent all sums of money required of him for closing costs, pro-rates, and clearance of encumbrances which are not to remain on property he is conveying.

__Exchange Realty__ of __1021 Phoenix Avenue__ __342-1964__
Broker   Address   Phone No.

is hereby authorized to act as broker for all parties hereto and may accept fees therefrom. Should second party accept this offer, first party agrees to pay

said broker a fee for services rendered as per listing and/or separate agreement, or as follows: __$2700 plus applicable__

__sales tax in cash at closing.__

Should second party be unable to convey an insurable title to his property then first party shall be released from payment of any fees, unless he elects to accept the property subject thereto. First party agrees that broker may cooperate with other brokers and divide fees in any manner satisfactory to them.

In consideration of herein named agent using his best efforts to procure an acceptance of this offer, this offer is exclusively and irrevocably binding on

the below party of the first part for __3__ days after date.

In consideration of mutual promises herein it is further agreed that should either party fail to perform and carry out his part of this agreement, such party so failing shall pay all of the brokers' fees which the parties have agreed to pay by reason of this transaction, this promise being made directly for said brokers' benefit. In this connection, the first and second parties agree to and with the undernamed broker or brokers that failure on the part of any party hereto to fix the amount of his broker's fees prior to the signing hereof by the other party shall be no defense against the broker's recovery of such fees, and said defense is hereby waived.

Time is the essence of this contract, but Broker may, without notice, extend for a period of not to exceed one month the time for the performance of any act hereunder, except the time for the acceptance hereof by second party. This is a legally binding contract, if not understood seek competent advice. All words used herein in the singular shall include the plural and the present tense shall include the future and the masculine gender shall include the feminine and neuter.

Dated __February 3__, 19__76__   _Nate Leonardo_
                                          Marie Leonardo

ACCEPTANCE

Second party hereby accepts the foregoing offer upon the terms and conditions stated.

__Growth Realty__ of __3419 22nd Street__ __411-6634__
Broker   Address   Phone No.

is hereby authorized to act as broker for all parties hereto and may accept fees therefrom, and may cooperate with other brokers and divide fees in any manner satisfactory to them. Second party agrees to pay said broker a fee for services rendered as per listing and/or separate agreement, or as follows

__$3100 plus applicable sales tax in cash at closing.__

Should first party be unable to convey an insurable title to his property then second party shall be released from payment of any fees unless he elects to accept the property of the first party subject thereto.

Date __February 4__, 19__76__   _Richard Blackman_

Figure 5–1 (cont'd.)

consideration. This was accomplished by inserting one clause in the purchase offer submitted by Starline Cleaners, Inc., which reads as follows:

> This agreement is contingent on Starline Cleaners purchasing real property acceptable to Ed Baily and exchanging said acquired property as consideration for Baily's property in lieu of the cash offered. It is understood and agreed that Baily has no right to the cash in this transaction and said cash is to be used only by Starline to acquire exchange property acceptable to Baily. If Starline is unable to acquire property suitable to Baily within 180 days, this agreement will become null and void and all deposits will be refunded.

In this case, Starline made a written offer to purchase with no intention of becoming involved in an exchange. Baily sought advice from his Realtor, who took over and proceeded to complete the counter-offer with the above clause. For consistency, the title of the "purchase" offer was change to read "exchange agreement."

In addition, the Realtor took responsibility for locating suitable exchange property. Within 90 days, an apartment complex was found and a standard purchase agreement was written by Starline with a special contingency clause concerning the exchange required by Baily:

> This offer to purchase is solely for the purposes of exchange and is contingent on that certain agreement to exchange between Starline Cleaners and Ed Baily dated July 1, 1975.

To summarize, Baily was able to take advantage of a firm offer to purchase without sacrificing a portion of his equity to taxes and giving up the monthly income he needed. The procedure used to accomplish this exchange was as follows:

1. Starline offered to buy Baily's property in writing on a standard preprinted purchase agreement.
2. Baily countered Starline's purchase offer with the contingency that Starline purchase other property and exchange it to Baily.
3. Suitable exchange property was located within the time limit and Starline committed to purchase it contingent on the agreement with Baily.
4. An escrow was opened, and the properties were transferred as contracted for in the agreements.

This transaction is a clear example of how an exchange can be made using preprinted purchase agreements, provided that the correct clauses are used. It's what actually happens that counts, not the name at the top of a printed form. The point here is that there is a legal and binding agreement between the parties to exchange whether the title of the form is changed or not. As long as the taxpayer receives only qualifying like kind property in exchange for qualifying like kind property, with no constructive receipt of cash, an exchange occurs—even if it began as a purchase offer. (1) The agreements used for this transaction appear in Figures 5–2 and 5–3.

How to Make an Exchange More Attractive to a Purchaser by Including an Obligation to Sell

Usually the party making an offer to purchase is not interested in pursing an exchange unless there is some assurance the property will be acquired even if exchange property

Exchange Agreement
~~XXXXXX XXXXXX~~
of
Exchange Realty Inc.

Received of **Starline Cleaners Inc.** Address **3514 Main N.W.**

Phone **432-9124**, the sum of **$1000.00** in the form of cash_____ Note_____ Check **X** dated **7/1/75**

_____ as deposit to be escrowed with broker as part payment for the Purchase of **Retail Center**

Type of property

_____ located at (address) **3514-3522 Main N.W.**

legal description **Lot 7, Block 14 Valencia Addition**

_____ Albuquerque, New Mexico,

and to include the following improvements: **All existing.**

together with all planting and improvements except **No exceptions.**

THE FULL PURCHASE PRICE is $ **75,000.00** to be paid as follows: total down payment including above deposit to be approximately $ **50,000.00** cash, plus or minus prorations, upon execution of formal instruments; the Purchaser(s) assume(s) and agree(s) to pay the existing mortgage or lien of record, current as of date of transfer in the approximate amount of $ **25,000.00** with monthly payments of approximately $ **250.00** on said mortgage and balance, if any, to be paid as follows: **This agreement is contingent on Starline Cleaners purchasing real property acceptable to Ed Baily and exchanging said acquired property as consideration for Baily's property in lieu of the cash offered. It is understood and agreed that Baily has no right to the cash in this transaction and said cash is to be used only by Starline to acquire exchange property acceptable to Baily. If Starline is unable to acquire property suitable to Baily within 180 days this agreement will become null and void and all deposits will be refunded.**

Seller shall make payments due on above incumbrance(s) before closing date, Purchaser thereafter. Survey, if required, to be furnished as expense of **N/A**. Warranty deed and ~~XXXXXXXX XXXXXXXX XXX~~ a policy of title insurance in Purchasers name, ~~XXXXXXXX XX XXXXXX~~ showing merchantable title clear of liens and assessments except as set out herein, to be furnished at Sellers expense as soon as practicable. Lien of Conservancy Districts, easements, restrictions, zoning and patent reservations, if any, to be assumed by Purchaser.

Paving **is paid.**, to be paid by **N/A**. Existing trust funds in the approximate amount of **N/A** to be assigned to buyer at **N/A** expense. Rent, taxes, interest, hazard and FHA mortgage insurance, if any, water, sewer and garbage charges, if any, are to be prorated to **closing**. Seller agrees to keep property adequately insured and to give possession of the premises to Purchaser on **closing** and certifies that property will be in the same condition, reasonable wear and tear excepted, as of the date of this agreement. ~~XXXXXXXX XXXXXXX XXXXXXX XXXXX XXXXXXX, XXXXXX XXXXX XXXXXX XXXXXX XXXXXXXX XXX XXXXXXX XXXXXX XXX XXXXXX XX XXXXXX XXXXXX XX XXXX XXXX.~~

Closing date **As soon as possible but not later than December 31, 1975**

The Broker herein is not in any way responsible for the condition of the property and in no way warrants the same.

All parties undersigned agree to complete closing within 72 hours after notification that papers are ready. Purchaser agrees to buy and Seller agrees to sell according to the terms and conditions set out hereinabove. Time is of the essence. This instrument comprises the entire understanding and agreement of the parties hereto on the subject matter herein contained and shall be binding upon and inure to the benefit of the parties, their heirs, executors, administrators, successors and assigns. Purchaser and Seller agree to pay their customary share of costs of closing the transaction, unless other arrangements are written above. Purchaser pays his own attorney fees.

In event Seller accepts this offer and Purchaser refuses or fails to consummate the purchase, Seller shall have the option of retaining the earnest money as partial liquidated damages and terminating this contract or of enforcing the same. Purchaser(s) hereby give(s) broker hereinafter named a specific period of **3** days to complete this purchase agreement, and agrees to keep this offer open for that time. If broker is unable to complete this agreement, earnest money is to be refunded in full to Purchaser and this agreement cancelled.

In the event the Seller remains in possession of the premises herein after all the instruments have been filed transferring title, then he will pay to the Purchaser $**N/A** per day as rental. In the event Purchaser occupies the property he shall pay to Seller the sum of $ **N/A** each day until the closing day, such advance to be computed in the closing, such rental to be paid unless other arrangements are made in writing between the Purchaser and Seller.

Dated this **1st** day of **July**, 19**75**, at **9:30** (A.M) ~~XXX XXX~~

Starline Cleaners Inc.

[signature]

Pre**s**ident
_____
Purchaser

By **Exchange Realty Inc.**
_____
Purchaser

'we hereby accept above offer to purchase and agree to pay agent a commission of **six** % on the full purchase price plus 4% New Mexico sales tax on the commission. In the event purchase is not consummated and earnest money forfeited, said earnest money is to be divided between Seller and Agent according to the Listing Contract.

[signature]
_____   _____
Seller   Seller

Date of Seller's Signature **July 2, 1975**

Figure 5-2

PURCHASE AGREEMENT
of

Exchange Realty Inc.

Received of <u>Starline Cleaners Inc.</u> Address <u>3514 Main N.W.</u>

Phone <u>432-9124</u> the sum of <u>$1,000.00</u> in the form of cash<u>   </u> Note<u>   </u> Check <u>X</u> dated <u>9/2/75</u>

<u>   </u> as deposit to be escrowed with broker as part payment for the Purchase of <u>Apartment Complex</u>
Type of property

<u>   </u> located at (address) <u>1517 Ogoshi Place S.E.</u>

legal description <u>Lots 15 through 25, Block 3 Valley Heights Addition</u>

<u>   </u> Albuquerque, New Mexico,

and to include the following improvements: <u>all existing.</u>

together with all planting and improvements except <u>no exceptions.</u>

THE FULL PURCHASE PRICE is $ <u>300,000.00</u> to be paid as follows: total down payment including above deposit to be approximately $ <u>50,000.00</u> cash, plus or minus prorations, upon execution of formal instruments; the Purchaser(s) assume(s) and agree(s) to pay the existing mortgage or lien of record, current as of date of transfer in the approximate amount of $ <u>200,000.00</u> with monthly payments of approximately $ <u>1801.67</u> on said mortgage and balance,

if any, to be paid as follows: <u>The balance of $50,000.00 to be paid by a note secured with a</u> <u>second mortgage on 1517 Ogoshi Place S.E. Said note to payable at $500.00 or</u> <u>more per month including 8% interest per year. This agreement to purchase is</u> <u>being made solely for the purpose of exchange and is contingent on that certain</u> <u>agreement between Starline Cleaners and Ed Baily dated July 1, 1975.</u>

Seller shall make payments due on above incumbrance(s) before closing date, Purchaser thereafter. Survey, if required, to be furnished as expense of <u>seller</u>. Warranty deed and ~~abstract xxxxxxxxx xx xxxx xx~~ a policy of title insurance ~~xx xxxxxxxx~~ ~~xxxxx xx xxxxxx xx xxxxx~~ showing merchantable title clear of liens and assessments except as set out herein, to be furnished at Sellers expense as soon as practicable. Lien of Conservancy Districts, easements, restrictions, zoning and patent reservations, if any, to be assumed by Purchaser.

Paving <u>is paid.</u> to be paid by <u>N/A</u> Existing trust funds in the approximate amount of <u>$5000.00</u> to be assigned to buyer at <u>seller's</u> expense. Rent, taxes, interest, hazard and FHA mortgage insurance, if any, water, sewer and garbage charges, if any, are to be prorated to <u>closing</u>. Seller agrees to keep property adequately insured and to give possession of the premises to Purchaser on <u>closing</u> and certifies that property will be in the same condition, reasonable wear and tear excepted, as of the date of this agreement. ~~Xxxxxxx xxxxxx xxxxxx xxxxxxx xxxxx xxxxxx~~ ~~xxxxx xxxxx xxxxx xxxxx xxxxxxx xxxxx xxxxxxxx xxxxxxxx xxxxxxxx xxxxxxxx xxxxxx xxxxx~~

Closing date <u>October 1, 1975</u>

The Broker herein is not in any way responsible for the condition of the property and in no way warrants the same.

All parties undersigned agree to complete closing within 72 hours after notification that papers are ready. Purchaser agrees to buy and Seller agrees to sell according to the terms and conditions set out hereinabove. Time is of the essence. This instrument comprises the entire understanding and agreement of the parties hereto on the subject matter herein contained and shall be binding upon and inure to the benefit of the parties, their heirs, executors, administrators, successors and assigns. Purchaser and Seller agree to pay their customary share of costs of closing the transaction, unless other arrangements are written above. Purchaser pays his own attorney fees.

In event Seller accepts this offer and Purchaser refuses or fails to consummate the purchase, Seller shall have the option of retaining the earnest money as partial liquidated damages and terminating this contract or of enforcing the same. Purchaser(s) hereby give(s) Broker hereinafter named a specific period of <u>3</u> days to complete this purchase agreement, and agrees to keep this offer open for that time. If broker is unable to complete this agreement, earnest money is to be refunded in full to Purchaser and this agreement cancelled.

In the event the Seller remains in possession of the premises herein after all the instruments have been filed transferring title, then he will pay to the Purchaser $ <u>N/A</u> per day as rental. In the event Purchaser occupies the property he shall pay to Seller the sum of $ <u>N/A</u> each day until the closing day, such advance to be computed in the closing, such rental to be paid unless other arrangements are made in writing between the Purchaser and Seller.

Dated this <u>2nd</u> day of <u>September</u>, 19 <u>75</u>, at <u>2:30</u> ~~XXXX~~ (P.M.)

Starline Cleaners Inc.

Jauno Lingo
President
Purchaser

By <u>Exchange Realty Inc.</u>
Purchaser

I/we hereby accept above offer to purchase and agree to pay agent a commission of <u>6</u> % on the full purchase price plus 4% New Mexico sales tax on the commission. In the event purchase is not consummated and earnest money forfeited, said earnest money is to be divided between Seller and Agent according to the Listing Contract.

Ray Baker
Seller

Seller

Date of Seller's Signature <u>9-3-75</u>

Figure 5–3

is not located. (7) This can be accomplished by the addition of one sentence to the clause in the previous example as follows:

> In the event acceptable exchange property is not located and the exchange is not closed by _____(date)_____, we shall be obligated to convey the subject property within 30 days of said date on the following terms:

The clause requires additional caution in that it gives the taxpayer a legal right to cash after a certain date. Care must be taken to either extend the date for closing the exchange before it arrives if exchange property isn't found or to close the exchange before the sale date. Failure to do one or the other will destroy the nontaxable benefits of the exchange.

Writing an Offer to Exchange with a Cash Take-Out

Another problem occurs when an exchange offer is initiated and the party receiving the offer wants cash instead of property. Fortunately, the problem can be solved and the exchange saved. A standard two-way exchange agreement is used by the party making the offer. The party receiving the exchange offer accepts, under the condition that a purchaser is located for the property offered in exchange. (29)

An example of this occurred when an exchange was made by Apartment Investment, Inc. which offered vacant land for an apartment complex owned by Dale and Mary Simpson. The Simpsons did not want the vacant land but did want to sell their apartments. To accomplish this, the following clause was inserted above their signature prior to acceptance:

> This agreement is contingent on arranging a purchase out of escrow of the exchange property offered by Apartment Investment, Inc. If a purchase satisfactory to the Simpsons cannot be arranged within 180 days of this acceptance, this agreement will become null and void and all deposits will be refunded.

By using this approach, you actually convert an exchange offer to a purchase offer for one of the participants, while protecting the exchange benefits for the taxpayer.

The specific wording of clauses used to accomplish a desired exchange can vary depending on the legal and tax advice obtained by the principals in the exchange. These clauses are presented in the hope that they will prove to be useful tools for the reader in the daily practice of real estate.

A buyer was located for the 10 acres offered by Apartment Investment within the 180-day time limit, and the exchange was closed. The buyer, Equity Investors Group, acquired 10 acres by purchase. The sellers, Dale and Mary Simpson, sold their apartments for cash to loan. Apartment Investment, Inc. exchanged 10 acres for 84 apartments tax-free. (See Figure 5–4.)

How to Tie Two-Party Exchanges into One Multiple Transaction Escrow

One of the necessary variations of the two-party exchange occurs when both parties want to exchange in principle but the property offered is not acceptable to one of them.

EXCHANGE AGREEMENT

Apartment Investment Inc. ...., the first party, offers to exchange

The real property situated in the City of Albuquerque ...., County of Bernalillo ...., State of New Mexico ....

described as: Tract 2 South Lomas Addition to the City of Albuquerque ....

consisting of: 10 acres valued at $260,000.00 ....

encumbered as follows:

Loans	Approximate Balance	Monthly Payment	Annual Interest %	Lender
none				

Leases	Remaining Term	Monthly Rentals	Other Terms	Lessee
none				

for the real property of: Dale and Mary Simpson ...., the second party,

which property is situated in the City of Albuquerque ...., County of Bernalillo ...., State of New Mexico ....

described as: Lots 1-25 block 4 Loma del Oeste Addition to the city of Albuquerque

further known as West Field Apartments

consisting of: 84 unfurnished apartments valued at $840,000.00 ....

encumbered as follows:

Loans	Approximate Balance	Monthly Payment	Annual Interest %		Lender
first	$580,000	$7000	8 1/2		First Savings

Leases	Remaining Term	Monthly Rentals	Other Terms	Lessee
scheduled to be furnished by second party				

ADJUSTMENT: Any net difference between the approximate loan balances shown above and the actual remaining balances of said loans at close of escrow shall be adjusted as follows: ☒ Cash ☐ Other:........................, provided that said loans shall not be reduced in excess of obligatory payments to principal made after this date, without the written consent of the other party to this agreement.

ENCUMBRANCES: In addition to any encumbrances referred to above, both parties shall take title subject to: 1) Real Estate Taxes not yet due and 2) Covenants, conditions, restrictions, reservations, rights, rights of way and easements of record, if any, which do not materially affect the value or intended use of the property.

TERMS AND CONDITIONS: Apartment Investment Inc. agrees to assume and pay the existing first mortgage on the West Field Apartments in the approximate amount indicated above.

EXAMINATION OF TITLE: 15 (fifteen) days from date of acceptance hereof are allowed each of the parties hereto for examination of title to the properties to be acquired by them and to report in writing any valid objections thereto. Any exceptions to title which would be disclosed by examination of the records shall be deemed to have been accepted unless reported in writing within said 15 days. If any objections are reported, the conveying party shall use all due diligence to remove such exceptions at his own expense within 60 days thereafter. But if such exceptions cannot be removed within the 60 days allowed, all rights and obligations hereunder shall terminate, unless the party acquiring the property so affected elects to accept the property subject to such exceptions.

EVIDENCE OF TITLE. Evidence of Title shall be in the form of ☒ a policy of title insurance, ☐ other: ....

to be paid for by the parties on the properties they are ☒ conveying, ☐ acquiring.

CLOSE OF ESCROW: Within 180 days from acceptance hereof, or upon removal of any exceptions to title, as provided above, whichever is later, both parties shall deposit in escrow all funds and instruments necessary to complete the exchange in accordance with the terms and conditions hereof.

Escrow holder shall be First American Title Co.

PRORATIONS: Rents, taxes, premiums on insurance acceptable to the party acquiring the property insured thereby, interest and other expenses of the herein properties shall be prorated as of the date of recordation of the deeds. Security deposits, advance rentals or considerations involving future lease credits shall be credited to the party acquiring title.

MAINTENANCE: Until possession is delivered, each party agrees to maintain heating, sewer, plumbing and electrical systems and any built-in appliances and equipment in his property in normal working order and to maintain the grounds.

NOTICES: Both parties warrant that they have no notice of violations relating to their respective properties from City, County or State agencies.

EXPIRATION: This offer shall expire unless a copy hereof with written acceptance is delivered to the First Party or his agent within 3 days from date.

TIME: Time is of the essence of this agreement.

BROKERAGE FEE: Upon acceptance hereof, the undersigned First Party hereby agrees to pay a brokerage fee for services rendered to:

Exchange Realty Inc.

as follows: $26,000 plus gross receipts tax in cash at closing

Should Second Party be unable to remove any exceptions to title objected to by First Party, as provided under the paragraph entitled "Examination of Title," then First Party shall be released from payment of any fee, unless he elects to accept the property subject thereto.

Exchange Realty Inc. ....is hereby authorized to act as agent for all parties hereto, may accept fees from all parties hereto, may cooperate with other agents and divide the fees in any manner satisfactory to them.

The undersigned First Party hereby acknowledges receipt of a copy hereof and acknowledges further that he has not received or relied upon or statements or representations by the agent, which are not herein expressed.

DATED: May 3, 1974

Exchange Realty Inc.	Agent	Apartment Investment Inc. _____ First Party
1301 Regals N.E.	Address	_President_ _____ First Party
234-4105	Phone	_____ First Party
By George Harrison GH		_____ First Party

FORM 102 (1-18-73)

CONTINUED ON REVERSE SIDE

Figure 5-4

ACCEPTANCE

The undersigned Second Party accepts the foregoing offer and agrees to exchange the herein described properties on the terms and conditions herein specified.

This agreement is contingent on the Simpson's arranging a purchase out of escrow of the exchange property offered by Apartment Investment, Inc. If the Simpsons cannot arrange a purchase satisfactory to them within 180 days of this acceptance, this agreement will become null and void and all deposits will be refunded.

BROKERAGE FEE: The undersigned Second Party agrees to pay a brokerage fee for services rendered to:

Exchange Realty Inc.

as follows: $50,000 plus gross receipts tax in cash at closing

Should First Party be unable to remove any exceptions to title objected to by Second Party, as provided under the paragraph entitled "Examination of Title," then Second Party shall be released from payment of any fee, unless he elects to accept the property subject thereto.

Exchange Realty Inc. ....is hereby authorized to act as agent for all parties hereto, may accept fees from all parties hereto, may cooperate with other agents and divide fees in any manner satisfactory to them.

The undersigned Second Party hereby acknowledges receipt of a copy hereof and acknowledges further that he has not received or relied upon any statements or representations by the agent, which are not herein expressed.

DATED: 5/4/74

Exchange Realty Inc.	Agent	_Dale Simpson_ _____ Second Party
1301 Regals N.E.	Address	_Mary Simpson_ _____ Second Party
234-4105	Phone	_____ Second Party
George Harrison GH		_____ Second Party

Figure 5–4 (cont'd)

To solve the problem and keep the transaction alive, the exchange can be accepted contingent on locating acceptable property.

An example of this occurred when Gary Brown offered to exchange his property for that of John Sutton. Although Sutton wanted an exchange, he did not want Brown's property. Since an exchange offer was in writing, signed by Brown, and both parties agreed in principle, Sutton accepted, provided acceptable property was located to replace Brown's. This was accomplished by inserting the following clause prior to Sutton's signing:

> This agreement is contingent on the location and exchange of other property in lieu of that offered by the first party.

Brown (actually his broker) then attempted to find real estate Sutton would accept. Suitable property was located and approved by Sutton within the specified time. Brown then offered to exchange his property for the property Sutton wanted, owned by Mike Butler, contingent on the original agreement with Sutton. The following clause was used for that contingency:

> This exchange is contingent on that certain exchange agreement dated February 13, 1975, between Gary Brown and John Sutton.

This clause tied the original two-way agreement into a multiple transaction involving three people and three properties. One week after this second agreement was signed, an unanticipated difficulty arose with Sutton's property, and Brown backed out. Having gone this far, the brokers involved didn't want to see the whole transaction fall apart, so they took on the task of finding other property acceptable to Brown. Within 30 days, property owned by Dave Richards was located and approved by Brown. Another agreement was written wherein Sutton and Richards agreed to exchange, contingent on the original February 13, 1975 agreement between Brown and Sutton.

At this point, the exchange became a four-party transaction in which neither of the two original parties received the property initially offered.

Map an Exchange by Using the Owners' Names

To get a clear picture of the activity in this multiple transaction, we can diagram the offers, final ownership and deed transmittal.

Offer Diagram	*Final Ownership Diagram*	*Deed Diagram*
Brown wants Sutton	Brown gets Richards	Brown deeds to Butler
Sutton wants Butler	Sutton gets Butler	Sutton deeds to Richards
Butler wants Brown	Butler gets Brown	Butler deeds to Sutton
—Change—	Richards gets Sutton	Richards deeds to Brown
Brown doesn't want Sutton		
Brown wants Richards		
Richards wants Sutton		

There are a number of dynamic elements which interact in keeping a multiple exchange like this alive. For the most part, success depends on the efforts of the brokers and the cooperation of the owners. This effort and cooperation permeates the entire process and is difficult, if not impossible, to measure except indirectly by the results of the exchange.

EXCHANGE WORK SHEET

BALANCING EQUITIES

	Gary Brown		John Sutton		Mike Butler		Dave Richards	
	Transferred	Received	Transferred	Received	Transferred	Received	Transferred	Received
	Apts	Offices	Offices	Apts	Apts	Apts	Offices	Offices
1. Market Value	$60,000	$70,000	$75,000	$90,000	$90,000	$60,000	$70,000	$75,000
2. Existing Loans	44,000	54,000	61,000	72,000	72,000	44,000	54,000	61,000
3. New Loans								
4. Equity (L.1 less L.2 & 3)	16,000	16,000	14,000	18,000	18,000	16,000	16,000	14,000
5. Cash Boot			4,000			2,000		2,000
6. Other (Boot) Property								
7. Loan Proceeds								
8. Balance	$16,000	$16,000	$18,000	$18,000	$18,000	$18,000	$16,000	$16,000

NETTING CASH

	Gary Brown	John Sutton	Mike Butler	Dave Richards
9. Cash Received (L.5 + L.7) Or (Paid) (L.5)	-0-	($4000)	$2000	$2000
10. Commissions	3600	4500	5400	4200
11. Transaction Costs	600	750	900	700
12. Total Capitalized Costs (L.10 + L.11)	(4200)	(5250)	(6300)	(4900)
13. Net Cash Received Or (Paid) (L.9 less L.12)	($4200)	($9250)	($4300)	($2900)

Figure 5–5

EXCHANGE AGREEMENT

__Gary Brown__

hereby agree to exchange the following described property, situated in the City of __Grants__
County of __Valencia__, State of __N.M.__, to wit: __Lot 10, Block 12 Volcano__
__Addition__   Address: __1521 North 90th Street__

including all planting and improvements and __no exceptions.__

FOR the property of __John Sutton__
situated in the City of __Grants__   County of __Valencia__, State of __N.M.__
To wit: __Lot 3, Block 5 Tower Addition__   Address: __321 Alamo, N.E.__

including all planting and improvements and __no exceptions.__

on the following TERMS AND CONDITIONS:

1. The market value of 1521 North 90th Street is $60,000; subject to a
note and first mortgage in the approximate amount of $44,000 payable at
$400 per month including 8% interest per year which the acquiring party
agrees to assume and pay.

2. The market value of 321 Alamo N.E. is $75,000; subject to a note and
first mortgage in the approximate amount of $61,000 payable at $500 per
month including 7 1/2% interest per year which the acquiring party agrees
to assume and pay.

3. John Sutton agrees to pay $4,000 into escrow to balance equities.

    This agreement is hereby amended and is contingent on the
location and exchange of other property to Brown in lieu
of that offered by Sutton.

The risk of loss or damage to said premises by fire or otherwise, until delivery of the deed or other conveyance, is assumed by the owner of each of the said properties respectively.

The title insurance policies or abstracts to be furnished in connection with this exchange shall show titles to be merchantable and free of all liens and encumbrances except current year's taxes, Conservancy District liens, easements, restrictions and patent reservations of record, and such liens and encumbrances as may be otherwise provided for herein. Each party shall pay for title insurance or abstracting fees for the property to be conveyed.

Should errors appear in the titles to any of said properties, such errors shall be corrected by and at the expense of the owner thereof. Should any error be uncorrected by 120 days from date, then this agreement shall terminate, unless the time for correcting errors be extended by the parties hereto, or unless the title to the properties affected be accepted subject thereto.

In the event that either party is assuming a loan against one of the above properties, and the grantor thereof is the owner of a Tax and Insurance Account or Trust Fund maintained with the lender, this account shall be transferred to the new owner, who agrees to pay seller the amount of such account.

Closing date __March 30, 1975__ All parties undersigned agree to complete closing within 72 hours after notification that papers are ready.

Rents, taxes, interest, hazard and FHA mortgage insurance, if any, water, sewer and garbage charges, if any, are to be prorated to __closing__ The date of possession shall be on ~~XXXXX~~ __closing__

The __Realty Exchange__ of __Albuquerque__ is hereby authorized to act as broker for all parties hereto and may accept commission therefrom. Should said broker cooperate with another broker or other brokers in this exchange, the commission may be divided by such brokers in any manner satisfactory to them. Receipt of $ __1,000__ earnest money deposit is hereby acknowledged.

By _(signature)_

Dated __February 13, 1975__   _(signature) Gary Brown_

ACCEPTANCE:

The undersigned hereby accept the foregoing offer upon the terms and conditions stated and agree that said broker may act broker for all parties hereto and may accept commission therefrom.

__This agreement is contingent on the location and exchange of other__
__property in lieu of that offered by the first party: Gary Brown. GB__

(signature) John Sutton

Dated __2/17/75__

Figure 5–6

EXCHANGE AGREEMENT

Gary Brown
_____

hereby agree to exchange the following described property, situated in the City of __Grants__
County of __Valencia__ , State of __N.M.__ , to wit: __Lot 10, Block 12 Volcano__
__Addition__   Address: __1521 North 90th Street__

including all planting and improvements and __no exceptions.__

FOR the property of _____ __Mike Butler__
situated in the City of __Grants__ _____ County of __Valencia__ _____, State of __N.M.__
To wit: __Lots 5,6,7 Block 3 Richman Addition__ Address: __4225 Simpson, S.E.__

including all planting and improvements and __no exceptions.__

on the following TERMS AND CONDITIONS:

1. The market value of 1521 North 90th Street is $60,000; subject to a
note and first mortgage in the approximate amount of $44,000 payable at
$400 per month including 8% interest per year which the acquiring party
agrees to assume and pay.

2. The market value of 4225 Simpson S.E. is $90,000; subject to a note
and first mortgage in the approximate amount of $72,000 payable at $625
per month including 7% interest per year which the acquiring party agrees
to assume and pay.

3. Mike Butler to be credited with $2000 in escrow to balance equities.

4. This exchange is contingent on that certain exchange agreement dated
February 13, 1975 between Gary Brown and John Sutton.

The risk of loss or damage to said premises by fire or otherwise, until delivery of the deed or other conveyance, is assumed by the owner of each of the said properties respectively.

The title insurance policies or abstracts to be furnished in connection with this exchange shall show titles to be merchantable and free of all liens and encumbrances except current year's taxes, Conservancy District liens, easements, restrictions and patent reservations of record, and such liens and encumbrances as may be otherwise provided for herein. Each party shall pay for title insurance or abstracting fees for the property to be conveyed.

Should errors appear in the titles to any of said properties, such errors shall be corrected by and at the expense of the owner thereof. Should any error be uncorrected by 120 days from date, then this agreement shall terminate, unless the time for correcting errors be extended by the parties hereto, or unless the title to the properties affected be accepted subject thereto.

In the event that either party is assuming a loan against one of the above properties, and the grantor thereof is the owner of a Tax and Insurance Account or Trust Fund maintained with the lender, this account shall be transferred to the new owner, who agrees to pay seller the amount of such account.

Closing date __March 30, 1975__ _____ All parties undersigned agree to complete closing within 72 hours after notification that papers are ready.

Rents, taxes, interest, hazard and FHA mortgage insurance, if any, water, sewer and garbage charges, if any, are to be prorated to __closing__ The date of possession shall be on ~~XXXXX~~ __closing__

The __Realty Exchange__ of __Albuquerque__ _____ is hereby authorized to act as broker for all parties hereto and may accept commission therefrom. Should said broker cooperate with another broker or other brokers in this exchange, the commission may be divided by such brokers in any manner satisfactory to them. Receipt of $ __1000__ earnest money deposit is hereby acknowledged.

By. _____

Dated __March 2, 1975__ _____   _Gary Brown_ _____

ACCEPTANCE:
The undersigned hereby accept the foregoing offer upon the terms and conditions stated and agree that said broker may act broker for all parties hereto and may accept commission therefrom.

Mike Butler _____

Dated _____ __3-4-75__ _____   _____

Figure 5–7

EXCHANGE AGREEMENT

_____John Sutton_____

hereby agree to exchange the following described property, situated in the City of _Grants_____
County of _Valencia_____, State of _N.M._____, to wit: _Lot 3 Block 5 Tower Addition_
_Address: 321 Alamo, N.E._____

including all planting and improvements and _no exceptions_____

____FOR the property of _____Dave Richards_____
situated in the City of _Grants_____ County of _Valencia_____, State of _N.M.___
To wit: _Lots 3 and 4 Block 8 Crossroads Addition. Address: 1305 Grand, N.W._

including all planting and improvements and _no exceptions._____

on the following TERMS AND CONDITIONS:

1.   The market value of 321 Alamo N.E. is $75,000; subject to a note and

first mortgage in the approximate amount of $61,000 payable at $500 per

month including 7 1/2 % interest per year which the acquiring party agrees

to assume and pay.

2.   The market value of 1305 Grand N.W. is $70,000; subject to a note and

first mortgage in the approximate amount of $54,000 payable at $600 per

month including 7 3/4% interest per year which the acquiring party agrees

to assume and pay.

3.   Dave Richards to be credited with $2000 in escrow to balance equities.

4.   This exchange is contingent on that certain exchange agreement dated

February 13, 1975 between Gary Brown and John Sutton.

The risk of loss or damage to said premises by fire or otherwise, until delivery of the deed or other conveyance, is assumed by the owner of each of the said properties respectively.

The title insurance policies or abstracts to be furnished in connection with this exchange shall show titles to be merchantable and free of all liens and encumbrances except current year's taxes, Conservancy District liens, easements, restrictions and patent reservations of record, and such liens and encumbrances as may be otherwise provided for herein. Each party shall pay for title insurance or abstracting fees for the property to be conveyed.

Should errors appear in the titles to any of said properties, such errors shall be corrected by and at the expense of the owner thereof. Should any error be uncorrected by 120 days from date, then this agreement shall terminate, unless the time for correcting errors be extended by the parties hereto, or unless the title to the properties affected be accepted subject thereto.

In the event that either party is assuming a loan against one of the above properties, and the grantor thereof is the owner of a Tax and Insurance Account or Trust Fund maintained with the lender, this account shall be transferred to the new owner, who agrees to pay seller the amount of such account.

Closing date _March 30, 1975_____ All parties undersigned agree to complete closing within 72 hours after notification that papers are ready.

Rents, taxes, interest, hazard and FHA mortgage insurance, if any, water, sewer and garbage charges, if any, are to be prorated to _closing___ The date of possession shall be on ~~before~~ _closing_____

The _Realty Exchange_ of _Albuquerque_____ is hereby authorized to act as broker for all parties hereto and may accept commission therefrom. Should said broker cooperate with another broker or other brokers in this exchange, the commission may be divided by such brokers in any manner satisfactory to them. Receipt of $_1000____ earnest money deposit is hereby acknowledged.

By _____

Dated _March 21, 1975_____   _John Sutton_____

ACCEPTANCE:

The undersigned hereby accept the foregoing offer upon the terms and conditions stated and agree that said broker may act as broker for all parties hereto and may accept commission therefrom.

_____

_____

_____   _Dave Richards_____

Dated _____3/22/75_____

Figure 5-8

But the mechanics and the legality of this approach are well defined and based on the net result as it affects the individual taxpayer in question. (30), (43) A multiple exchange should be tied to one escrow by including a contingency that cites the original (Brown-Sutton) exchange agreement in all the agreements. When Brown backed out, the transaction was held together by amending the original agreement to provide for the location of property suitable to Brown in lieu of Sutton's. Modification of any exchange agreement is possible if it is done prior to closing. Finally, the deeds were transferred directly without the unnecessary formality of running people who don't end up owning the property through title. (23), (43) The completed agreements for this transaction appear in Figures 5–5 through 5–8.

Note the following clause, which was inserted in the original Brown-Sutton agreement as an amendment to keep the transaction alive:

> This agreement is hereby amended and is contingent on the location and exchange of other property to Brown in lieu of that offered by Sutton.

Flexibility Is the Key to Successful Exchanging

The two-party exchange is far from being the restricted and impossible-to-work transaction that it is often thought to be. With a flexible attitude and the basic tools of the trade, you can turn what sometimes seems a hopeless situation into a solid opportunity for a successful exchange.

All too often, an offer to exchange is never put in writing because the taxpayer thinks the other owner won't accept his property. But that worry need not stop a transaction before it gets in writing. Availability of the alternative courses of accepting an exchange offer with a "cash take-out" contingency or "in lieu of" locating acceptable property can greatly increase the chances of success for any exchange.

Furthermore, having "just the right form" is not necessarily going to make the exchange succeed. In fact, trying to make an exchange perfect on paper can often stand in the way of getting the job done. A potentially beneficial exchange should never be allowed to run aground because of disagreement over the form used to describe the facts of the transaction.

Each Real Estate Association will usually have its own approved form. The following samples (Figures 5–9 through 5–12) illustrate the variations that occur from state to state. The "Exchange Contract" is widely used in New Mexico and is a very binding form that has been around for several years. Then follow the forms used in California, Arizona and Colorado, which are excellent because they provide ample blank space for explanation of the terms and conditions of the exchange. Since real estate law varies in custom and practice from state to state, it is always wise to have local legal counsel approve a form before it is put into wide use.

Exchange Contract

THIS CONTRACT, Made and entered into this................day of.........................., 19......, by and between

....
of................County, State of................, hereinafter called "first party," and...

....
of................County, State of................, hereinafter called "second party";

1. Witnesseth: That first party, for and in consideration of the covenants hereinafter contained has bargained and exchanged, and does hereby agree to convey or cause to be conveyed to second party, by................................the following described real estate situated in................County, New Mex., to wit: ....

....

....

....

with all improvements thereon, and fixtures of a permanent nature, said improvements and fixtures to be in their present condition, ordinary wear and tear accepted.

Subject to building restrictions, if any, of record; free and clear of all taxes and assessments both general and special which can be paid at date hereof, and all incumbrances whatsoever, except the following to be assumed by second party:........................

....

....

....

First party, in addition, does hereby agree to pay the second party $.............. in cash upon consummation of this exchange.

2. In consideration whereof second party has bargained and exchanged, and hereby agrees to convey or cause to be conveyed to said first party, by................................, the following described real estate situated in.............County, New Mex., to wit:..

....

....

....

with all improvements thereon and fixtures of a permanent nature, said improvements and fixtures to be in their present condition, ordinary wear and tear excepted.

Subject to building restrictions, if any, of record; free and clear of all taxes and assessments both general and special which can be paid at date hereof, and all incumbrances whatsoever, except the following to be assumed by first party: ....

....

....

....

Second party, in addition, does hereby agree to pay the first party $................in cash upon consummation of this exchange.

3. Possession and income of the respective properties shall go to the respective grantees at and from the date of transfer of title unless herein otherwise specified.

4. Taxes for the current year, based upon the previous year's taxes, together with rents, water rents, interest, insurance and special assessments shall be apportioned between the parties as of the date of................................. Also allowance shall be made where any reduction in incumbrance balance resulting from obligatory payments is made after date of this contract.

5. Special conditions: ....

....

....

....

6. Each party shall, within.............days from date hereof, deliver to and at the office of...

....deeds or contracts to their respective properties to be delivered to the respective grantees upon completion of this contract, and shall, at the same time and place, deliver complete Abstracts of Title to their respective properties or title insurance policies with binder, certified to the date of this agreement.

7. Each party shall have...........days from date of such delivery for examination of title and to report, in writing to the other party, at ...., the defects, if any, found therein.

8. Either party whose title, by such examination and report is found to be defective shall, within........................days from date of such written notice, correct and remove such defects; and unless such defects be corrected within said time and no extension of time be given—time being the essence of any entire contract—this contract shall be null and void, at the option of the party not in default, and the abstracts be returned to their respective owners; or party not in default may pursue his legal remedies.

9. Each of said parties shall deposit with...the sum of $.....................
as a guaranty of good faith, to be returned to the respective parties when the transaction is completed, and agents commissions are paid; but if either party shall fail to perform this contract, said deposit made by him shall be paid to his agent herein to apply on his commission, and the deposit of the party not in default shall be returned to him, but such payment shall not affect the right or liabilities of said parties hereunder; and the party so failing to perform shall pay all agents' commissions herein provided for and such agents may sue him directly on this contract for same.

10. It is understood that each party to this transaction agrees to pay forthwith to his agent a Real Estate Commission as provided by separate agreement.

....Agent of 1st Party   ....Agent of 2nd Party

11. This contract is made subject to approval by............. party within ....days from date hereof, and upon approval hereof shall become a valid and binding contract between 1st and 2nd parties. This contract shall inure to the benefit of and be binding upon the heirs, legal representatives, successors and assigns of each of said parties.

12. Upon failure of...............party to approve this contract, deposit of the other party to be refunded.

In witness whereof said parties have hereunto set their hands and seals, the day and year first above written.

.... (Seal)   .... (Seal)

.... (Seal)   .... (Seal)

Figure 5–9

EXCHANGE AGREEMENT

CALIFORNIA ASSOCIATION OF REALTORS STANDARD FORM

....

....

first party, hereby offers to exchange the following described property, situated in...

.... County of .... California:

....

....

....

....

....

For the following described property of..

.... second party, situated in

.... County of .... California:

....

....

....

....

Terms and Conditions of Exchange:

....

....

....

....

....

....

....

....

....

The parties hereto shall execute and deliver, within...............................days from the date this offer is accepted, all instruments, in writing, necessary to transfer title to said properties and complete and consummate this exchange. Each party shall supply Preliminary Title Reports for their respective properties. Evidences of title shall be California Land Title Association standard coverage form policies of title insurance, showing titles to be merchantable and free of all liens and encumbrances, except taxes and those liens and encumbrances as otherwise set forth herein. Each party shall pay for the policies of Title Insurance for the property to be acquired ☐ conveyed ☐

If either party is unable to convey a marketable title, except as herein provided, within three months after acceptance hereof by second party, or if the improvements on any of the herein named properties be destroyed or materially damaged prior to transfer of title or delivery of agreement of sale, then this agreement shall be of no further effect, except as to payment of commissions and expenses incurred in connection with examination of title, unless the party acquiring the property so affected elects to accept the title the other party can convey or subject to the conditions of the improvements.

Taxes, insurance premiums (if policies be satisfactory to party acquiring the property affected thereby), rents, interest and other expenses of said properties shall be pro-rated as of the date of transfer of title or delivery of agreement of sale, unless otherwise provided herein.

....of...Calif..
Broker   Address   Phone No.

is hereby authorized to act as broker for all parties hereto and may accept commission therefrom. Should second party accept this offer, first party agrees to pay said broker commission for services rendered as follows:-

....

....

Should second party be unable to convey a marketable title to his property then first party shall be released from payment of any commission, unless he elects to accept the property subject thereto. First party agrees that broker may cooperate with other brokers and divide commissions in any manner satisfactory to them.

This offer shall be deemed revoked unless accepted in writing within...............................days after date hereof and such acceptance is communicated to first party within said period. Broker is hereby given the exclusive and irrevocable right to obtain acceptance of second party within said period. Time is the essence of this contract.

....

....

....

Dated...19...................   ....

A C C E P T A N C E

Second party hereby accepts the foregoing offer upon the terms and conditions stated and agrees to pay commission for services rendered, to:-

....of...Calif..
Broker   Address   Phone No.

as follows:-...

Second party agrees that broker may act as broker for all parties hereto and may accept commission therefrom, and may co-operate with other brokers and divide commissions in any manner satisfactory to them.

Should first party be unable to convey a marketable title to his property then second party shall be released from payment of any commission, unless he elects to accept the property of first party subject thereto.

....

....

....

Dated...19...................

For these forms address California Association of Realtors 505 Shatto Place, Los Angeles 90020. All rights reserved. Copyright 1972 by California Association of Realtors

FORM E 14   REVISED APRIL, 1972

Note: Changes are made frequently to reflect new regulations and laws. The reader should be sure he has an up-to-date form before using it in business.

Figure 5–10

R
REALTOR

AGREEMENT FOR THE
EXCHANGE OF PROPERTY

Agreement No. _____

By _____

Date _____

_____ , Arizona   _____ , 19____

Agent for both parties to this agreement shall be:

WITNESSETH THAT:

Party of the First Part, hereinafter for convenience referred to as:

hereby offers and agrees to convey and exchange the following described property, including all buildings or improvements located thereon and any rights appurtenant thereto:

SUBJECT TO:

FOR THE PROPERTY NOW OWNED BY:

Party of the Second Part, hereinafter for convenience referred to as:

hereby agrees to convey and exchange the following described property, including all buildings or improvements located thereon and any rights appurtenant thereto:

SUBJECT TO:

Form approved by Arizona Association of Real Estate Exchangors 3/74

Figure 5–11

TERMS AND CONDITIONS OF EXCHANGE

All words used herein in the singular shall include the plural, and the masculine gender shall include the feminine and neuter, and the present tense shall include the future.

Until possession is given, each party agrees to maintain the property to be exchanged in working order, and to maintain the grounds and leave the premises in substantially the same condition as currently exists.

In the event that any Party to this Agreement or Broker is required to employ legal counsel to enforce any of the terms of this Agreement, the prevailing party shall be entitled to recover his reasonable attorney's fees and costs incurred.

All parties agree to pay said broker's commission or fee for services rendered in accordance with the provisions of separate agreements pertaining thereto, and they also agree that Brokers may cooperate with other duly licensed Brokers and divide commissions or fees in any manner satisfactory to them.

All parties to this Agreement hereby acknowledge that they have investigated the respective properties and the Brokers are hereby released from all responsibility regarding valuation and representation of condition.

All understandings and agreements heretofore and between the parties are merged into this Agreement which alone fully and completely expresses their understanding, and neither party is relying upon any statement or representation as to valuation or condition of the property, not embodied herein, made by the other.

This Agreement shall be binding upon all parties, their heirs, personal representatives, successors and assigns.

Time is of the essence of this Agreement.

_____shall act as Escrow Agent for closing of this transaction and all funds and necessary instruments, with the exception of the earnest money deposit, shall be deposited with it. Escrow fees are to be divided equally between the Parties.

All taxes, insurance premiums, impoundments and assessments, including liens assessed but not yet of record, and encumbrances, rental and water charges on respective properties, shall be prorated as of _____, 19 _____, and each Party shall deliver possession of the property he now owns to the other party as of date of closing. All properties conveyed shall also be subject to: all restrictions of record, utility easements, and zoning ordinances. Closing date of this transaction shall be on or before _____, 19 _____.

Should a party be unable to furnish marketable title to the property he is exchanging, such party shall have thirty (30) days from the date of this Agreement to perfect the same. Should a party be unable to convey marketable title to the property he is exchanging, then the other Party shall be released from payment of any commission or fee unless he elects to accept the property subject thereto, provided, however, Broker shall still be entitled to his fee from the Party who was unable to deliver marketable title to his property.

We, the undersigned Party of the First Part, do hereby give the below named Broker exclusive right to and including _____

19 _____, to obtain the acceptance by Party of the Second Part of this exchange of property, and when so accepted shall become a binding Agreement to convey to party of the Second Part in substantially as good condition as of this date, said property, which we now own as hereinabove described, as per terms and conditions stated herein. We further agree that Broker may act as agent for all parties to any transactions in connection with the above described property and may accept from any or all parties to consummated transactions, commissions or fees for services rendered including commissions of fees from both parties. On closing we agree to furnish title insurance on the property which we are conveying and to pay customary sales expenses.

Dated _____, 19 _____

BROKER: PARTY OF THE 1st PART

_____   _____

_____   _____

ACCEPTANCE

We, the undersigned Party of the Second Part, hereby accept the foregoing offer and agree to convey to the Party of the First Part, the property which we now own as hereinabove described as per terms and conditions stated herein. On closing we agree to furnish title insurance on the property which we are conveying and to pay customary sale expenses. Should Party of the First Part be unable to convey a marketable title to his property, then Party of the Second Part shall be released from payment of any commission or fee unless he elects to accept the property of the First Party subject thereto.

Dated _____, 19 _____   Address _____

BROKER: PARTY OF THE 2nd PART

_____   _____

_____   _____

Figure 5–11 (cont'd.)

MULTIPLE LISTING SERVICE
OF GRAND JUNCTION, COLORADO

CONTRACT TO EXCHANGE REAL ESTATE
(With Valuations)

THIS AGREEMENT made and entered into this_____day of_____, 19_____, by and between_____whose address is
_____, hereinafter referred to as "First Party" and_____
_____whose address is_____
_____, hereinafter referred to as "Second Party,"

WITNESSETH,

1. First Party agrees to convey to Second Party the following described real estate, situate in the_____
County of_____, State of Colorado, to-wit:

with all easements and rights of way appurtenant thereto, all improvements thereon and all fixtures of a permanent nature, if any, in their present condition, ordinary wear and tear excepted, known as_____ ___
_____ and the following personal property:

by good and sufficient_____warranty deed (and bill of sale). Said real (and personal) property, for the purpose of this contract, has a gross valuation of $_____. Said property will be conveyed subject to the following encumbrances which the Second Party (will) (will not) assume and agree to pay:

If an encumbrance is to remain on the property after conveyance, the second party agrees to pay a loan transfer fee not to exceed $_____ and it is a condition of this contract that there will be no change in the terms or conditions of said encumbrance except_____
_____

2. Second Party agrees to convey to First Party the following described real estate, situate in the_____
County of_____, State of Colorado, to-wit:

with all easements and rights of way appurtenant thereto, all improvements thereon and all fixtures of a permanent nature, if any, in their present condition, ordinary wear and tear excepted, known as_____
_____and the following personal property:

by good and sufficient_____warranty deed (and bill of sale). Said real (and personal) property, for the purpose of this contract, has a gross valuation of $_____. Said property will be conveyed subject to the following encumbrances which the First Party (will) (will not) assume and agree to pay:

If an encumbrance is to remain on the property after conveyance, the first party agrees to pay a loan transfer fee not to exceed $_____ and it is a condition of this contract that there will be no change in the terms or conditions of said encumbrance except_____
_____

No. EX 30-7-71 Contract to Exchange Real Estate (With Valuations)

Figure 5–12

3. The difference between the values of the respective properties, after having considered and deducted the encumbrances above described, shall be deemed for the purposes of this agreement to be $_____ and said sum shall be due and payable by_____ Party to_____ Party as follows:

4. Title shall be merchantable in the respective parties hereto. Each party agrees, at his option and expense, to furnish to the other party, on or before_____, 19_____, an abstract of title to his property, certified to date, or a current commitment for title insurance policy. If either party elects to furnish said title insurance commitment, that party will deliver the title insurance policy to the other party after closing and pay the premium thereon. Each party shall have_____days from date of delivery of such evidence of title, to examine title and report, in writing to the other party, the defects, if any, found therein. Either party whose title by such examination and report is found to be defective, shall within 60 days from date of such written notice, correct and remove such defects; and unless such defects be corrected within said time (and if no extension of time is given) this contract shall be null and void at the option of the party giving notice, and each party shall be released from all obligations hereunder and any payments made herewith shall be returned forthwith to the party who made such payments, upon return of any abstract furnished to that party.

5. General taxes for 19_____ (based on 19_____ levy and 19_____ assessment), personal property taxes, prepaid rents, water rents, sewer rents, FHA mortgage insurance premiums, interest on encumbrances, if any, and_____shall be apportioned to date of delivery of deeds with respect to each property. Each party shall give credit at closing for any tenant security deposits. Loan balances are to be adjusted at the time of closing. Any encumbrances required to be paid, may be paid from the proceeds of this transaction.

6. Each party agrees to execute and deliver his deed to the other party on_____, 19_____, or, by mutual agreement, at an earlier date, conveying his property free and clear of all taxes (including special improvements now installed, whether assessed or not unless specifically hereinafter excepted), except general taxes for the year of closing which said other party assumes and agrees to pay subject to the adjustment herein provided for. The property of each party shall be subject to building and zoning regulations pertaining thereto and shall be subject to any tenancies hereinafter set forth and shall be free and clear of all liens and encumbrances except those hereinabove described, and except:

*As to the property described in paragraph one

*As to the property described in paragraph two

7. The hour and place of closing shall be designated by_____

8. Possession of the premises shall be delivered to each purchaser concurrently with the transfer of title or as follows: _____

The property described in paragraph one shall be subject to the following leases or tenancies:

and the property described in paragraph two shall be subject to the following leases and tenancies:

*There should be inserted here any reservations, restrictive covenants, easements, rights of way, special taxes or any other exceptions to which the property is subject.

No. EX 30-7-71

Figure 5-12 (cont'd.)

9. In the event that the premises to be conveyed by either party are substantially damaged by fire, flood or other casualty between the date of this agreement and the date of transfer of title, this agreement may, at the option of the other party, be declared null and void and any obligations hereunder terminated.

10. Both parties have examined the properties and accept the same in the present condition. Neither party is relying on representations of the other party or real estate broker or agent, as to zoning, other than as specifically set forth herein.

11. It is agreed that_____is

acting as broker for the first party and_____

_____, is acting as broker for the second party. If the broker named for each party herein shall be same, then each of the parties agrees that said broker may act as broker for each party and may receive such commissions from each party as may be established by separate agreement.

12. First party herewith deposits with broker for the second party $_____ by (cash) (check) (note) and second party herewith deposits with broker for the first party $_____ by (cash) (check) (note), as a guaranty of good faith, to be returned to the respective parties when the transaction is completed.

13. Time is of the essence hereof, and if any payment or other condition hereof is not made, tendered or performed by either of the parties hereto as herein provided, then this contract, at the option of the party who is not in default may be terminated. In case of such termination, any deposit made by the defaulting party shall be retained by the broker for the non-defaulting party, on behalf of said non-defaulting party, and the payments so retained shall be divided between the said broker and the nondefaulting party one-half thereof to the broker, but not to exceed a sum equal to the agreed commission, and the balance to the nondefaulting party. In the event of such termination, any payments made by the nondefaulting party shall be returned to said party, and the nondefaulting party may recover such additional damages as may be proper. In the event however the nondefaulting party elects to treat this contract as being in full force and effect, then nothing herein shall be construed to prevent its specific performance.

14. This contract shall be binding upon and shall inure to the benefit of the parties hereto, their heirs, successors, and assigns.

15. Additional Provisions:

16. In the event this agreement is not signed by all parties hereto on or before_____ 19_____, this agreement shall become void and of no effect

IN WITNESS WHEREOF the parties hereto have set their hands and seals.

	Date			Date
	( )			( )
	( )			( )
First Party	( )		Second Party	( )
Broker	( )		broker	( )

By:_____   _____

No. EX 31-7-71

Figure 5–12 (cont'd.)

6

Writing Multiparty
Agreements That Will
Make the Exchange Work

A well-written multiparty exchange agreement is one of the most useful tools in exchanging. It can make money for you.

In this chapter, we will see how an agreement can be set up to accomplish an exchange regardless of the difficulties in the transaction. This chapter will provide:

- strategies for dealing with uncooperative participants in the exchange;
- the complete sequence from the initial agreement to acquisition of the exchange property; and
- methods of modifying strategy to meet requirements often imposed by the buyer.

A Multiparty Agreement Should Conform
to the Facts of the Transaction

The primary objective in a multiparty exchange is to structure the written agreements in a way that meets the practical requirements of getting the job done without sacrificing the nontaxable aspects of the exchange. There are two common types of multiparty exchanges: (1) The ABC Multiparty Exchange, which occurs when "B" buys "C" and exchanges it for "A," and (2) the ACB Multiparty Exchange, which occurs when "A" and "C" exchange and "B" agrees to buy "A" from "C" out of escrow, fulfilling a contingency of the exchange. The second approach is an exchange with a cash take-out, and it is essentially a variation of the two-way exchange. The first sequence forms the standard multiparty exchange and is the subject of this chapter. It's the structure that characterizes the majority of exchanges that have made it to tax court—and it's the method most frequently used to solve the typical real estate tax problem under Section 1031.

99

There are several techniques that can be used to fit the mechanics to the circumstances of a multiparty exchange. In fact, the techniques for completing the agreements used in a multiparty exchange are as important practically as the agreements are legally. And circumstances restricting the participants—what they will and won't do—to a large extent determine the approach that must be taken to accomplish an exchange.

For example, if the buyer is a large corporation in another city, is it really going to be practical to get signed offers and counters on the exchange property? It's hard to imagine a real estate transaction that doesn't go through some form of written negotiation. What should you do if the buyer agrees to exchange but doesn't want to be bothered by making offers for exchange property until closing? Is there a danger of losing tax benefits if the taxpayer looks for exchange property and negotiates the acquisition? Is it possible for the taxpayer to tie up the exchange property for purchase by the buyer? These are the practical problems that the agreements must solve.

Adapting Multiparty Exchange Agreements to the Circumstances of the Transaction

The final measure of whether an exchange succeeds is the execution of the documents in the transaction—did each piece of paper get signed step by step? When it is impossible to obtain signatures on an essential document, and the exchange falters because of some external factor, all the tax planning and financial analysis suddenly become academic. It is the completion of the documents that makes the transaction a reality.

Therefore, the methods used to carry out the exchange must conform to the practical restraints of the transaction, and the agreements used must adapt to these restraints, without attempting to force circumstances to conform to the agreements beyond reasonable expectations. And under no circumstances should an agreement be the cause of the destruction of an otherwise well-structured exchange. If the facts of the transaction and the necessary mechanics of getting the job done conflict with the agreements, try changing the documents, not the facts.

Problems of mechanics in a multiparty exchange usually relate to the buyer of the exchange property. This is a practical problem which can be classified in three general categories that describe the degree of cooperation exhibited by the buyer of the exchange property. Each situation has a different set of problems and consequently requires a different set of documents to get the job done:

1. A Cooperative Local Buyer
   a. An exchange agreement signed by the taxpayer and buyer.
   b. A letter from the taxpayer to the buyer designating acceptable exchange property.
   c. A purchase agreement signed by the buyer and owner of the designated exchange property.
   d. In some cases, a document extending the original exchange agreement.

This is probably the most easily completed exchange. If the buyer has a cooperative nature and will put up with a lot of purchase offers that don't work, a number of problems and fears of losing tax benefits and the resulting delays can be eliminated. Unfortunately, though, a buyer willing to participate in the negotiation of an acquisition is not always there when you need him to sign an offer.

2. A Cooperative Out-of-Town Buyer
   a. An exchange agreement signed by the taxpayer and buyer.
   b. A limited power of attorney signed by the buyer designating an agent (usually his attorney) to sign offers to buy exchange property within the limits of the exchange agreement.
   c. A letter from the taxpayer to the buyer's agent designating acceptable exchange property.

     d. A purchase agreement signed by the buyer's agent and the owner of the exchange property.

     e. In some cases, a document extending the original exchange agreement.

This second strategy differs from the first only in that an agent is substituted for the buyer. This technique solves a problem that could cause an expensive bill for air travel. The important thing in this approach is that the agent must be comfortable in knowing that the purchase agreement does not obligate his client beyond the terms of the initial exchange agreement. This can easily be accomplished by a clause that makes the offer contingent on the terms and conditions of the exchange agreement. Correctly written, the contingency would void the purchase agreement if the terms of the exchange were inadvertently violated.

But the real problem in a multiparty exchange arises when the buyer is out-and-out-unwilling to cooperate.

  3. An Uncooperative Buyer (Note: This approach has a number of practical advantages regardless of the circumstances and was tested in two cases. (1) (13))

     a. An exchange agreement signed by the taxpayer and buyer in which the buyer agrees to accept assignment of purchase agreements signed by the taxpayer.

     b. A purchase agreement or option signed by the *taxpayer* and owner which contains a clause allowing the taxpayer to assign all of his rights and obligations under the purchase agreement to the buyer (thus creating a novation).

This strategy allows the taxpayer to negotiate in writing for the exchange property essentially as agent for the buyer. (1) Then he completes the transaction by transferring his rights and obligations to purchase to the buyer under the terms of the exchange agreement.

The document used to acquire the exchange property could be in the form of an option provided all the steps are taken to clearly exercise the option and obligate the buyer. (13) But from a practical standpoint, a purchase agreement negotiated by the taxpayer has distinct advantages:

  1. The buyer is out of the picture—one less person to deal with.

  2. The offer is an enforceable document and will carry more weight during negotiations than an option.

  3. Standard preprinted agreements can be used, saving time and expense.

Some lawyers feel uneasy about using the taxpayer as agent for the buyer. Any technique is open to challenge by the IRS. We can only look to the authority for the method and then make a prudent judgment weighing the risk of both using and not using a given technique—and this should only be done with the guidance of the taxpayer's counsel. If not taking a relatively risky approach kills the deal, was the tax benefit lost worth less than the risk of not taking action? It's your decision.

Writing a Standard Multiparty Exchange Agreement

The agreement you use should be written by the taxpayer's lawyer. He's the one who will have to defend the transaction in the event of challenge, therefore, if he doesn't write them, he should at least approve the legality of each document signed by the taxpayer.

The model agreements presented here are designed as guides to help get the transaction started. They are flexible and can be easily adapted to your situation. They are not the only agreements possible. As long as the agreement allows the taxpayer to receive only property for property with no right to cash, it can—as far as Section 1031 is concerned—contain or omit anything necessary to make the exchange work.

EXCHANGE AGREEMENT

THIS AGREEMENT, made this <u>27th</u> day of <u>March, 1975</u>, between Alamo Ranch, Inc., a New Mexico Corporation ("Alamo") and Norman S. Purcell of Denver, Colorado ("Purcell").

Alamo is Owner of the following land, located near Mesita, Valencia County, New Mexico:

18,000 acres, more or less, of deeded land with buildings and other improvements, as more fully described in Appendix A and referred to as the "Montana Ranch."

Alamo wants to exchange the Montana Ranch for other qualifying like kind property under the nontaxable provisions of Section 1031 of the Internal Revenue Code.

Purcell wants to acquire the Montana Ranch but does not presently own property ("exchange property") acceptable to Alamo.

Alamo is currently attempting to locate exchange property for Purcell to acquire and exchange for the Montana Ranch.

The parties, therefore, agree as follows:

1. Purcell will pay First American Title Company, designated as escrow agent, the sum of ten thousand dollars ($10,000) cash on execution of this Agreement, as a deposit to be applied to the purchase price of the exchange property.

2. It is agreed that the fair market value of the Montana Ranch is $990,000. The current encumbrances are approximately $390,000, and Alamo's equity is $600,000.

3. Alamo agrees to exchange the Montana Ranch for property which it will locate and designate as acceptable.

4. Purcell agrees to acquire the exchange property designated by Alamo and exchange it for the Montana Ranch.

5. Alamo shall have no right to the cash in this exchange and said cash is to be used by Purcell solely to purchase exchange property acceptable to Alamo. In the event that the equity of the exchange property is in excess of Alamo's equity in the Ranch, Alamo shall pay the excess to Purcell. In the event the equity of the exchange property is less than Alamo's equity in the Ranch, Purcell shall pay the difference to Alamo.

6. Alamo agrees to use its best efforts to locate acceptable property or properties and agrees to promptly designate the same and notify Purcell of the conditions of acquisition.

7. Both parties shall receive adequate assurances of merchantable title and proof of liens and encumbrances, presently existing upon the respective properties in accordance with accepted practices. Property taxes, rents, operating expenses and other appropriate items shall be prorated to the date of closing. Each party shall pay the closing costs associated with the property conveyed.

8. At closing, each party will be totally released from any continuing liability under the respective encumbrances: Alamo will have no remaining liability relating to the Montana Ranch, and Purcell will have no liability for encumbrances of the exchange property. Closing shall occur within 180 days of this date.

9. It is understood that this Agreement is binding on our heirs, executors, administrators, successors and assigns.

10. This Agreement is complete and may be modified only in writing.

ALAMO RANCH, INC.

By _____
President

_____
Norman S. Purcell

How to Modify an Exchange Agreement
So the Taxpayer Can Act as Agent for the Buyer

This agreement can be easily modified by inserting or deleting paragraphs that cover the terms of your specific exchange.

In the event it becomes necessary for the taxpayer to make offers for exchange property, the following paragraph could be added:

> It is mutually agreed that Alamo may write offers to acquire exchange property on behalf of Purcell. Purcell hereby agrees to accept the assignment of said offers to purchase.

If this approach is taken, it will be necessary to use a "right to assignment" clause in the purchase offers on the exchange property. The right to assign the purchase offer is then automatically agreed to by the owner of the exchange property when he signs it. Any general right to assignment clause will do, provided it is part of the purchase agreement and clearly assigns *both* the rights and obligations of the taxpayer, thus creating a novation.

> Alamo Ranch, Inc. shall have the right, without the need of any further approval or consent of sellers, at any and all times during the term hereof and prior to the completion of the acquisition of the subject property, to transfer and assign all of its rights and obligations under this agreement to Norman S. Purcell (or to any corporation, partnership or limited partnership of which he is a General Partner), pursuant to the contractual obligation of said party to purchase the subject property hereunder in accordance with the terms and provisions of that certain Exchange Agreement entered into between Alamo Ranch, Inc. and Norman S. Purcell on March 27, 1975. It is hereby agreed by and between the parties hereto that upon such assignment having been made by Alamo Ranch, Inc., effective forthwith upon seller's receipt of written notice of the same, Alamo Ranch, Inc. shall have no further rights, obligations or liabilities hereunder, all such rights, obligations and liabilities having been fully and finally transferred and assigned to Norman S. Purcell.

When the purchase agreement is accepted, the taxpayer must assign it to the buyer. This requires a separate document that effects the transfer of rights and obligations as provided for by the above clause. It is signed by the taxpayer and the buyer.

Assignment of Purchase Agreement

For value received, we hereby grant, set over and assign unto Norman S. Purcell all rights, obligations and liabilities under that certain purchase agreement between Alamo Ranch, Inc. and Realty Development Company dated June 6, 1975, a copy of which is attached and marked exhibit "A."

Witness our hands and seal this 10th day of June, 1975.

Alamo Ranch, Inc.

By _____
                                    President

Assignee's Acceptance

The undersigned assignee named in the above assignment of that certain purchase agreement between Alamo Ranch, Inc. and Realty Development Company dated June 6, 1975 hereby approves and accepts the assignment and agrees to be bound by all of the terms and conditions contained in the above described purchase agreement.

Witness my hand and seal this 10th day of June, 1975.

_____

Norman S. Purcell

Therefore, it takes three things to modify a standard multiparty agreement to permit the taxpayer to act as agent for the buyer:

1. A clause in the initial exchange agreement obligating the buyer to accept assignment of purchase offers from the taxpayer.
2. A clause in the purchase offer giving the taxpayer the right to assign the agreement to the buyer.
3. An "Assignment of Purchase Agreement," which actually transfers the taxpayer's rights and obligations to the buyer. The seller should be sent notice that the assignment was completed.

These are the documents you need to use a purchase agreement signed by the taxpayer. In the event his tax attorney is reluctant to have the taxpayer sign the purchase agreement, you might consider using an option.

Using an Option to Tie Up the Exchange Property

Although there is some conflict of opinion among tax attorneys as to the safety of using a purchase offer signed by the taxpayer, there is usually little resistance given an option.

Using an option requires only a slight modification of the above sequence. In the place of the purchase agreement use an option, negotiated and signed by the taxpayer. The right of assignment clause and actual assignment remain essentially the same.

The reason an option is often more acceptable to the taxpayer's lawyer is that there is a case in which it was used that went in favor of the taxpayer. (13) It does not obligate the taxpayer—it only gives him a right that he may or may not exercise.

The major disadvantage of an option is that the element of negotiation is weakened. Furthermore, owners normally want to be compensated for the time their property is off the market under option; that is, they want compensation over and above the value of the property.

Using an Agent Other than the Taxpayer
to Acquire Exchange Property

If you decide that the best approach for you is to use an agent other than the taxpayer, you can often make the deal with little difficulty. In fact, this may prove the best approach in the following circumstances:

1. When the taxpayer is reluctant to act as agent for the buyer.
2. When direct involvement of the buyer is impractical (due to lack of cooperation or absence from town).

A likely candidate for the buyer's agent is his attorney. The advantage here is that the buyer's attorney will represent his interests and make sure the offers to acquire exchange property are within the provisions of the original exchange agreement concerning the balancing of equities and commitment to unexpected liability. There are three documents you need to accomplish this technique.

1. A limited Power of Attorney signed by the buyer designating his attorney as agent for the purpose of making offers and, in some cases, conveying exchange property.
2. When the time comes, a letter to the agent from the taxpayer designating the price and terms for acquisition of the exchange property to be acquired.
3. A purchase agreement prepared for the agent's signature.

The offer on the exchange property would normally be drawn by the broker handling the exchange. The agent would then be presented with the designation letter authorizing an offer on the exchange property and the purchase agreement ready for his signature. A standard limited power of attorney form may be used to appoint the buyer's agent.

POWER OF ATTORNEY

THIS POWER OF ATTORNEY is made and executed this 30th day of March, 1975, by Norman S. Purcell of Denver, Colorado.

1. *Power of Attorney.* Norman S. Purcell of Denver, Colorado, has made, constituted and appointed, and by this appointment does hereby make, constitute and appoint John S. Campbell, Attorney and Counselor at Law, of Albuquerque, State of New Mexico, as his true and lawful attorney, and does grant him the full power and authority to do and perform all and every act and thing whatsoever requisite and necessary to be done as he might or could do if personally present as more specifically set out in Paragraph 2 hereof.

2. *Limits of Authority.* John S. Campbell, Attorney at Law, is specifically authorized to act in my name, place and stead, and on my behalf for the purpose of discharging my duties and responsibilities under that certain Exchange Agreement executed on the 27th day of March, 1975, by and between Norman S. Purcell and Alamo Ranch, Inc., a New Mexico corporation, wherein Norman S. Purcell agreed to acquire certain exchange property acceptable to Alamo Ranch, Inc. and for the purpose of conveying said property to Alamo Ranch, Inc. for the purpose of consummating an exchange within the meaning of Section 1031 of the Internal Revenue Code of 1954. John S. Campbell is authorized and empowered to do all of the things necessary to negotiate and effect said acquisition and subsequent conveyance including, but not limited to, the execution of all contracts, deeds, and other legal documents.

It is contemplated that the acquisition of said property will be by payment of a sum of cash not to exceed the equity of Alamo Ranch, Inc. in that certain property known as the Montana Ranch, Valencia County, New Mexico (approximately $600,000).

John S. Campbell, Attorney and Counselor at Law, shall have no further authority and power other than that delineated in this paragraph, it being understood that this Power of Attorney is granted solely for the purpose of discharging duties and obligations pursuant to the Exchange Agreement referred to herein.

3. *Ratification.* I hereby ratify and confirm all things that John S. Campbell, Attorney at Law, shall lawfully do or cause to be done by virtue of this Power of Attorney.

IN WITNESS WHEREOF, I have executed this Power of Attorney on the day and year above first written.

_____

Norman S. Purcell

STATE OF COLORADO   )
) ss.

COUNTY OF   )

The foregoing document was acknowledged to before me this 30th day of March, 1975.

_____

Notary Public

My Commission Expires:

_____

Designating the Exchange Property and Writing the Offer

The mechanics of applying the attorney-as-agent-for-the-buyer approach require a letter designating the exchange property acceptable to the taxpayer. This letter is addressed to the buyer and is delivered to his agent with the completed purchase agreement ready for signing. When he signs the agreement, it becomes a firm offer requiring only the acceptance of the seller. When the seller signs, the exchange is fully negotiated and the parties can proceed to work out the problems that must inevitably be solved before closing. The designation letter follows. Figure 6–1 is the purchase agreement.

June 6, 1975

Mr. Norman Purcell
402 North 4th Street
Denver, Colorado

Dear Mr. Purcell:

As provided in the exchange agreement between us dated March 27, 1975, you are hereby advised that exchange property acceptable to Alamo Ranch, Inc. has been located and is hereby designated as that property described in the attached purchase agreement, known as the Cibola Bank Building, 3400 West 98th Street, Albuquerque, N.M. The cash down payment will not exceed the cash equity of the Montana Ranch.

This letter is written as required under the terms of the above-mentioned exchange agreement which remains in full force and effect according to its terms.

Alamo Ranch, Inc.

By _____
President

How to Provide for a Sale if Exchange Property Is Not Located

A multiparty exchange agreement will normally provide for sale of the taxpayer's property in lieu of an exchange if acceptable exchange property is not found by a certain date. (7) There are two advantages to this provision.

PURCHASE AGREEMENT
of
EXCHANGE REALTY, INC.

Received of ___Norman S. Purcell___ Address ___Denver, Colorado___

Phone_____, the sum of ___$10,000___ in the form of cash____Note____Check____dated ___March___
27, 1975___ as deposit to be escrowed with ~~Broker~~ First American Title as part payment for the Purchase of ___Cibola Bank Building___
                                                                    Type of property

_____ located at (address) ___3400 West 98th. Street___

legal description ___Tract A of the West Height Addition, Bernalillo County,___

_____ Albuquerque, New Mexico,

and to include the following improvements: ___All existing including 70,000 square feet of___
___gross leaseable area situated on 10 acres___

together with all planting and improvements except ___No exceptions___

THE FULL PURCHASE PRICE is $ ___1,800,000___ to be paid as follows: total down payment including above deposit to be
approximately $ ___500,000___ cash, plus or minus prorations, upon execution of formal instruments; the Purchaser(s)
assume(s) and agree(s) to pay the existing mortgage or lien of record, current as of date of transfer in the approximate amount of
$ ___1,200___ with monthly payments of approximately $ ___1,300,000___ on said mortgage and balance,

if any, to be paid as follows: ___N/A___

.Seller understands that Purchaser is acquiring the subject property solely
for the purpose of exchange as provided in that certain exchange agreement
between Alamo Ranch, Inc. and Norman S. Purcell, dated March 27, 1975, the
terms and conditions of which shall become part of this agreement and control
and rule herein.

Seller shall make payments due on above incumbrance(s) before closing date, Purchaser thereafter. Survey, if required, to be furnished
as expense of ___seller___. Warranty deed and ~~Bill of Sale or other~~ a policy of title insurance in Purchasers
name, at option of Seller, showing merchantable title clear of liens and assessments except as set out herein, to be furnished at Sellers
expense as soon as practicable. Lien of Conservancy Districts, easements, restrictions, zoning and patent reservations, if any, to be
assumed by Purchaser.
Paving ___if any___, to be paid by ___seller___ Existing trust funds in the approximate amount of ___N/A___
to be assigned to buyer at ___N/A___ expense. Rent, taxes, interest, hazard and FHA mortgage insurance, if any, water,
sewer and garbage charges, if any, are to be prorated to ___N/A___. Seller agrees to keep property adequately
insured and to give possession of the premises to Purchaser on ___close of escrow___ and certifies that property will be in the same
condition, reasonable wear and tear excepted, as of the date of this agreement. ~~Vendor and Vendee agree that in case of loss or damage~~
~~to property by fire or other cause between date of this agreement and date of transfer, said loss is to be assumed by property owner.~~
Closing date ___July 15, 1975___
The Broker herein is not in any way responsible for the condition of the property and in no way warrants the same.
All parties undersigned agree to complete closing within 72 hours after notification that papers are ready. Purchaser agrees to buy
and Seller agrees to sell according to the terms and conditions set out hereinabove. Time is of the essence. This instrument comprises
the entire understanding and agreement of the parties hereto on the subject matter herein contained and shall be binding upon and
inure to the benefit of the parties, their heirs, executors, administrators, successors and assigns. Purchaser and Seller agree to pay their
customary share of costs of closing the transaction, unless other arrangements are written above. Purchaser pays his own attorney fees.
In event Seller accepts this offer and Purchaser refuses or fails to consummate the purchase, Seller shall have the option of retaining the
earnest money as partial liquidated damages and terminating this contract or of enforcing the same. Purchaser(s) hereby give(s)
broker hereinafter named a specific period of ___one___ days to complete this purchase agreement, and agrees to keep this
offer open for that time. If broker is unable to complete this agreement, earnest money is to be refunded in full to Purchaser and
this agreement cancelled.
In the event the Seller remains in possession of the premises herein after all the instruments have been filed transferring title, then
he will pay to the Purchaser $ ___N/A___ per day as rental. In the event Purchaser occupies the property he shall pay to Seller
the sum of $ ___N/A___ each day until the closing day, such advance to be computed in the closing, such rental to be paid
unless other arrangements are made in writing between the Purchaser and Seller.

Dated this ___6th___ day of ___June___, 19 ___75___, at ___2:00___ ~~A.M.~~ (P.M.)
        NORMAN S. PURCELL   EXCHANGE REALTY, INC. _____

        By _[signature]_   By _[signature]_
___John S. Campbell, his attorney-in-fact___   _____
                Purchaser   Purchaser

I/we hereby accept above offer to purchase and agree to pay agent a commission of ___6___ % on the full purchase price
plus 4% New Mexico sales tax on the commission. In the event purchase is not consummated and earnest money forfeited, said earnest
money is to be divided between Seller and Agent according to the Listing Contract.

___REALTY DEVELOPMENT COMPANY___ by _[signature] R.J. Jordan_ President
                Seller   Seller
        Date of Seller's Signature ___6-6-75___

Figure 6–1

1. It ensures acquisition of the taxpayer's property by the buyer, thus encouraging him to go along with the search and purchase of exchange property—he knows he'll get the property eventually even if the exchange fails.

2. It puts a deadline on the exchange and motivates the participants to make the transaction work or suffer loss of the tax benefits.

Providing for a sale may be a necessary requirement for acceptance of the initial exchange agreement. Fortunately, this can be done very easily by the addition of one clause to the initial exchange agreement:

> In the event that the acceptable exchange property is not located and designated by Alamo within 180 days from the date of this Agreement, Alamo shall then be bound to sell the Ranch to Purcell, and Purcell shall be bound to buy the Ranch from Alamo upon completion of customary papers and on the close of escrow on the following terms:
> Payment on December 1, 1975, of the sum of Twenty Thousand Dollars ($20,000) in cash, in addition to the $10,000 deposit, which shall be released by the escrow agent to Alamo to apply on the purchase price. The balance is to be paid in cash on January 15, 1976.

The danger in setting a date for sale in lieu of exchange is that it automatically establishes a time when the taxpayer will have a right to cash (constructive receipt). As a result, extreme care must be taken to either close the exchange by the sale date or extend the date prior to its arrival.

Challenges to multiparty exchanges by the IRS have for the most part been limited to transactions that involve a sale for cash in lieu of an exchange. The reason for this danger can be found in the definition of an exchange—the receipt of property for property rather than the receipt of cash or other nonqualifying consideration.

Therefore, in any multiparty exchange structure—and there are some skillfull variations on the standard approach—it is essential that the initial exchange agreement limit the taxpayer's right to any cash involved when a sale in lieu of an exchange is permitted. (11)(24)(35)

There are three circumstances that typically cause the taxpayer to realize a taxable transaction by having the right to cash.

1. When one of the parties to the exchange does not sign the agreement. (35)

2. When the *buyer* assigns the right to purchase exchange property to the taxpayer and causes the transfer of cash to him for that purpose. (11)

3. When there is a date agreed upon after which the taxpayer must sell for cash and that date passes without a prior extension by the parties.

Extending an Exchange Agreement

If the exchange agreement does provide for the sale of the taxpayer's property, it may be necessary during the search for exchange property to extend the time limit. This extension must occur before the date arrives. There are two ways to accomplish such an extension.

1. By increasing the number of days provided by the exchange agreement. For example, 180 would be crossed out and 210 inserted and initialed by both parties.

2. By a separate extension agreement signed by both parties.

An example of a separate agreement that fully states the circumstances of the transaction.

EXTENSION OF EXCHANGE AGREEMENT

THIS AGREEMENT is made this 14th day of July, 1975, by and between Alamo Ranch, Inc., a New Mexico Corporation, hereinafter referred to as Alamo, and Norman S. Purcell, of Denver, Colorado, hereinafter referred to as Purcell.

WHEREAS, the parties are signatories to that certain Exchange Agreement executed on the 27th day of March, 1975, whereby Alamo and Purcell agreed to exchange certain properties so as to qualify the conveyance by Alamo as a like kind exchange pursuant to Section 1031 of the Internal Revenue Code of 1954; and

WHEREAS, said exchange is to be made on or before August 22, 1975; and

WHEREAS, the parties are presently attempting to effect said transfer; however, because of complications in securing instruments from third parties, it is anticipated that there will be a delay in closing the exchange; and

WHEREAS, the parties desire to extend their Exchange Agreement.

NOW THEREFORE, in consideration of the mutual covenants and agreements contained herein, it is agreed as follows:

1. *Extension.* The Exchange Agreement, as aforesaid, and the time in which the exchange therein agreed to be made may be made is hereby extended by thirty (30) days to September 21, 1975.

In the event that acceptable exchange property has not been located as designated by Alamo within that time, Alamo shall then be bound to sell that certain Ranch, known as the Montana Ranch, to Purcell and Purcell shall be bound to purchase said Ranch from Alamo as provided for in the Exchange Agreement, as aforesaid.

2. *Ratification.* Each and every other term not inconsistent with this Amendment is hereby ratified and continued in full force and effect.

WHEREAS, this Agreement has been executed the day and year above first written.

ALAMO RANCH, INC.

By ——————————————————
President

——————————————————
Norman S. Purcell

Writing a Multiparty Exchange Agreement That Combines Three Alternatives in One Document and the Contingency of Refinance

Since flexibility is the key to success in an exchange, an agreement that provides the maximum flexibility will contribute most to the potential success of the transaction.

Many exchanges begin without the participants knowing what the outcome will be or the method that will ultimately be used to reach the objective—not because of lack of knowledge on the part of the people involved, but because there are so many techniques available to make an exchange work and so many unknowns that appear between beginning and closing.

One method that plays an important role in multiparty exchanges is the refinancing of the taxpayer's property to generate the cash to purchase exchange property. If this technique is part of the exchange, it must be in the agreement.

The following document is designed to provide the maximum flexibility by including three alternatives in one document: (1) a purchase for exchange, (2) an exchange with a cash take-out and (3) a sale for cash, all of which are contingent on the refinancing of the taxpayer's property by the buyer.

EXCHANGE AGREEMENT

THIS EXCHANGE AGREEMENT entered into this 12th day of July, 1975, by and between William C. Harris, a married man dealing in his sole and separate property, hereinafter called "Harris," and Charles B. Webster, a widowed gentleman, hereinafter called "Webster."

WHEREAS, Harris is the owner of certain real property located in Bernalillo County, New Mexico, being described as follows:

Lots numbered "1" and "2" in Block numbered Thirty-six (36) of O'LEARY AD-DITION, an Addition to the City of Albuquerque, New Mexico, as the same is shown and designated on the Map of said Addition filed in the office of the County Clerk of Bernalillo County, New Mexico,

including permanent and existing improvements, hereinafter referred to as "subject property."

WHEREAS, Harris is desirous of exchanging the subject property for property of a like kind and having the transaction qualify as an exchange under Section 1031 of the Internal Revenue Code of 1954.

NOW, THEREFORE, in consideration of the mutual convenants and agreements contained herein, it is agreed as follows:

1. *Exchange of Property.* Harris, in consideration of One Dollar ($1.00) paid, the receipt of which is hereby acknowledged, and the conveyance by Webster, hereinafter agreed to be made, hereby agrees to transfer and convey the subject property to Webster, at a valuation, for the purposes of the Exchange Agreement, of $200,000.

A portion of the total subject property value of $200,000 is hereby allocated to the personal property in the amount of $10,000.

The subject property is presently encumbered by the certain Mortgage by and between Harris and American Savings and Loan Association with an approximate balance of $30,000 and that certain Mortgage by and between Harris and Mountain Mortgage Company in the approximate amount of $27,000, referred to herein as "existing mortgages." Webster does hereby agree to assume and pay said Mortgages in full upon completion of this exchange transaction.

The premises will be conveyed free of all other liens and encumbrances other than current year's taxes, patent reservations, easements and restrictions of record.

2. *Transfer by Webster.*

(a) In consideration of the conveyance hereinabove agreed to be made by Harris, Webster hereby agrees to transfer and convey to Harris any property or properties of a like kind acceptable to Harris so as to qualify as an exchange under Section 1031 of the Internal Revenue Code of 1954. The exchange shall be made no later than ninety (90) days after the date that Webster secures a letter of commitment from a lending institution to loan Webster the sum of One Hundred Fifty Thousand Dollars ($150,000) in accordance with the provisions of paragraph 5 herein.

(b) Webster agrees to fully cooperate with Harris and to purchase property or properties which Harris may wish to receive in exchange for the subject property.

(c) Webster shall do all things necessary to effect the purchase of exchange property or properties, including making an offer or offers to purchase properties, in writing, dircted to the owners of said properties. Said offers shall be upon terms and conditions acceptable to Harris as stated by letter to Webster, but in no event shall Webster be required to offer cash in excess of Harris' equity in the subject property, approximately $143,000.

(d) Webster shall bear no additional cost or expense on account of the exchange transaction herein and shall not be required to assume any existing encumbrance or liability on any exchange property that may be acceptable to Harris.

3. *Alternative Method of Exchange.* Within the ninety (90) day period provided for in paragraph 2(a) hereof, Harris shall have the right to exchange the subject property for property of a like kind provided, however, that Harris will cause the person or persons who will become the owner or owners of the subject property to agree in writing as a contingency of exchange to immediately sell the subject property to Webster under the terms and conditions of this agreement, as provided for by paragraph 4 herein.

4. *Alternative Sale.* In the event that Harris has found no property acceptable as an exchange property such as would qualify as a like kind exchange pursuant to Section 1031 of the Internal Revenue Code of 1954 within the time hereinabove provided, the subject property shall be sold by Harris to Webster as follows:

(a) The total purchase price shall be $200,000 cash, including the existing mortgages to be paid in full at closing, plus or minus normal prorations as provided for herein.

(b) The subject property shall be free and clear of all liens and encumbrances other than those excepted in paragraph 1 hereof and all other liens and encumbrances shall be paid by Harris in full at closing.

5. *Contingency of Transaction.* This agreement is subject to and contingent upon Webster obtaining a conventional loan in an amount equal to no less than seventy-five percent (75%) of the value of the subject property ($200,000). The terms of said loan shall be not less than twenty-five (25) years at an interest rate of nine and three-quarter percent (9-$\frac{3}{4}$%) per year or less together with a maximum of two (2) points. In the event that Webster is able to secure financing at less than nine and three-quarters percent (9-$\frac{3}{4}$%), then and in that event the maximum points payable by Webster shall be three (3) points. Webster agrees to immediately make an application for said financing with an appropriate lending institution and to do all things necessary to obtain said financing. Webster shall bear all expenses of financing including any additional fees required by the lending institution for issuing a loan commitment letter, appraisal fees and other similar expenses.

In the event that Webster is unable to obtain said financing, this agreement shall be null and void and all monies paid by Webster as deposit on this transaction shall forthwith be returned to him.

6. *Title Insurance.* Harris shall provide title insurance for Webster showing title to be merchantable and free and clear of all liens and encumbrances except current year's taxes, conservancy district liens, if any, easements, restrictions and other reservations of record.

7. *Return of Earnest Money.* The parties acknowledge that Webster has deposited $10,000 earnest money with First American Title Company. In the event that this agreement is declared null and void pursuant to paragraphs 5 or 11 hereof, all earnest money shall be returned to Webster forthwith. In the event that Webster is able to secure financing but for any other reason fails to complete and close this transaction, then and in that event the earnest money deposited herein shall be retained by Harris and shall be divided equally between Harris and Exchange Realty, Inc.

8. *Management of Premises.* Between the date of this agreement and the closing date hereof, Harris agrees to retain U.S. Management, Inc. to manage the premises and agrees to pay U.S. Management, Inc. a fee of five percent (5%) of the gross rentals collected.

9. *Prorations.* The following items shall be prorated between the parties as of the date of closing: Real estate taxes for the calendar year, 1975, water and sewer charges, prepaid insurance, mortgage interest, and prepaid rents, if any. In addition, Harris shall turn over to Webster any security deposits held under any leases or agreements with tenants.

10. *Costs of Transaction.* The parties to this agreement shall each bear one-half ($\frac{1}{2}$) of attorney's fees incurred in connection with the closing of this transaction and one-half ($\frac{1}{2}$) of the escrow fee charged by First American Title Company to close this transaction. In the event that a survey is required by the title company before insuring title, all costs of survey shall be borne by Webster.

11. *Casualty.* If, prior to closing hereof, any of the improvements on the subject property are destroyed, or if there has been damage by fire or any other casualty, which destruction or damage is repairable, and such repairs shall not have been completed on or prior to the closing date, then Webster shall have the option of cancelling this contract. In the event of such cancellation, all monies deposited hereunder by Webster shall be returned to him. In the event that Webster does not cancel this contract, all insurance monies payable as a result of such casualty shall be turned over to Webster for the purpose of making the required repairs, except to the extent that such insurance monies must be paid to, or must be turned over to, the holders of the existing mortgages on the subject property.

12. *Documents at Closing.* At the closing hereof, Harris shall:

(a) Execute, acknowledge and deliver to Webster a General Warranty Deed conveying to Webster a fee simple title to the premises free and clear of all items and encumbrances except as herein provided.

(b) Assign to Webster any and all leases then in effect between Harris and the tenants of the premises.

(c) Execute and deliver to Webster a Bill of Sale with Affidavit of Title to all the personal property included in the transaction.

13. *Date of Closing.* This transaction shall be closed not later than the ninetieth (90th) day after the date that Webster secures the letter of loan commitment provided for in paragraph 5. Closing shall be held at the offices of First American Title Company, Albuquerque, New Mexico.

14. *Brokerage.* Harris agrees to pay in cash, at the time of closing, a commission of six percent (6%) plus applicable New Mexico Gross Receipts Tax to Exchange Realty, Inc. of Albuquerque, New Mexico.

15. *Notices.* Any notices required to be given hereunder shall be given in writing to Harris, c/o John S. Campbell, 2500 Louisiana Blvd. N.E., Albuquerque, New Mexico, 87110, and to Webster, c/o James R. Jacobson, 4201 Indian School Rd. N.E., Albuquerque, New Mexico, 87110.

16. *Indemnity.* Harris hereby indemnifies and agrees to hold Webster harmless from any and all excess tax liability, if any, that may be caused or that Webster may incur as a result of his execution of this Exchange Agreement. For the purpose of this Agreement, excess tax liability shall mean any incidence of taxation that would not otherwise have been imposed on Webster and that is caused by the execution of this document.

17. *Binding Effect.* This contract shall be binding upon the parties hereto, their successors, personal representatives, assigns and heirs.

WHEREFORE, this Agreement has been executed the day and year above first written.

Exchange Realty, Inc.

By _____ _____
George T. Harrison   William C. Harris

U.S. Management, Inc.

By _____ _____
Samuel C. Chavez   Charles B. Webster

7

How to Write
Listing and Commission
Agreements That Will
Protect You in an Exchange

    As in all areas of real estate, exchanging requires the use of written agreements to prevent misunderstanding over brokerage commissions and fees. Even with their use, however, problems often arise.

    Three areas will be discussed in this chapter.

1. Listing agreements
2. Commission and fee agreements
3. Commission and fee split agreements between brokers

    More bickering, hard feelings and unfortunate circumstances surround brokerage commissions in a real estate deal than any other aspect of the transaction. For example, if the seller isn't trying to get the broker to cut his fee, the buyer is trying to get the broker to pay for an unexpected expense. And if it's not the principals in the transaction, then it's the other brokers refusing to split the commission equally—possibly because they had more salesmen or had legal expenses they weren't used to. Occasionally, an outside party will even try to step in to get a referral fee for a phone call—something he never wanted until he smelled someone else making money.

    Disputes tend to follow commissions. And problems of this nature are created more easily in an exchange because of the specialized knowledge necessary, the additional work required, which many people don't understand, and the relative lack of conventionally accepted methods of dealing with the fees. Combine these circumstances with innate human greed, and real problems can easily develop.

Guidelines to Getting Paid

There are general principles that you can use to try to preserve hard-earned commissions regardless of the source of attack:

1. If it involves money, get it in writing before it's apparent the deal will go through. This goes for fees or commissions paid by owners and especially splits with other brokers.
2. If you didn't get it in writing, expect to get less than you thought you were going to.
3. If you did get it in writing, expect someone to try to take it away from you.
4. To make sure you get paid, learn to say no and maintain control of the closing.
5. Have the fee written in the closing or settlement sheet, collected at closing by the escrow agent and then paid to you on recording.

These guidelines can help in any real estate transaction but are doubly important in an exchange. However, sometimes nothing works. In one case, a broker had actually listed two parcels of land. The listing agreement covered either sale or exchange. He brought the two principals together, wrote the exchange agreements and closed the transaction. At closing, one of the principals refused to pay the commission he had previously committed himself to in the listing agreement. The broker went ahead with the closing anyway, accepting a commission on the other parcel in the exchange. He then sued the reluctant owner for the commission, but lost the case. The judge didn't understand the exchange (too complicated apparently) and felt it wasn't equitable for the broker to receive two commissions, although the question was one of enforceability of a contract (the commission payment in the listing agreement). Evidently, the fact that each owner was only to pay one commission didn't matter. So, in this case, the taxpayer got a nontaxable exchange and got out of paying a commission.

Even with written agreements an element of control over the transaction from inception to closing must be maintained. In some cases, it's a question of who blinks first. If you are the only one who understands the entire exchange—that is, all the possible pitfalls relating to the tax consequences and mechanics of expressing the transaction in the agreement and on the closing statement—then control can be maintained right down to recording and getting paid, which of course is the usual reason for being in this unpredictable business anyway.

Writing an Exchange Listing Agreement

One of the important tools that can help protect your commission in an exchange is the owner's *written* agreement to pay. This can be accomplished by listing the property for exchange only, as distinguished from a listing for sale. Although most listing agreements refer to "sale or exchange" and in some cases "lease," it is sometimes necessary to make a clear-cut distinction when there is concern over nonqualification if the property is placed on the market for sale. In certain strategies, it may be essential to use a listing agreement specifically designed for the exchange of real estate.

This may be the case when there is some question about qualifying the property being exchanged as held for investment or use in trade or business. For example, if the property were acquired by exchange, a listing for sale might imply that it was being held for sale, not investment, thus destroying the tax benefits of the previous exchange. A more serious danger may arise when the taxpayer owns property held for resale as well as investment property. To build a case for the exchange, it may be advisable to clearly separate the exchange property from the sale property by using an exchange listing agreement.

There are additional reasons to list property for exchange only:

1. It establishes from the start that the owner intends to avoid tax as permitted by Section 1031.

2. It is a good first step toward psychological preparation for an exchange, a necessary step with certain owners.

3. It establishes a fee specifically for the exchange.

The following exchange listing agreement is a general format which can be adapted to different localities.

EXCLUSIVE RIGHT TO EXCHANGE REAL PROPERTY

THIS AGREEMENT made this 10th day of August, 1974, between Thomas A. Christ, of 1521 Mesa Street, Albuquerque, New Mexico, hereinafter called the "Owner" and Exchange Realty, Inc., of 42 West 53rd Street, Albuquerque, New Mexico, hereinafter called the "Broker."

1. *Exclusive right to exchange.* In consideration of the promise of the Broker to use its best efforts to exchange the herein described real estate of the Owner, located in Albuquerque, New Mexico, known as the Royal Apartments and more fully described in exhibit "A" attached hereto, the Owner hereby grants the Broker the sole and exclusive authorization and right to offer for exchange and to exchange such property through its efforts at a fair market value of $575,000.

2. *Duration of agreement.* This agreement shall remain in force for a period of six months from the date of this agreement and shall continue thereafter until either party terminates it with not less than 30 days written notice.

During the period of six months specified above, this agreement shall be irrevocable.

Should the Owner withdraw the property from the market during the period of this agreement or otherwise prevent the Broker from exchanging the property, the Broker will be entitled to its commission in full.

3. *Authority of broker.* During the term of this agreement, the Broker is granted the sole authority to advertise the property for exchange, to place a sign on the same and to take all steps necessary to bring about the exchange thereof. The Owner agrees to refer all inquiries or offers he may receive to the Broker.

4. *Representations.* The Owner represents that he is the Owner in fee simple of the property and that there are no encumbrances thereon and hereby agrees to furnish the Broker a title binder on the property within 14 days from the date of this agreement.

The Broker makes no representations or guarantee of exchange.

5. *Right of broker to act on own behalf.* The Broker shall have the right to acquire the property or participate as a principal in an exchange thereof and, in such case, title to the property shall be conveyed to the Broker or its designee.

6. *Fee.* The Owner agrees that if the property is exchanged through the efforts of the Broker, or in the event that the property is exchanged while this agreement is in force, by the Owner or anyone else, the Broker will be paid a fee in the amount of $50,000 in cash at close of escrow.

7. *Right of broker to represent both parties to exchange.* If there is an exchange of properties, the Broker may represent and receive fees from both parties and cooperate with other brokers and divide the fee with them in any manner agreed upon.

8. *Sale or exchange after termination of agreement.* If a sale or exchange is consummated after the termination of this agreement, to a party or on behalf of a party to whom this property was submitted by the Broker, the Broker will be paid its full fee of $50,000 in cash at close of escrow.

In witness whereof the parties hereto have executed this agreement on the date first above written.

_____

Thomas A. Christ

Exchange Realty, Inc.

By _____

President

Model Preprinted Listing Agreement

A preprinted listing agreement that has stood the test of time and benefited from the input of several users over the years can expedite the process of listing property for exchange. Listing forms that incorporate both the essential legal language and detailed property information are the most efficient.

They not only can save time, they also reduce items that might otherwise be negotiated to routine points. Of particular importance is the term of the listing—enough time must be allowed to meet the objective while protecting the time the broker has already invested in the project.

Possibly the most helpful function of a listing form is the ease with which it provides for the collection of detailed property information. One of the most important tasks in preparing a property for marketing—whether for sale or exchange—is the collection of accurate property data.

A preprinted listing form can provide for this while placing the burden of accuracy and liability on the owner where it belongs. Accurate property information is essential for the potential new owner to correctly decide which property to acquire.

An example of a preprinted listing form appears in Figure 7–1.

Using a Fee Instead of a Percentage Commission

In exchanging, there has traditionally been a preference for charging a set fee rather than a percentage commission tied to the property value. The amount is usually related to the difficulty the broker anticipates in the transaction. In some cases, the time required to complete the exchange is greater than it would have taken to sell the same property. Consequently, the fee is more appropriately tied to the problem surrounding the property and the time necessary to solve it.

Sometimes the value of the property in an exchange, and the percentage commission that would result in no way reflects the amount of work necessary to meet the owner's objectives. This is one of the main reasons exchangors have moved toward a set fee and away from the use of a percentage commission—a fee is compensation for representing an owner's interests, not a percentage charge for disposing of property.

EXCLUSIVE AUTHORIZATION TO EXCHANGE

The undersigned Owner hereby grants the undersigned Broker the EXCLUSIVE AUTHORIZATION and RIGHT, for a period commencing this date and terminating at midnight of.., 19......., to solicit offers to exchange Owner's real property situated in the City of..,

County of ...., State of ....;

described as: ....

....

consisting of: ....;

for other real property acceptable to Owner, subject to the following terms: ....

....

Owner agrees to pay Broker as compensation for services rendered a fee of ...., IF:

1. The herein described property is exchanged, sold, leased for a period of more than 12 months, or otherwise transferred during the term hereof through the efforts of the Broker or by Owner or through any other source.

2. This authorization is revoked during the term hereof, or if the Owner otherwise prevents the performance hereunder by the Broker.

3. An exchange, sale, or other transfer of the property is made within three (3) months after the termination of this authorization with persons with whom Broker shall have negotiated during the term hereof and whose names Broker shall have submitted in writing to Owner within ten days after termination of this authorization.

If suit is brought to collect the compensation or if Broker successfully defends any action brought against Broker by the Owner arising out of the execution of this authorization or any agreement of exchange, sale or other transfer relating to the herein described property, Owner agrees to pay all costs incurred by Broker in connection with such action, including a reasonable attorney's fee.

Owner agrees that Broker may act as agent for all parties to any exchange in connection herewith, may accept fees from any or all parties to such transaction, may cooperate with other brokers and divide the fees in any manner satisfactory to them.

Owner agrees to make available to Broker all data, records and documents pertaining to the property, to allow Broker, or any other broker with whom Broker chooses to cooperate, to show the property at reasonable times and upon reasonable notice and to commit no act which might tend to obstruct the Broker's performance hereunder.

In the event of an exchange, Owner will promptly, upon Broker's request, deposit in escrow all instruments necessary to complete the exchange.

Owner warrants the accuracy of the information furnished herein with respect to the above described property and agrees to hold the Broker harmless from any liability arising out of incorrect or undisclosed information. Owner agrees to notify Broker within seven days of any changes in rentals and/or expenses of the property.

The undersigned Owner warrants that he is the owner of record of the property or has the authority to execute this agreement.

In consideration of the execution hereof, the undersigned Broker agrees to use diligence in effecting an exchange of said property.

Receipt of a copy hereof is hereby acknowledged.

DATED:..

....Broker   ....Owner

....Address   ....Owner

....Phone   ....Address

By...   ....Phone

The following changes and/or additions are herewith incorporated in this authorization: ....

....

This authorization is herewith extended until midnight of..., 19.......
All other terms shall remain the same.

DATED:...

....Broker   ....Owner

By...   ....Owner

Address: ....Fair Market Value $..

Corner...Between....................................and..

District..............................Lot Size/Acreage...Zoning.................................

Taxes $.........................Allocated to Land:.........................Allocated to Improvements:.........................

Existing Encumbrances:

1st Loan $......................., $..................... Mo. @...........%, Including Impounds ☐, Lender...................Loan No...........

2nd Loan $......................., $..................... Mo. @...........%, Due on Sale ☐, Due Date...........................

3rd Loan $......................., $..................... Mo. @...........%, Due on Sale ☐, Due Date...........................

Motivation: ....

Exchange for: ....

Remarks: ....

Figure 7–1

FLOOR PLAN	BED ROOMS	SIZES	BATH ROOMS	SHOWERS Stall	SHOWERS O-Tub	LIV.R. SIZE	DIN.R. SIZE	KIT-CHEN	OTHER ROOMS	STOR-AGE	KITCHEN		GARAGE		GROUNDS	
3rd Floor											Blt-In R&O		No. Cars		Improved	
2nd Floor											Disposal		Side by Side		Fenced	
1st Floor											Dishwash		Tandem		Sprinkler	
Street Lev											Fan		Attached		Patio	
Cellar											Hood		Detached		BBQ	
TOTAL											Bkfst Area		Car Port		Pool	

No. Stories		Floors		Transp. Blks.		Cond. Grounds			
Attached		Fireplace		Shops Blks.		Cond. Exterior			
Detached		Heat		Elem. School		Cond. Interior			
Style		Air Cond.		Jr. High School		Occupant			
Year Built		W/Stripped		High School		Owner ☐		Tenant ☐	
Builder		Insulated		Paroch. School		Phone			
Exterior		Interior Walls		Carpets		To Show			
Roof		Laundry		Drapes		Lock Box			
Sq. Ft.		220 Wiring		Inter-Com		Key At			
Level/Slope		Copper Pipes		Possession					
View		Sewer		Rental					

Units	Rms	Bdrms	Baths	Furn	Refr	Sq.Ft.	CONDITION	TENANTS	Phone Nos.	Lease E/D	Monthly Rent	ANNUAL STATEMENT	
												Taxes	
												Insur.	
												Licenses	
												Util/Wat	
												Trash	
												Mgr/Jan	
												Elev.Serv	
												Gardener	
												Pool Serv.	
												Mangmnt.	
												Legal/Acct	
												Maint.	
												Gross Inc	
					INCOME FROM: LAUNDRY ☐	GARAGES ☐					Less Exp	
UNITS				SQ. FT.				TOTAL MONTHLY INCOME				Net Inc.	

RES. MGR.				APT.#		PHONE:		TO SHOW:					
No. Stories		Floors		Laundry Rm.		Fire Sprinklr.		Transp. Blks.					
Elevator		Carpets		Washr-Dryer		Copper Pipes		Freeway Blks					
Type Constr.		Drapes		Owned/Lease		Sep.Gas Meters		Shops Blks.					
Exterior		Fireplaces		Storage		Sep.Elec.Meters		Cond. Ground					
Year Built		Inter-Com		Recreatn.Rm.		Lawn Sprink.		Cond. Exter.					
Builder		TV Outlets		Hall Floors		Pool		Cond. Halls					
Level/Slope		Blt-In R & O		Heat		Garages		Cond. Apts.					
View		Fan & Hood				Car Ports							
Basement		Garb. Disp.		Air Cond.		Parking Lot							
Roof		Dish Washer		Garb. Chutes									

LESSEE		TYPE BUSINESS		Sq. Ft.	Rent P/Sq. Ft.	OVERAGE	Tax Clause	Lease E/D	INCOME	ANNUAL STATEMENT	
										Taxes	
										Insur.	
										Utilities	
										Services	
										Salaries	
										Mangmt.	
										Legal/Acct	
										Maint.	
										Gross Inc	
										Less Exp	
										Net Inc.	

Advert. Value		Load Access		Type Constr.		Amps		Fire Sprinklers	
Dist. Main Highw.		Room F/Expans		Exterior		Voltage		Load. Dock	
Trans. Blks.		Size Bldg.		Roof		Plumbing		Spec. Equipmnt	
Spur Track		No. Stories		Height Clear.		No. Toilets		Front Ft.	
Traffic Count		Basement		Floors		Heat		Square Ft.	
Parking		Age Bldg.		Load Factor		Air Cond.		Office Area	
Restrictions									

HIGHEST & BEST USE:		DISTANCE TO:							
Farm		Transp.		Easements		Storm Drain		Bonds	
Ranch		Main Highway		Restrictions		Sewerage		Front Ft.	
Timber		Railroad		View		Water		Square Ft.	
Industrial		Metrop. Area		Above Grade	Ft	Gas		Dedication	
Commercial		Bus. Distr.		Below Grade	Ft	Power		Fire Hydrant	
Motel		Shop. Center		Contour		Phone		Traffic Count	
Resort		Schools		Fill Required		Street			
Subdivision		City Limits		Depth Bedrock		Sidewalks			
Building Lot				Sub-Soil		Curbs			
				Zoning		Gutters			

The Owner of the herein property verifies the accuracy of the information contained herein ——————————— Owner

Figure 7-1 (cont.)

Exchanging often requires specialized knowledge and contacts that go beyond the usual requirements of real estate brokerage; that is, the best representation available in this specialized area can often command a fee above the standard commissions paid in brokerage. Of course, it works both ways. A given transaction can also warrant a fee less than the usual commission. In the last analysis, the fee is a judgment arrived at by the exchangor and agreed to by the owner. Regardless of the amount, however, basis of a fee is on representation of the owner, not the value of his property.

A separate fee agreement is necessary in certain circumstances, such as in cases in which no listing exists or there is a listing for sale only and in situations in which it is not appropriate to state the fee on the exchange agreement. The purpose of a fee agreement is to specify the compensation due the broker on closing of the exchange.

An exchange fee agreement can be a preprinted form or a simple letter agreement. It can be general or tied to an exchange agreement already in force. The following clause does the job in a letter agreement.

FEE AGREEMENT

I agree that on exchange of my property described in exhibit "A" (attached) to pay Realty Exchange, Inc. a fee of $35,000, plus applicable gross receipts tax in cash at closing. I understand that Realty Exchange Inc. will use its best efforts to effect an exchange of my property on satisfactory terms. This agreement shall remain in force for 180 days and will extend automatically and remain irrevocably in force in the event an exchange agreement is signed.

| _____ | _____ |
| Date | Owner |

A different form is sometimes used for exchanges in which the property to be exchanged is specified and the transaction is virtually agreed to. Both formats can be set up for preprinted forms. But the best and safest approach is to use a complete "Exclusive Authorization to Exchange."

EXCHANGE FEE AGREEMENT

It is agreed by the undersigned that in the event an exchange of the property located at _____

on the terms stated in the Exchange Agreement dated _____ 19__, or upon any other terms agreed on, I will pay a fee to _____ in the amount of $_____ in cash at close of escrow.

_____	_____
Date	Owner
_____	_____
Date	Owner

Splitting Fees Between Brokers

It is essential to a smooth transaction that there be no misunderstanding between the brokers as to the amount of the commission each will receive. There are several methods that can be used to establish an equitable division of fees.

COMMISSION AGREEMENT
BROKER SPLIT

_____
Date

It is agreed by the undersigned that if the transaction described as

_____

_____

_____

is closed, the parties will contribute commission/fees as outlined below:

PRINCIPAL	FEE
_____	$ _____
_____	_____
_____	_____
_____	_____

It is further agreed that the total sum of these fees is _____ and this sum will be divided between the participating brokers in the following manner:

_____

_____

_____

_____

As a participating broker, I agree to the above split.

_____	_____
_____	_____
_____	_____
_____	_____

Figure 7–2

1. All the commissions attached to the various properties in the exchange may be pooled and divided equally among the brokers.
2. The broker providing the exchange know-how may require most of the commission, with the other less-experienced broker (who is doing no work on the exchange) receiving a listing commission on the property he listed.
3. Each broker may receive the fee agreed to by the owner he represents.

Regardless of the guidelines followed or the amounts agreed to verbally, as with all business arrangements, the final agreement should be in writing and signed by all brokers involved. The following is a typical agreement format. Figure 7–2 presents a preprinted split agreement.

COMMISSION SPLIT AGREEMENT

It is hereby understood and agreed that the combined total commissions of that certain exchange agreement date February 13, 1975, between *Gary Brown*, party of the first part, and *John Sutton*, party of the second part, will be divided in the following amounts:

Exchange Realty, Inc. will receive a total of $8,500, plus gross receipts tax due thereon. American Brokerage Co. will receive $7,500, plus gross receipts tax due thereon.

Approved and agreed to this 13th day of February, 1975.

Exchange Realty, Inc.   American Brokerage Co.

By _____   By _____

8

The Mechanics of
Closing an Exchange

Closing an exchange is the final step in carrying out the terms of the agreements. When the agreements are properly written and clearly understandable, the closing follows naturally.

This chapter presents the mechanics of closing the following three types of exchanges:

1. A two-party exchange
2. A multiple exchange
3. A multiparty exchange

The principles that apply when each type of exchange is closed are the same regardless of the number of people or properties in the transaction. The overriding principle is that the parties to the exchange are viewed separately, with the understanding that the tax impact on one is not a factor in determining the tax effect on another. Keeping this in mind will help avoid confusion when you are closing the exchange.

The fact that a transaction may have involved a sale or purchase will not endanger the nontaxable exchange or require an attempt to illustrate that the buyer acquired the taxpayer's property by a two-party exchange rather than an interdependent step in a multiparty exchange. For example, in a multiparty exchange, there are actually three types of closing statements documenting the different position of each participant: the taxpayer with an exchange, the buyer with a purchase and the seller with a sale. The closing statement for each is nothing more than an accounting of transaction costs and the values transferred and received, whether property or cash. Closing statements neither support nor dispute the claim that a nontaxable exchange occurred—they can only account for the financial facts of the transaction in a manner consistent with the exchange agreement.

The closing statements, transfer of deeds and recording process are all part of the formalities that document the financial position of the participants at the end of escrow.

In fact, the closing statement *only* presents the financial aspects of the exchange—the exchange agreement documents the facts that establish the tax benefits. Consequently, the exchange agreement should not be relied on to present the final financial picture, nor should the closing statements be looked at as a determining factor in supporting qualification under Section 1031. But during a tax audit, the closing statement can help if it clearly reflects that the taxpayer closed an exchange.

In some states, title or escrow companies require written escrow instructions, which are signed by all parties when the escrow is opened. Closing, then, is referred to as "close of escrow." But in most areas, the exchange agreement is the only source of written instruction to the escrow company. In the event you are closing with written escrow instructions, these instructions should conform to the exchange agreement so that what actually happens during escrow is consistent with the nontaxable exchange intended.

Closing a Two-Party Exchange

Exchange closing statements have taken many forms through the years. To the extent that each approach correctly documented the financial position of the participants at the end of the transaction, it was a proper approach. There is no one way that is right and another that is wrong, just some that are more nearly accurate and easier to understand than others.

In some closings, letters to the taxpayer are used which state only the transaction costs of the exchange without reference to the values of the properties transferred and received. At the other extreme, title companies often use four closing statements for a two-party exchange—a separate sale and purchase statement for both taxpayers showing each selling and purchasing property from the other. This method of documentation is quite common because it provides a familiar structure for the escrow officer.

But both of these methods have a major drawback when the taxpayer is examined by the IRS—they lack consistent and clear documentation of the exchange. The best way to structure an exchange ensures that substance, form and documentation conform throughout the transaction—from intent through recording.

It is always easier to prove to an IRS agent that an exchange occurred if the taxpayer's closing statement says it did, rather than by presenting two documents that say "purchase" and "sale" or a letter that gives no property values, presenting only a summary of transaction costs.

Closing Statements Account for Values and Costs

The problem of documentation of an exchange closing can be easily solved if you remember one overriding principle—the closing statement should present your transaction costs and the value you gave (put in the pot) and received (from the pot) and the form it was in (cash, property).

If the closing statement clearly documents these elements, you have all you need for final calculation of your tax treatment and basis transfer on one document signed by a third party, the escrow officer. A clear presentation of the facts on a closing statement combined with an exchange agreement can make short work of a tax audit.

The exchange closing statements that appear in Figures 8–2 and 8–3 illustrate this method of documenting the closing for both taxpayers in a two-party exchange. This exchange involves a duplex owned by Charles and Marie Morrison which they exchanged for an 8-unit complex owned by Harrison and Cynthia Barnhart. The duplex was valued at $42,000 and had a first mortgage of $20,000. The 8-unit complex was valued at $98,000, with a first mortgage of $57,000. The equity difference was therefore $19,000, owed by Morrison to Barnhart. Barnhart agreed to carry back a second mortgage of $10,000, secured by the 8-unit complex, provided Morrison paid the additional $9,000 in cash at closing.

The Exchange Work Sheet in Figure 8–1 presents the estimated transaction costs and the cash each party will pay or receive. The Morrisons' closing statement details the property values and costs, resulting in the net amount they must pay, including boot and transaction costs, after offsetting credits for deposits and property taxes.

The Barnharts' statement presents the net cash they will receive from the title company, which includes $9,000 boot from the Morrisons less commissions and transaction costs. As both the Exchange Work Sheet and closing statement reflect, the majority of the cash paid to the Barnharts was offset by the commissions and transaction costs.

The Exchange Work Sheet is not intended to be a final statement of costs, but is a tool to help structure the equity balance and estimate the cash necessary to close. The final tax treatment and new basis calculation will be taken from the figures on the closing statement. Note also that the transaction costs on line 11 are net after offsets for prorations.

Closing a Multiple Exchange

The process of closing a multiple exchange is a logical expansion of the steps involved in a two-party transaction. The only difference is that there are more people and a corresponding increase in closing statements.

In the following example, three individuals owned acreage in a mountain resort area, which they held for investment. In 1974, after a series of changes in plans, they decided to exchange property. Each parcel was in a subdivision that could not be further divided, and they varied in size from 10 to 25 acres. The transaction was based on a $250-per-acre value, and each party agreed to assume the existing land sale contract outstanding on the property acquired.

The transaction was a standard CBA multiple exchange. The agreement stated that Arnoff would receive Barlow's lot, Barlow would receive Causway's lot, Causway would receive Arnoff's lot and each would receive the same value in equity or cash as they contributed. The exchange appears on the work sheet in Figure 8–4. (See also Figures 8–5 through 8–7.)

Documenting a Multiparty Exchange Closing

The closing process that involves the greatest variation occurs in the standard ABC multiparty exchange involving a buyer, a seller and the taxpayer who accomplishes an exchange.

In the exchange between Aloha Investments, Ltd. and Vino Batista, Aloha agreed to exchange the Westway Shopping Center for property that Batista was to acquire. When Aloha located suitable exchange property, Batista committed to purchase it, thus partially completing his obligation under the exchange agreement. In settlement of the transaction that followed, Aloha had an exchange, Batista had a purchase and Graham Cantrow, owner of the office building, had a sale.

Although each was bound by the exchange agreement, only Aloha Investments, Ltd.

WILLIAM T. TAPPAN JR., INC.

COMMERCIAL INVESTMENT REAL ESTATE
6400 UPTOWN BOULEVARD, N.E., SUITE 366 WEST
ALBUQUERQUE, NEW MEXICO 87110

505 - 299 - 1031

EXCHANGE WORK SHEET

BALANCING EQUITIES

	MORRISON		BARNHART			
	Transferred	Received	Transferred	Received	Transferred	Received
	Duplex	8 Units	8 Units	Duplex		
1. Market Value	$ 42,000	$ 98,000	$ 98,000	$ 42,000		
2. Existing Loans	20,000	57,000	57,000	20,000		
3. New Loans		10,000				
4. Equity (L.1 less L.2 & 3)	22,000	31,000	41,000	22,000		
5. Cash	9,000			9,000		
6. Other (Boot) Property						
2nd Mortgage				10,000		
7. Loan Proceeds						
8. Balance	$ 31,000	$ 31,000	$ 41,000	$ 41,000		

NETTING CASH

	MORRISON	BARNHART	
9. Cash Received (L.5 + L.7) Or (Paid) (L.5)	($ 9,000)	$ 9,000	
10. Commissions	$ 2,600	$ 6,600	
11. Transaction Costs	(300)	1,400	
12. Total Capitalized Costs (L.10 + L.11)	(2,300)	(8,000)	( )
13. Net Cash Received Or (Paid) (L.9 less L.12)	($11,300)	$ 1,000	

Figure 8–1

First American Title Company

2601 LOUISIANA BLVD. N.E.   801-3300 87110
3736 EUBANK BLVD. N.E.   292-1595 87111
4603 FOURTH ST., N.W   881-3300 87107

MAILING ADDRESS: P.O. BOX 30066 STATION D. ALBUQUERQUE, NEW MEXICO 87110

EXCHANGE   CLOSING ESCROW STATEMENT   EXCHANGE

GF # __1237503__   Charles and Marie Morrison transferring 9123 Harvard, N.W.

Date __9/1/75__   receiving in exchange 1501 North Regal Place

Legal: Lot 5, Block 2, College Addition - transferred

Lots 3 through 6, Block 10, North Heights Subdivision - received

	Debits	Credits
Value of property received (1501 North Regal Place)	$ 98,000.00	
Mortgage to N. W. Savings " "		$ 57,000.00
Mortgage to Barnharts " "		10,000.00
Property taxes 1/1/75 through 8/31/75 "		1,000.00
Damage Deposits "		400.00
Loan Transfer Fee "	50.00	
Recording	5.75	
Value of property transferred (9123 Harvard, N.W.)		42,000.00
Mortgage to Federal Savings " "	20,000.00	
Property taxes 1/1/75 through 8/31/75 "	400.00	
Damage Deposits "	200.00	
Escrow Fee (1/2) "	75.00	
Title Insurance "	306.00	
Commission $2,500, plus $100.80 tax "	2,620.80	
Due from Charles and Marie Morrison		11,257.55
	$121,657.55	$121,657.55

Taxes for the year __1975__ are estimated to be __$600.00__ and the proration hereinabove used is based upon the assessment. This estimate is hereby agreed upon by Buyer and Seller and no liability is assumed by First American Title Insurance Company for any increase or decrease in taxes caused by changed valuations or rates.

We, the undersigned, hereby approve this statement in its entirety.

Charles Morrison

Marie Morrison

FIRST AMERICAN TITLE COMPANY

By _____
Escrow Officer

Figure 8–2

First American Title Company

2601 LOUISIANA BLVD. N.E.   801-3300 87110
3736 EUBANK BLVD. N.C.   292-1595 87111
4603 FOURTH ST., N.W   881-3300 87107

MAILING ADDRESS: P.O. BOX 30066 STATION D, ALBUQUERQUE, NEW MEXICO 87110

EXCHANGE   CLOSING ESCROW STATEMENT   EXCHANGE

GF # __1237503__   Harrison and Cynthia Barnhart transferring 1501 North

Date __9/1/75__   Regal Place receiving in exchange 9123 Harvard, N.W.

Legal: Lots 3 through 6, Block 10, North Heights Subdivision – transferred

Lot 5, Block 2, College Addition – received

	Debits	Credits
Value of property received (9123 Harvard, N.W.)	$ 42,000.00	
Mortgage to Federal Savings " "		$ 20,000.00
Property taxes 1/1/75 through 8/31/75 "		400.00
Damage Deposits "		200.00
Loan Transfer Fee "	50.00	
Mortgage from Morrisons	10,000.00	
Recording	5.75	
Value of property transferred (1501 North Regal Place)		98,000.00
Mortgage to N. W. Savings " "	57,000.00	
Property taxes 1/1/75 through 8/31/75 "	1,000.00	
Damage Deposits "	400.00	
Escrow Fee (1/2) "	75.00	
Title Insurance "	547.60	
Commission $6,370, plus $270.73 tax "	6,640.73	
Due to Harrison and Cynthia Barnhart	880.92	
	$118,600.00	$118,600.00

Taxes for the year __1975__ are estimated to be __$1,500.00__ and the proration hereinabove used is based upon the assessment. This estimate is hereby agreed upon by Buyer and Seller and no liability is assumed by First American Title Insurance Company for any increase or decrease in taxes caused by changed valuations or rates.

We, the undersigned, hereby approve this statement in its entirety.

_____

_____

FIRST AMERICAN TITLE COMPANY

By _____
     Escrow Officer

Figure 8–3

WILLIAM T. TAPPAN JR., INC.
COMMERCIAL INVESTMENT REAL ESTATE
6400 UPTOWN BOULEVARD, N.E., SUITE 366 WEST
ALBUQUERQUE, NEW MEXICO 87110

505 · 299 · 1031

EXCHANGE WORK SHEET

BALANCING EQUITIES

	ARNOFF		BARLOW		CAUSWAY	
	Transferred	Received	Transferred	Received	Transferred	Received
	10 ac.	18 ac.	18 ac.	25 ac.	25 ac.	10 ac.
1. Market Value	$ 2,500	$ 4,500	$ 4,500	$ 6,250-	$ 6,250	$ 2,500
2. Existing Loans	1,675	3,015	3,015	4,188	4,188	1,675
3. New Loans						
4. Equity (L.1 less L.2 & 3)	825	1,485	1,485	2,062	2,062	825
Cash	660		577			1,237
6. Other (Boot) Property						
7. Loan Proceeds						
8. Balance	$ 1,485	$ 1,485	$ 2,062	$ 2,062	$ 2,062	$ 2,062

NETTING CASH

	ARNOFF	BARLOW	CAUSWAY
9. Cash Received (L.5 + L.7) Or (Paid) (L.5)	($ 660)	($ 577)	$ 1,237
10. Commissions	$ 260	$ 468	$ 650
11. Transaction Costs	60	82	146
Total Capitalized Costs (L.10 + L.11)	(320)	(550)	(796)
13. Net Cash Received Or (Paid) (L.9 less L.12)	($ 980)	($1,127)	$ 446

Figure 8–4

First American Title Company

2601 LOUISIANA BLVD. N.E.   801-3300 87110
3736 EUBANK BLVD. N.C.   292-1593 87111
4603 FOURTH ST., N.W   881-3300 87107

MAILING ADDRESS: P.O. BOX 30066 STATION D, ALBUQUERQUE, NEW MEXICO 87110

EXCHANGE   CLOSING ESCROW STATEMENT   EXCHANGE

GF # __03256__   Charles Arnoff transferring 10 acres

Date __6/1/74__   receiving in exchange 18 acres

____Legal: Lot 12, Mountain View Subdivision - transferred____

_____Lot 17, Mountain View - received____

	Debits	Credits
Value of property received (Lot 17)	$ 4,500.00	
Land Sale Contract to Reclots, Inc. (Lot 17)		$ 3,015.00
Property taxes 1/1/74 through 5/31/74 "		37.50
Recording	1.75	
Value of property transferred (Lot 12)		2,500.00
Land Sale Contract to Reclots, Inc. (Lot 12)	1,675.00	
Property taxes 1/1/74 through 5/31/74 "	20.83	
Escrow Fee (1/3)	50.00	
Title Insurance	25.00	
Commission $250, plus $10 tax	260.00	
Due from Charles Arnoff		980.08
	$ 6,532.58	$ 6,532.58

Taxes for the year __1974__ are estimated to be __$50.00__ and the proration
hereinabove used is based upon the assessment. This estimate is hereby agreed upon by
Buyer and Seller and no liability is assumed by First American Title Insurance Company
for any increase or decrease in taxes caused by changed valuations or rates.

We, the undersigned, hereby approve
this statement in its entirety.

_____   FIRST AMERICAN TITLE COMPANY

_____   By _____
                                    Escrow Officer

Figure 8–5

First American Title Company

2601 LOUISIANA BLVD. N.E.   801-3300 87110
3736 EUBANK BLVD. N.E.   292-1593 87111
4603 FOURTH ST., N.W   881-3300 87107

MAILING ADDRESS: P.O. BOX 30066 STATION D. ALBUQUERQUE, NEW MEXICO 87110

EXCHANGE   CLOSING ESCROW STATEMENT   EXCHANGE

GF #   03256   Baird Barlow transferring 18 acres

Date   6/1/74   receiving in exchange 25 acres

Legal: Lot 17, Mountain View Subdivision - transferred

Lot 21, Mountain View Subdivision - received

	Debits	Credits
Value of property received (Lot 21)	$ 6,250.00	
Land Sale Contract to Reclots, Inc. "		$ 4,188.00
Property taxes 1/1/74 through 5/31/74 "		52.08
Recording	1.75	
Value of property transferred (Lot 17)		4,500.00
Land Sale Contract to Reclots, Inc. "	3,015.00	
Property taxes 1/1/74 through 5/31/74 "	37.50	
Escrow Fee (1/3)	50.00	
Title Insurance	45.00	
Commission $450, plus $18 tax	468.00	
Due from Baird Barlow		1,127.17
	$ 9,867.25	$ 9,867.25

Taxes for the year 1974 are estimated to be $90.00 and the proration hereinabove used is based upon the assessment. This estimate is hereby agreed upon by Buyer and Seller and no liability is assumed by First American Title Insurance Company for any increase or decrease in taxes caused by changed valuations or rates.

We, the undersigned, hereby approve
this statement in its entirety.

FIRST AMERICAN TITLE COMPANY

By _____
     Escrow Officer

Figure 8–6

First American Title Company

2601 LOUISIANA BLVD. N.E.   881-3300 87110
3736 EUBANK BLVD. N.E.   292-1595 87111
4603 FOURTH ST., N.W   881-3300 87107

MAILING ADDRESS: P.O. BOX 30066 STATION D. ALBUQUERQUE, NEW MEXICO 87110

EXCHANGE   CLOSING ESCROW STATEMENT   EXCHANGE

GF # __03256__   Arnold Causway transferring 25 acres

Date __6/1/74__   receiving in exchange 10 acres

Legal: Lot 21, Mountain View Subdivision - transferred

Lot 12, Mountain View Subdivision - received

	Debits	Credits
Value of property received (Lot 12)	$ 2,500.00	
Land Sale Contract to Reclots, Inc. "		$ 1,675.00
Property taxes 1/1/74 through 5/31/74		20.83
Recording	1.75	
Value of property transferred (Lot 21)		6,250.00
Land Sale Contract to Reclots, Inc. "	4,188.00	
Property taxes 1/1/74 through 5/31/74 "	52.08	
Escrow Fee (1/3)	50.00	
Title Insurance	62.50	
Commission $625, plus $25 tax	650.00	
Due to Arnold Causway	441.50	
	$ 7,945.83	$ 7,945.83

Taxes for the year __1974__ are estimated to be __$125.00__ and the proration hereinabove used is based upon the assessment. This estimate is hereby agreed upon by Buyer and Seller and no liability is assumed by First American Title Insurance Company for any increase or decrease in taxes caused by changed valuations or rates.

We, the undersigned, hereby approve this statement in its entirety.

FIRST AMERICAN TITLE COMPANY

By _____
    Escrow Officer

Figure 8–7

made a nontaxable exchange. After the smoke cleared, Batista owned the Westway Shopping Center, Aloha owned the office building and Cantrow had cash in his pocket.

In order to be accurate, the closing statements must reflect what each party contributed to the exchange escrow and received from escrow. Batista contributed cash and received property—a purchase; Cantrow contributed property and received cash—a sale; Aloha contributed property and received property—an exchange. Therefore, Batista's closing statement reflects a purchase, Cantrow's closing statement reflects a sale and Aloha's closing statement reflects an exchange.

Each closing statement presents an accounting of the transaction from the viewpoint of the party receiving the statement. Differences in the method of presenting the closing do not endanger the qualification of the exchange. Aloha's exchange is protected by conforming the exchange to the contractual commitment with Batista. The closing statements can't change that fact regardless of the form they take. Figure 8–8 presents the work sheet and Figures 8–9, 8–10 and 8–11 present the closing statements for this transaction.

Closing an Exchange from the Title Company's Point of View

As in all real estate transactions, the title company in an exchange is a fiduciary agent whose powers are limited by the instructions of the principals. But because of the potential challenge to an exchange by the IRS, the title company must take special care to ensure that the action it takes on behalf of the principals conforms to their written instructions.

In states such as California in which escrows are "opened" with the signing of specific instructions, the instructions should in no way deviate from the terms of the exchange agreement and thereby change the facts of the transaction. In states in which written instructions are not used and there is doubt as to the mechanics, it is best to request written instructions from the tax attorney who represents the taxpayer seeking Section 1031 treatment.

The main danger during escrow occurs in multiparty exchanges in which action taken by the parties circumvents the intent of the exchange agreement, resulting in the constructive receipt of cash by the taxpayer. In closings that involve qualifying property only, there is virtually no way to endanger the tax benefits during escrow.

WILLIAM T. TAPPAN JR., INC.
COMMERCIAL INVESTMENT REAL ESTATE
6400 UPTOWN BOULEVARD, N.E., SUITE 366 WEST
ALBUQUERQUE, NEW MEXICO 87110

505 - 299-1031

EXCHANGE WORK SHEET

BALANCING EQUITIES

	ALOHA		BATISTA		CANTROW	
	Transferred	Received	Transferred	Received	Transferred	Received
	Center	Offices	Cash	Center	Offices	Cash
1. Market Value	$1,200,000	$1,875,000		$1,200,000	$1,875,000	
2. Existing Loans	500,000	1,200,000			1,200,000	
3. New Loans				900,000		
4. Equity (L.1 less L.2 & 3)	700,000	675,000			675,000	
5. Cash		25,000	$300,000			$275,000
6. Other (Boot) Property						
7. Loan Proceeds						400,000
8. Balance	$ 700,000	$ 700,000	$300,000	$ 300,000	$ 675,000	$675,000

NETTING CASH

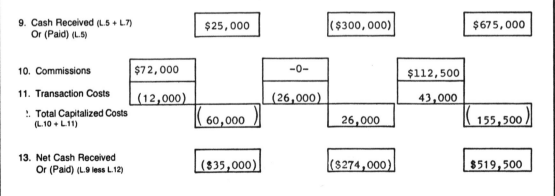

	ALOHA	BATISTA	CANTROW
9. Cash Received (L.5 + L.7) Or (Paid) (L.5)	$25,000	($300,000)	$675,000
10. Commissions	$72,000	-0-	$112,500
11. Transaction Costs	(12,000)	(26,000)	43,000
12. Total Capitalized Costs (L.10 + L.11)	(60,000)	26,000	(155,500)
13. Net Cash Received Or (Paid) (L.9 less L.12)	($35,000)	($274,000)	$519,500

Figure 8–8

First American Title Company

2601 LOUISIANA BLVD. N.E.   801-3300 87110
3736 EUBANK BLVD. N.C.   292-1595 87111
4603 FOURTH ST., N.W   881-3300 87107

MAILING ADDRESS: P.O. BOX 30066 STATION D, ALBUQUERQUE, NEW MEXICO 87110

EXCHANGE   CLOSING ESCROW STATEMENT   EXCHANGE

GF # 19423

Date 10/15/73

Aloha Investment, Ltd. transferring the Westway Shopping Center, receiving in exchange the Cantrow Plaza

Legal: Tract A, Westway Addition - transferred

Lots 1 through 12, Block 1, Ridgemont Subdivision - received

	Debits	Credits
Value of property received (Cantrow Plaza)	$ 1,875,000	
Mortgage to Western Insurance "		$ 1,200,000
Property taxes 1/1/73 through 10/15/73 "		29,687
Tenant Deposits "		11,125
Loan Transfer Fee "	250	
Recording	12	
Value of property transferred (Westway Center)		1,200,000
Mortgage to N. W. Savings "	500,000	
Property taxes 1/1/73 through 10/15/73 "	19,000	
Tenant Deposits "	8,670	
Escrow Fee (1/3)	300	
Title Insurance	907	
Commission	72,000	
Due from Aloha Investment, Ltd.		35,327
	$ 2,476,139	$ 2,476,139

Taxes for the year 1973 are estimated to be $24,000 and the proration hereinabove used is based upon the assessment. This estimate is hereby agreed upon by Buyer and Seller and no liability is assumed by First American Title Insurance Company for any increase or decrease in taxes caused by changed valuations or rates.

We, the undersigned, hereby approve this statement in its entirety.

ALOHA INVESTMENTS, Ltd.

by _____
President

FIRST AMERICAN TITLE COMPANY

By _____
Escrow Officer

Figure 8–9

First American Title Company

2601 LOUISIANA BLVD. N.E.   801-3300 87110
3736 EUBANK BLVD. N.E.   292-1595 87111
4603 FOURTH ST., N.W   881-3300 87107

MAILING ADDRESS: P.O. BOX 30066 STATION D. ALBUQUERQUE, NEW MEXICO 87110

CLOSING ESCROW STATEMENT

GF #   19423   Vino Batista, receiving by agreement to exchange, the

Date   10/15/73   Westway Shopping Center

Legal: Tract A, Westway Addition

	Debits	Credits
Value of property received	$ 1,200,000	
New mortgage to Western Insurance		$ 900,000
Property taxes 1/1/73 through 10/15/73		19,000
Tenant Deposits		8,670
Escrow Fee (1/3)	300	
Recording	8	
Due from Vino Batista		272,638
	$ 1,200,308	$1,200,308

Taxes for the year 1973 are estimated to be $24,000 and the proration hereinabove used is based upon the assessment. This estimate is hereby agreed upon by Buyer and Seller and no liability is assumed by First American Title Insurance Company for any increase or decrease in taxes caused by changed valuations or rates.

We, the undersigned, hereby approve this statement in its entirety.

FIRST AMERICAN TITLE COMPANY

By _____
Escrow Officer

Figure 8–10

First American Title Company

2601 LOUISIANA BLVD. N.E.   881-3300 87110
3736 EUBANK BLVD. N.E.   292-1595 87111
4603 FOURTH ST., N.W   881-3300 87107

MAILING ADDRESS: P.O. BOX 30066 STATION D. ALBUQUERQUE, NEW MEXICO 87110

CLOSING ESCROW STATEMENT

GF # __19423__   Graham Cantrow, transferring the Cantro Plaza

Date __10/15/73__

Legal: Lots 1 through 12, Block 1, Ridgemont Subdivision

	Debits	Credits
Value of property transferred	$	$ 1,875,000
Mortgage to Western Insurance	1,200,000	
Property taxes 1/1/73 through 10/15/73	29,687	
Tenant Deposits	11,125	
Escrow Fee (1/3)	300	
Title Insurance	1,050	
Commission	112,500	
Due to Graham Cantrow	520,338	
	$ 1,875,000	$ 1,875,000

Taxes for the year ___1973___ are estimated to be __$37,500__ and the proration hereinabove used is based upon the assessment. This estimate is hereby agreed upon by Buyer and Seller and no liability is assumed by First American Title Insurance Company for any increase or decrease in taxes caused by changed valuations or rates.

We, the undersigned, hereby approve this statement in its entirety.

FIRST AMERICAN TITLE COMPANY

By _____
Escrow Officer

Figure 8–11

9

How to Use
the Nontaxable Exchange
to Improve Investment
Performance

The application of exchange strategies and techniques goes far beyond the limits usually considered in the average real estate transaction. This chapter deals with three strategic areas of exchanging:

1. Exchanges that yield tax savings.
2. Exchanges to increase return on investment.
3. Approaches to securing personal benefits and solving real estate problems.

The strategies covered here focus on the direct benefits possible for the taxpayer when he accomplishes a specific real estate objective, what you can plan for and expect from certain applications of the nontaxable exchange.

The reasons behind a particular real estate transaction often extend beyond the stated economic objectives of the owner. In fact, there is probably no limit to the reasons why real estate is transferred. Reasons range from attempts to prevent repossession for back mortgage payments to the elimination of management problems.

This chapter presents the economic, tax and personal reasons that often make an exchange the best action to take—not the causes isolated after the fact, but the objectives that can be planned and accomplished. As in all business activity, an exchange should be structured with a specified objective in mind, one which will result in a range of benefits for the taxpayer, whether economic, personal or both.

Exchanges Designed to Preserve Equity from Tax

Conservation of Capital

Preservation of job and income-producing capital is the underlying wisdom of the nontaxable exchange. It provides a method of transferring property tax-free when its essential nature isn't changed in the process; that is, converted to cash or boot. So you can virtually establish an exchange simply by not converting the property to a different type of asset.

This simple fact is why an investor or business with plans to sell real estate and reinvest part or all of the proceeds in different real estate should structure a nontaxable exchange. Why sell outright, convert property to money, pay tax and then take what's left and buy the same kind of property when you can end up at the same place without paying tax?

For example, an individual who sells property with a zero basis for $200,000 cash may have a capital gains liability of approximately $65,000, depending on the tax rates in effect when the property is sold. The $65,000 paid in tax is not only a loss to the taxpayer, it is investment capital taken directly out of circulation unnecessarily. The nontaxable exchange is specifically intended by Congress to prevent this and thus keep job-producing investment capital in the hands of investors and business.

Furthermore, taking advantage of a tax-free exchange can result in substantial long-range economic benefits. In this example, the $65,000 paid in tax could have produced an annual before-tax income of $6,500 if capitalized at 10%. And with an aggressive acquisition program, the $65,000, when leveraged at 10%, represents purchasing power of $650,000. Is there any doubt that, in certain circumstances, a nontaxable exchange is the only logical and responsible business decision?

Compare:

Sale		Exchange
Sale Price	$200,000	$65,000 × 10% = $6,500/yr. income
Basis	–0–	or
Gain	200,000	$65,000 ÷ 10% = $650,000 in
Tax (approximate depending on the tax rate at sale date)	− 65,000	acquisition power
Net Equity	$145,000	

An exchange is often turned to only when the tax is so large that there's no choice or when the seller stumbles in contact with a knowledgeable Realtor, but it doesn't have to be that way. Exchanging can and should be a simple, routine investment tool.

Increase in Basis

Basis forms the foundation for calculating gain when real estate is sold; it also determines the starting point for computing depreciation, which contributes to sheltered income. Depreciation write-off, in turn, preserves a portion of income from tax to provide for replacement of improvements as they wear out. Again, this is a benefit of law designed to keep capital in the economy.

Property that has been held for several years often has little or no basis remaining and consequently relatively little depreciation to shelter income. This lack of depreciation can be a problem when rents increase with inflation and interest payments decrease as loans are amortized. The end result is often an owner paying tax on income which goes to mortgage payments rather than into his pocket. When a large amount of tax is paid on money locked up in loan principal reduction, serious problems can result.

Fortunately, the problem can be solved by an exchange structured to increase depreciable basis while concurrently increasing net after-tax cash flow by sheltering a larger portion of income with the increased depreciable basis. An exchange up for property with a larger fair market value and a larger loan can significantly improve after-tax return by sheltering more cash flow. The entire process can be accomplished while protecting the entire appreciated equity from capital gains tax.

Complete investment analysis requires that all income be considered in the context of net after-tax return. In fact, the nature of real estate ownership makes this calculation one of the more significant benefits. A nontaxable exchange is a very effective way to increase net after-tax return by increasing depreciable basis. If the economics of the circumstances dictate the soundness of an exchange, then why not do it and maximize the performance of the asset?

James Garrett, for example, owned a 10-apartment complex which he exchanged in a multiparty transaction involving a cash takeout. He received a 40-apartment complex as consideration for his 10 apartments. The objective for Garrett was to increase the depreciable basis of his real estate and thereby shelter a larger portion of cash flow from tax.

Figure 9–1 illustrates the effect of the exchange on Garrett's basis.

Transferring Basis from Vacant Land to Improved Real Estate

An exchange structured to transfer basis from land to improved real estate can often result in substantial tax savings. This approach is best illustrated in the case of an investor who has a large earned income and vacant land holdings. The ownership of land usually provides no income and, consequently, no annual return on investment, and may even require the monthly payment of debt service.

Futhermore, land provides no income shelter, and the only return occurs when it's sold. An analysis of your real estate investment portfolio may indicate that an exchange of vacant land for improved real estate would result in an overall increase in performance; that is, the addition of income and tax shelter to the appreciation, which was the only benefit of owning the land.

The benefit of owning improved real estate with income is a fundamental incentive for investment in real estate. Obtaining this benefit through a nontaxable exchange is an effective method of improving real estate investment performance.

In one case, Dr. Wallace Warris had invested over the years in well-located vacant land. Land value increased as the years passed, and so did the doctor's earned income. Heavy mortgage payments on the land, a large portion of which went to principal and was not deductible, combined with a high tax bracket to substantially reduce his discretionary income. Dr. Warris had three objectives.

1. To retain his investment in real estate
2. To get out from under mortgage payments
3. To avoid diminishing his appreciated land equity as a result of tax

EXCHANGE BASIS COMPUTATION

TRANSFERRING BASIS

1. Adjusted Basis of Qualifying Property Transferred	$ 5,000	
2. Adjusted Basis of Other (Boot) Property Transferred	_____	
3. Cash Paid	_____	
4. Liabilities On All Property Received	350,000	
5. Total (L1+2+3+4)		$355,000
6. Cash Received	_____	
7. Liabilities on All Property Transferred	10,000	
8. Total (L.6+L.7)		10,000
9. Difference (L.5 less L.8)		345,000
10. Gain Recognized		-0-
11. Total (L.9+L.10)		345,000
12. Loss Recognized on Other (Boot) Property Transferred		-0-
13. Basis of All Property Received (L.11 less L12)		345,000

ALLOCATING BASIS

14. Basis of All Property Received (L.13)	345,000	
15. Market Value of Other (Boot) Property Received*	_____	
16. Basis Allocated to Qualifying Property (L.14 less L.15)		345,000
17. Market Value of Improvements on Qualifying Property	400,000	
18. Market Value of Qualifying Property Received	460,000	
19. Percentage Allocated to Improvements (L.17÷L.18)		87%
20. Basis Allocated to Improvements on Qualifying Property (L.19×L.16)		$300,000

*The basis of the boot property received is the same as its market value as indicated on line 15.

Figure 9–1

These three objectives and more were accomplished by structuring an exchange of Dr. Warris' various land investments for a shopping center.

	Land Investments		Shopping Center	
Value	$800,000	$2,100,000	
Loans	200,000	1,500,000	
Equity	600,000	600,000	
Income (payment)	($18,000)	45,000	base rents
Depreciation	N/A	−44,444	($1,400,000 to
Net taxable	N/A	($556)	improvements)

Not only did this exchange meet the primary objectives, the doctor's discretionary income increased by approximately $63,000 ($18,000 + $45,000). Figure 9–2 illustrates the calculation of basis in this example.

Reallocation of Basis

Real estate with a high land value and relatively low improvement value may not have adequate depreciation available to shelter rental income. Since the value of improved property must be allocated between improvements and land in proportion to the fair market value of each, an investor who owns real estate with a high land and a low improvement value can improve after-tax income by arranging an exchange for property with a higher relative building value. This strategy maximizes after-tax income by increasing the value allocated to improvements, as the following case illustrates.

Bill Phillips purchased an office building for $100,000. Due to the age of the building and the location of the land (a reviving downtown area), only 20% of the total value, or $20,000, could be allocated to improvements. Therefore, the land was valued at $80,000. Consequently, over a 20-year period it was possible to take depreciation based on only 10% of the total property value. To increase after-tax rental income, an exchange was structured which increased the allocation of value to improvements.

Example:

	Property Transferred	Property Acquired
Total Value	$100,000	$100,000
Land	80,000	10,000
Improvements	20,000	90,000

Exchanging to Increase Return on Equity

This section presents several situations in which exchanging is used specifically to increase investment performance. The tax advantage in an exchange increases the opportunity to improve profitability—investment strategy can be concentrated on economics without concern about tax. Since you don't have to worry about losing equity to tax, more attention can be given to the market factors that determine the worth of an investment.

Aggressive exchange strategy centers around moves designed to improve the taxpayer's investment by making equity more productive than it would have been if the exchange had not taken place. An investment attitude that places relative improvement

EXCHANGE BASIS COMPUTATION

TRANSFERRING BASIS

1. Adjusted Basis of Qualifying Property Transferred $ 400,000

2. Adjusted Basis of Other (Boot) Property Transferred

3. Cash Paid   80,000

4. Liabilities On All Property Received   1,500,000

5. Total (L1+2+3+4) $1,980,000

6. Cash Received

7. Liabilities on All Property Transferred   200,000

8. Total (L.6+L.7)   200,000

9. Difference (L.5 less L.8)   1,780,000

10. Gain Recognized

11. Total (L.9+L.10)   1,780,000

12. Loss Recognized on Other (Boot) Property Transferred

13. Basis of All Property Received (L.11 less L12)   1,780,000

ALLOCATING BASIS

14. Basis of All Property Received (L.13)   1,780,000

15. Market Value of Other (Boot) Property Received*

16. Basis Allocated to Qualifying Property (L.14 less L.15)   1,780,000

17. Market Value of Improvements on Qualifying Property   1,659,000

18. Market Value of Qualifying Property Received   2,100,000

19. Percentage Allocated to Improvements (L.17÷L.18)   79%

20. Basis Allocated to Improvements on Qualifying Property (L.19×L.16) $1,400,000

*The basis of the boot property received is the same as its market
value as indicated on line 15.

Figure 9–2

ahead of perfection is a sign of flexibility. And it's flexibility that maximizes success. Exchanges just don't happen, they must be set up and made to work.

Pyramiding Real Estate Ownership

Pyramiding is a process of acquiring real estate of increasingly greater value by nontaxable exchange. The word "pyramid" refers to the movement of ownership from lower to higher total value—each exchange is a move up. The objective is to use the tax-free benefit to increase the compounding effect of equity appreciation. In other words, by making nontaxable exchange a part of your acquisition program, that portion of equity that would go to payment of tax is used to acquire more real estate.

Pyramiding is effective because of the equity saved by exchanging. But if you are able to acquire real estate below market value or improve it in a few ways that will immediately increase its value, you will be that much further ahead.

Normally, pyramiding is a gradual process which occurs over a period of years. One fortunate investor began the process by acquiring a rental duplex in a university area on the verge of rapid expansion. Fortunately, the seller didn't want a lot of cash, so the investor was able to buy the property for $500 down—a helpful first step in pyramiding. Over the next five years, due to increased rents, unusually rapid appreciation in real estate values and loan amortization, the duplex equity increased to $10,000.

The leverage of a very low down payment got him off to the right start. When the opportunity came to step up by exchange, he was ready. The duplex was exchanged tax-free for a 12-unit apartment complex, which, after two years of patient ownership, resulted in a significant increase in total benefits. The new property, because of its size, provided larger value appreciation, greater debt reduction (equity build-up) and a much higher net cash flow than the duplex would ever have been able to produce.

Exchanging for Property with Faster Appreciation

An exchange for greater appreciation is based on the sound reasoning that if you are holding property for increase in incremental value, it should be appreciating as fast as possible. If your investment real estate is located in an area that is going downhill or not appreciating at the rate you think it should, an exchange may solve the problem. Keeping in mind that real estate is a vehicle for reaching broader personal goals, look at the sections of your city to determine the path of progress. The direction of population growth and new building indicates where the fastest appreciation is and the area in which to find exchange property—provided the growth is the result of natural supply and demand factors.

To apply this strategy, establish an appreciation trend by geographic area. Which areas are declining? Which are developing? Where is property most in demand? Which type of property is in demand in a given area; i.e., improved, vacant land, residential rental, commercial? Then compare your property and the area it's in to what's available in other areas. There's no limit to the size of the area for consideration—block, subdivision, quadrant, city, state, climatic region. Why not consider as many possibilities as you feel comfortable with?

One investor moved his holdings in a series of exchanges from a slum area in a large city to a small mining town which later boomed due to the demand for energy. It took patience, but the potential was recognized before the first step, and within three years the plan paid off.

If the investment objective is maximum appreciation, well-planned exchanges can move your ownership to locations that meet the goal—without the tax.

Exchange for Loan Value

Exchanging often results in a significant increase in equity return. But in order to increase the percentage of return on equity, it is sometimes necessary to refinance, thus reducing the relative amount of equity.

Unfortunately, there are certain types of properties that lending institutions won't make loans on, and there are properties they will loan on but shouldn't. In any event, an exchange for real estate that is acceptable for loan purposes can generate cash, increase percentage return on equity and result in a more secure investment.

To analyze this possibility, establish the property's current return on equity. What is it compared to what it could be? Then, can it be refinanced—just what is the loan value: 70%, 75%, 80% or nothing? Maybe the age, location and condition eliminate the possibility of refinancing. Or is it that loans aren't available for commercial property and an exchange into residential income will solve the problem? When potential exchange property is found, establish its loan value and make sure a loan will be possible before committing yourself to the transaction.

In one case, an investor exchanged free and clear commerical rental property with no loan value for a free and clear apartment complex. His basis was transferred from the commercial property to the apartments. After the transaction closed, he financed the apartments, increasing the *percentage* return on equity. He then reinvested the tax-free loan funds and increased the total size of his real estate portfolio.

Exchange for Property with a Lower Debt Service Payment

Exchanging for property with lower debt payments can solve a number of problems while increasing equity return. High interest rates, short-term loans and balloon payments tend to reduce return. Acquiring property with equal equity and expenses but lower loan payments automatically increases return on equity.

The first step in this strategy is to establish the percentage relationship between gross scheduled income, operating expenses and debt service. For example, an investor owned a 16-unit apartment complex in which:

Gross Scheduled Income	=	100%
Vacancy	=	5%
Operating Expenses	=	42%
Debt Service	=	48%
Cash Flow	=	5%

By concentrating on debt service and setting up an exchange that will lower it to 40%, you can increase cash flow automatically to 11% if all other variables are held constant. This can be accomplished by locating property with established loans or by negotiating a carry-back loan with lower interest rate and generally favorable terms not possible with conventional financing. But when this type of exchange is called for, return on equity is often not the major consideration. An investor saddled with loan payments that the property doesn't support can be faced with more of a personal than an investment problem.

This is a widespread problem in situations involving vacant land payments that cut into discretionary income.

One of the most effective applications of this exchange strategy is in obtaining relief from vacant land payments. In one case, an investor had a substantial equity in 10 acres that was not producing income. Due to changes in his job situation, the large land payments became prohibitive and he was in danger of foreclosure. By structuring an exchange for income property, he not only protected the land equity but also received cash flow equal to the amount of the land payments.

Exchange a Nonproductive Equity for Income

Return on equity can take a real jump when land is traded for income-producing real estate. Farmers have experienced this benefit when faced with the fact that certain land is more valuable as a subdivision than as a farm.

A 640-acre farm purchased 20 years ago at $100 per acre and valued today at $1,000 an acre is a real retirement asset. In fact, a 10% return on its value today is equal to the original cost—the farm equity of $640,000 can be expected to produce an annual income of $64,000 when exchanged for income-producing real estate. What better way to retire with a larger income than ever possible to consistently earn by farming and at the same time leveraging the transaction to increase the estate size?

The exchange strategy applies equally well for all land owners, including ranchers, investors and city lot owners. The objective is to receive maximum return on appreciated equity in today's dollars without the diminishing effect of paying tax on a sale.

Exchanging to Solve Problems and Secure Benefits That Go Beyond Tax and Business Considerations

The benefits available through exchanging are not limited to tax and business considerations. Exchanging plays a large part in solving problems and meeting personal objectives in ways not possible by selling. These are the situations that broaden the meaning of value and separate it from price. The distinction between value and price is created by the effect of the transaction on the owner—in problem real estate the value of the exchange to the owner psychologically may far exceed the market value of the property. To establish the price of real estate without considering the value of a specific transaction for the owner is an incomplete analysis. Price is one factor contributing to value, but the effect of an exchange on the owner may be more important and must ultimately figure in the decision to go ahead with a specific transaction.

Putting people before property in considering a real estate move is essential to good judgment in any transaction. Opportunities to secure benefits are almost unending in real estate. Real estate is a means to an end—a vehicle to carry people to relatively better circumstances. The value of real estate is in what it can do for people. A dollar price established arbitrarily at some passing moment is a shot in the dark at a fixed value. At best, a price set out of context from an owner is a hollow abstraction—unreal and meaningless. It is only by introducing real people with needs, desires, and unique objectives that value can be established. No doubt that is why real estate negotiation is so often a difficult process. Value is in the use of the property to a living person and a concept completely separate from price.

What seems too high a price today often proves, in restrospect, to have been a bargain.

Going one step further to define real estate value in terms of what it can do for you is the only way to protect yourself from making the wrong decision. It seems that more people kick themselves for not making an acquisition at what seemed a high price at the time than those who do make such an acquisition.

Don't make the error of confusing value with price. Value is where the real estate vehicle will take you as an individual. Price is someone else's shot in the dark at dollars. Not making a move because the price set by some stranger seems "too high (or if you're selling, too low) for today's market" can result in a loss of real, personally measurable value. Money is only an abstraction; people are real, and the only determinant of value.

Consolidation of Assets

The management demand of real estate that is scattered over a large geographic area can often become an unbearable energy drain on the owner. Although rental houses and duplexes acquired through the years may represent hard-earned equity dollars, the effect on health and life style of trying to take care of them can overshadow the investment benefits. Consolidation of several properties into one large complex can eliminate the management problems without loss of equity to tax.

The primary benefit of a consolidation exchange is management centralization. A pyramiding step-up in overall value can also be a natural by-product. And the entire process can be tax-free.

In making this strategy work, it is reasonable to assume that the owner of a large income property wouldn't want several scattered houses and duplexes any more than the person disposing of them. The solution is to find a wholesale buyer for the scattered property or, if practical, individual buyers to cash the houses out of escrow. This approach sets up a multiparty transaction, resulting in a nontaxable exchange for the consolidating taxpayer, a sale for the income property owner and a purchase for the new owner of the houses and duplexes.

Arrange a Transaction Not Otherwise Possible

An exchange is sometimes the only way to complete a real estate transaction. Take, for example, the expansion necessitated by a successful business. A business that must have a specific parcel of real estate, which the owner refuses to sell because of the tax consequences, is a natural exchange opportunity. Multiparty exchanges probably solve more acquisition problems of this type than any other technique. This problem normally arises when the business wants only the property in question and the owner can't afford to sell because of taxes.

The solution is the standard ABC multiparty exchange in which the business agrees to acquire real estate designated by the owner and exchange it for the desired parcel. There's no other way the transaction can go through. The business must own the property. But with a low basis the owner may have practically no equity left after taxes if he sells. Both objectives are met in an exchange. The business owns the property it needs, and the taxpayer acquires other real estate with possibly more potential and income than he had before. A transaction that would not have occurred without the nontaxable exchange benefits of Section 1031 is completed.

Acquisition of Property Without Cash

Contrary to popular opinion, real estate is acquired every day without cash or, more accurately, without the acquiring party's cash. This rewarding process is accomplished through the use of the several financing and negotiation techniques that are in Part II of this book. The nontaxable exchange is a frequent method of acquiring property by using appreciated value of property instead of cash.

This process is a natural by-product of exchanging. To put it in action simply requires the completion of an exchange. In effect, the equity of the original property serves as the value placed as down payment on the acquired property. One of the major benefits of exchanging is the acquisition of real estate of equal equity but with greater total value, resulting in an overall increase in the size of the owner's portfolio. Used in combination with one or more of the financing techniques, an exchange can maximize leverage as much as a cash purchase.

In one such case, the taxpayer exchanged a fourplex for a 16-unit apartment complex with management problems. By negotiating a favorable carryback loan on the 16-unit complex, he was able to use the fourplex equity as down payment and literally finance himself into the balance of the complex without paying into the deal.

Initiate an Exchange for a Cash Takeout

An exchange with a cash takeout (ACB multiparty exchange) can be initiated by "C," the participant who supplies exchange property. This strategy would normally be used as a method of disposing of real estate that has not been easy to sell. Not that you would expect anything to be inherently wrong with the property—there might be a shortage of buyers, the timing could be wrong or the marketing effort might be inadequate. Regardless of the reason, there is a real opportunity for a seller to initiate a nontaxable transaction, supply the exchange property and receive cash.

This approach is the other side of the coin in an ACB multiparty exchange. Given a taxpayer who has property he wants to exchange (A) and a buyer (B) with cash who wants the property, the transaction is completed with location of the exchange property (C). This strategy reverses the process. The owner with the potential exchange property seeks out the exchange. The end result is a sale for "C"—he puts property into the exchange escrow and receives cash. In fact, he begins the exchange by offering property for exchange provided a cash buyer is located who will buy the property he receives from "A."

This technique was used in a situation in which a partnership ("C") had attempted to sell an office complex for over a year without success. By actively offering it for exchange, they located a group (A) that was trying to complete a multiparty exchange. Subsequently, a buyer (B) was located for the property owned by the partnership. The exchange between A and C was closed with the conditional purchase of "A's" property from "C" by "B."

By initiating the exchange, "C" completed a cash sale. If the strategy had not been changed to an exchange, the partnership would probably still own the complex. Obviously, the benefit here for "C" was receiving the cash without expectation of tax-free treatment.

Exchange for Investment Property That Is Easier to Sell

If you've tried to sell and can't, an exchange may help solve the problem. Exchanging property that is difficult to sell for a number of rental houses, duplexes and triplexes as part of a consolidation exchange can greatly increase the ease of a sale. The strategy here is different than that of an exchange with a cash takeout.

This strategy involves completing the exchange and holding the more saleable property for income or investment. When the property has appreciated to the investment objective over a reasonable period of time, sell it.

The distinction between this procedure and exchanging with a contingent cash takeout is that the property received is not sold at closing. It is held for investment (not sale) and sold when the market is right for taking an investment profit. Being involved in a multiparty exchange as the supplier of exchange property who receives cash at closing is one transaction—a capital gain sale. But closing an exchange and later selling the real estate received results in two transactions. Therefore, care must be taken to avoid any implication that the property acquired in the exchange was held for sale rather than investment if you want to avoid tax on the exchange.

Exchange for New Circumstances

If you want to retain an investment in real estate but need a change in lifestyle, consider exchanging. Retirement and travel plans don't mix with the management demands of rental property. An exchange for well-located land can eliminate the management problems and provide other benefits as well.

This situation occurred with a retiring civil service worker who had acquired a number of older rentals over the years. Although he had built a sizeable equity, the net income from the ten rental houses was small and not worth forgoing travel plans.

The solution was to stay in real estate ownership but get out of rentals; that is, exchange circumstances. If you accept the concept that real estate is a vehicle to reach personal objectives, it follows that if the objectives change it may be necessary to change vehicles. This is exactly what happened with the retired civil service worker.

He had sold retirement income and didn't need the small amount contributed by his rentals. But what he did want was the stability and security of a well-placed real estate investment. He got just that by exchanging the rental houses for acreage located about five years away from the major residential growth of the city. Returning from five years of travel would place him in a position to sell the land at long-term capital gains—a gain estimated to be much greater than that anticipated for his old rentals. But, more importantly, he eliminated management responsibility without sacrificing equity and was able to travel with peace of mind.

Intrinsic Benefits of Exchanging

There are several benefits that follow naturally from exchanging. Although they are minor compared to the sometimes tremendous tax savings and increases in equity return, they deserve mentioning.

Aside from the specific tax or business objectives, an exchange often results in a general change in the circumstances surrounding an owner's life. Transferring real estate can solve a whole set of personal problems. For example, high monthly land payments that are beyond the financial capacity of the owner have more than once strained family relations. What was once a long-term investment may become a symbol of bad judgment or a deal in which you "got taken." When this type of thinking starts, it's time to get out.

Lifetime estate conservation is another benefit inherent in the nontaxable exchange. If lifetime estate conservation is carried to its logical extreme, you can acquire real estate and continue to exchange throughout life without ever selling. You could pyramid equity on equity, never paying tax. Transaction after transaction can be made without one cent lost to tax—a very efficient way to build an estate.

Making an exchange also automatically provides the decision of where to invest funds—a decision that is difficult for some of us to make. In a tax-free exchange there's no problem of what to do with money—the decision is made by the nature of the transaction. Equity is not converted to money; it stays in the form of real estate.

Keeping investment capital in real estate is a benefit in itself. To someone who has seen his hard-earned capital disappear in the stock market or vanish overnight in the commodities market, real estate offers welcome security. After an exchange, there's no temptation to enter the more volatile investment areas.

All of the tax, business and general exchange benefits can appear separately and in combination in any given transaction. In fact, the complexity of some exchanges tends to obscure the advantages until it's all over and the smoke clears.

A Combination of Acquisition Techniques Is Often What Makes an Exchange Work

There's no black or white in exchanging—it's all complex, often conflicting negotiation. To fit the puzzle of each principal's objectives together in one closed transaction requires a trade-off of desires and a balance secured by acquisition techniques. The seemingly unending list of real estate acquisition and financing techniques may, at first glance, seem unrelated to exchanging. But an exchange is a tax and economic structure held together by these very techniques. They provide the means to trade off the principals' often conflicting objectives and balance the transaction. Part II of this book is composed entirely of techniques and is designed for daily reference to help you put deals together.

It's difficult to imagine how complicated a transaction can get until you get into it. To overcome the complexity it is essential to have principals who want the exchange to go through. Without everyone pulling together in a spirit of give and take, few exchanges would ever close.

10

Using Formulas to
Make Exchanges Work

The heart of exchanging is the application of sound economic practice within the limitations of tax law. Knowing the tax consequences of your transaction is essential. But to mke an exchange work financially, to make it fit the requirements of the participants, it is necessary to have a full range of formulas and techniques from which to draw. Each exchange demands unique solutions for the problems that inevitably arise before closing. These formulas and techniques are simply solutions that make an exchange work.

This chapter presents formulas that are used in the daily practice of exchanging. They are the methods that make the difference between wasted effort and efficient results. They are the glue that holds a transaction together—the ideas that when put in practice can meet each investor's unique objective. Some apply to a particular combination of circumstances. Many can be used in combination. They all should be modified as needed to fit the individual requirements of a transaction.

Saving the Exchange with a Note Takeout

Cash is sometimes a rare commodity in real estate transactions and even moreso in exchanges. This recurring problem is often solved by the use of personal notes secured by real estate in the exchange. Although notes can eventually lead to more problems than they solve, when used properly they can save a transaction.

Locating property that is on the market specifically for exchange is difficult. The only viable solution is to make offers to exchange for property that is for sale.

If the offer to exchange is refused (it's always possible that it will be accepted), consider a counteroffer that structures a sale by note out of escrow, contingent on closing the exchange. A third party, possibly one of the brokers involved in a transaction, might agree to accept the property offered in exchange if it could be bought on favorable terms—a personal note with easy payments.

The sequence is as follows: (1) Taxpayer offers to exchange for Seller's property, which is on the market for sale. (2) Seller refuses the exchange offer. (3) The offer to exchange is resubmitted contingent on a sale out of escrow by note on terms satisfactory to a third party (Buyer) already located. (4) Taxpayer receives Seller's property by exchange, and (5) the Seller receives the Buyer's personal note secured by Taxpayer's original property. (6) The Buyer receives Taxpayer's property.

This procedure is obviously a negotiation problem. In fact, once the mechanics of any transaction are put in motion, the ongoing challenge is negotiating it through to closing. Certainly cash can play a helpful role in completing the exchange, provided it is available. Fortunately, cash is sometimes available in an exchange.

Eliminating Mortgage Relief by Paying Down the Loan

Taxable gain due to mortgage relief is an exchange-killing problem that can be eliminated by planning. If a problem exists with mortgage relief and the taxpayer has enough cash, he can pay down the principal amount of the loan and solve the problem. This should be done prior to closing the exchange escrow, with the taxpayer's own money.

Reducing the loan balance will increase the equity of the taxpayer's property; that is, the difference between the loan balance and the market value will be larger.

If this procedure creates a difference in the equities of the properties being exchanged, they can be rebalanced with paper, cash or other assets. It may even be possible to solve the mortgage relief problem and balance equities at the same time.

Example:

	Rich	Garcia
Market Value	$125,000	$125,000
Loan	− 100,000	− 90,000
Equity	$ 25,000	$ 35,000

In the above example, Rich could pay $10,000 on the principal amount of his loan, which would increase his equity by $10,000. This would eliminate loan relief to Rich and balance equities. The observant reader might say that the same result could be achieved by having Rich pay $10,000 in cash to Garcia since boot paid is netted against loan relief. The reason for not doing this is that it will result in cash received by Garcia—a tax liability. If Rich pays down the loan by $10,000, Garcia would receive no boot and equities would automatically balance.

Offsetting Mortgage Relief with Boot

There are situations in which the payment of boot is desirable. Keeping in mind the expenses of an exchange, it might be that the taxpayer can pay boot and at the same time offset mortgage relief, while providing cash for the other party to pay commissions and transaction costs. But with the payment of boot it may be possible to structure the exchange so that neither party will have a tax liability.

Let's take the same example but in this case have Rich pay Garcia $10,000 in boot.

Example:

	Rich	Garcia
Market Value	$125,000	$125,000
Loan	−100,000	−90,000
Equity	25,000	35,000
Boot Paid	10,000	–0–
Balance	$ 35,000	$ 35,000

Rich offsets anticipated loan relief by paying $10,000 in boot. Now Garcia has a tax liability because he received $10,000 cash. Assume for the sake of the example that he also has commission and transaction costs amounting to $10,000. Receipt of $10,000 in boot would then be offset by the payment of $10,000 in expenses, thus eliminating the tax liability. (55)

Under these conditions, neither party pays tax on the exchange. Rich's potential liability as a result of mortgage relief is wiped out by the cash he paid. Garcia's potential liability as a result of receiving cash is eliminated by netting it against commissions and transaction costs. Unfortunately, cash is not always available to solve a mortgage relief problem.

Eliminating Mortgage Relief by Increasing the Loan on the Acquired Property

When cash is not available to pay down the principal amount of the loan on the property transferred to eliminate mortgage relief, the opposite approach can be taken. Increase the loan on the property acquired prior to closing. If the acquired property is being financed as part of the exchange, there may be some degree of control possible over the amount of the loan.

If new financing is not part of the exchange, it may be possible to increase the total loans by using a carryback loan. Although this approach will eliminate mortgage relief for the party assuming the increased loan amount, it will result in boot to the other party in an amount equal to the carryback loan.

Example:

	Serato	Garcia
Market Value	$110,000	$110,000
Loan	−80,000	−70,000
Equity	$ 30,000	$ 40,000

Serato is faced with payment of $10,000 boot to balance equities and a potential liability of $10,000 due to mortgage relief—two concurrent problems. But if Garcia agrees to carry back a second mortgage of $10,000, both problems are solved simultaneously. Equities are balanced and mortgage relief is eliminated in one step.

It may not always be possible to accomplish the task this neatly, but if a portion of the tax liability is reduced, it is like money in the bank. Although both the boot requirement and mortgage relief are eliminated for Serato, Garcia has a liability to pay tax on the boot he received in the form of the carryback loan. The receipt of boot is not always acceptable and can sometimes kill an otherwise sound exchange. Fortunately, there is a solution.

Balancing Equities with Like Kind Property

This solution to the problem of receiving boot is beautiful in its simplicity. In a situation in which one of the parties to the exchange will not accept boot in any form because of the tax liability, you can solve the problem by balancing equities with like kind property.
Example:

	Quito	*Brownstone*
Market Value	$150,000	$200,000
Loan	− 100,000	− 130,000
Equity	50,000	70,000
Difference	20,000	–0–
Balance	$ 70,000	$ 70,000

In this example, Quito owes Brownstone $20,000 in value. But Brownstone will not complete the exchange if he has any additional tax liability (he already has loan relief of $30,000). Quito can solve the problem by purchasing free and clear real estate valued at $20,000 and adding it to the exchange. This step balances equity and results in no additional increase in tax liability for Brownstone.

This example uses free and clear real estate to balance equities. But there is no reason why mortgaged like kind property could not be brought into play to solve the problem; in fact, that may be a better solution. For example, if Quito were to purchase a rental house or duplex encumbered with a loan of $30,000 and an equity of $20,000 and add that to the exchange, the end result would be that both mortgage relief and the receipt of boot would be eliminated for Brownstone. That is, he would receive additional property, increasing total loans received to $130,000 and equity to $70,000.

The essential requirement is that the additional property received be of like kind—real estate. Although the obvious solution is to use free and clear land, sustituting property that is already encumbered may be a more efficient solution.

Offsetting Negative Cash Flow in an Exchange

One of the recurring problems in the real estate industry is marketing income property that is losing money. Negative cash flow can result from a number of things, including incompetent management, poor location, inappropriate use, overfinancing and an endless number of other causes.

Converting property with a history of negative cash flow into a well-managed, successful operation is one of the best opportunities for profit. But marketing property with negative cash flow often requires an added incentive to compensate for the operating loss. In an exchange, there are several ways to offset a loss.

Step 1: Establish the fair market value of the property, based on considerations other than income; for example, replacement costs and comparable sales.

Step 2: Calculate the total operating loss projected over certain time periods—one year, three years, five years.

Step 3: Now, armed with a reasonably accurate estimate of future losses, you can establish a compensating factor that may give a potential new owner the incentive needed to exchange.

There are several methods that can be used in an exchange to compensate for negative cash flow.

1. Decrease the market value in an amount equal to the total anticipated loss.
2. Increase the market value of the property received.
3. Increase the interest and payments on carryback loans paid by the transferor of the negative cash flow property until the loss is wiped out—then lower them.
4. Increase the amount of the note or the amount of the boot paid by the owner of the negative cash flow property.

In each case, the adjustment should reflect the present value of the total anticipated loss. These are techniques to help an exchange make it through closing when one of the properties is operating at a loss. The key is to use them during marketing and negotiation so that they are clearly recognized as added incentives specifically designed to offset a loss.

Acceptance of one of these approaches depends on realizing that over the long term the loss is eliminated. Furthermore, the loss has, in fact, lowered the market value. Even though replacement cost and comparables indicate a higher value, the loss may necessitate an adjustment for actual marketing.

The Real Estate Owned Exchange

Banks and savings and loan associations are forced by circumstance to repossess real estate from time to time. But they are restricted by law as to the length of time they can hold repossessions. Generally, they can only own real estate that is used in their business, such as for branches. Repossessed real estate must be disposed of—it's a legal requirement. The longer real estate is held, the more pressure the institution feels from the state banking examiners. Therefore, there is a strong desire to dispose of repossessed real estate. You can determine the value of this type of property by looking at the bank's Statement of Financial Condition, which must be published regularly in the local newspaper. Repossessed real estate is listed on the financial statement as "Real Estate Owned" (REO).

There are three strategies for taking advantage of this situation.

1. Exchange with the bank and arrange a purchase out of escrow if necessary.
2. Find property the bank wants, buy it, and make the exchange.
3. Exchange with the bank and buy back your original property. But don't expect to get any tax benefits on this alternative—it's a financing incentive for the bank and lacks substance from a tax viewpoint.

Regardless of the structure you use, the objective remains the same—to acquire property by exchange from a motivated seller on favorable terms. The tax considerations are of secondary importance.

The incentive for the bank or savings and loan association lies in the opportunity to take real estate they are not permitted to own off their financial statement and replace it with a receivable in the form of a note and mortgage or different real estate that they can use. The advantage to you is that they may not be too particular as to the terms of the note on a cash takeout or buy-back arrangement.

Exchange with a Buy-Back Option

An exchange with an option to buy back the original property provides a method of using frozen equity to acquire more property while retaining the potential of future appreciation in the property transferred. This is a method of using all of the benefits available through an exchange without losing the future potential of the original exchange property. Before you plan to receive the tax benefits of this exchange formula, make sure the option doesn't create a retained real interest under your state law. If it does, there may be a question as to qualification of the transaction under Section 1031. (8), (17)

This variation on a two-way exchange anticipates the reluctance of an owner to dispose of potentially valuable property. It is not only an investment technique designed to preserve future appreciation, it is also a negotiation method for use when one of the parties to an exchange is reluctant to cooperate because he feels the value of his property warrants continued ownership.

Exchange Leaseback

Exchanging land and leasing it back can be a very effective incentive for the other party to accept the exchange. With certain variations, a number of benefits can be accomplished. For example, Smith owns a lot valued at $25,000. Jones owns a lot valued at $20,000. They exchange, and Jones pays Smith $5,000 in cash. Smith then leases back his original lot, providing income to Jones.

Smith now has a free and clear lot, $5,000 in cash and a leasehold interest in his original property. This gives him the opportunity to continue investing using the free and clear lot and cash. Furthermore, he may develop the leasehold land or sublease it to a user, such as a used car lot dealer or parking lot company.

Jones owns free and clear land that is providing income via the leaseback by Smith. He can now move forward with income-producing land, possibly exchanging it, subject to the lease, for other real estate.

The exchange leaseback has a number of applications. The above example provides a method specifically designed to increase the attractiveness of vacant land. It can also be used on improved property; for example, in situations in which the person acquiring the leased-back property is unable to or doesn't want to manage the acquired property, usually because of location, time or experience considerations. Therefore, acceptance of the exchange is made conditional on the original owner leasing back the income property for a certain time to insure the return and transfer management responsibility from the new owner. A number of variations and combinations can be used with the exchange leaseback to make property easier to exchange.

Making Free and Clear Land Easier to Exchange

Trying to exchange free and clear land is sometimes difficult because it usually produces no income. Furthermore, land that is outside the path of development may have no immediate hope of resale. But there are ways to make land more interesting to potential new owners.

The obvious incentive is to offer the land in combination with cash. This is sometimes one of the few ways that work in attempts to exchange subdivision land in remote development areas. Adding cash to a land-offering transaction may serve to compensate for the sometimes lengthy period necessary to realize appreciation in outlying development projects.

Another approach is to offer to exchange land encumbered with a note and mortgage secured by only half the land. This step reduces the total equity of the land but makes up for it with the note and mortgage. The other half would be left free and clear and, therefore, available for future exchanges. The new owner then receives half of the property free and clear and half of the property encumbered by a note and mortgage, both of which he assumes and pays.

The income from the note goes to the original owner. By reducing the land equity with the addition of a note, making it a smaller package, you increase the possibility of finding someone to accept it.

The reverse of this approach may also be used. That is, secure the note and mortgage with the property received by the former landowner and make it payable to the new landowner, leaving the land entirely free and clear. The note income would act as an incentive for the new landowner to accept an exchange that would have othewise not resulted in income.

These techniques facilitate the exchange of land by reducing the equity size and by adding income from notes to either side of the exchange.

BLM and Forest Service Exchanges

The Bureau of Land Management (BLM) is a consistent exchanger of land in the United States. It does not exchange for tax purposes but, rather, for consolidation of land with the cooperation of ranchers, state governments and the U.S. Department of Forestry.

The BLM exchanges primarily to round off its holdings. For example, it may own a section of land right in the middle of a ranch, and on the edge of the ranch it may own a few hundred sections. In order to consolidate its holdings in one block of property, the BLM will exchange the section in the middle of the rancher's property for a section at the outer boundaries of the ranch adjacent to the BLM's larger tract.

Like the BLM, the Forest Service also exchanges property in order to consolidate and increase the size of some of its forests and round off its holdings. Exchanges with the Forest Service may occur in situations in which development is encroaching on Forest Service land and there is pressure from the developer, who wants more property to subdivide. The developer will then purchase land of equal value that the Forest Service wants and exchange it for the property he needs for the subdivision. The situation may be reversed when the Forest Service wants property located in the middle of a forest that is owned by an individual.

General Services Administration Exchange

The General Services Administration (GSA) of the U.S. Government is a separate holding organization for various assets, supplies and property used by other branches of the government. The GSA has a separate budget and a separate management and is accountable for all of the property it supplies to other branches. It is a center for the purchasing and distribution of government property.

When it sells an asset, the proceeds must go back to the general treasury fund and do not remain within the General Services Administration operating account.

Since the GSA is charged with supplying property and services for other government branches, occasionally the need arises to acquire real estate in various geographical locations. If the budget is tight and there are not funds available to purchase the necessary property outright, a problem develops, which may be solved by an exchange. Even though the GSA may own real estate it would like to sell, it can't because the funds would go back into the general treasury and out of GSA control.

To retain control over the asset and provide the necessary services to other branches of government, the GSA will sometimes arrange an exchange—not to avoid tax, of course, but to avoid a sale and the subsequent reversion of the proceeds to the general fund.

Flight Capital Exchange

Citizens of the United States who own real estate located outside of the United States and who would like to transfer the equity back to the States can do so by nontaxable exchange.

This technique not only avoids tax under Section 1031, it also avoids converting the property to foreign currency. The legal mechanics of this technique no doubt vary from country to country depending on their laws—or lack of them. With the restrictions that many countries have against taking currency out of the country, the tax benefits may be of secondary importance.

After the exchange, the new owner of the U.S. property could refinance it and pull out his cash. Special attention should be paid to certain restrictions and requirements of other countries placed on foreigners (citizens of the U.S.) owning real estate.

From the standpoint of the American citizen, there is no tax problem. The nontaxable provisions of Section 1031 apply. (53) What is important on the American side of the transaction is conforming with the laws of the country in which the real estate is located. This technique may be helpful to companies doing business in foreign countries when they are acquiring new business locations.

Eliminating Recapture in an Exchange

One of the most costly and often unexpected aspects of a real estate transfer, including an exchange, is the tax effect of recapture.

The problem arises most frequently in an exchange in which improved property is exchanged for vacant land. If accelerated depreciation has been taken on the property transferred, depreciation in excess of straight line will be recaptured as ordinary income, prior to calculation of capital gains.

This can be prevented by insuring that there are improvements on the property acquired that have a value equal to or greater than the recapture liability. The recapture liability would then be absorbed by the improvements received.

Caution should also be exercised in the transfer of personal property in connection with the sale or exchange of real estate.

Personal property transferred in connection with the exchange of real estate is considered boot and creates a taxable event for the person receiving the personal property. The person transferring the personal property may be subject to recapture of all depreciation taken. In certain circumstances, there can be tax liability not only for the person receiving boot in the form of personal property but also for the person transferring the property, if it is subject to recapture.

Converting an Exchange to a Sale

An exchange can be converted to a sale just as easily as a sale can be converted to an exchange. It can even be done while the nontaxable aspect of the transaction is being protected for the party who wants it.

The objective of this technique is to preserve the nontaxable exchange for the person making the offer when the person receiving the offer refuses to exchange. The solution to such a refusal is conditional acceptance of the exchange by the reluctant party provided a sale of the property is made out of escrow contingent on closing the exchange.

This take-out contingency can be readily structured by adding a clause similar to the following:

This exchange agreement is contingent on a satisfactory sale of the property offered in exchange.

The party making the offer accomplishes a nontaxable exchange, and the party receiving the offer makes a sale.

11

Advanced
Exchange Techniques

The number of techniques for exchanging real estate under Section 1031 grows every year. Historically, the nontaxable exchange has been misunderstood and, consequently, feared. But in recent years, with the help of national seminars for real estate brokers, this situation has been improving. Gradual understanding and acceptance of exchanging has contributed to the effective application of what is now the greatest area of opportunity for tax savings in the real estate industry.

The techniques in this chapter cover the more advanced formulas, including multiparty exchange structures, fractional interests and the exchange of divided free interests.

Formulating the Multiparty Exchange

A multiparty exchange can be structured to fit two distinct sets of circumstances. The first set of circumstances arises when the taxpayer has not located suitable exchange property but does have a buyer for his property (the ABC multiparty exchange). The second set of circumstances arises when the taxpayer has located the exchange property he wants but the owner of the exchange property refuses to take the taxpayer's property unless a buyer is found to purchase it out of escrow (the ACB multiparty exchange).

In applying the multiparty exchange to the first set of circumstances, it is necessary to first establish a written agreement between the taxpayer and the person who wants to buy his property (the buyer). The exchange agreement obligates the buyer to acquire property acceptable to the taxpayer and exchange it for the taxpayer's real estate.

The first step in carrying out the agreement is to locate exchange property satisfactory to the taxpayer. Once this barrier is passed (and it can be a time-consuming effort), the buyer must obligate himself contractually to acquire the designated exchange property by signing an agreement to purchase it.

After the exchange agreement is signed and the exchange property is located and tied up by purchase agreement, the transaction can be closed. There are two ways to handle the transfer of deeds in a multiparty exchange: by the seller deeding to the buyer and the buyer then deeding to the taxpayer or, more simply, by the seller of the exchange property deeding directly to the taxpayer and the buyer transferring the cash directly to the seller. It is not necessary for the buyer to go into title to satisfy the terms of his obligations under the exchange agreement. It is also unnecessary for him to go into title to protect the taxpayer from adverse tax consequences, provided the buyer is contractually obligated to purchase the exchange property. (23), (43)

The second set of circumstances that falls in the multiparty category involves a slightly different approach. In this situation, the taxpayer has already found exchange property but the owner will not exchange—he wants to sell. This eliminates one problem (the location of satisfactory exchange property), but it creates another problem. In order to gain acceptance of the exchange by the reluctant seller, it is necessary to locate a buyer for the exchange property (the ACB multiparty exchange). So the situations are reversed. In the first set of circumstances, we had to locate a seller; now we have to locate a buyer. Since the owner of the exchange property wants cash instead of the taxpayer's property, it is necessary to write an exchange agreement contingent on locating a purchaser for the taxpayer's property.

The agreement then establishes a contingency on the exchange, requiring a sale out of escrow, with the proceeds going to the seller.

To protect the nontaxable aspect of the exchange for the taxpayer, the agreement must clearly establish that the seller accepts the exchange contingent on receiving cash at closing. When a buyer is found, the cash that goes to the seller must be restricted so that it cannot be construed as having been received by the taxpayer.

Again, there are two methods for handling the transfer of deeds. The taxpayer can deed to the seller and the seller then deed to the buyer; or the taxpayer can deed directly to the buyer. The choice of method is a formality and does not change the substance of a legally correct exchange.

These two approaches form the standard mechanics of multiparty exchanging. They are, in the last analysis, problem-solving techniques, solutions that hold a transaction together and preserve the benefits of Section 1031 for the taxpayer.

The Mineral Rights Exchange

It is a little-known fact that under certain conditions you can exchange mineral rights for a fee interest in real estate. The application of Section 1031 to mineral rights was established in a 1941 case. (17)

There are two requirements that must be met to protect the nontaxable aspect of a mineral rights exchange. The mineral rights must be considered real property rights by the law of the state in which they are located. Also, the transfer of the mineral rights must be absolute and irrevocable. The person transferring the rights can retain no interest whatsoever in them.

This technique can be quite useful with farm and ranch property because the owner can retain the surface real estate while exchanging the mineral rights for land, income-producing real estate or even different mineral rights. Transferring mineral rights under Section 1031 with all the benefits of a nontaxable real estate exchange adds that much more value to the rights—the tax savings.

This strategy is the result of dividing the real estate fee between surface rights and the mineral rights. The owner is able to retain the crop-producing surface rights and exchange the mineral rights for income-generating real estate without loss of equity by paying tax.

The Nontaxable Exchange of Water Rights

Water rights may also be exchanged under the provisions of Section 1031 for improved real estate or land without recognition of gain. (42) In many western states, the use of surface and underground water rights is controlled by state government. Each owner is allowed a certain limited use of water based on the number and kind of rights owned. Usually water rights are measured based on acre units, which vary depending on use— domestic, grazing or irrigation.

In states in which moisture is relatively scarce, water rights are often sold by an owner who no longer needs them to a farmer or commercial user who does. The rights are transferred with state permission from one owner and location to another. Normally, there are restrictions on moving water rights from their original water basin.

In states in which water rights are considered real property, an opportunity exists for a nontaxable exchange, including the use of a multiparty exchange in any of its variations.

In situations in which owners of water rights are reluctant to sell, a multiparty exchange that allows the choice of alternative real estate combined with the tax-free benefits can provide the incentive necessary for an owner to let go of the water rights.

The Exchange of Leasehold Interests

Section 1031 provides that a leasehold interest with a term of 30 years or more may be exchanged tax-free for other real property. The leasehold interest is considered to merge with the fee and, therefore, is treated as real property.

As the leasing of land becomes more widespread, this application of exchanging will no doubt grow in popularity. A leasehold exchange may begin, for example, when an investor leases land for the construction of a shopping center. The owners of the land agree to subordinate to construction and permanent financing obtained by the investor in an amount equal to the cost of improvements.

Provided 30 years or more remain on the land lease, the investor-lessee has the option of exchanging the leasehold interest (land lease and improvements) without recognition of gain. Of equal importance, it may be received in exchange for other real property without recognition of gain by the taxpayer receiving it. Simply put, a leasehold interest with 30 years or more remaining is considered like kind property for purposes of Section 1031.*

If the term of the lease is less than 30 years and you want to use the property in an exchange, see Revenue Ruling 78–72 which permits you to include options to renew when calculating the 30-year requirement.

* For the Court's position see CARL E. KOCH V. COMMISSIONER 71TC5 (1978).

Saving a Two-Way Exchange by Creating a Multiple Exchange

One of the frequent stumbling blocks in a two-way exchange is the refusal by one of the parties to accept the property offered. The question is often asked: "How can I ever make an exchange? I've got to find property I want, and the owner must want my property."

With all the techniques available, there is no reason to be stopped by this concern. It is a problem, but one with a solution.

The direct solution is for the reluctant party to accept the exchange offer, provided other suitable property is located and substituted for the property he doesn't want. This conditional acceptance is the beginning of a three-way multiple exchange.

The mechanics can be easily set up by inserting one clause establishing the contingent acceptance of the initial exchange offer. The clause can be worded many ways. The following is one approach:

> This offer to exchange is irrevocably accepted provided that different property, satisfactory to me, is located and conveyed to me instead of the property offered. If acceptable property is not located within 180 days from this date, this agreement will become null and void and all deposits will be refunded.

This technique is designed to keep an exchange alive and provide the motivation to locate satisfactory property and close the exchange. With an accurate understanding of the objectives of the parties involved, completion of the exchange can naturally follow. It may even be possible for a third party to purchase acceptable property and put it in the deal.

To a large extent, the efficiency of the transaction will depend on the brokers' understanding of what their clients want to accomplish.

The Equal Partnership Exchange

This technique is designed to bring two owners together in an equal equity position when they are acquiring one property. In the following example, each partner owns real estate, and they both want to consolidate their equities by exchanging for one larger property as tenants in common.

Woods has equity valued at $70,000, and Brownwell has equity valued at $50,000. They have located property with an equity of $100,000, which they want to acquire as equal partners. The owner of the property they want has agreed to accept the two properties owned individually by Woods and Brownwell. The problem is that they both want to have an equal ownership percentage in the new property.

To solve the problem, Woods exchanges his $70,000 equity and, in addition to 50% of the new property, receives a $20,000 note secured by a mortgage on the property he transferred. Therefore, he receives a $20,000 note and $50,000 in equity for a total of $70,000 in value. Brownwell, of course, exchanges his $50,000 equity for 50% of the new property.

This gives an equal ownership percentage to both Woods and Brownwell. The former owner of the property they receive gets a total of $100,000 in equity represented by two properties, one of which is the security for the $20,000 note payable to Woods.

Any number of variations can be made on this method. The objective is to balance equities and control the percentage ownership in a way that meets the objectives of the participants. The exchange of partial interests can be made quite safely under Section 1031 provided the partners are exchanging like kind property and not securities. (17)

The Exchange of Partial Interests

From the standpoint of Section 1031, exchanging a partial interest in real estate is no different from exchanging a 100% interest.

The percentage of the ownership doesn't restrict the qualification of an exchange any more than the size of the equity does. Nor does a partial interest require a different set of procedures.

For example, Hughes owned an undivided one-third interest (valued at $25,000) in 10 acres. Jackson owned an undivided one-fifth interest (valued at $30,000) in an apartment complex. They exchanged property by deed, and Hughes paid Jackson $5,000 cash to balance equities.

Since they both owned a partial interest in real property rather than a limited partnership share, the exchange qualifies under Section 1031. (17), (31)

The Business Exchange

Business property that is held for productive use or investment, whether real or personal in nature, may be exchanged tax-free under the provisions of Section 1031. In essence, you can, with proper planning, exchange your business for another without tax on the transaction.

This technique requires that the assets involved be clearly separated by "kind." To ensure maximum benefit, personal and real property should be handled as separate exchanges. Furthermore, care must be taken to distinguish personal and real property from receivables and inventory held for sale to customers.

When the values are correctly allocated between the various kinds of properties as defined by Section 1031, an agreement can be written that maximizes the tax benefits of the exchange. That is, after the market values are established, an agreement can be written that provides for a separate exchange of personal and real property in each business.

If personal property is the only mutually owned asset (each business owns personalty, which is being exchanged) and one of the businesses owns real estate, which is used to balance equities, the real estate may constitute boot. Real estate is considered boot when it is used to balance equities in an exchange of personal property. If this is the way the exchange is planned, care should be taken because an installment sale of the real estate may be more advantageous. The same caution should be used when personal property is used to balance a real estate exchange—an installment sale might be better for both parties. (32)

Another application of Section 1031 to the transfer of businesses involves offering to exchange real estate for a business. This strategy is designed to solve a problem related to financing older income real estate.

If you own real estate that is too old to refinance, consider exchanging for a going business. Commercial banks look for sound business loans, but they avoid older real estate. With a strong market for new homes and multifamily dwellings, it's difficult to get a savings and loan association or insurance company to consider a loan on older property.

This strategy is initiated by an offer to exchange for a business that is either free and clear or encumbered with loans that are smaller than the total debt the business could normally support. The preferred situation is a business with real estate of equal or greater value than the property transferred, which opens the opportunity to structure a tax-free exchange.

The crucial element is to locate a business with sufficient earnings to support the loan you need. If you want to avoid receiving cash as part of the exchange, the loan must be made after closing without contingency on the transaction. It can work most smoothly when both properties are free and clear, but neither property has to be. Equity balance can be arranged with personal notes or other property and in any way that contributes to the ultimate objective of financing the business after closing.

Exchanging Property You Don't Own

It is well established that you may enter into an exchange agreement for property that you do not own but can acquire. (23) This technique is part of the foundation of the multiparty exchange. Although it may appear somewhat abstract, taking the time necessary to fully understand this approach will be time well invested, as illustrated by the following case example.

A real estate broker, named Good, approached he owner of a lot in a resort area, proposing to the owner, named Hadley, that he exchange his Lot 6 for the adjacent Lot 7, owned by Thomas. In order to complete the transaction, Good requested that Hadley pay him a commission of $1,500. Hadley refused to pay a commission but was willing to exchange lots.

In order to accomplish the transaction and get paid for his efforts, Good, acting as principal, arranged to purchase Lot 7 from Thomas for $7,000 and signed a purchase agreement to that effect. He then contacted Beal, the owner of Lot 5, who had expressed an interest in acquiring Lot 6 to expand the size of his holdings. As a result of the meeting, Good signed a contract in which he agreed to sell Lot 6 to Beal for $10,000.

Next, Good signed an exchange agreement with Hadley that committed Hadley to exchange Lot 6 for Lot 7 with no cash consideration. Up to this point, Good had signed three documents: (1) an agreement to purchase Lot 7 from Thomas, (2) an agreement to sell Lot 6 to Beal and (3) an agreement to exchange Lot 7 for Lot 6 with Hadley.

At closing, instead of going into title to Lot 7, then exchanging it with Hadley for Lot 6 and, subsequently, selling Lot 6 to Beal, Good requested that Thomas deed Lot 7 directly to Hadley and that Hadley deed Lot 6 directly to Beal. Beal then paid the money for Lot 6 directly to Good.

After all the dust settled, Beal owned Lot 6 by purchase; Hadley owned Lot 7, which he acquired by exchanging Lot 6; Thomas sold Lot 7 for $7,000. Good received $10,000 directly from Beal and paid $7,000 of that to Thomas, leaving a $3,000 profit for Good. This was a pleasant turn of events for a transaction that occurred because one principal refused to pay a commission.

At no time was Good in title to any of the properties involved in the transaction. But he was contractually obligated throughout to the other three parties.

In a similar situation, the courts ruled that an exchange does occur when the taxpayer carries out a contract made with another person even though the other person does not receive title to the exchange property or to the taxpayer's property, provided the parties are obligated by contract to complete the exchange. (23)

Acquiring Exchange Property by Loan

Under certain conditions, you can borrow money from the other principal in the transaction to buy property to exchange with him. (20) This technique is helpful when one of the potential exchange participants doesn't own exchange property but does have an option to acquire it.

In one case, the taxpayer owned an option on property that an insurance company wanted to acquire; but the taxpayer didn't have the cash needed to exercise the option. The option was part of a 10-year lease, which gave the taxpayer the right to purchase the building for $500,000 cash at any time during the lease term. The insurance company originally approached the taxpayer in an effort to acquire the property by purchase.

After extensive negotiation, a contract was arranged in which the insurance company agreed to loan the taxpayer $500,000 cash necessary to purchase the exchange property, and the taxpayer agreed to exchange the acquired property for the insurance company's current location.

In carrying out the plan, the insurance company made the loan to the taxpayer (secured by his property), who then exercised the option and closed escrow. Next, the taxpayer conveyed the acquired property by deed, subject to the $500,000 loan, and received in exchange the insurance company's current location, subject to a $600,000 mortgage.

This technique provides a method of arranging a tax-free exchange when the taxpayer doesn't have money to acquire property to exchange. It can be used in cooperation with banks acquiring new locations, developers acquiring land, and any number of similar situations.

Using a Lease to Provide Possession Before Closing an Exchange

In a multiparty exchange, it is sometimes necessary for the buyer to go into possession of the taxpayer's property before exchange property is located. One of the safest solutions to this problem is a standard lease agreement.

The first step is for the taxpayer to contractually obligate himself to exchange his property for property to be purchased by the buyer or, if suitable property is not found, to sell his property to the buyer. The buyer, in turn, is obligated to purchase exchange property and exchange it for the taxpayer's property or, if property is not located, to purchase the taxpayer's property after a given date.

Concurrently with the exchange contract a separate agreement to lease the taxpayer's property to the buyer is executed at the fair market rental. It is best to start the lease term a few months later than the date of the exchange contract so that possession would not be given until a reasonable attempt to locate exchange property had been made. If the exchange is not completed prior to the effective date of the lease, the taxpayer would automatically turn over possession to the buyer and receive a fair rent.

This technique is used as a method to get the taxpayer out from under management and financial responsibilities when it is evident his health and personal well-being are jeopardized. It is also a method of meeting the buyer's objective of possession prior to closing the exchange. Use of a lease can, in certain cases, keep the tax-free exchange alive when the buyer won't cooperate because of the time necessary to find exchange property.

Leasing can also be helpful when several diverse properties are being exchanged, such as in an exchange of rental houses in which occupancy is essential to the transaction.

For example, a taxpayer owned six rental houses. He wanted to consolidate management by acquiring an apartment complex by tax-free exchange, but he couldn't locate one taker for all six houses without discounting them.

He solved the problem by locating buyers for each house, who all agreed to a multiparty exchange. They contracted to purchase or contribute to the purchase of like kind property in an amount equal to the equity they were to acquire in the houses. Buyers for the houses signed an exchange agreement and lease for one year. The lease was written to automatically terminate if the exchange closed before the lease ended. If exchange property wasn't located within the year, the buyers had the right to acquire them for cash.

All of the houses were occupied on leases by persons who agreed to acquire exchange property. Leasing fulfilled the obligation of immediate occupancy without destroying the exchange benefits for the taxpayer. When exchange property was located, the taxpayer exercised the exchange contracts and closed the transaction. He got full value for his rentals since he didn't have to wholesale them to one buyer. And the new owners were not inconvenienced by the exchange.

Building a Building Solely for Exchange

Constructing a building for exchange eliminates the search and unknown time factor involved in a conventional ABC multiparty exchange. The qualification of this technique under Section 1031 is now well established. (3), (8), (13), (60)

For example, a corporation wanted to transfer manufacturing to a new location. An investor was ready, willing and able to purchase the existing facility. Since the corporation wanted a new plant, the following transaction was structured to prevent a taxable event.

The corporation and investor entered into an agreement that required the investor to purchase land designated by the corporation and construct a building to meet its manufacturing requirements. The investor went into title to the tract of land and was obligated on the contract for construction of the building. On completion, and pursuant to the original exchange agreement, the investor and corporation exchanged property.

This technique is one of the most tried and practical methods of accomplishing a nontaxable exchange. It really proves the point that there's no reason to sell, pay tax, and use what's left to buy different property. Elimination of the time delay for location of suitable exchange property is an additional and significant element of this approach—the taxpayer who doesn't like anything on the market can draw the building he wants and have it built.

12

How to Change
a Sale into a
Multiparty Exchange

It is rarely too late to change your mind and take advantage of Section 1031. Sales have been changed to exchanges many times in the past and will no doubt be changed many times in the future. In fact, it is often the case that the parties to a sale do not discover the benefits (or necessity) of exchanging until they are analyzing the tax consequences of a purchase offer.

An owner's sudden realization of the equity that will be lost in payment of tax has probably created more exchanges than any broker could ever hope to initiate.

It is now well-established that a contract for sale can be amended to provide for a nontaxable exchange (1). A verbal offer or statement of intent to purchase can easily be countered with an exchange. A written purchase offer can be modified almost as easily. An option to purchase can also be modified to set up an exchange without fear of losing the benefits of Section 1031 (13).

If a sale hasn't closed, it probably can safely be changed to an exchange. The essential procedure in any sale or option modification is to make the changes before you have actual or constructive receipt of money (11), (24).

If you make the transition from a sale to an exchange prior to receipt of cash and in a way that restricts your right to the cash that would have gone to you in a sale, you more than likely have a safe exchange.

How to Make the Transition from a Purchase to an Exchange

It seems that more emergencies are created by purchase offers than loan defaults. Certainly this is often the case when a seller realizes the impact of taxes and discovers the benefits of making an exchange. When the necessity of exchanging becomes apparent and a purchase offer is in hand with a time limit, there is a simple way to save the deal.

Practically speaking, the offer to purchase should not be rejected. In fact, the offer would be accepted and signed with the addition of a simple amendment that:

1. permits you to modify the purchase contract with the buyer's cooperation to accomplish an exchange, and
2. makes it clear to the buyer that a deal has been made contingent on completion of the documents necessary for your tax-deferred exchange, and that a sale will go forth in the event an exchange is not made.

The first document in this process is a simple addendum to the initial purchase offer. From that point on the steps that follow are the same as the basic steps of a multiparty exchange.

The objective, therefore, becomes to locate satisfactory exchange property, which will be acquired by the buyer offering to acquire your property, and transferred to you. Essentially, this is the same sequence as a multiparty exchange with a slight variation on the documentation because the transaction began as a purchase.

The steps required to convert an offer to purchase to an exchange are:

Step 1: You receive the initial purchase agreement, offering to buy your property.

Step 2: You add a purchase agreement addendum, declaring your intent to complete an exchange and binding the buyer to execute the necessary documents.

Step 3: You sign the purchase agreement acquiring the exchange property with the right to assign this agreement to the buyer of your property.

Step 4: You assign the purchase agreement acquiring the exchange property, which transfers the contractual rights and obligations to the buyer.

Step 5: You execute the exchange escrow instuctions, which outline the exchange and the transfer of titles to complete the transaction. The simplicity of this approach lies in the use of standard purchase agreements, which are slightly modified to accommodate the practical requirements of completing an exchange.

A Simple Purchase Agreement Addendum That Protects an Exchange

There are any number of ways to vary the wording of an addendum to a purchase agreement in order to initiate the exchange process. These variations should be made with the guidance of your lawyer and presented in a manner that will be acceptable to the buyer of your property.

The following example works. Slight variations won't endanger the process as long as the buyer is clearly committed to signing the documents (escrow instructions and deeds) necessary to complete the exchange. Note that the following example provides for setting up an escrow for a delayed exchange.

Purchase Agreement Addendum

It is understood and agreed between the parties hereto that seller's intent is to convert this transaction from a purchase and sale to a tax-deferred exchange under Section 1031 of the Internal Revenue Code. The parties hereto, therefore, agree to fully cooperate, one with the other, in executing whatever additional documents or amendments, which may be required in order to properly effect a tax-deferred exchange, at such time as seller has located other acceptable property for the purpose of completing the exchange.

The parties hereto further understand and agree that seller is attempting to locate acceptable exchange property and to restructure this transaction as a multiparty, concurrently closing, tax-deferred exchange. In the event seller has not located acceptable exchange property, or is unable to close the acquisition of such property on or before the closing date herein, or fails to establish an escrow arrangement providing for a delayed closing of the exchange escrow, then this transaction shall become a purchase and sale on the original terms provided herein.

The language for the addendum can be worded in various ways provided the buyer is legally bound to execute the necessary documents to protect your tax-free exchange. The agreement on the part of the buyer to cooperate is not enough. The buyer must agree to sign all the documentation.

A Longer-Form Addendum for Converting a Purchase to an Exchange

The following addendum contains more specific language for converting to an exchange. It works equally well, but does not provide for setting up a delayed exchange.

Both addendum forms are provided to illustrate the process of converting a purchase offer to an exchange. The specifics of the wording can vary based on your lawyer's preference.

ADDENDUM TO AGREEMENT OF PURCHASE AND SALE AND RECEIPT FOR DEPOSIT OF _____, 19__

Provided, however, that in lieu of the sale of the subject property by Owners to Buyer, Owners shall have the right to locate other real property for the purpose of effecting a tax-deferred exchange of the subject property and to arrange for the terms of purchase thereof with the Seller.

In the event Owners have done so and have notified Buyer in writing of the same on or before ___(c.o.e.)___, 19__, Buyer shall enter into a written contract with said Sellers to purchase said property and shall, upon said acquisition, transfer and convey the ownership thereof from Buyer to Owners, in consideration of, and concurrently with, the transfer of the subject property to Buyer, provided, however, that in no event shall Buyer be required to make a total cash payment for said exchange property, including all costs and expenses of such purchase, in excess of the cash payment which would otherwise have to be made to Owners had Buyer completed the purchase of the subject property from Owners hereunder; and provided further that in no event shall Buyer be required to assume any secured loan on any of the properties to be so acquired by Buyer or to execute any promissory note or other evidence of indebtedness in connection with any such acquisition which would impose any personal liability upon Buyer for its payment.

Owners shall make a good-faith, diligent effort to locate the property to be exchanged hereunder by Buyer, and Buyer shall make a good-faith, diligent effort to acquire the same once it has been located and its purchase negotiated for by Owners; provided, however, that only in the event that Owners are unable to locate, or Buyer is unable to acquire the exchange property within the time provided for herein to do so, Buyer agrees to purchase and Owners agree to sell the subject property to Buyer for the price and on the terms set forth above.

In the event of such an exchange being made in lieu of purchase, Buyer shall pay to Owners, in cash, a sum equal to the difference, if any, between the total cash payment that would otherwise be made to Owners in such a purchase and the total cash payment made to said Seller, including all of Buyer's cost of escrow, title insurance premiums expended to acquire said other properties, documentary transfer taxes and all prorations, and real estate brokerage commissions, all of which shall be approved by Owner before Buyer enters into said agreement of purchase with said Sellers.

In the event that through no fault or lack of performance by Buyer, the intended exchange is not completed on or before ___(c.o.e.)___ , 19__ , Owners covenant and agree to forthwith transfer and convey title to the subject property to Buyer on that date in accordance with the terms and provisions of sale set forth above.

OWNERS:
(Exchangor)

_____

Dated: _____

BUYER:

_____

Dated: _____

Protecting the Right to Assign the Purchase Agreement

After you have located acceptable exchange property and have negotiated a firm contract to acquire it, the next step is to assign that agreement to the buyer. In order to protect your exchange benefits, certain language should be included in the purchase agreement when it is written.

Specifically, you must retain the right to assign the purchase agreement. A simple way to do this is to make the offer to purchase in your name followed by "or assigns." Depending on the nature of the negotiations for the exchange property, you may also want to add a paragraph clarifying that it is being acquired to complete an exchange. For example:

> This property is being acquired for purposes of completing an exchange and this agreement is contingent on a concurrent closing of said exchange pursuant to that certain agreement dated _____.

Making sure that you have the right to assign the agreement acquiring the exchange property is essential to the success of the transaction. All rights and obligations must be transferred to the buyer who wants your property. The following addendum is a more complete and preferred format for accomplishing this task.

ADDENDUM TO DEPOSIT RECEIPT
AND/OR ESCROW INSTRUCTIONS

Buyers shall have the right, without the need of any further approval or consent of Sellers, at any and all times during the term hereof and prior to the completion of the purchase of the subject property, to transfer and assign all of their rights and obligations under this Agreement to _____ pursuant to the contractual obligation of said parties, and each of them, to purchase the subject property hereunder in accordance with the terms and provisions of that certain Agreement of Exchange entered into between Buyer and said parties on _____, 19__. It is hereby agreed by and between the parties hereto, that upon such assignment having been made by Buyer, effective forthwith upon Seller's receipt of written notice of the same, Buyer shall have no further rights, obligations or liabilities hereunder, all such rights, obligations and liabilities having been fully and finally transferred and assigned to the above-named parties.

SELLER: BUYER: ("Owner" of previous property/exchangor)

_____   _____

Dated: _____

Note: *Addendum to be attached (or included) in offer to purchase property by Exchangor. (Exchangor is putting Seller on notice that Exchangor is acting as the agent for the Buyer of the Exchangor's property.)*

Documenting the Assignment of the Purchase Agreement

Not only must you retain the right to assign the purchase agreement, you must actually assign it to the buyer who wants your property. This is easily accomplished by a simple assignment such as the following.

Assignment

___(Exchangor/Taxpayer)___ does hereby transfer, assign, and convey to ___(Buyer)___ the right and obligation to purchase the real property commonly known as 1000 Park Office Plaza pursuant to the terms of the purchase agreement which is attached hereto.

Dated: _____   ___(Exchangor/Taxpayer)___

Accepted:

Dated: _____   ___(Buyer)___

Converting a Sale to an Exchange Is a Step-by-Step Process

Although there may seem to be a lot of pieces to the puzzle, when they are kept in sequence they can fall into place quite naturally. So far we have reviewed the following documents.

1. An addendum to the initial offer to purchase your property, which allows you to proceed with the exchange process by signing the offer contingent on the buyer's agreement to sign subsequent documentation converting the transaction to an exchange.
2. An addendum allowing you to assign the purchase agreement acquiring the exchange property, which allows you to negotiate the acquisition of the exchange property acting as agent for the buyer who wants your property.
3. An assignment, which actually transfers the right and obligation to purchase the exchange property to the buyer who wants your property.

After these preliminary documents are out of the way it is time to set up the escrow instructions that establish the heart of the exchange.

Guideline Escrow Instructions for Converting a Sale to an Exchange

The exchange escrow instructions tie the whole exchange process together. They must be signed by the taxpayer/exchangor who wants the nontaxable exchange and the buyer who wants the taxpayer's property.

The escrow instructions actually form the exchange agreement and outline the procedure for completing the transaction. They review the background of the exchange and specify the steps the escrow company must take to meet the requirements necessary to protect the tax benefits of Section 1031.

The transaction these escrow instructions were taken from involved two separate escrow companies. This is not a necessity, and in fact complicated the mechanics of closing. It is much more simple to close through one escrow or title company. If you are in a state that does not close through title companies this is not a problem.

ADDENDUM AND JOINT ESCROW INSTRUCTIONS

This Agreement is made as of this, the 11th day of March, 191X, by and among John Smith (herein "Smith") and Sam Jones (herein "Jones").

Background:

A. Smith and Jones are parties to an "Offer to Purchase and Agreement of Purchase and Sale" dated January 28, 191X (the "Purchase Agreement"), wherein Jones has agreed to sell and convey to Smith and Smith has agreed to purchase from Jones, all of Jones's right, title, and interest in certain property located in Bernalillo County, New Mexico (the "Property").

B. Pursuant to the "Addendum" attached to the Purchase Agreement, Smith has agreed to cooperate with Jones in effecting a nontaxable exchange pursuant to Section 1031 of the Internal Revenue Code of 1986.

C. Jones does not desire to sell the Property to Smith but desires to transfer the Property to Smith in exchange for like kind property designated by Jones.

D. Jones has located suitable like kind property, commonly known as 1000 Park Office Plaza, Albuquerque, New Mexico and desires Smith to purchase and acquire such property and to transfer such property to Jones in exchange for the Property.

E. The parties desire to amend the Purchase Agreement to further document their agreements and understandings with respect to the exchange and to establish joint escrow instructions for the facilitation of the exchange transaction.

Now, therefore, it is agreed:

1. *Transfer by Smith.* Smith shall purchase the property commonly known as 1000 Park Office Plaza (the "Exchange Property") pursuant to the terms and conditions of that certain Purchase Contract, a copy of which is attached hereto as Exhibit "A" (the "Exchange Contract") and shall transfer the Exchange Property to Jones in exchange for the Property. Smith's obligation to purchase the Exchange Property shall be subject to the following limitations and conditions:

(a) Smith's maximum liability shall be to pay to the sellers of the Exchange Property an amount equal to purchase price payable by them for the Property under the Purchase Agreement, less the costs, expenses, and prorations chargeable to Jones pursuant to the terms of the Purchase Agreement.

(b) Any additional consideration due to the seller of the Exchange Property shall be paid by Jones.

(c) Smith shall not be required to incur any liability whatsoever in connection with the purchase of the Exchange Property.

(d) Smith shall acquire the Exchange Property in the condition provided for in the Purchase Contract attached hereto as Exhibit "A" and shall transfer the Exchange Property to Jones by Special Warranty Deed, without further warranties, both as to title or condition.

2. *Transfer by Jones.* In consideration of Smith's agreement to acquire the Exchange Property and to transfer the Exchange Property to Jones, Jones shall transfer the Property to Smith, in accordance with the terms of the Purchase Agreement.

3. *Covenants.* Smith agrees to accept the Property from Jones subject to the Restrictive Covenants attached hereto and marked Exhibit "B" (herein the "Covenants").

4. *Escrow Instruction.* On the Closing Date, as defined in the Purchase Agreement—

(a) Jones shall deposit with First American Title Insurance Company (herein the "Title Company") a good and sufficient Warranty Deed conveying the Property to Smith in the condition required by the terms of the Purchase Agreement and shall execute such other documents and instruments as may be required to consummate his obligations under the Purchase Agreement. Jones shall also deliver to the Title Company the Covenants in recordable form.

(b) Smith shall deposit with the Title Company the balance of the Purchase Price required to be paid under the Purchase Agreement. Smith shall also deliver to the Title Company a good and sufficient Special Warranty Deed to the Exchange Property, conveying the Exchange Property to Jones, with the transfer date left blank, and shall execute such other documents and instruments as may be required to consummate their obligations under the Purchase Agreement.

(c) Jones shall have no right to any amounts deposited by Smith with the Title Company hereunder and the Title Company shall hold such funds subject to the terms and provisions of this Paragraph 4.

(d) When the Title Company has received all of the funds and items required to be deposited hereunder and is in a position to issue an owner's title insurance policy to Smith as required by the terms of the Purchase Agreement, the Title Company shall record, in the following order, (1) the Covenants and (2) the Warranty Deed from Jones.

(e) When the Title Company has recorded the Covenants and Warranty Deed and is in a position to issue an owner's policy of title insurance to Smith as aforesaid, it shall disburse the funds held by it hereunder as follows:

(1) In payment of all costs, expenses, and prorations required to be paid by the terms of the Purchase Agreement, including the Title Company's fees and title insurance premiums;

(2) The balance to Albuquerque Title USA, the title insurance company responsible for closing the sale and purchase of the Exchange Property, but subject to the following conditions: that Albuquerque Title USA shall be authorized to disburse any of such funds only at such time as all of the conditions to closing under the Purchase Contract have been satisfied in full, that the Exchange Property has been conveyed to Smith in the condition required by the Purchase Contract and the deed of conveyance has been recorded, and that it is in a position to issue an owner's policy of title insurance as required by the terms of the Purchase Contract to the purchasers—then such policy of title insurance be issued to Jones. Such instruction shall also provide that if for any reason the purchase of the Exchange Property cannot be consummated for any reason by March 15, 19X1, the funds shall be redelivered to the Title Company. If such funds are redelivered to the Title Company, the Title Company shall continue to hold such funds until the purchase of the Exchange Property may be consummated or until April 30, 19X1, which ever occurs earlier.

(f) When the Title Company has been notified by Albuquerque Title USA that the Exchange Property has been transferred to Smith and that the deed of conveyance has been recorded, the Title Company shall complete the transfer date and record the Special Warranty Deed conveying the Exchange Property to Jones.

(g) In the event that the purchase of the Exchange Property cannot be consummated for any reason by April 30, 19X1, the Title Company shall distribute the balance of the funds held by it to Jones. As set forth above, Jones shall have no right to require payment to him of any portion of the funds held by the Title Company hereunder except as provided for in this subsection, in the event that the purchase of the Exchange Property cannot be consummated by April 30, 19X1.

5. *Indemnity*. Jones does hereby indemnify and hold Smith harmless from and against all costs, expenses, loss, and liability incurred by Smith as a result of cooperation with Jones in the exchange transaction herein provided for or arising out of accepting and conveying title to the Exchange Property, including reasonable attorney fees.

_____

John Smith

_____

_____

Sam Jones

Accepted:

First American Title Insurance Company

By _____

The Buyer Has No Liability When Cooperating in an Exchange

One of the major concerns in an multiparty exchange is the possible liability incurred by the buyer who wants the taxpayer/exchangor's property. As the escrow instructions clearly point out, the buyer is fully indemnified against any cost or liability as a result of this cooperation.

Furthermore, there is no tax liability whatsoever because the buyer is acquiring property, not disposing of it. The fact that the buyer went through title momentarily is not a taxable event because there was no profit made.

13

Documenting and Closing
a Delayed Exchange

Over the years Section 1031 of the Internal Revenue Code has been virtually untouched by direct legislative change. This came to an end in 1984 when a couple of issues, which had caused conflict with the IRS, were clarified: Partnership interests were excluded from nontaxable exchanges under Section 1031 and the time period for accomplishing a delayed exchange was established.

By limiting the time period for completing a delayed multiparty exchange, Congress also put the legislative stamp of approval on the basic multiparty exchange structure, which until this point had been validated only through case law. Furthermore, the application of the multiparty exchange was expanded. Now, when you receive an offer to purchase, you can set up the paperwork for an exchange and convey your property to the buyer before you even locate property you want in exchange.

The Subtle Trap of the New Delayed Exchange Guidelines

It is important to remember that the new time limits imposed on a delayed multiparty exchange changed nothing in the procedural requirement for making a nontaxable exchange—you must receive qualifying like-kind property in exchange for qualifying like-kind property without the actual or constructive receipt of the cash used to acquire the exchange property.

Consequently, if you attempt to make a delayed exchange by selling your property and placing the money in a regular escrow account and then purchasing the replacement property, you will not meet the test of a tax-free transaction.

Properly written and duly executed exchange agreements and escrow instructions are essential to avoiding this trap. These agreements must legally restrict your right to receive the cash used to purchase exchange property.

The time limit placed on receipt of replacement property in a delayed multiparty exchange does not mean that the requirements of Section 1031 have been relaxed. The money used for purchase of exchange property cannot be placed in an unrestricted escrow account or simply "held in escrow" until you find suitable exchange property. Consequently, the exchange agreement for a transaction that involves a delay between the transfer and receipt of property should be drafted by a competent tax attorney. The main legal objective is to avoid the constructive receipt of the money used to purchase exchange property within the limits established by the new law.

Applying the New Guidelines for a Delayed Exchange

The guidelines for a delayed multiparty exchange are simple to understand, but difficult to apply within the practical limitations of today's market.

There are two parts to the delayed exchange law, which allow you to receive property in exchange even though you have already deeded your property.

(1) You must designate the property you want in exchange not later than 45 days from the date you transfered title to your original property.

(2) You must receive title not later than 180 days from the date you transfered title to your original property, or the due date of your tax return—whichever comes first. (In other words, you have 45 days to designate and 180 days to close. But, you must close before the due date of the tax return for the year in which the initial title transfer occurs.)

How to Establish the Structure for a Delayed Exchange

Because of the time restraints inherent in a delayed exchange, it is probably best to view its use as an alternative to a standard multiparty strategy rather than a replacement. The most common multiparty exchange involves an agreement with a potential buyer that allows sufficient time to locate exchange property, which is then purchased and exchanged for your property.

One of the main difficulties with this approach is obtaining the buyer's cooperation for the extended time normally required to locate satisfactory exchange property. It is not easy to find good real estate buys these days. Consequently, it is essential to insure that the buyer gets the taxpayer's property after a certain date even if exchange property isn't found.

To meet the requirements of the buyer for eventual ownership as well as the demands of the marketplace, a standard multiparty exchange agreement with enough time to locate exchange property and close the exchange is still a reasonable structure. As a general rule, under this procedure, if the closing date is not extended, the taxpayer is obligated to sell and the exchange is no longer possible.

In effect, the new provisions of Section 1031 serve to meet the needs of the buyer while extending the time period the taxpayer can still successfully complete an exchange. Put in a positive light the new law simply gives everyone 45 days *more* to locate suitable exchange property.

Practically speaking, the new law provides a very clear and legally airtight time extension for completing an otherwise standard multiparty exchange; not to mention that by doing so it has also validated the legal soundness of the basic multiparty exchange. Consequently, we can look at the new law not as a structure that must be applied, but as an alternative to meet the ownership requirements of the buyer if the time period for locating property provided by the initial exchange agreement is inadequate.

Documenting a Delayed Exchange

The documents necessary to close a delayed exchange are essentially the same forms needed to complete an exchange that closes concurrently. The main difference, of course, is the added requirement of escrow instructions which guard against the constructive receipt by the taxpayer of the cash used to acquire the exchange property.

The following documents outline a delayed multiparty exchange from the amendment of the purchase agreement to the designation of exchange property. The essential first step is to amend the buyer's offer to purchase to create an exchange. This addendum allows the transfer of the taxpayer's property to the buyer with the understanding that the funds will be held in escrow and used only for acquisition or exchange property.

EXCHANGE ADDENDUM

This Exchange Addendum amends that certain agreement by and between R. C. Growth (herein "Seller") and Southwest Cattle, Inc., a Montana corporation (herein "Purchaser") for the purchase and sale of real property dated January 5, 19X1 (the "Agreement"), whereby Seller has agreed to sell to Purchaser certain real property located in Sandoval County, New Mexico (the "Property").

In addition to the terms and conditions set forth in the Agreement the parties hereto agree as follows:

1. *Exchange.* It is acknowledged by the Purchaser that Seller desires to arrange for suitable property or properties to be exchanged in connection with the transaction contemplated in the Agreement in order to complete a tax-free exchange or exchanges under the provisions of Section 1031 of the Internal Revenue Code of 1986. Purchaser agrees to accommodate Seller in completing such an exchange, subject to the following conditions;

(a) Seller shall, at any time within 45 days after the date that the transaction contemplated in the Agreement is to be closed (the "Closing"), designate one or more parcels of real property as suitable exchange property. Thereafter, within 180 days after the Closing, the Purchaser shall acquire for and cause to be transferred to Seller one or more of such exchange properties, upon terms and conditions acceptable to Seller. Purchaser agrees not to retain any direct, indirect, partial, or beneficial interest in the exchange property, but shall cause title in the form of a warranty deed to be transferred directly from the owner of the exchange property to Seller.

(b) Seller expressly agrees that Purchaser's total cash obligation in connection with the purchase of property to be acquired and transferred to Seller hereunder shall not exceed the amount which Seller would otherwise be entitled to receive pursuant to the Agreement in the event that no exchange were contemplated. In the event the purchase of exchange property shall require execution of any purchase money debt or instrument, Purchaser shall not be required to assume or incur any personal liability thereon.

(c) Seller acknowledges and agrees that in the event Purchaser participates in an exchange transaction, its participation therein is merely an accommodation to Seller and that in so cooperating, Purchaser makes no representation or warranty whatsoever that any such exchange will comply with the applicable Internal Revenue Code provisions governing like kind exchanges under Section 1031. Seller acknowledges that he is relying solely on his own information, inquiry, and assessment as to the effect of such a transaction with respect to nonrecognition of gain under Section 1031 of the Code. The Purchaser shall, as necessary, execute a purchase agreement or purchase agreements provided that such agreement provides that Purchaser's liability is limited as set forth herein.

(d) Seller agrees to indemnify and hold purchaser harmless from and against any and all obligations, losses, liabilities, claims, and expenses (including all costs and reasonable attorneys' fees) of any kind whatsoever which may in any way arise in connection with Purchaser's participation in the exchange of properties herein provided. If in connection with the purchase of exchange property it is necessary for a purchase money note and mortgage or other debt instrument to be executed with respect to additional purchase money to be paid, then and in that event, nothing contained herein shall require Purchaser to incur any personal liability for the payment of such additional purchase money whether pursuant to a purchase money note and mortgage or debt instrument, or otherwise. In the event that the purchase of exchange property requires the payment of monies in excess of the money Purchaser is obligated to pay to Seller pursuant to the Agreement, then and in that event, Seller shall pay all additional consideration required in connection with the purchase of exchange property.

(e) Purchaser shall have the right to review and approve all documents to be executed by Purchaser in connection with any such exchange, and said approval shall not be unreasonably withheld.

(f) Pending the Purchaser's completion of the purchase of the exchange property, as required herein Purchaser shall establish an escrow account with First American Title Company ("Title Company") into which the Purchaser shall deposit the net proceeds that would otherwise be due to Seller in the event of a sale of the Property pursuant to the Agreement. Purchaser shall enter into an Escrow Agreement with Title Company in the form attached hereto as Exhibit A and incorporated by reference herein. Purchaser agrees to enter into such other and further agreements, including one or more escrow or similar agreements, if reasonably necessary to effectuate such a delayed exchange.

(g) Seller shall, within 45 days of the Closing designate, in writing, one or more suitable exchange properties. If Seller has not been able to find suitable exchange property within such 45 days he shall notify Purchaser. The Purchaser shall thereupon join with Seller in notifying Title Company and instructing Title Company to deliver all escrowed funds to Seller.

If, within such 45 days, one or more exchange properties have been designated by Seller, thereafter (within the 180-day period after the Closing) promptly upon Seller's request to do so, Purchaser will execute such purchase agreements as Seller may require (provided that such agreements comply herewith) and shall join in such notices to the Title Company as are required under the Escrow Agreement to enable Title Company to deliver escrow funds for the purchase of exchange property.

If, on the expiration of such 180-day period, any funds remain in escrow, Purchaser shall join with the Seller in notifying Title Company in regard to the Escrow Agreement.

2. *Additional Consideration.* To induce Seller to convey the Property prior to the locating of suitable exchange property, Purchaser agrees to pay to Seller the interest earned on the funds held in escrow (less the escrow fees).

3. *Effect.* This Exchange Addendum shall have the same force and effect as if a part of the Agreement and shall be binding on the parties and their successors in interest and assigns.

DATED: January 20, 19X1   _____

_____

How to Set Up an Escrow to Protect a Delayed Exchange

The following escrow agreement is designed specifically to protect the taxpayer from constructive receipt of the cash used to acquire the exchange property. The key element here is that the funds held in escrow remain the property of the buyer and can only be used for acquisition of exchange property. The taxpayer has no right to this cash.

ESCROW AGREEMENT   (Exhibit A)

This Agreement is made this 20th day of January 19X1 by and between Southwest Cattle, Inc., a Montana corporation (herein "Southwest") and First American Title Company, a New Mexico corporation (herein "Escrow Agent").

Recitals:

1. Pursuant to the terms and conditions of that certain Agreement dated January 5, 19X1 (the "Agreement") as amended by the Exchange Addendum of even date herewith (the "Amendment") (herein collectively the "Exchange Agreement"), between Southwest and R. C. Growth (herein "Growth"), Southwest has agreed to acquire and transfer to Growth certain real property designated by Growth (the "Exchange Property") in exchange for property transferred by Growth to Southwest. Pursuant to the Exchange Agreement, Southwest has an obligation to expend the net proceeds to Growth from the purchase of Growth's property in cash to purchase the Exchange Property and has agreed to deposit such cash in escrow (herein the "Exchange Funds"). The Exchange Funds include the additional consideration provided for in Paragraph 2 of the Exchange Agreement.

2. Pursuant to the terms of the Exchange Agreement, the Exchange Funds must be held in escrow by an independent escrow agent until such time as Growth has located suitable Exchange Property, or until a date that is 180 days after the date on which Growth's property is transferred to Southwest (the "Exchange Period"), whichever is earlier. When Exchange Property is located, all or a portion of the Exchange Funds are to be used to purchase the Exchange Property. If, on the expiration of the Exchange Period, (the "Sale Date") the Exchange Funds have not been used in whole or in part to acquire the Exchange Property, or if, within 45 days of the date on which Growth's property is transferred to Southwest, Growth has not designated suitable Exchange Property (the "Designation Date"), all funds held in escrow hereunder shall be forthwith delivered to Growth.

3. While in escrow, the Exchange Funds are to remain the property of Southwest. At no time shall Growth have the right to demand or receive any portion of the Exchange Funds held in escrow except on the Designation Date (if no Exchange Property has been designated) or the Sale Date, pursuant to the Exchange Agreement and pursuant to the terms hereof.

4. Southwest desires to constitute and appoint the Escrow Agent to hold the Exchange Funds pursuant to the terms and conditions of this Agreement.

NOW, THEREFORE, IT IS AGREED:

1. *Appointment of Escrow Agent.* Southwest does hereby constitute and appoint First American Title Company as its escrow agent for the purpose of accepting and receiving the Exchange Funds. The Escrow Agent shall hold the Exchange Funds for the benefit of Southwest pursuant to the terms and conditions of this Agreement. At no time shall Growth have any influence over, right to receive, or demand payment of the Exchange Funds, except as set forth in Paragraph 2 hereof. It is understood and agreed that the Escrow Agent is not the Agent of Growth.

2. *Disposition of Items Held in Escrow.* The Escrow Agent shall hold the Exchange Funds and shall deliver such items as follows:

(a) If prior to the Sale Date the Escrow Agent receives a signed statement (the "Notice") from Southwest and Growth that: (i) Southwest desires to purchase Exchange Property for transfer to Growth; (ii) setting forth the amount of the Exchange Funds to be used; and (iii) that Growth has approved and designated the property as the Exchange

Property and has approved the terms of purchase, then and in that event, the Escrow Agent shall deliver to the title company named by Southwest as being the closing agent as to the purchase of such Exchange Property, that portion of Exchange Funds then held by the Escrow Agent, up to the whole thereof, necessary as required to purchase the Exchange Property designated in the Notice.

(b) If, for any reason, by the Sale Date all of the Exchange Funds have not been used to acquire the Exchange Property, the Escrow Agent shall, forthwith and without further notice or demnd or other consent, deliver to Growth an amount equal to the remaining Exchange Funds.

(c) If, after the Designation Date, the Escrow Agent receives a notice signed by Southwest and Growth that no Exchange Property has been designated, then the Escrow Agent shall deliver all of the funds to Growth.

(d) Upon proper delivery by the Escrow Agent of the Exchange Funds in accordance with this Paragraph 2, all of the Escrow Agent's liabilities hereunder shall thereupon cease.

3. *Fee.* The Escrow Agent shall receive a fee that is customary and reasonable for acting hereunder, to be paid out of the monies deposited hereunder.

4. *Position of Agent.* The Escrow Agent acts hereunder as depository only and is not a party to be bound by any agreement or undertaking which may be evidenced by or arising out of any items deposited with the Escrow Agent hereunder, and is not responsible or liable in any manner for the sufficiency, correctness, genuineness, or validity of any such items and undertakes no responsibility or liability for the identity, authority, title, or rights of any person.

5. *Liability of Agent.*

(a) The Escrow Agent shall not be liable for any error of judgment or for any act done or omitted by it in good faith. The Escrow Agent shall be liable only for intentional wrongful acts or omissions, willful neglect, or gross negligence in the performance of its duties hereunder. No liability will be incurred by the Escrow Agent if, in the event of any dispute or material question as to the construction of the directions set forth herein, it acts in accordance with the reasonable opinion of its legal counsel; or in the event of an irreconcilable dispute among Growth, Southwest or any other person, or between the Escrow Agent and any of such parties, it deposits in the District Court for the Second Judicial District of Bernalillo County all of the monies deposited with it hereunder. In the event that the Escrow Agent elects to institute an appropriate action and deposit all monies escrowed hereunder with the District Court, all of the Escrow Agent's expenses incurred in connection with such action, including its reasonable attorneys' fees and costs, shall be satisfied out of the funds held in escrow hereunder.

(b) The Escrow Agent is authorized to act upon any document reasonably believed by it to be genuine and to be signed by the proper party or parties, and will incur no liability in so acting.

(c) In the event of any disagreement or the presentation of adverse claims or demands in connection with or for funds held in escrow hereunder, the Escrow Agent shall at its option, be entitled to refuse to comply with any such claims or demands during the continuance of such disagreement and may refrain from delivering any monies hereunder, and in so doing the Escrow Agent shall not become liable to Southwest or Growth or to any other person, due to its failure to comply with any such adverse claim or demand. The Escrow Agent shall be entitled to continue to refrain from delivering any monies held hereunder without liability, (i) until the adverse claims or demands are fully and finally adjudicated by a court having jurisdiction over the parties and the monies affected, after which time the Escrow Agent shall be entitled to act in conformity with such adjudication; or (ii) until all differences shall have been adjusted by agreement and the Escrow Agent shall have been notified thereof and shall have been directed in writing signed jointly or in counterpart by Southwest or Growth and by all persons making adverse claims or demands, at which time the Escrow Agent shall be protected if acting in compliance therewith.

(d) Southwest shall, but solely to the extent of the monies held in escrow hereunder, in such amount as is from time to time held by the Escrow Agent, indemnify and hold harmless the Escrow Agent against and from any and all costs, expenses, claims, losses, liabilities, or damages (including reasonable attorneys' fees and costs) that may arise out of or in connection with the Escrow Agent's acting as escrow agent hereunder, except with respect to any claims due to or caused by intentional wrongful acts, omissions, willful neglect, or gross negligence of the Escrow Agent. Nothing contained herein shall be construed as imposing personal liability on Southwest to indemnify the Escrow Agent, and the Escrow Agent shall look solely to the monies held in escrow hereunder.

6. *Investment of Funds*. The Escrow Agent shall deposit all monies received by it in a separate interest bearing account or such certificates of deposit, governmental obligations, repurchase agreements, or money market investments as Southwest shall designate and shall not commingle such money with any other monies of the Escrow Agent. All interest earned on the Exchange Funds shall belong to Southwest; provided that such interest shall be used to satisfy Southwest's obligations under the Exchange Agreement. At such time as the Escrow Agent is required to disburse such funds, all such funds may be disbursed on the Escrow Agent's check payable to the order of the parties entitled thereto.

7. *Duties of Escrow Agent Limited*. The Escrow Agent shall have no duty to determine the performance or nonperformance of any term or condition of any item deposited in escrow or of any contract or agreement between the parties hereto, except as specifically stated herein. The Escrow Agent shall not be responsible for notifying any of the parties hereto or any person executing any document or instrument deposited in escrow of any transaction or action involving any of the items deposited in escrow.

8. Amendment. This Agreement may not be altered, amended, or modified unless in writing signed by the parties hereto.

9. *Effect*. This Agreement shall inure to the benefit of the parties hereto and their successors and assigns.

IN WITNESS WHEREOF this Agreement has been executed this 20th day of January, 19X1.

ESCROW AGENT: First American Title Company

By: _____

SOUTHWEST: Southwest Cattle, Inc.

By: _____

Designating the Exchange Property

The most impractical aspect of the law providing for a delayed exchange is the 45-day designation limit. It is difficult to find suitable exchange property anyway, but to find it in a 45-day period is not realistic, given the nature of the real estate market.

Nevertheless, when we look at the details of a transaction there are ways to stretch out the time for locating exchange property. For example, when a purchase offer is received there is normally a minimum of 30 days allowed for closing and often more if new financing is needed or soil samples are required. This is time that can be used to search for exchange property. In fact, there is no reason not to set the closing date at a comfortable time in the future, provided you don't lose the buyer.

In any event if you get down to the wire and you have been unable to locate one property that you are sure you can close on it is possible to designate more than one exchange property candidate. They should be designated in the order of preference and attempts to acquire them should be made in order of preference. In order to meet the designation requirement it is necessary that failure to acquire the target exchange property be due to contingencies beyond the control of the taxpayer, such as failure to get financing or a desired change in zoning.

Designation of the exchange property can occur by contract and by designation letter. For example, the purchase agreement acquiring the exchange property is, by definition, designation of the exchange property. But, what if you designate only one property within the 45-day limit and forces beyond your control prevent closing? With this thought in mind and depending on the specifics of your primary target property, it might be wise to designate more than one exchange property. This can be done by a Designation Letter, which should specify any contingencies that might prevent the acquisition of the preferred property.

DESIGNATION LETTER

To: Southwest Cattle, Inc., A Montana Corporation

Pursuant to that certain agreement between R. C. Growth (herein "Seller") and Southwest Cattle, Inc. (herein "Purchaser") for the purchase and sale of real property dated January 5, 19X1, plus amendments thereto, Seller hereby designates the following property for the like kind exchange under Section 1031 of the Internal Revenue Code.

1. Lots 2 and 3, Block 15, of the West Sandoval Office Park Subdivision Bernalillo County, New Mexico, commonly known as The Garcia Office Complex. (This acquisition is contingent on R. C. Growth obtaining new financing on this property.)
2. Tract 12 of Sandia Ranch Subdivision, Bernalillo County, New Mexico.

R. C. Growth

Date: February 26, 19X1   _____

RECEIVED: Southwest Cattle, Inc.

Date: February 26, 19X1   By: _____

Notifying the Escrow Agent of the Designated Property

After you have designated the exchange property it is necessary to notify the escrow agent to proceed with the transaction as outlined in the original Escrow Agreement. The following instructions are designed to accomplish that task.

Instructions to Escrow Agent

To: First American Title Company
      Albuquerque, New Mexico

Pursuant to that certain Escrow Agreement dated January 20, 19X1 by and between Southwest Cattle, Inc. and First American Title Company, you are hereby notified that R. C. Growth has located suitable exchange property and desires to have Southwest Cattle,

Inc. acquire, in full satisfaction of Southwest Cattle, Inc.'s obligations under the Exchange Addendum between R. C. Growth and Southwest Cattle, Inc., dated January 20, 19X1, the real property described in Exhibit "A" attached hereto. You are hereby instructed to utilize 100% of the remaining Exchange Funds, presently held by you in escrow, for the purpose of effecting the purchase of such property.

At such time as you have utilized those funds and delivered the funds to the seller in connection with the purchase of the exchange property, your duties hereunder shall cease and you shall be relieved of all further liability and obligation hereunder.

Dated: February 26, 19X1

Southwest Cattle, Inc.

By _____

R. C. Growth

_____

After the exchange property has been designated you can begin the process of closing. The law gives you 180 days from the date you convey your property to the buyer to close on the acquisition of the replacement property. Assuming you designated exchange property on the 45th day, that leaves 135 days to work out the details of financing, building inspections, soil testing, and any other contingencies related to closing on the exchange property.

Acquiring Exchange Property in a Delayed Exchange

A delayed exchange, of course, is closed at different times. First you close on transfer of the taxpayer's (exchanger's) property to the buyer, subject to the terms of the exchange agreement (Exchange Addendum and Escrow Agreement in this example) and then you close on acquisition of the exchange property and its transfer to the taxpayer.

Acquisition of the exchange property is done by purchase agreement, which is negotiated and signed by the taxpayer-exchanger. Consequently, when the exchange property is designated and a purchase agreement is signed by the taxpayer, subject to the conditions of the exchange, the purchase agreement must be assigned to the buyer of the taxpayer's property.

The following Assignment and Agreement is designed for that purpose:

ASSIGNMENT AND AGREEMENT

This Assignment and Agreement is made as of this the 26th day of February, 19X1 by R. C. Growth (herein "Growth") in favor of Southwest Cattle, Inc., a Montana corporation (herein "Southwest").

BACKGROUND:

1. Pursuant to that certain "Exchange Addendum" dated January 20, 19X1 Southwest has agreed to acquire and transfer to Growth such real property as Growth shall designate.

2. Growth desires to have Southwest acquire certain real and personal property located in Bernalillo County, New Mexico, described generally as Lots 2 and 3, Block 15 of the West Sandoval Office Park Subdivision Bernalillo County, New Mexico (herein "Property") from Park Partnership.

3. To enable Southwest to effect such acquisition, Growth desires to transfer to Southwest all of its rights, duties, and obligations under the Purchase Agreement of the Property, all as set forth herein.

NOW THEREFORE, IT IS AGREED:

1. *Assignment.* Growth does hereby transfer, assign, and convey to Southwest all of its right, title, and interest in and to the Purchase Agreement on the Property. Southwest does hereby accept the Assignment and, except as provided herein, does hereby agree to acquire the Property described therein upon the terms and conditions set forth in the Purchase Agreement on the Property, and does hereby agree to simultaneously transfer and convey the Property or cause the Property to be transferred and conveyed to Growth, in full satisfaction of Southwest's obligations under the January 20, 19X1 Agreement, described above.

2. *Additional Consideration.* It is understood and agreed that Southwest's total obligation in connection with such purchase is the payment to the seller, Park Partnership, of the sum of 100% of the Exchange Funds held by First American Title Company. The additional consideration required to be paid pursuant to the Purchase Agreement on the Property shall be paid or provided for by Growth. The acquisition by Southwest of the Property and the subsequent transfer by Southwest of the Property to Growth shall be effected simultaneously.

3. *Conveyance of Title.* Southwest shall either (i) convey title to the Property to Growth by Special Warranty Deed, in such condition of title as Growth shall approve; or (ii) cause Park Partnership to convey title to the Property directly to Growth by General Warranty Deed, in the condition of title as Growth shall direct. Southwest shall cause the title insurance, which is to be delivered to the purchaser of the Property, to be issued directly to Growth, without endorsement or additional charge.

It is understood and agreed that if title is conveyed directly to Growth by Park Partnership, such conveyance is for convenience only and Southwest shall be deemed the purchaser of the Property for the purpose of the provisions of Section 1031 of the Internal Revenue Code.

4. *Additional documents.* Growth shall execute such documents as are required to effect the foregoing transactions, including a notice to that certain Escrow Agent.

IN WITNESS WHEREOF, this Assignment has been effected and executed the day and year above first written.

R. C. Growth

_____

ACCEPTED: Southwest Cattle, Inc.

By: _____

APPROVAL:

Park Partnership does hereby approve the foregoing assignment and agrees to sell the property described above to Southwest, and if required to do so by Southwest to transfer title to the Property to Growth.

Park Partnership

By: _____

The Essential Documents of a Delayed Exchange

Multiparty exchanges tend to begin with an offer to purchase. This is the case whether the exchange closes concurrently or evolves into delayed exchange. In this chapter we reviewed a delayed exchange that started with an offer to purchase that was amended to allow for a delayed exchange. The following documents formed the transaction into an exchange.

1. *The Exchange Addendum.* This document amended the offer to purchase and set up the procedure for a delayed exchange.
2. *The Escrow Agreement.* This document established the escrow for holding the funds from the buyer of the taxpayer's property in a manner that prevented constructive receipt of the cash, thus protecting the exchange benefits until suitable exchange property could be found.
3. *The Designation Letter.* This document designated the exchange property as required within 45 days of the transfer of the taxpayer's property to the buyer.
4. *The Instructions to Escrow Agent.* This document fulfilled a requirement of the Escrow Agreement, informing the escrow agent that the exchange property had been designated and authorizing its acquisition with the exchange funds.
5. *The Assignment and Agreement.* This document assigned the purchase agreement used to acquire the exchange property to the buyer of the taxpayer's property. (From a practical standpoint the taxpayer actually negotiates and makes written offers on the exchange property, then assigns the final accepted agreement to the buyer for acquisition and completion of the exchange.)

There are variations on the way any document can be written. The essential requirement is to have all the agreements prepared by a competent tax lawyer who has a real estate background.

How to Amend a Purchase Offer to Establish a Delayed Exchange

It is possible to set up an exchange from a purchase offer in a manner that will provide for a delayed exchange, a standard multiparty exchange, or an exchange through a third-party title transfer. The following Addendum to Agreement is designed as a multi-use amendment to a purchase offer to provide for virtually all types of exchange structures.

ADDENDUM TO AGREEMENT

This Addendum is to that certain agreement by and between _____ (herein "Sellers") and _____(herein "Purchasers") for the purchase and sale of real

real property dated _____, (the "Agreement"), whereby Sellers have agreed to sell to Purchasers certain real property located in _____(the "Property").

In addition to the terms and conditions set forth in the Agreement, the parties additionally agree as follows:

1. *Like Kind Exchange.* It is acknowledged by the Purchasers that Sellers may desire to arrange for suitable property or properties to be exchanged in connection with the transaction contemplated in the Agreement so as to effectuate a tax-free exchange or exchanges pursuant to Section 1031 of the Internal Revenue Code of 1986. Purchasers agree to accommodate Sellers in effecting such an exchange, subject to the following conditions:

(a) Sellers may, at any time within ten (10) days prior to the date that the transaction contemplated in the Agreement is to be consummated and closed (the "Closing"), elect to have Purchasers purchase one or more parcels of real property, upon terms and conditions acceptable to Sellers and to concurrently convey the same to Sellers by special warranty deed in exchange for the Property. In order to effectuate such a tax-free exchange, Sellers may extend the Closing Date set forth in the Agreement for a maximum of ____days.

(b) Sellers expressly agree that Purchasers' total dollar obligation in connection with the purchase of property to be exchanged hereunder shall not exceed the amount which Purchasers would otherwise be required to pay pursuant to the Agreement in the event that no exchange were completed. If at all possible, the purchase of exchange property by the Purchasers shall be consummated simultaneously with the purchase and sale contemplated under the Agreement unless Sellers otherwise designate hereunder. Notwithstanding the foregoing, in the event that Purchasers are unable to purchase the exchange property due to the failure or inability of the Sellers thereof to convey title or consummate the agreement under which such exchange property is to be purchased, then and in that event, the purchase and sale transaction contemplated by the Agreement shall be consummated without regard to the provisions of this paragraph.

(c) Sellers acknowledge and agree that in the event Purchasers participate in an exchange transaction, their participation therein is merely as an accommodation to Sellers and Purchasers—(1) make no representation or warranty whatsoever that any such exchange will comply with the applicable Internal Revenue Code Provisions governing nonrecognition of exchange under Section 1031. Sellers acknowledge that they are relying solely on their own information, inquiry, and assessment as to the effect of such a transaction with respect to nonrecognition of gain under Section 1031 of the Code; and (2) will have no responsibility to make any offers or otherwise negotiate for the purchase of exchange property; it being acknowledged that Sellers shall have the sole responsibility for making all decisions as respects the exchange property.

(d) Sellers agree to indemnify and hold Purchasers harmless from and against any and all obligations, losses, liabilities, claims, and expenses including all costs and reasonable attorneys' fees, of any kind whatsoever which may in any way arise in connection with Purchasers' participation in the exchange of properties herein provided. If in connection with the purchase of exchange property it is necessary for a purchase money note and mortgage or other debt instrument be executed with respect to additional purchase money to be paid, then and in that event, nothing contained herein shall require that Purchasers incur any personal liability for the payment of any such additional purchase money whether pursuant to a purchase money note and mortgage or debt instrument, or otherwise. In the event that the purchase of exchange property requires the payment of monies in excess of the money Purchasers are obligated to pay hereunder, then and in that event, Sellers shall pay all additional consideration or shall incur any purchase money indebtedness necessary or required in connection with the purchase of exchange property.

(e) Purchasers shall have the right to review and approve all documents to be executed by Purchasers in connection with any such exchange, and said approval is not to be unreasonably withheld.

(f) In the event that the Sellers are unable to locate suitable exchange property, the purchase of which can be consummated simultaneously with the Closing of the transaction contemplated by the Agreement, then and in that event, the Sellers may notify the Purchasers and require the Purchasers, pending the Purchasers' completion of the purchase of the exchange property, to establish an escrow for deposit of the net purchase money that would otherwise be due to Sellers in the event of a sale of the Property. Purchasers agree to enter into such other and further agreements, including an escrow or similar agreement, necessary to effectuate such a delayed exchange.

(g) In connection with effecting a like kind exchange, the Sellers may transfer the Property to a third party subject to the terms of the Agreement. Thereafter the third party shall consummate the Agreement. In this event the Purchasers will release the Sellers from all liability hereunder.

2. *Effect.* This addendum shall have the same force and effect as if a part of the Agreement and shall be binding on the parties and their successors in interest and assigns.

Dated _____

_____

_____

How to Apply the Reverse Delayed Exchange

Both the delayed exchange and the reverse delayed exchange are forms of the multiparty exchange with nonconcurrent transfer of title. In a standard multiparty exchange, the buyer agrees to purchase property you designate and exchange it for your property in an interdependent transaction. The standard delayed exchange occurs when you transfer property to the buyer before he transfers the exchange property to you. In the standard delayed exchange, the buyer is located first.

In the reverse delayed exchange, the property you want is located before the buyer for your property is found. This delay technique is also a variation on a form of the multiparty exchange. The regular form of this technique is often referred to as an exchange with a cash take-out. It is used when the exchange property you want is found before a buyer for your property. Therefore, you and the owner agree to exchange provided a buyer is found for your property prior to closing. In the reverse delayed exchange, the owner of the property you want transfers title before you transfer title to your property. Consequently, there is a delay between acquisition of the target property and completion of the exchange.

In a delayed exchange, the buyer is found first and then the target property. In a reverse delayed exchange, the target property is found first and then the buyer for your property.

How to Overcome the Problems of a Reverse Delayed Exchange

It is one thing to hold cash for acquisition of property. It is quite another to hold title with the full burdens of ownership while a buyer is found. In the reverse delayed exchange scenario, you must find someone who is willing to acquire the property you have located and hold it pursuant to an agreement to exchange when the buyer for your property is located. When the buyer is found, he acquires the target property from the intermediary and completes the exchange.

Obviously, this proceedure raises a number of barriers that must be overcome. You cannot take title during the delay period (*Bloomington Coca Cola Bottling Company v. Commissioner*, 189 F 2d 14). Consequently, an accommodating party must be used. This party must have the full benefits and burdens of owning the property, which presents a number of risks, especially if a buyer can't be easily found for your property. Furthermore, the property must be financed or purchased for cash and the additional cost of this capital outlay must be factored in as a risk.

Given the problems that are readily apparent, there are a couple of solutions that can be used to set up the reverse delayed exchange. For example, try to acquire vacant land rather than income property. This will tend to eliminate many of the liabilities, risks, and problems of management during the delay period.

The main problem of how to find an accommodating party without paying an excessive fee to cover the liability and risks can be accomplished if you have a corporation. The corporation should be a legitimate business venture and not formed solely to make the exchange.

As with all of the exchange techniques that have developed through the years, the reverse delayed exchange evolved out of the changing nature of the marketplace. When property is in demand and there is an active market, buyers are easier to find than acceptable exchange property and the delayed exchange is common. The advent of the reverse delayed exchange* indicates that property is easier to find than buyers and that supply is indeed catching up with demand.

* See *Lee v. Commissioner*, TC Memo 1986–294.

II

REAL ESTATE
ACQUISITION TECHNIQUES

The word "exchange" implies movement in two directions. To exchange you must give and get, transfer and receive, divest and acquire. It is understandable, then, that acquisition techniques are extensively used in connection with exchanging. The successful completion of an exchange often depends on the acquisition formulas used to move the deal through closing.

Consequently, it is essential to have a source of methods you can draw from to overcome the problems that are inevitable in all exchanges. The problems usually relate to financing or difficulty with one of the principals—a difficulty that must be overcome if the transaction is to close.

The following techniques are intended for continuing reference. They are presented in a manner that allows rapid understanding of the concept while permitting you to fill in the details, combining and customizing as needed for your unique transaction, whether it is an exchange or a deal that grew from the technique itself. In many cases the technique is a potential transaction, a starting point for acquiring real estate.

Part II is divided into seven chapters:

14. How to Use Cycles in a Real Estate Acquisition Strategy

15. Techniques for Acquiring Real Estate Without Cash

16. Institutional Financing Techniques

17. Private Financing and Negotiation Techniques

18. Using a Lease to Acquire and Finance Real Estate

19. Acquisition with Options

20. Acquisition Techniques for Special Deals

These techniques form an important segment of exchanging because few exchanges are closed without problems. Without methods such as these of solving these problems, few exchanges would ever close. It is hoped that they will help you get your exchanges through closing. Maybe as an added benefit one of the following techniques will be a formula you can use to initiate and close a transaction that is not related to exchanging.

14

How to Use Cycles
in a Real Estate Acquisition
Strategy

Real estate is a cyclical industry. It expands and contracts with the fluctuations of the supply-demand forces that permeate our economy.

The housing cycle is the most regular. It tends to peak every seven years. At least this has been the case for the last three cycles, which reached high points in 1972, 1979, and 1986. If this relatively even time spacing between cycle crests recurs, the next peak will be about 1993.

The primary defining factor in all real estate cycles is activity. There is more buying and selling, which constitutes activity, during the expansion phase and a major drop in activity during the contraction phase.

Generally, this cyclical process follows the supply-demand dynamics of:

1. The industry segment: offices, retail space, industrial, and apartments.
2. Regional supply-demand forces: a technological boom may be underway in the northeast at the same time an oil-induced depression is going on in the southwest.
3. The expansion and contraction of the general economy, which during the past 130 years has moved through somewhat regular business cycles that average 51 months from trough to trough.

There are two factors that interact to influence the level of activity in real estate. Expanding employment opportunity is the primary force behind demand for real estate. More jobs attract more people. When the job market contracts, houses go on the market, apartments become vacant, and retail space empties. During a contraction, demand for real estate shrinks as supply grows—not new supply, but offices, stores, and apartments that were once occupied and then become vacant, adding to a growing inventory.

Interest rates and the availability of loans are of virtually equal importance to the health of the real estate market. Nevertheless, if there are no jobs and no people, low interest rates are of little help in stimulating real estate activity.

Consequently, the primary influence on the health of the real estate market is employment expansion. In fact, employment expansion is the major defining factor of economic health in our general economy. Here too, interest rates and the availability of money play a major role as the Federal Reserve manipulates interest rates in an attempt to keep the economy growing without allowing inflation to get out of control—a difficult job at best and a major contributor to our regular recessions.

The Great Inflation Cycle of the 1970s

Every 54 years or so a major cycle peak occurs in our economy. The last one occurred in the seventies as the OPEC cartel increased the price of oil, resulting in a general price increase in goods and services throughout our economy. But it was not only the price of oil. During the early 1970s gold was released from governmental control and allowed to trade at free market levels. Concurrently, a grain sale of major proportions was made with the Soviets, resulting in a sudden increase in commodity prices.

These basic changes in our economy laid the foundation for a major shift in attitude toward real estate by the general public. When the economy moved out of the major recession of the mid-1970s a public perception of ongoing inflation grew as prices increased through the efforts of stimulative governmental policy.

The price of oil, gold, and real estate increased as the public expectation of further price increases and visions of riches and financial independence became firmly implanted in the collective psyche. Speculation regardless of the cost became the controlling factor in real estate.

Ads for books and seminars on how to get rich in real estate presented by a seemingly never-ending string of new geniuses who got lucky during the great inflation cycle appeared throughout the newspapers of our major cities. Historically, one of the characteristics of a peak in speculation is an increase in books on how to get rich speculating in the particular asset that has enjoyed the run-up in price. Unfortunately, the books came out after the prices had already increased substantially, taking advantage of the public popularity for an investment that is already priced at levels of extreme risk.

Furthermore, the basics of economics kicked in and the increase in prices attracted more supply—oil exploration increased and major conservation measures were implemented; more grain was planted and new real estate developments were started.

The Role of Debt Expansion in the Real Estate Cycle

Real estate is a debt-dependent asset. It is the leverage afforded through borrowing that accelerates price appreciation in real estate. This is especially true when interest rates are lower than the rate of inflation and the rate of price appreciation as was the case during much of the 1970s. It is leverage that provides the major benefit when prices and rents increase at a higher rate than the cost of borrowing money to acquire the property.

Unfortunately, it seems like we are always fighting the last war. Adapting to the current reality of investment life is difficult. It is especially difficult in real estate where public perceptions can be years behind actual price trends. This tendency causes people to buy when they shouldn't—that is, after prices have risen so high that it becomes difficult for the property to support the debt attached to it.

The most obvious effect of this speculative, and in some cases fraudulent excess, is the great debt liquidation of the savings and loan industry during the 1980s. The savings and loan industry was deregulated at the same time the great real estate inflation cycle was reaching a crest. Values were high and consequently, so were the appraisals that were used to justify an increasing number of loans—loans to farmers for land and equipment acquisition to take advantage of increased grain prices; loans to real estate developers to take advantage of the boom in the southwest due to the increase in oil prices; loans to investors to acquire real estate due to the increase in price of real estate. Wait a minute. Does it make sense to borrow money to buy real estate because the price has increased in the past? No—it makes sense because you think prices will increase in the future. In other words, past performance is not expected to be the same in the future when viewed in the context of cyclical fluctuations.

But what if prices stop increasing? That, of course, is what happened. It is also what anyone with a basic understanding of cycles would expect to happen. The government imposed an embargo on grain sales to the Soviets, shooting down the farm expansion it had encouraged only a few years earlier and the price of oil fell as OPEC went the way of all cartels into overproduction and internal disarray. In 1986 Congress ended the favorable tax policy of 1981 throwing the real estate investment market that was actually spawned by government policy into a major contraction. Concurrently, the loans that seemed justified by high real estate appraisals caught up with the savings and loan industry.

The Great Debt Liquidation of the 1980s

It is natural for growing demand to result in higher prices until new supply is brought on line to meet the new demand. It takes higher prices to justify the cost of expansion. It is also the price mechanism that checks demand that gets out of hand. When prices get too high, demand tends to slow at the same time new supply is arriving at the marketplace. It can really be a kind of double whammy: Serious problems occur when the forces that caused prices to increase evaporate suddenly, leaving a mountain of debt and no price structure to support it. Debt liquidation is the primary characteristic of the long-wave cycle contraction that tends to hit the economy at about 54-year intervals.

Consequently the banks, and especially the savings and loans in the southwest, have become real estate holding companies. Once-quiet bankers have been converted into real estate salesmen as they grope to sell repossessed property (REOs). This is indeed an uncomfortable position for those who happen to realize their new status. And even the federal workers who head up the FSLIC and the FDIC have become salesmen as they scramble to find solvent institutions to buy the growing number of insolvent savings and loan associations. Under it all it seems we are a nation of commodity speculators and salesmen, expanding our businesses as grain and oil prices increase and then trying to sell our way out as they fall.

It seems also that the major national banks were at heart commodity speculators in the late 70s and early 80s as they "recycled" petro-dollars from the far east into Latin American loans, some of which were ironically for the expansion of oil production in Mexico. Unfortunately, where there is easy money there is also corruption and much of these loans never made it past the pockets of the officials in control. Historically, these loans tend not to be repaid. This is important to note because major loan defaults occurred in Latin America during the long-wave contraction of the 1930s, adding further evidence that the 1980s constitute a major cycle trough.

Currently, we are in the process of liquidating the billions in debt secured by real estate in the midwest and southwest resulting from farm and oil industry expansion and the general real estate boom of the late 1970s and early 1980s. Over the last ten years we have seen the completion of a long-wave inflation cycle and the beginning of the steps toward completion of the debt liquidation that is the natural end result of the process. Ultimately, there may be psychological damage. The process of debt liquidation may take a very long time in many areas of the country and is likely to damage public acceptance of real estate as a sure-thing investment. This change in attitude will lay the foundation for a new cycle and a new opportunity to acquire real estate for the next long-term cycle of inflation and debt liquidation.

The Impact of Economic Cycles on Real Estate

A broad economic perspective is useful whether your goal is to build personal wealth or acquire real estate for your company's pension fund. A balanced perspective requires an understanding of the very long-term cycles that contain the regular business recessions and recoveries. This type of understanding will not only help to protect your portfolio from unnecessary risk, but will also allow you to take advantage of the extended economic contractions that present major opportunities for long-term acquisitions. There are four aspects to this broad perspective.

1. Inflation is built into the economy and will continue as long as population and employment growth is sustained.
2. Through the decades real estate has appreciated as the population has grown and the general standard of living has increased.
3. The free world economy moves in long waves of industrial expansion and contraction, which measure about 54 years from trough to trough.
4. Real estate activity fluctuates in irregular, but somewhat predictable cycles, corresponding to and sometimes overlapping the normal business cycle, which has averaged 51 months from trough to trough for about 130 years.

The business cycle and the long-wave industrial cycle are time-related market characteristics which can serve as real estate acquisition timing guides. The normal fluctuation in real estate activity is the basis for timing acquisitions. The trough in the normal business cycle is the chance every several years to invest with relatively low risk and negotiate the most advantageous price and terms. The long-wave contractions every 54 years or so present a once-in-a-generation opportunity for major acquisitions. The indications that we are in the middle of a long-wave contraction during the late 1980s are all around us, not least of which is the highest number of bank failures since the depression of the 1930s.

The major impact of cyclical fluctuations on real estate is the reduction of activity during the contraction phase and an expansion of activity during the expansion phase. Generally, prices and terms ease during the contraction as demand slacks off. This, of course, is the best time to acquire real estate. In contrast the time to sell is at the end of the expansion phase while demand is strong and the majority of the public is buying.

Four Ways to Make the Most of Economic Cycles

1. Maintain a certain portion of investment funds in real estate for long-term appreciation.
2. Avoid highly leveraged acquisitions, and therefore large debt obligations, at the peak of the business cycle.
3. Make long-term real estate investments, which you plan to hold during severe contractions, as nearly free of debt as possible.
4. Use cyclical peaks in the economy as opportunities to sell short-term investments when demand and prices appear to have increased excessively—when public optimism and interest in real estate is high.

How Investor Expectations Affect Real Estate Activity

Expectations of continuing inflation, steady growth, expanding employment, reasonable interest rates, and a favorable federal tax policy; or, in contrast, recession, unemployment, and high real interest rates and an unfavorable federal tax policy all work in concert to determine market sentiment and influence investment decisions. For example, a reduction in the tax benefits (Tax Reform Act of 1986) of owning real estate can bring a sudden halt to investment activity. This is especially true if the general price level has increased substantially due to a prior liberal tax policy (Economic Recovery Act of 1981).

It is interesting to note that a major reduction in the tax benefits of owning real estate followed on the heels of a major increase in the benefits of owning real estate just at the point in the long-wave cycle where a 54-year trough was due. This is a typical trigger event that ends a speculative run-up in prices.

The expansion in real estate activity that occurred in the late 1970s was followed by an artificially induced extension of activity as a result of the liberal depreciation rules of the 1981 tax law, which brought still more supply to an already peaking market. This made the reduction in tax benefits that came with the Tax Reform Act of 1986 all the more damaging to the real estate market. It is another confirmation of a market top for an outside event to occur that triggers a drop in prices. The trouble with real estate is the debt it usually carries can obscure the price reduction, especially if the property isn't sold. How could property be worth less than the loan on it? To answer this question just ask the largest real estate holding companies in the country—the savings and loan associations that have repossessed property that can't even be sold for the amount of the loans made just a few years earlier.

How to Recognize and Profit from Speculative Patterns

The speculative increase in prices to extremes is a curious process with a long history involving many types of assets, including real estate. It is a curious process because the same psychological factors play a major role in the pattern regardless of the assets involved or the level of expertise or wealth of the participants. The process is re-enacted time and again in different financial arenas without the majority of the participants realizing that they are part of a scenario with a recognizable pattern.

For example, toward the end of the acquisition phase it is almost as if a buying frenzy takes precedence over reason as buyers acquire more at ever increasing prices in the hope of getting, and fear of missing, the "sure" profits made by those who bought earlier. Toward the end of the boom, fear of loss crowds out fear of missing a profit and hope of riches, as the specter of repaying the debt used to buy the asset becomes psychologically dominant. The characteristics of the process are:

1. *Excessive credit expansion.* Loans are easy to get when secured by the asset that is rising in price. The funds from the new loans are used to buy more of the speculative asset.

2. *Visions of wealth dominate the participants' consciousness.* Pursuit of "more" takes hold as the participants attempt to expand their holdings and increase their standard of living in line with new-found self-importance and impressions of financial genius.

3. *The participants "realize" they have it made.* Confidence takes over. Owners refuse to sell except at very high prices because of the obvious permanent value. At this stage the press and how-to-get-rich books spread the word of past successes, drawing in the late-comers who buy at high prices with new debt commitments in a topping market.

4. *A trigger event stops the market rise and prices fall of their own weight.* For example, the grain embargo, the inability of OPEC to hold oil prices up, and the unfavorable tax treatment of real estate imposed in 1986 all served to end market activity, allowing prices to fall.

5. *Debt pressures mount as participants attempt to sell into a weak market.* Fear takes over at this stage as participants worry more about lack of cash to pay loans than missing out on future price increases. Lenders realize their loans are in trouble and try to salvage what they can by working with borrowers, even if it means extending more credit.

6. *Debt liquidation begins as foreclosures mount.* Assets are taken by the lenders, as values drop below the amount of the loans. Loans are written down as no buyers are found. An increasing number of lenders get in trouble and the government is forced to step in with taxpayers' money. In extreme cases the process can take years.

7. *Loss of investor confidence eventually follows.* This is the opposite extreme of the blind speculation found at market tops. It is a time to wait and watch for opportunity and the beginning of the recovery when the cycle starts up again. Patience is the key at this stage. Things will get better. They always have. Cycles will continue, bringing both the good and the bad. And after this stage is over it will be time for the good again.

Obviously, there is a relationship between patterns of speculation and the expansion and contraction of the economy. Extreme speculation tends to involve government intervention—either to prevent damage to the banking system as occurred with the Hunt's silver binge, or unintentionally as when the grain embargo caused havoc in the farm community.

Furthermore, the timing of the cycles tends to fit with the events that occurred during the previous cycle point, containing many similar if not identical events. For example, the trade protection movement growing in Congress today is not unlike the protectionist legislation of the late 1920s which has been cited as a contributing cause of the 1930s depression.

In the last analysis, the normal flow of the economy through cycles is the basis for growth and the natural corrections inherent in our system. It is also the basis of opportunity for those who are willing to adapt and take advantage of the ebb and flow of cycles within the real estate market.

How to Time Acquisitions to Take Advantage of Real Estate Cycles

One way you can work toward profiting from market conditions is to analyze the real estate cycle in the context of the activity stages that are the most easily recognized characteristics. The natural tendency we all have is to focus attention on isolated events, which form only part of the ongoing real estate cycle.

It's very difficult to define and isolate a process until a major terminal event defines it as completed. That is, the beginning of a process is easy to overlook until the process itself ends, often with some dramatic occurrence. For example, the speculative excesses of the stock market in 1929 and 1987 were easy to overlook until prices fell. The process was then framed and obvious. Few people saw it coming and virtually no one initially realized the extent of the fall in prices.

Prices boom, then bust, and few see the boom in perspective until the bust is in place. Real estate is not exempt from this process. It just moves more slowly as a market and lacks rapid price quotes. But real estate prices do rise and fall. And that cyclical activity is the basis of opportunity.

Real estate investment processes follow activity stages which contain the supply-demand and purchase and sales activity that reflect investor expectations—expectations that prices will rise forever, or never rise again; expectations that inflation will never end or that the deflation we are experiencing will never work out of the system.

There are four activity stages that define the complete real estate cycle:

1. *Activity basing*—Real estate activity is low, as excess supply is very gradually absorbed. Sellers give concessions, which amount to lower prices. Public expectations reach a low point. Liquidity is the prime concern, cash is in demand, and risk avoidance dominates investor psychology.

2. *Activity rising*—Interest in real estate picks up as demand begins to absorb the existing supply. Prices rise, terms tighten, and construction activity starts up in an attempt to take advantage of the growing demand.

3. *Activity topping*—Supply starts to catch up with demand. Construction activity starts to taper off, but public awareness of the profit made by others is at a high point. The outlook is generally optimistic, and the greatest fear is missing a profit. New construction hangs on as long as lenders are willing to lend.

4. *Activity falling*—Too much supply is available for demand. Rents and prices stop rising and sellers are forced to give concessions on terms. Public expectation of profit diminishes as market activity decreases and credit becomes increasingly restrictive. Pessimism increases to balance the previous optimism as investors pull back to avoid risk and reduce debt exposure.

After activity falls the basing stage starts again. Normally the complete cycle takes years to complete in the slow-moving real estate market. Activity in different segments of the real estate market is simply a reflection of the combined interaction of supply and demand for that type of real estate—whether apartments, offices, retail, or single family housing.

15

Techniques for
Acquiring Real Estate
Without Cash

Knowing what is possible gives you the opportunity to accelerate real estate acquisition. If you learn what others have done, you simply increase your chances by drawing on their knowledge. This is the purpose behind the following techniques—to give you the advantage that comes from knowing specific ways of getting the job done.

Some of the techniques may solve an immediate problem and pave the way for closing an acquisition that you've had your eye on for some time. Others will not fit your needs today, but someday they may. In any event, the objective is to give you the widest possible range of alternatives to choose from. Look at these techniques as the starting point. They are meant to be modified. Try to combine and customize them to fit your specific needs.

Mortgage Out

By definition, you mortgage out when the permanent loan is equal to or larger than your total acquisition costs. The mathematical key is to keep land and construction costs at the same percentage of appraised value as the financing. With existing projects, the sales price must equal the loan value of the property.

Mortgaging out is probably the most sought after objective of builder-developers. Meeting this increasingly elusive objective requires a combination of cost control and solid income tenants. Developers have found mortgaging out increasingly difficult as land and construction costs have increased. Nevertheless, rents have also moved up, and with a shrewd approach you can still build value into certain projects that will do the job.

If your rents are high enough to generate an appraisal based on income that is comfortably above your costs, you are in business. Since lenders base their estimate of value on the income-producing ability of the property, you have a built-in chance. Everything from ranches to shopping centers have been acquired using this technique.

The objective is to keep costs of land and construction to about 70 or 80 percent of appraisal, depending on the percentage of value you will receive from the loan. Investors who have an inventory of commercial land acquired years ago have a definite advantage. Land that was acquired just a few years ago will probably contribute to appraised value far in excess of its original cost. But there are a couple of other alternatives if land costs are a problem in your area:

(1) Carefully negotiate a long-term land lease with low payments at the outset to give you the margin for borrowing the initial development money you need.

(2) Work in small towns before land values move up out of sight.

Big name, grade A tenants and a shopping center developer-builder who can leave his profit in the project add to the ease of mortgaging out.

Refinance with the Seller Carrying Back a Second

This technique is a natural for acquiring older property (especially apartments) that can be refinanced. The primary objective of this approach is to obtain a new first mortgage large enough to pay both the existing loans and the down payment required by the seller. The down payment actually comes from the proceeds of the new first mortgage.

The balance of the sales price is then carried by the seller on a second mortgage. It may also be possible for you to structure the terms of the transaction so that a portion of the loan proceeds are used for renovation of the property. The proceeds of the new loan, therefore, can meet three objectives:

(1) to pay the existing loans;
(2) to make the down payment; and
(3) to upgrade the property.

As with most acquisition techniques, this one works smoothly when the seller wants out and trusts your management ability. The challenge here is to make the seller accept a totally financed acquisition. It is equally important to build enough value into your loan presentation to get the largest possible first mortgage. This requires a very complete presentation of the changes you will make in the property, the benefits of the management system you will implement, and the steps you will take to increase the income. Your objective is to convince the seller and lender that you are the best possible buyer and their interests will be better cared for when you own the property.

There are a couple of direct benefits to the seller:
(1) He steps out of the liability of the existing loans because you have refinanced;
(2) and he gets the down payment he wants from the proceeds of the new loan.

Since he was probably prepared to carry back a second position anyway, nothing has changed substantially. The main negotiating block may be over the amount of the second mortgage. But this need not be a problem if the seller has confidence in the income-producing power of the property and your ability to manage it professionally.

Create Paper

Solid real estate equity is buying power. And in times of high inflation it is a source of capital appreciation—the only type of gain that can keep your estate even with or ahead of inflation. Creating paper is a method of using the purchasing power of your home or other real estate equity without refinancing or selling.

The mechanics of this approach are simple. You sign a note, usually payable in monthly installments, which is secured by a second mortgage on real estate you own. The note buys out the seller's equity in the property you are acquiring. It is the down payment. If you default on the note, the seller gets your other property. As added security, the terms could be written so that in the event of default the seller would get the property he sold you as well.

Of course, you would not want to use this technique if there were the least possibility of default. The income must be there to support the payments. Using your residence as security can be a means of ensuring the seller that the note for the down payment will be paid.

A personal note backed with solid collateral that meets the income needs of the seller often makes more sense than a lot of cash when you calculate the tax benefits. Spreading out payment of the seller's equity spreads out the tax on his profit. Why should a seller demand a lot of cash when receiving the cash may actually increase the total amount that passes through his hands on the way to the federal government? The only logical reason is to meet a desire for security. Using your residence as security for the note is designed to meet this need.

Refinance Your Home

The steady, unrelenting increase in single-family home values is probably the major factor contributing to the broad acceptance of real estate as an investment. The equity in your home that grows each month as a result of paying the loan and from market value appreciation is now widely recognized as being just like money in the bank. Home ownership is replacing savings, often by necessity rather than by choice.

Recognition of home equity as solid security has moved what used to be viewed as a consumer item into the area of acceptable low-risk investment. Consequently, savings and loans and banks are fighting to develop new types of home loans.

Cities are even entering the market by issuing bonds for inter-city home loan funds. This is evidently the political motive in competition with the profit motive.

Putting the home in the spotlight increases the opportunity for aggressively using equity for investment. You can turn your equity into cash two ways: (1) refinance completely, or (2) add a second mortgage. The rapid increase in home values is a chance to put solid equity to work acquiring additional investment real estate. It is also a chance to become overextended. But with proper prudent planning and financial analysis your home equity can be a safe source of investment capital.

The challenge here is to put the cash, which of course is tax free, to work earning investment dollars. Using the refinance proceeds for consumer goods doesn't make sense since no income or capital gains are produced to repay the debt.

The obvious requirement of this technique is that the money earned by the real estate acquired with the refinance proceeds be sufficient to offset the risk of additional debt on such an important personal asset as your personal residence. Carefully weigh the balance between risk and reward before using this approach.

Professional Services as Down Payment

If you don't have cash, what do you have? That is the basic question to thoroughly explore as you negotiate any acquisition. Often the answer falls back on what you can do that is of benefit to the seller.

Sellers who really want to get out and avoid getting back in will often look to your management ability. Just knowing that their equity will be protected by good management and that they will eventually be paid from the improved operating efficiency of the property can be enough to swing the deal. If you can provide this kind of assurance and add another benefit, you may be in good shape.

Do you have a professional skill the seller might need that would meet part or all of the down payment requirement? For example, if the seller is interested in the stock market and you are a computer programmer, how about creating a program to trade stocks or test his system and manage the transactions.

Lawyers and doctors have an advantage with this technique because of the high costs of the professions. Furthermore, eventually almost everyone seems to need their services. Contractors and related building trades also have an edge here because real estate sellers often have other property that may need work. This is a natural opportunity to trade for the down payment.

Knowing the seller is often half the battle. If you have an idea of what he wants out of life, you may be able to jump the cash gap and go directly to his objective. There are probably several things any seller will do with the cash he has, whether it comes from a down payment or his job—what can you provide without the intermediate step of cash?

Effort Equity

There are several applications of effort equity. It can be used to acquire a home through FHA as well as an interest in a partnership.

If you are putting a partnership together for real estate acquisition, a percentage of the ownership may be appropriate compensation. It is often an expected incentive that is built into the project from the beginning.

FHA has a provision that allows the use of the buyer to apply "sweat equity" to the down payment requirement. You receive credit for the labor you put into the property to bring it up to FHA standards.

The purpose of this technique is for you to receive credit toward the down payment for the value of the effort you contribute to the property or project. In complicated investment transactions, it is usually one person who creates the idea for a real estate transaction and puts the pieces together that result in a finalized transaction. Without this type of effort few deals would close. More often than not, the value of the property is enhanced as a result. When this is being done for the benefit of a partnership, it is only appropriate that the creating member be compensated for the extra effort. Equity in the property is one solid form of compensation. It is also a method of ensuring a profitable outcome of the investment when the partners look to the same person for the management and ultimate sale of the property.

Real estate brokers who work with out-of-town investors have an edge here. There is a degree of added comfort when you know that someone is there who will stand behind the property and work out the problems. A right to participate in ownership makes good business sense when the primary owner depends on the guy putting in the effort for his profit. It is the same reasoning that is behind stock option compensation for corporate executives.

Borrow Against Paper

If you own second mortgages, trust deeds, or real estate contracts secured by property you have previously sold, consider using them as collateral for acquisition funds.

A second mortgage is a depreciating "debt" investment. Real property is normally considered to be an appreciating "equity" investment. Borrowing against your depreciating paper to buy appreciating income property is a method of converting the asset to cash without disposing of it.

As payments are received on your paper-collateral, they are applied directly to repayment of the loan. The value stored in the paper which was formerly diminishing with each principal payment and each jump in inflation is now stored in an appreciating investment. The transition step in getting there was borrowing against the paper to generate the cash necessary to meet the down payment requirements of the seller. The net effect of the procedure is reinvestment of a portion of your capital gain while deferring the tax on the balance.

The amount you can borrow against secured paper will depend somewhat on your relationship with the lender. Standard practice uses about 50 percent of the face value of the paper as a rule-of-thumb. The amount may vary up or down based on your equity and lien position. The condition and value of the property securing the paper will also be a factor. You may be able to borrow more if the property securing the paper is sound and if you have a solid position that will allow a quick discount sale in the event of default.

This technique is based on the principle of moving the value you have to the property you want. You just hitch a ride on borrowed cash to make the move.

Seller Pays Buyer

It may be somewhat of a surprise to you that a seller of real estate in today's market would actually pay someone to buy his property. But, really, when you consider the spectrum of human nature, the scenario leading to this technique is not difficult to understand. The instances in which I have seen this happen were both rather large properties with correspondingly large debt. Sellers were anxious to get out from under the obligations and use their energies in more productive pursuits. Furthermore, it was going to take some cash to turn the performance of the properties around.

In some cases an overextended property owner who doesn't have the expertise or inclination to deal with real estate that is losing money and becoming a drain on other income and a threat to his healthy assets can be a most willing negotiator. His cooperation can even extend to providing the cash necessary to offset the risk he is transferring to the buyer. Cases like this illustrate the fact that all real estate is not necessarily appropriate for all investors. In any event, this technique allows an owner to get out of a bad situation which may even be damaging his health.

As a practical matter, the cash advanced by the seller may by necessity be put back into the property to finance the changes needed to make it productive. This cash outlay by the seller is not necessarily a negotiated gift. It can also be structured as a loan secured by the acquired property. Consequently, the seller can act as lender, selling to someone who can do the job and financing his efforts to do it. There are situations in real estate as in general business, that require an infusion of cash to operate productively. A seller who puts up money to protect his equity and other assets may be making a sound business move.

Acquire with Future Profits

If you are going into a project that has doubtful cash flow, this technique may balance part of the risk. It is a deferred down payment method that is tied to the profitability of the property you are acquiring.

The value of the target property may be there based on comparable sales and replacement cost analysis, but it may lack the income to justify the owner's equity requirement. The source of the income problem may be poor management, a lack of demand, or a mistake in the design of the property, such as inadequate parking. Regardless of the cause, you should see a ready solution before taking on the problem.

This is the type of opportunity that will allow you to negotiate your way into ownership and pay for it by virtue of your entrepreneurial and management skills. As the property begins to show a net profit above a predetermined monthly amount, the seller receives a payment toward his equity. Every dollar above the agreed-upon monthly minimum goes to the seller. The faster you turn the property around, the faster the seller is paid. He shares the risk by waiting for payment until the property produces.

The objective of this technique is to give you enough margin to make a losing investment a producer without the pressure and risk of laying out a cash down payment. It is a method of making a property pay its own way while giving the right buyer an incentive to see that the job gets done.

Acquire with Closing Credits

This is an approach that uses time to your direct advantage. It combines the mechanics of closing with planned timing to offset the net cash you must pay at closing. This technique uses routine closing calculations to your advantage.

When you buy toward the end of the tax year but before property taxes are due, and a few days after the rent on the property is due, you are in line for certain cash benefits. Although the net effect may depend on the type of loan you're assuming, the proration of taxes and rents will usually reduce the amount of cash needed to close.

When you close after a significant portion of the year has passed during which the seller was liable for property taxes, you will be credited with the amount of the seller's tax liability. Then when the property tax bills come due, you will pay them directly for the entire year. Until the tax bills are due you have use of that money. And the routine first use is to credit you with a portion of the down payment.

Of equal importance is the proration of rents. When you close a few days after the rent is due, you will usually receive credit for the balance of the rent representing the remaining days in the month. You own the property as of the day of closing, so you get the rent for the rest of the month. Timing your purchase and planning the routine math in your favor can significantly reduce the cash due at closing and often entirely eliminate it when combined with other techniques. Always figure out your net cash due at closing *after prorations* before deciding you don't have enough money for a down payment.

Assign the Rents

When you are borrowing the down payment from a bank and need additional security, this approach may help out. The income stream from the property you are acquiring is itself a source of security. It has value and can be used as loan collateral.

If the terms of the existing loans on the property you are acquiring do not stipulate that the rents have previously been assigned, you have made it past the first barrier. All you need is an "assignment of rents" agreement drawn by a knowledgeable real estate lawyer and a loan officer willing to accept it as backup for your signature on a loan.

A properly written assignment gives the lender the right to impound the rents to pay the loan in the event of default. This added security for the down payment loan may just be the edge you need to satisfy your banker.

Of course, you are negotiating what is essentially a commercial signature loan, and the bank will normally look to your total financial statement and credit history in making the decision. Any form of security you can provide will simply make your chances of success that much better. By assigning the rents, you give the bank additional collateral to meet the ever-present need of satisfying bank examiners—a requirement your loan officer must always keep in mind. When you know of ways to beef up the security for your loan, you just make it that much easier for a loan officer to help you. Keep in mind that a cash-flow history and projection on the property you are acquiring is required backup material when you are applying for a down payment loan, regardless of the security you offer.

Acquire with a Repair Partnership

Property that needs rehabilitation may be a headache for the owner but it is an opportunity for you to put together a repair partnership. Start by determining potential partners who have skills that will upgrade the property. A plumber, an electrician, a carpenter, and other needed trades contribute their work toward the down payment. Each receives a percentage of ownership equal to the value of the work contributed. The improvements increase the property's value, thereby replacing the seller's need for some evidence that the buyers won't default.

The seller takes his equity on a purchase money mortgage and in effect has greater security by virtue of the rehabilitation than with a nominal cash down payment.

The work done by the partners serves as security to the seller that the buyers have put true value into the property and won't readily default on the loans. The sales price can even be negotiated upward to reflect the added value as a result of the renovation contributions if necessary. This would increase the face amount of the purchase money mortgage.

There is also a way of determining the sales price based on the rehabilitation costs. If the work contributed by the partners represents 20 percent of the ultimate market value of the property after repairs, the sales price would then be 80 percent of that figure.

Consequently, the note and mortgage to the seller is 80 percent of the eventual value, which may be more or less than the original asking price.

Sometimes the only way to save a property from going downhill is to bring it back up with an infusion of long overdue repairs. A seller who realizes this may ultimately come out ahead and avoid the serious loss that may otherwise have occurred if the deterioration of the property had not been stopped.

The Note Partnership

Several small notes signed by a number of individuals can be better security than one large note signed by one person. Ten $9,000 notes from different people, each having a net worth of $90,000, is sounder security than a note from one person with a net worth equal to the face value of the note. Acquisition partnerships that realize the negotiation advantage of buying as a group can be quite successful.

An additional advantage to this method is the flexibility it provides the seller. If he needs cash from time to time, he can discount and sell one of the notes without stepping into a tax liability for the entire profit—installment reporting can be protected.

Security for the notes can be handled in a couple of ways. A mortgage on the acquired property could serve as security for all the notes. Another approach is to have each of the partners secure his note by a separate mortgage placed on different property owned outside the partnership. In fact, for example, individual residences may prove to be better collateral in the eyes of the seller than the property he sold.

If the property acquired is used to secure the notes, it is important to word the documents so that a default by one partner would trigger default of the entire property. This is to protect the seller. The notes and mortgage should also be written to protect the other partners by giving them the right to step in and cure a default by one of the other members.

Negotiating a no-cash acquisition can sometimes be accomplished more easily by spreading the liability (and security) among several people.

Advertise for a Private Loan

This method of raising acquisition capital proves the rule that you never really know what is possible until you try. Venture capital provided by individuals and privately owned companies has historically been the foundation of new business. It is no different in real estate. One young real estate entrepreneur turned a steady credit line provided by a wise and trusting widow into a multimillion dollar company. The right kind of financial backing has helped more than one hard-working person to the top, and it can just as easily happen to you as the next guy.

If you have found what seems to be one of those rare opportunities to buy that come along when you are least prepared financially, consider advertising for a private loan. With a project that has solid potential, you can offer higher-than-usual interest and a percentage of the profits if necessary. You may be surprised at the response if your ad request clearly reflects the unique opportunity you perceive in the property.

There are people with money who know a good opportunity when it is presented to them and want an above-average return for their willingness to take a chance. You may already know of someone like this or of a company that specializes in what is traditionally considered high-risk venture capital lending. If you do, it may not be necessary to advertise. But if you don't, why not try an ad?

With the general acceptance of real estate as a solid hedge against inflation, many of the difficulties of long ago are reversed. People are now searching for ways to participate in the growth of real estate. One way without the management demands of direct ownership is by lending money to people who have found a good buy.

Commission as Down Payment

This acquisition technique illustrates one of the real benefits of being a licensed real estate agent. I have met people who have entered the real estate brokerage business mainly because of the commission benefit when they acquire property for their own account.

In some ways, being active in the real estate brokerage business is very similar to having a seat on the New York Stock Exchange. You are in the middle of the action and can see opportunities while they are still in the formative stage. And you can cut the cost of entry by the amount of your own fee when you buy for your own account.

Real estate commissions are generally paid in cash at closing of the transaction. The net effect of paying a commission is to reduce both the sales price and the cash received by the seller. Conversely, when a broker invests for his own account, the net effect of receiving a commission is reduction of both the price and cash required for down payment.

From a practical standpoint, this technique is applied during negotiation to eliminate the unnecessary payment and repayment of cash between buyer and seller. There is really no need to run the commission through the hands of the escrow agent from the buyer to the seller as down payment and back to the buyer in the form of commission. The obvious alternative is to agree during negotiation to reduce the sales price by the amount of the commission and deduct it from the cash down payment.

Credit Union Loan

If you are a member of a credit union, you have an inside track for getting an acquisition loan. Furthermore, the interest rate and terms are often more easy to digest than those of the neighborhood bank.

Employee credit unions exist essentially for the benefit of the employees. If you have the good fortune of belonging to an institution that has a credit union, it should be considered among your first sources for an acquisition loan.

The process is not unlike that of a bank. It is just easier sometimes because of the inter-relationship between the credit union, your job, and your employer. There is less risk from the credit union's point of view—they know you have a job and the degree of your security in that job.

The amount of the loan and the type of collateral, if any, will vary based on your income and the money you have on deposit with the credit union. But the point is that the credit union is there for your benefit, and using it for real estate acquisition capital is one of the best ways to get your benefit out.

Real Estate Equity as Down Payment

This technique is really a form of real estate exchange and has an amazing number of very effective applications. For our purposes, though, it is useful in developing a somewhat different view of the ways you can use the real estate you now own.

Equity in real estate is one of the most effective forms of purchasing power available to investors today. It can be a tax-free, inflation-resistant, and relatively liquid asset when you know the unique exchange techniques.

As you may know, when certain legal requirements are met you can exchange investment real estate for different investment real estate without paying tax on the profit. This special real estate opportunity is provided by Section 1031 of the Internal Revenue Code and has an incredible number of variations.

For example, if you have located a larger investment property which better suits your objectives than the property you now own, consider making an exchange. In effect, when you exchange, the equity in your property serves as the down payment for the property you acquire. If you receive no cash or other boot and assume larger loans, you will pay no tax on the disposition of your original property. This tax advantage alone makes exchanging mandatory in many cases for wise investors—why sell and pay tax when you can exchange tax-free?

In addition, when you use exchanging to build your estate you can eliminate the need to raise cash. The erroneous objection that has often unnecessarily stopped sound exchanges is the unfounded assumption that the owner of the property you want doesn't want your property. You never know until you try. And even if the seller won't accept your property, there is an easy and routine method of structuring an exchange for you and a sale for him. You simply enter into an agreement to exchange, contingent on the sale of your property out of escrow.

Using the real estate you have to acquire the real estate you want makes good sense when the alternative is selling, paying tax, and buying with the money you have left over.

Family Loan

Don't overlook the possibility of borrowing from family members to raise the cash you need for a worthwhile investment. How many people have been forced by circumstances to borrow occasionally from close family to get through difficult times? Borrowing to acquire solid-investment real estate makes a lot more sense in many ways.

When the investment opportunity is unique and liable to slip through your fingers if you don't act fast, consider talking it over with the people who care about you the most. There are a lot of benefits here: no credit check, probably a fast OK, and the loan application can probably be made over the dinner table. Seriously, though, you may actually be doing a family friend a favor by providing good security and higher interest than a savings account. Furthermore, giving someone a chance to help you is often more rewarding for them personally than leaving unneeded money in the bank to be chewed away by inflation.

The point here, as with all acquisition techniques, is that you must consider all funding alternatives and combinations of alternatives, and borrowing among family is one of the most often-used and successful ones.

Acquisition with Soft Paper

Soft paper refers to loans that have low initial payments. The terms can be structured for interest only at the beginning, with an increased principal reduction later. The term of the loan is also lengthened in certain cases to meet the objective of this technique, which is to "soften" the impact of the payments on the buyer. Therefore, when you acquire real estate with soft paper, the transaction is set up to make the monthly payments easy for you.

High prices have forced many lenders to accept longer term financing for new car loans as well as government-sponsored and conventional home mortgages. This continuing institutional trend has made the use of soft paper more easily accepted in real estate negotiations. In the past, soft paper was normally used on purchase money mortgages when prices ran up and credit tightened. Now it is the only way many people can afford a car or home.

Soft paper allows you to acquire the property you want even when the price is higher than the property's income can support under a conventional lending situation.

When the seller is adamant about his price but not concerned about when he gets it, soft paper can often make the deal workable. If you can pay the asking price, although high, by making the down payment with a soft second mortgage, it is possible to come out ahead in the long run, provided inflation continues.

Although finding sound real estate is the major problem, getting control of it is equally challenging. Property priced at the top price for today's value may be cheap after a few years' appreciation, but it won't do you any good if you cannot gain control today. Try paying the full price with a low-interest, low-payment second mortgage that the income can cover. Be sure to cover your risk by avoiding personal liability. In the event of default, limit the seller to repossession of the property. If you think the property you want shows enough promise to warrant paying top dollar and the seller also thinks it is that valuable, there should be little worry about default. If you are concerned about losing it, maybe you should look for another deal.

Acquire with a First and Second—Then Sell the First for Cash

If you are negotiating the acquisition of free and clear property and the seller wants more cash than you have, here's a method of supplying it.

First mortgages are more easily sold and at less of a discount than second paper. In this cashless approach, the seller receives two purchase money mortgages: a first mortgage and a second. The purchaser pays no cash.

The purchase agreement is made contingent on locating a buyer for the first mortgage at a price satisfactory to the seller. The sale of the first mortgage therefore occurs concurrently with your acquisition of the property. But it doesn't have to. The seller may get a better price for the mortgage by waiting until it is seasoned. The seller receives the net proceeds from the sale of the first mortgage and keeps the second mortgage. The buyer pays no cash, yet the seller gets the cash he wants.

The purpose of splitting the acquisition between a first and second lien position is to establish a relatively large equity and security position for the buyer of the first mortgage. This will usually reduce the discount necessary to sell the paper.

If the seller doesn't like the idea of discounting the sales price by virtue of the first mortgage sale, you can make up the difference with the second. Just increase the face amount of the second by the amount of the discount. Work in an equal discount amount for an early pay-off of the second. Another alternative is to compensate the seller for the discount by adding periodic balloon payments in addition to the regular monthly payments on the second. The point here is to negotiate whatever is necessary to gain control of the property, provided the ultimate profit you make will offset the risk you take.

Collateral Security Agreement

If an owner will not sell without a down payment because he is worried about "getting the property back," this approach may serve to quiet his concerns.

Offer to buy the property with no cash down on a purchase money second. In addition, offer to secure your performance on the second by providing other property you own as collateral.

The equity value of the collateral property should at least equal the amount of the down payment previously requested. You get in for no cash and the seller gets the security he needs to offset his fears about getting the property back.

The security agreement should be properly drawn by your lawyer and tied to the payment of the mortgage on the property you are acquiring. It should provide for transfer of the collateral to the seller if you default. It should also provide for release of the additional collateral when the second is paid down to a certain figure. For example, you might include a provision that automatically releases the collateral when the mortgage is reduced by an amount equal to the down payment the seller had originally requested.

Another alternative is to provide for release of the collateral when the acquired property exceeds a certain value as verified by independent appraisal. Calculation of the release provision under this formula is based on the percentage relationship between the new owner's equity and the balance of the loans. When the balance of the mortgage is 75 percent of the property value, it is in effect the same as making a 25 percent down payment.

Borrow Against Your Trust

If you have money that is tied up in a trust, consider the possibility of borrowing against it. You may not be able to bust the trust and you may not even want to. But if you are fortunate enough to have located sound investment real estate and need to raise acquisition funds, this can be a solid approach.

Bank trust departments often have a difficult time making money on their investments, much less keeping up with inflation or matching the performance of real estate. Taking a hard-nosed business look at what the trust department is doing to your money may be a good idea anyway. You may find a move to investment real estate long overdue.

Trusts generally must meet certain liquidity requirements. This makes trust assets excellent collateral. Also there is usually an attempt to balance the portfolio with income producing assets—normally stocks and bonds that have no aura of risk attached to them.

Consequently, you may have two advantages in borrowing against a trust. You have liquid assets that can usually be converted to cash within a few days and you have income that can be applied toward reducing the money you borrow.

Borrowing against your trust income now to get into sound income producing and appreciating real estate can greatly improve the overall performance of the trust portfolio when you finally do gain full control.

Land Sale Lease-Back

In the last analysis land is the true source of real estate appreciation. Improvements may cost more temporarily due to inflation, but eventually they will waste away. Insurance companies have recognized this long-term value of land and are actively acquiring well-located commercial income properties. This growing acceptance of the pivotal role of land values in the economic future is the basis for an effective acquisition technique.

With certain types of property you can raise down payment funds by setting up a land sale lease-back. The process involves arranging a sale of the land under the improvements you're acquiring and leasing it back. The land sale is made prior to your closing, subject to the existing first mortgage, but provides protection for the new landowner by allowing him to step in if there's a default on either the mortgage or the land lease. The proceeds from the land sale go to the seller of the property you are acquiring as down payment to cash out his equity.

Consequently, you in effect acquire a leasehold interest without cash. You receive the direct benefit from rental income and tax shelter for the life of the lease.

Although you are giving up fee ownership with this approach, you may be making a transaction not otherwise possible. There is also the possibility of another benefit here. Depending on the mathematics of the transaction, you may actually be able to sell the land for more than the necessary down payment and pocket the difference. This technique is generally suitable only for larger transactions that have appeal to real estate investment trusts and other large institutional investors with long-range appreciation in mind.

The Lease Down Payment

When you are buying from someone who is both owner and tenant of the property, this technique can help offset the down payment.

Consider offering the seller use of the property as down payment. If he plans to keep his business in the same location anyway, you have an opportunity to cover part of the down payment. Essentially, you trade a short-term lease for the down payment.

The seller gets continuing use of his established business location for the term of the lease instead of a cash down payment. You get the property with all its burdens and benefits but without the outlay of cash.

The purpose of this technique is to make a direct move between buyer and seller without the unnecessary step of running cash through the hands of the buyer, then to the seller, and back to the buyer again. Furthermore, if you are able to negotiate beneficial use of the rent before you receive it, you pick up a time value advantage which makes the rent worth more when applied in lump sum to the down payment than it was when received monthly.

The Installment Down Payment

This technique allows you to acquire property now but pay the seller's equity by making installment payments as you raise the cash. The income from the acquired property offsets the down payment installments, permitting you to avoid a lump sum cash outlay at closing.

For example, if you negotiate quarterly down payment installments of $3,000 and the cash flow is $500 per month, your net out-of-pocket cost will be only $1,500 per quarter.

The installment payments are secured by placing a purchase-money second mortgage on the property you are acquiring. As an alternative, consider negotiating an unsecured personal note payable to the seller.

This method can be helpful when you need time to raise a down payment but have competition for the property from other buyers. A pipeline to commercial loan funds won't do you any good if the property is bought out from under you. Tying it down by offering a deferred down payment arrangement such as this is far better than missing a good buy. Lenders and other funding sources often can't move as fast as you need to maintain a competitive stance in fast moving markets.

Assume the Mortgage—Seller Keeps the Land

This technique permits the seller to retain the long-term benefits of land appreciation while realizing the income benefits of selling the improvements. The seller keeps the land under the improvements instead of receiving a down payment.

There are several ways of structuring this acquisition method that allow you to vary the negotiations to fit the details of the property. As buyer, your primary objective is to acquire the income and tax benefits of ownership by leaving the long-term land benefits to the seller. Retaining land ownership with lease income can be quite an incentive to the seller. Of course, the incentive for you is acquisition of sheltered income without cash.

Although this is technically a leasehold acquisition, you do assume the existing loans and all the burdens and benefits except land ownership.

One key to negotiating the offer is to accurately split the asking price between the land and improvement values. An imbalance between the two is not desirable. Any difference between the land value and the balance of the existing loans would be paid on a purchase-money second mortgage.

It is conceivable then that you may end up making three monthly payments: the first mortgage, the purchase-money second, and the land lease. Obviously, it is important to make sure that the income is there to meet the payments. After all, this technique is designed to acquire tax-sheltered cash flow. A real danger in any leased land acquisition is the escalation clause which is generally negotiated by the seller. It is worth a fight to keep any lease payment increase to a minimum.

The Executive Incentive Plan

If you work for a successful privately owned company, the solution to your real-estate acquisition program may be at the office. Incentive programs have long been recognized as essential to maximum employee performance. This fact of business life combines with the inflation hedge benefits of real estate to form a technique with solid benefits.

There are several ways to work this cashless acquisition method into a company incentive program. In one case an insurance agency had trouble attracting and keeping good salesmen. In an attempt to provide an incentive that would solve the problem, the owner set up an inter-company real estate sharing program. The company acquired a large office building and arranged for sales staff ownership participation which increased to a certain percentage based on time with the company. If an employee left without working a reasonable time period, he forfeited ownership in the building. The sales staff grew and made monthly income while building an appreciating net worth because of the foresight of this creative businessman.

Another approach to this acquisition formula is founded on individual employee initiative. If you have a secure relationship with your employer, consider asking to use the company credit line to back up your signature for a down payment loan. Both private and institutional lenders look favorably on loans that are backed by successful corporations. Any loan agreement of this sort should provide for release of the corporation when an appropriate principal reduction is made.

The 100 Percent Solution

One of the most straightforward ways to acquire real estate without cash is to assume the existing first mortgage and execute a second-position purchase money mortgage for the entire amount of the seller's equity.

If the seller does not need cash and is satisfied with your track record, a second mortgage secured by his property may be all that is needed to make the deal. This technique is especially designed for sellers who have faith in their property and its future income potential.

A frequent application of this technique occurs when the seller just wants out and is willing to take what equity he has on paper. In this type of situation, the purchase-money mortgage you offer has more value to the seller than his property. There are more benefits in not owning some property for some sellers than owning it, regardless of the potential you may see in it. This opportunity usually follows depressed markets and is a rare find in high growth areas.

It is a fact of real estate that you are better off not assuming what a seller will do. If you want a certain property, you owe it to yourself to offer to buy it any way you can. Anybody with experience in real estate acquisition will tell you that it is filled with more surprises than you could possibly anticipate—and many of them will be in your favor.

The Performance Second

The performance second is used in various applications including acquisitions with and without cash. It is a downright test of the seller's faith in the value he places on his property.

With this approach you agree to pay the seller's asking price but make the payments on the second-purchase money mortgage contingent on the income of the property. The selling price is calculated based on the return that the seller represents you will realize from the property. Consequently, you are in effect asking the seller to share your estimate of risk since you are accepting his estimate of value.

If the cash flow is not there, the seller doesn't get paid on the purchase-money second mortgage. But if the property performs as the seller represents it will, the payment is made for that month. As an incentive to accept this performance-based payment method, you can negotiate an increase in the payments if the property is more profitable than the seller projected. Setting it up this way allows you and the seller to benefit if he is right. The main purpose, of course, is to protect yourself from overpriced deals by tying the down payment to the property's performance.

Of course, to fairly measure the income, you must separate operating and capital expense items so that one-time replacements are amortized over their useful lives rather than charged in lump sum against a certain month's cash flow. If the seller refuses to cooperate with this approach, you might question the accuracy of the property's performance projections.

Broker as Lender

If you are working with a successful broker, don't overlook the possibility of approaching him as a lending source.

When you consider that he will receive a commission out of the down payment, provided the deal goes through, you can see that he has a real stake in the success of the negotiations. It may be that your broker doesn't have an immediate need for the cash from the commission other than finding a high return investment.

By giving him the opportunity to loan you the cash you need to make the deal, you both benefit. He generates income and places it in a debt investment at the same time. When the alternative is failure because you are short of cash, an aggressive broker will usually lend a helping hand. And for a real estate broker there's no better pay-off than saving a transaction that almost slips through his fingers.

The Hidden Co-Signer

If you have found solid investment property, you have the most difficult job behind you. When you reach this point don't let not having enough money to close stand in your way. There is always a method of getting the job done—you just may not have found it yet.

One of the most easily overlooked sources of that all-important credit line so essential to real estate acquisition may be closer than you think. If you have located that right deal but the bank won't lend you the money to make the down payment, look for a co-signer. An old friend may be more than interested in helping out. A rich aunt who thinks the world of you may be overjoyed to start you on your way to building a solid estate. All possibilities must be considered when the alternative is losing a unique real estate buy. You may be pleasantly surprised at the help you can find when you strongly believe in what you are doing.

The Insurance Policy Loan

If you have built up cash value in a life insurance policy over the years, consider the direct benefits of borrowing against it to buy real estate. Insurance policy loans are one of the cheapest sources of money around. And borrowing against your cash value is like getting your own money back while using it for loan collateral at the same time.

Furthermore, you provide the best additional collateral possible—your own life. And when you think about it, it's hardly a loan—it's really your money which you, in fact, have a right to under the qualifying conditions of the insurance policy. Many young couples have bought their first house when the husband suddenly realized that the insurance policy a friend sold him in college was like money in the bank.

Issue Stock

Form a corporation and issue stock to sellers for their equity. It solves the sellers' management problems and starts a real estate business for you.

The property owner receives an equity position in the corporation and the corporation gets an asset. This approach not only reduces the management responsibilities of the owner, but it also provides a degree of diversification.

A real estate corporation with several properties is able to spread the risks of ownership and increase the possibility that some of the properties will perform profitably.

Trade Stock at Purchase Price

Both listed and unlisted stocks and bonds offer a method of acquiring real estate even if the market price of the stock has fallen below your purchase price.

Try trading your stock at the price you paid for it. Who knows—you may find out that the owner has more faith in the stock than in his real estate.

In cases where management requirements are a problem, it is possible that the release from the burdens of ownership would appeal more to the seller than the relative value of your stock.

Furthermore, it is possible that both the property and the stock will increase in value.

Signature Loan

One of the most often used methods of acquiring real estate is to borrow the down payment on your signature. The loan is granted based on your ability to repay. Your job and future income prospects are looked to by the lender.

The objective is to repay a portion of the loan with income from the property and renew it if necessary, eventually repaying it in full with income from the property.

This is essentially a fast method of borrowing money for a good investment opportunity, which uses income from the real estate to repay the loan.

Employer Advance

Under the right job conditions, it may prove feasible to borrow or get a salary advance from your employer to use as a down payment. Then use the income from the property and a portion of your salary to pay your employer back.

Of course, this approach requires the right conditions. But an understanding employer may be relieved to loan you money when the alternative is to give you a long overdue salary increase.

Furthermore, your job becomes security for the loan and your loan becomes security for your job. What employer wants to fire an employee and lose the source of repayment for a loan?

Credit for Services Certificate

By an agreement between buyer and seller, the buyer may reduce the balance of a note held in escrow by sending a credit certificate signed by the seller and buyer, instructing the escrow company to reduce the principal balance by an agreed amount.

For example, a dentist who buys property may make an agreement with the seller to trade dental work for loan reduction payments on owner-carried financing.

This method allows the payment of a note held in escrow with services. It is also a good method of keeping a record of the amount paid by services. A coupon book of certificates can be printed for ongoing use.

Secured Corporate Note

If you are acquiring real estate for your corporation, offer a corporate note secured by specific assets of the corporation—but, not secured by the real estate you are acquiring.

Essentially the note becomes the down payment, with additional owner financing secured by the property. In some cases it may be possible to acquire the property free of debt, using the corporate assets as full security for the loan necessary to acquire the property.

You may want to require release of certain corporate assets as the principal amount of the loan is reduced.

Multiple Notes—One Mortgage

When you are acquiring real estate in a partnership without a down payment, the seller may be more willing to accept separate notes secured by only one mortgage on the property.

This method will provide greater flexibility if the seller plans to discount and sell the notes for cash as needed in the future.

Also, it places an obligation on the individual note signatories as members of the partnership. If one were to default, the others would be in danger of foreclosure and more likely to step in to preserve their equity.

Pledge Future Income as Down Payment

If you have a secure job or future investment income, negotiate with the seller to have your bank deduct a specific amount from your checking account each month until the amount the seller wanted as down payment is paid.

As additional security, you can give the seller a mortgage on other property to secure your performance under the agreement. You get immediate ownership, and the seller eventually gets the down payment.

16

Institutional
Financing Techniques

If you know the loan variations possible with institutional lenders you can increase your chances of getting the financing you need. Real estate is a credit-dependent industry, and when you know how to work with lenders you're ahead of the game.

Any loan officer will look more favorably on someone who applies for a loan with a sound plan in hand—especially one that will make a profit for his company with little or no risk.

Furthermore, even when what you propose is not within the power of the lender to grant, you establish a starting point for building a plan that is workable. Sometimes a slight change in the way your proposed financing is structured will make the deal.

Easy credit and tight money are the extremes of the lending industry. More than any other business group, lenders are at the mercy of the economics of politics. Government monetary policy will by necessity vary with the national economic cycle in continuing attempts to avoid depressions and moderate inflation.

From the standpoint of an individual investor who simply wants to operate profitably within the massive unknowns of the marketplace, a few rifle shot specifics of the lending industry can help. When you know what's possible, you can choose the approach that meets your needs. When you know both what's possible and what meets your needs, you know what to ask for.

New financing methods are being developed continually, especially in the area of government-backed programs. Often the solution to your financing needs is to ferret out that hidden government program no one else knows about.

Conventional lending policy varies throughout the country, depending on the local market and the money supply. When you are faced with a lender who is not familiar with what you propose, don't lose faith. No one can be aware of all possibilities in this fast moving industry. Furthermore, a technique unfamiliar to your lender is not necessarily an unworkable technique. The best institutional lenders compete for loans and pride themselves on their ability to creatively meet the needs of their customers. New technology in any industry spreads fastest when the profit motive is the driving force. Techniques used in one market can often work equally well in others and just because they haven't as yet been introduced doesn't mean they are unworkable. Lenders want to make loans that are risk-free and profitable. Any application for funds that you make must be designed to meet your objectives.

Wraparound Mortgage

A wraparound mortgage is an excellent method of obtaining a high loan yield without the usual requirement of lending the full face amount of the loan in cash. It is a method of refinancing and cashing out the seller without paying off the current loans.

For example, an older center priced at $400,000 with $100,000 down subject to an existing $100,000 first-mortgage-bearing $7\frac{1}{2}$% interest is a likely candidate. The new first mortgage is written subject to the existing first mortgage and "wraps around" it. In some areas this financing procedure is referred to as "all inclusive" and is set up with trust deeds.

You make loan payments to the new lender who is responsible for making the payments on the existing $7\frac{1}{2}$% first mortgage. The new loan has a face amount of $300,000 bearing $9\frac{1}{2}$% interest, but the new lender is required to provide only $200,000 cash. The additional $100,000 is covered by the first mortgage already on the property. Therefore, the lender collects $9\frac{1}{2}$% interest on the new $200,000 cash and an additional 2% interest on the $100,000 represented by the existing loan—$100,000 in capital the lender did not have to supply.

This approach is a solution to tight money and provides an incentive to the lender with no increase in acquisition costs. The wraparound lender is fully protected. The seller cashes out his position entirely and you are able to leverage the acquisition by establishing financing that might not otherwise be available.

Open End Mortgage

Under certain conditions you may borrow back the principal paid on conventional real estate loans. This type of equity loan has grown in popularity as real estate values have increased, but can vary greatly with money market conditions and lender's policies.

The basic approach works like this. If your original loan was $150,000 and over the years it was paid down to $125,000, you have the possibility of reborrowing the $25,000 you've paid and maybe more.

An open end mortgage allows you to generate nontaxable cash for reinvestment, for further development, or capital improvements on the property. The lender is able to increase the face amount of the principal and thereby increase the total dollar income from interest. Lenders normally charge fees for this service which are part of the incentive to do it and well worth the cost to you if you can make money with the new money you borrow.

Sale Buy-Back

This technique provides an additional source of profit for lenders and another source of incentive to provide financing. In this approach the developer sells his land to the lending institution and immediately buys it back on paper with release clauses. The developer gets cash from the sale to build, and the lender gets an equity position that increases its profit beyond the restrictions normally imposed by a loan. It also gives the lender maximum security.

This technique allows a developer to arrange financing in a tight money market by providing an incentive to a lending institution through equity participation at the buy-back point. The developer buys the land back on paper and uses the cash from the sale to develop the property.

Equity-Kicker

An equity-kicker can often mean the difference between closing a loan at a reasonable interest rate and not making the loan at all. It provides the lender with a percentage of the income generated by the property in excess of a certain amount.

For example, if the projected base income from a shopping center is $400,000 per year, the loan might stipulate that the lender will receive 15% of everything collected above $400,000. An equity-kicker may also call for a percentage of the sale price to go to the lender if the property is sold above a specified price during the first few years of the loan. A skillfully negotiated equity-kicker can attract financing in tight markets or with higher risk projects. It gives that additional incentive often needed to complete a loan— a potentially higher yield.

R.E.O. as Incentive to Finance

Lending institutions that are burdened with REOs, or "real estate owned" (repossessed property), look more kindly toward making a loan to an investor who concurrently arranges to buy an REO.

You can look on a bank's balance sheet and see the value of the "real estate owned." This property represents an undesirable asset for the lending institution because of the pressure from state banking regulations which limit the time period REOs can be carried on the books.

Repossessed property is a source of available real estate which can often be acquired on favorable terms. It can also serve as a point of negotiation if you're trying to work out a loan. Acquisition of an unwanted REO is contingent on the bank providing the financing you need.

There are many ways banks can help you reach financial objectives. The occasional availability of REOs is another reason it pays to develop a good banking relationship. It's a source of real estate, and, with the growing competition for property, every source of potentially profitable deals should be regularly cultivated.

Certificate of Deposit Delivery

When a lender is reluctant to refinance property, offer to deposit a portion of the refinance proceeds in the form of a certificate of deposit (time deposit). Redepositing funds from a loan or opening an account with a sizable deposit can often make the difference between getting a loan and not.

Using only part of the proceeds of the refinance to acquire additional real estate is better than not being able to raise the funds at all. Banks and savings and loans need deposits. If you can arrange deposits, chances are that your loan application will get a higher priority than that of someone who can't. The lender benefits by putting a new loan on the books, while concurrently obtaining additional deposits. In times of rapid savings withdrawal, this type of incentive makes a real difference in the decision as to who gets a loan.

Collateral Assignment

This technique is designed to help when you negotiate a first mortgage and the lender questions your ability to repay the loan or the adequacy of the real estate you offer as security.

To solve the problem, offer to assign different property as additional security for the loan. The security is encumbered by the bank until the loan is reduced to a certain amount. The process involves a simple pledge of assets by agreement. The collateral may be other real property or personal property. Listed securities are often used.

This technique can help you obtain a loan at a "higher loan to value" ratio. In certain situations, it can increase your leverage and significantly improve your return. But, as with all highly financed acquisitions, care must be taken to ensure that the investment will safely produce enough income to pay back the loan and show a profit—the potential reward must justify the obvious risk.

Negative Pledge

A negative pledge is used to protect a bank. It helps you obtain a commercial loan when the bank is relying on the condition of your financial statement at the point in time the decision is made to grant the loan.

The negative pledge differs from a regular pledge by stating that something will not be done. This contrasts with a traditional security pledge agreement which encumbers a specific asset.

A negative pledge states that you will not encumber or dispose of any of the assets listed on your financial statement without written permission of the bank. If you violate the pledge agreement, the loan automatically becomes due. The bank is lending money based on your financial statement and the net worth it reflects at the time of the loan. Consequently, with a negative pledge, the bank is ensuring that the basis for the loan remains sound. The negative pledge fixes your assets and if you want to take action that may change your financial position the bank has a chance to protect the loan. In a way this is a method for the bank to monitor your finances over the life of the loan.

Pledging to maintain a financial statement in the condition that it was in at the time that the bank agreed to make the loan is a small concession if the loan is important to you.

Letter of Credit

A letter of credit is a useful acquisition tool. Under the right conditions it's as effective as money. It can be used as an earnest money deposit or as a down payment collectible when and if the transaction closes and the documents are recorded. It is an excellent method of tying up and acquiring real estate.

A letter of credit can fit into a variety of situations. For example, it is advantageous when a financially weak but energetic entrepreneur is backed by a financially strong investment partner or group of partners. The backer does not have to come up with cash unless the limiting conditions in the letter of credit are met. A letter of credit is usually exercisable only after a certain date and only if certain agreed events occur.

When used as earnest money it may, for instance, be exercised only after a commitment for financing is secured. If the limiting conditions of the purchase agreement are not met by a certain date, it expires automatically. The key is to never exercise the letter of credit but gain time with it to arrange financing. Attempt to mortgage out before the letter is collectible or purchase property for resale and turn it over at a profit without exercising the letter of credit used as earnest money.

For a seller, the letter of credit is solid protection in the event of default on the purchase agreement. When you're acquiring property with it, it is an effective method of providing earnest money consideration with someone else's line of credit.

Compensating Balances

Many banks will loan money when they are assured of receiving compensating balances equal to the amount loaned. This allows a bank to maintain its deposit-loan ratio, and, in some cases, may be the only way it can make the loan without depleting reserves. Helping lenders meet the requirements imposed by regulatory agencies and corporate policy is often the only way to get the cash you need.

It is normal practice to loan only to clients who maintain accounts with the bank providing the funds. It's virtually a prerequisite. But if money is tight it sometimes takes even more to get the loan you need.

A solution that is quite effective involves arranging the deposit of compensating balances by a third party. Your line of credit is therefore offset by compensating balances placed with your bank through an arrangement with another business.

Normally the process is worked out with a company who wants your business. Title companies with large amounts of cash in transit can be helpful in this area when the end result is an increase in real estate closings for them.

Advance Payments Deposit

You can sometimes convince a lender of your ability to repay a loan by depositing a certain number of the monthly payments at the time the loan funds are disbursed. For example, your agreement might require deposit of the first year's payments at closing and the second year's payments at the beginning of the second year. You would actually be paying monthly payments in advance annually.

This technique is a way of buying time to establish credit in a new location. It's designed to demonstrate to the bank that, although your credit may not yet meet requirements, the source of loan payment funds is clearly established.

The purpose here is to offset weakness in credit history by strengthening the payback method. Keeping in mind that lenders look to credit history and a source of payback funds, this is one way of combining the two so the end result is adequate to get the loan you need.

Have Seller Move His Account to Your Bank

Since the seller has an interest in the success of your loan, consider ways you can work with him to get the money you need to buy his property. Banks like to make loans when they get additional deposits, and, in some cases, they require the checking accounts of the people to whom they lend. The seller may be more than willing to change banks if he knows that is what it will take for you to buy his property.

Will it help get the loan? That, of course, depends on the size of the account and competitive stance of your bank. In growing areas there are usually young banks in real need of new deposits. It can be a pleasure to borrow money when banks are in competitive battles—they can be quite accommodating.

If you're not working with a competitive lender consider moving elsewhere. In any event, if you are able to attract a new (and substantial) customer to your bank as a result of buying real estate with the money you borrow, you have a distinct advantage. The bank benefits on two counts: a new loan to you which yields a new customer for the bank—the seller.

Savings Account Transfer

When you are considering the transfer of business to the lender, don't overlook savings of relatives who may want to see you succeed more than they want their current bank or savings and loan association to profit. Transfer of an account can often be done without inconvenience to your helper and be timed to prevent loss of interest.

You may not think a new account is significant but banking is becoming increasingly competitive and loan officers earn management recognition when they bring in new business. If you help a loan officer build his business, chances are he will be more inclined to help you get your loan approved.

Sizable loans must go through loan committee approval. Every person you can get on your side can contribute to a favorable decision and approval of your loan request, and, when you bring a new deposit with your loan application, it's one more plus on your side.

Blanket Mortgage

A blanket mortgage is one note and mortgage that encumber two properties. It is used when the primary property borrowed against is not sufficient security for the size of the loan. Release of the additional security is normally provided for when the loan is reduced to an agreed amount and should be written into the mortgage terms.

One of the requirements for obtaining any real estate loan is demonstration that there is virtually no risk for the lender. A blanket mortgage is a method of substantially eliminating risk. In many cases it actually oversecures the loan, and that's what makes lenders happy.

With this technique you sign one note and one mortgage which encumber two separate properties. The additional real estate is essentially a method of making up a deficit in equity, and this is the clue to using a blanket mortgage as an acquisition method.

In the best of situations the property used as added security will in effect serve as a down payment (your equity). Consequently, the loan amount may be large enough for you to totally finance the new acquisition. The end result of the procedure is to provide sufficient security for the lender to make your loan. You can accomplish the same thing by selling your additional security property and making a down payment, but that would not be a wise business decision because of the tax consequences and loss of appreciation. Furthermore, it's not necessary when a blanket mortgage can be used to meet the lender's security requirements and provide the equity security you need to make the deal.

Participation

Participation is syndication of a loan among two or more lending institutions. It spreads the risk and allows small lenders to participate in a larger loan than would have been possible otherwise. It benefits the larger institution in essentially the same way by also reducing the risk.

Generally, two banks or thrift institutions join together to provide funds when one does not have sufficient reserves to undertake the project alone. Their mutual objective, of course, is higher profits at reduced risk.

If the loan you request is too big for your bank, participation with a larger institution may help out. It may take a lender from out of town to do the job. Corresponding banks in different cities have relationships designed for mutual benefit. If you live in a smaller town and have a big project, loan participation may be the solution for your plans.

Employer Influence

Having real trouble getting the loan? Banks don't like to lose business. Maybe a little pressure from a major depositor such as your employer would swing the deal. This can often work smoothly with small banks when competition is rough.

This type of approach is the other side of providing compensating balances. Instead of bringing business to the lender, you arrange for him to keep the business he has. Obviously, banks don't want to lose large accounts and normally do everything possible to make their clients happy. The exception to this general rule occurs when they are poorly managed, which does occasionally happen. In any event, a little influence from a friend or employer who is a major depositor may provide the incentive for the success of your loan application.

Joint Venture

Joint venture development projects are becoming increasingly popular as land and improvement costs escalate. The lender and developer enter into a profit-sharing partnership for development of a project such as lots in a residential subdivision. Usually the lender or its holding company will contribute some equity in the land and provide some development financing and permanent financing for the home buyers. The developer will also have an equity position in the land and handle all of the lot development engineering and preparation of the subdivision for sale to individual buyers.

Consequently, expertise and financing combine to produce a ready-to-build package for smaller builders. The joint venture group realizes the profit from lot sales and in the process provides an invaluable service.

Smaller builders are dependent on large companies specializing in packaged land sales. The tremendous increase in raw land costs combined with regulations for open land and environmental protection have forced all but the largest companies out of subdivision development. Joint venture projects have helped solve this growing problem and worked to keep lot costs within practical limits.

Long-Term Amortization—Halfway Due Date

This technique is used on older property or in situations where there is concern for the long-range economic stability of the area. The lender is protected by requiring full payment of the loan balance halfway through (or sooner) the amortization schedule.

This may appear to be a burden but you can cut the amortization term in half by paying an amount equal to the principal due each month in addition to the regular payment. The net effect is to pay off the loan before the halfway due date by increasing the payments each month by the amount of each principal payment. Although the due date approaches fast, you do have flexibility and time to get the rents up to cover the payments without cutting into cash flow.

This type of loan is designed to accomplish another profit-oriented objective of the lender that sparks its use with new property. The stated policy is to renew the loan at the halfway due date, but for a fee and at the rates in force at that time.

Therefore, the lender is not locked into an interest rate established years earlier that is much below future rates. It's also an opportunity for the lender to turn over loans more frequently and increase the net return of each loan investment. It's a more profitable loan for the lender and with strong cash flow can be a helpful refinance method.

You Buy Our Stock—We'll Make Your Loan

A lender with a stock offering that's going slowly is a lender who needs help. Offer to buy some stock if he or she will make your loan and thereby free up the cash you need to make the stock purchase. But do it informally so it won't be construed as a loan fee.

Again, this is one more back-scratching method. Help the lender and he'll help you. A loan officer selling stock by direction of management is usually willing to negotiate.

There are many ways to establish solid working relations with your bank. In the last analysis, though, they boil down to getting to know the people. If you're serious about acquiring real estate you must develop good banking relations. Stock ownership of the lending institution is definitely a foot in the door.

Standby Commitment

If you have a good project but permanent financing is not available or is too costly, look into the possibility of a standby commitment. It will allow you to get construction financing, build the project, and, if you haven't found permanent financing by then, you can exercise the standby commitment and pay off the construction loan. Commitments will often run as long as three years, giving you time to find permanent financing without making you wait to build and suffer the added cost of inflation in the meantime.

A standby commitment gives your construction lender the security he needs to make the interim construction loan. It permits you to get the project started without delay. There's another advantage here as well. It's often easier to find permanent financing when the lender can see the project unfold. In any event the standby commitment can be a help when money is tight and the prospects are good that it will be more readily available later.

Three Years with a Balloon

If you are buying property that you plan to sell within three years, this technique can increase your yield. Structure the loan for the down payment so monthly payments are low and there is a balloon at the time you are ready to sell. Then pay off the down payment loan with the profit from the sale.

When you structure this approach correctly, the return can be very high. You are able to borrow the entire amount of the down payment and then pay it off from the sale proceeds which flow from future appreciation. The property actually buys itself. The cash flow and ultimate resale proceeds are the down payment. You simply set up the transaction so the down payment is paid out of the profit rather than out of your pocket.

Less than Five Years Secured

Commercial banks don't like to loan money for more than five years, and for a loan of that length they normally want security. Knowing this in advance can help you structure your deal to meet their requirements and plan for the cash flow you need to make the deal work. The most beneficial approach is to structure the transaction so the cash flow from the property will pay off the down payment loan in five years. If you can negotiate a purchase with this in mind and then take a workable proposal to the bank, you have a head start on getting the loan.

Much of the success you have with banks depends on your loan presentation. When you're trying to borrow equity money (the down payment), thoroughness and accuracy go a long way toward soothing a loan officer's concern over risk. When the lender can see clearly that you know what you're doing, the level of risk associated with the loan drops drastically. Approach borrowing to acquire real estate the same way you would approach borrowing for a business.

Commercial banks specialize in business loans. If you go in for a down payment loan with an income and expense history of the property and a projection of its future performance, a real estate loan begins to look more like a business loan, and that is what banks feel more comfortable with. Set up your loan request as thoroughly and accurately as you would for a business loan. Look at your personal financial statement as a company balance sheet. Structure the property history like a business profit-and-loss statement with a projection for the future. The more business-like your loan request, the more likely the response will be positive.

18 Months Unsecured

If you plan to borrow on a personal note with no amortization, make the application for less than an 18-month term. This is generally the limit banks like to go on signature loans. If your signature is security enough and the short-term due date is manageable for you, this type of loan is a good source of down payment funds.

If you apply for the loan with a specific payback plan in mind, it makes it that much easier for the loan officer to approve the loan. There are two essential requirements which lenders must see in your loan request. First, there must be adequate security. Within certain limits your signature may be security enough if you are well-established in the community. Second, there must be a source of funds to repay the loan. Optimally the income from the property will meet this requirement. Possibly your salary will help also.

The Bridge Loan

If you're moving out of town and don't want to wait to sell your old house before buying a new one, this might be the answer. Before you leave, arrange a short-term loan with a local bank for a portion of the equity in your house and secure it with a second mortgage. The due date should be set far enough ahead to provide enough time to sell your old house but would be due in the event the sale occurred earlier. Another approach is to borrow the down payment from a bank in the town to which you are moving, with the understanding that it will be paid when your old house sells.

This is one application of a very helpful financing technique. When there is a time lag between two events and your funds depend on their concurrent completion, a bridge loan is a practical solution. The proceeds actually bridge the two points in time.

For example, if the seller must close within 30 days but your financing is not available for 90 days, there is a 60-day time gap that must be covered to save the deal. A bridge loan is the way to do it.

Finance Company Second

An increasingly popular source of loan money is from finance companies. They recognize the value of loaning on homes that have experienced a high degree of appreciation and are willing to loan money on the difference between your first mortgage and 80 percent of the appraised value. This permits you to borrow back a portion of the first mortgage you've paid plus a percentage of the appreciated value of your house. The interest rates are high, but you can generally stretch the payout over ten years and if the funds are wisely invested the loan can be worth the cost.

Although your home is solid security for the finance company, due consideration should be given certain aspects of the transaction. Will the profit from the investment of the loan proceeds pay the loan back, cover the interest costs, and yield a high enough return to justify the risk involved?

Care should also be taken that you don't take a deep step into debt just prior to a major economic contraction. It's when the good times look like they'll never end that you want to be careful, especially with your home. Consider also that capital debt must always produce a solid investment return and never be used for consumer purchases.

Commitment Letter

If you must close an acquisition now but the mortgage rates are high and show signs of going down soon, a commitment letter may help you. First, get a letter of commitment from a savings and loan association agreeing to lend the money you need at today's rates. Then, go to a commercial bank and use the commitment letter as security to borrow the money to close. When the bank loan is due (six to nine months later usually), the rates for permanent financing may be lower. But, if they're not, you can exercise the commitment and live with the higher interest.

The alternative is to let the commitment letter expire and apply for a loan at a lower rate. When a change in rates gets underway, the movement is fast regardless of the direction of the trend. Usually the turnaround points are reasonably identifiable and the trends in interest rate changes are obvious. If a change in trend indicates a lower interest cost a few months down the road, purchasing a commitment letter and setting up a short-term loan may be well worth the trouble.

17

Private Financing
and Negotiation Techniques

One look at the variety of methods for negotiating the acquisition of real estate is enough to light a fire in the heart of any serious entrepreneur. It's also a fair test for anyone who questions the strength of his interest. There are probably as many people scared by unstructured opportunity as there are people turned on by it.

People who are attracted by the virtually unlimited potential of real estate tend to do exceptionally well as they learn more of what can be done. Each new technique forms the basis for another chance to replace someone else's problem with an opportunity-creating solution.

Ultimately it's your application of the vast and growing body of real estate methods that will measure your success, and there's no better area for applying this solution-oriented approach than in negotiating the details of a privately financed acquisition.

A privately arranged acquisition that is not restricted by the mysterious reasoning of institutions or government sponsorship can take shape like a symphony. Real estate transactions are often orchestrated by artists in their fields and they are music to those who know how to hear.

Today's techniques are the starting point for what you can do. The more you know the more you can do to expand the opportunity before you. And when you are negotiating with flexible, creative people there's really no limit to what you can accomplish.

Builder's Bailout

Builders and developers who have an inventory of unsold homes are able to take advantage of this often-used technique. It helps the builder out of a tight spot and can help you acquire a home without a large down payment.

You actually bail the builder out of his construction loan. This is done by making a small down payment and having the builder carry back a portion of the difference between

233

the sale price and the first mortgage. For example, a $50,000 home is more easily sold to someone who can buy it with a minimum down payment. Under normal market conditions the down payment is approximately 20 percent of $50,000 ($10,000). But as a sales promotion for unsold inventory, the builder may be more than willing to sell with $1,000 down to qualified buyers. You arrange for a first mortgage of $40,000 and the builder carries back on a second mortgage for $9,000.

This technique gives the builder an aggressive sales plan for buyers who have high incomes, but not a large amount of cash. It allows a qualified buyer to purchase a home and receive the immediate benefits of ownership on terms that are quite an incentive. Builders have been saved from bankruptcy with this approach. It provides them with relief from the interest burden of carrying the construction loan and protects their profit with the second mortgage.

Overpay

Overpaying the asking price is a negotiation technique designed to secure benefits which are more valuable than the price. Applying this technique requires judgment and timing during negotiations. You certainly don't want to pay more if it's not necessary. You only want to offer more if it's the only way the seller will accept your offer.

In consideration for paying more than the seller is asking, you may negotiate easier payout terms, a smaller interest rate, or smaller down payment. It can also be used as a lever to obtain releases for certain portions of the real estate being acquired.

This technique is designed to provide an incentive for the seller to concede on terms which he might not otherwise consider—terms which are more important to you than the price of the real estate. You can't meet your profit objectives if you don't acquire the real estate. This technique is an effective method of making sure you get the property. The seller can be rapidly motivated when he realizes more total profit from the sale of his real estate than he had originally anticipated or even requested.

Contingent Price Sale

A contingent price sale is an acquisition at a value to be determined by the future performance of the property. The sales price is set as a function of the income production of the property.

This technique is often used in the sale of a business and can make the difference between a successful acquisition or a failure when you suspect hidden problems. There are a number of ways to structure the payout details with this approach. Generally, though, you should capitalize the operating income over a given time period to establish the total sales price. Although the seller may require a minimum base, you can establish the maximum total price by dividing the annual income by the return you want. For example, an average annual operating income of $50,000 divided by a 10 percent return results in a price of $500,000. If the income is $45,000 the sales price drops to $450,000 if you want a 10 percent return. This is just one way of many to structure a contingent price sale. A variation in the price formula may be necessary to account for the effect of the financing.

Another application is to avoid a base sales price and simply agree to pay the seller a specified percentage of the profits over a limited time period. If you are involved in a contingent price sale be sure to investigate the tax advantages to the seller. The general benefit is that gain from sales do not have to be reported until the sales price is final. With proper tax counsel, the seller may find the tax advantage worth the risk of a contingent price.

Private Wraparound

One of the most beneficial ways for a seller to carry the balance of his equity is a wraparound mortgage. This can be structured by using a number of different instruments such as a mortgage, trust deed, or real estate contract. The particular document used can best be determined by your state law—the financial benefits will be the same.

The procedure is simple. The seller receives a first lien position subject to the existing loan, which is paid monthly out of the buyer's payments on the new wraparound. The seller gets interest on the dollar balance of his equity, plus additional interest on the difference between the existing loan rate and the higher interest on the wraparound.

This is an excellent method for a seller and can offer an incentive for other concessions when you are negotiating an acquisition. If the existing loan is $80,000 at 8 percent interest and the seller agrees to a wraparound mortgage at $9\frac{1}{2}$ percent, here's how it would work. With a sales price of $160,000 and a $20,000 cash down payment the seller's equity balance is $60,000. But the face value of the wraparound mortgage is $140,000. Consequently, the seller receives interest of $9\frac{1}{2}$ percent on his equity of $60,000 and $1\frac{1}{2}$ percent on the underlying 8 percent mortgage of $80,000. This can be quite an incentive for a seller who knows how to calculate the long-term benefits of compound interest.

Seller as Short-Term Lender

This is a method of working with the seller to avoid high interest rates. If the seller wants terms that require refinancing but interest rates are too high for you, this approach may solve the problem.

Negotiate with the seller to carry the amount which would have been paid off by refinancing. Then set a due date a couple of years away at the maximum or sooner if you obtain a satisfactory loan rate.

This will allow you to close the transaction now and give you the chance to set up permanent financing at a lower cost as interest rates drop.

Vary the Loan Payments Based on Occupancy

This technique ties the payments on your purchase money mortgage directly to the occupancy of the property you acquire.

For example, if you're acquiring a 20-unit apartment complex with a questionable future, structure the financing with the seller so that if the occupancy rate is 90 percent the interest rate on the carry-back loan stays at 9 percent. But if occupancy drops to 80 percent the interest rate drops to 8 percent. The reduction would continue at a ratio of a 1 percent drop in interest for each 10 percent drop in occupancy.

There are a couple of variations to this approach which can be helpful. If occupancy drops below a certain rate, you might want a temporary suspension in amortization of loan principal and pay only the interest until things improve. Another variation is to decrease the total amount of the loan payment rather than just the interest. In some cases where the loans provide for a large monthly amortization of principal, it may not be necessary to decrease the amount of interest paid at all. The object is to decrease monthly debt service to avoid a negative cash flow. Whether you whittle the interest or principal portion of the payment depends on what the seller can live with.

Improvement Costs as Return of Down Payment

If you are acquiring property that is really run down and a questionable investment due to its present condition, consider putting the cash that would normally go to the down payment into repairs. You can protect your position and the seller by setting up the purchase to upgrade the property.

It's not unusual for property to be sold because the owner is unable or unwilling to spend the money necessary to bring it up to its market potential. Furthermore, it may be necessary to put a certain amount of money into the property just to protect it. By agreeing with the seller to divert the down payment to repairs, you will give him better protection on the equity he carries on a purchase money mortgage. It's certainly better than the alternative.

Consequently you are able to acquire real estate in a condition that ensures a profitable operation. The seller, of course, gets his full purchase price in the form of the purchase money mortgage, and you get your cash outlay (that would have gone to the seller) back in property value.

Putting the down payment into the improvements may be necessary to ensure a profitable operation and timely payment of the seller's carry-back mortgage, but there's another benefit as well. If the seller insists on cash, there's a possibility he may get more in the long run if the improvements are sufficient to permit refinancing. This would of course cash out the seller and may increase his willingness to take the deal.

Moratorium on Debt Service

If you are acquiring a one-tenant building and there is a question as to whether the lease will be renewed, some degree of protection can be insured by negotiating a stop to the loan payments if the building becomes vacant. Usually you will have to put a limit on the time of the moratorium, with the understanding that the purpose is to give you enough breathing room to find a new tenant. Three to six months is a good starting point.

By including this relatively minor provision in a purchase money mortgage, you may avoid a serious problem in the future. The objective is to lessen the risk of acquiring income property that depends on the continued occupancy of one tenant. A warehouse acquisition is a likely candidate for protection using this formula.

Automatic Discount

An automatic discount should always be part of your acquisition strategy. When you're acquiring property with a substantial purchase money mortgage and there's a possibility of refinancing it in the future, this technique can mean real savings.

For example, a $100,000 carry-back mortgage on a $150,000 purchase might provide for an automatic discount of 10 percent (about $10,000) if paid in full within two years. The objective of the seller is to provide an incentive for the buyer to cash him out. Consequently, a drop in the discount after two years to 5 percent is an appropriate extension of the technique. Of course, when you're acquiring the property and paying on the note, you want the longest time possible at the maximum discount the seller will accept.

This technique allows you to reduce the total sales price by transferring the bargaining point from the property to the note and mortgage. The possibility of a future cash-out is solid incentive for many sellers to reduce a sales price, and negotiating it into the future gives you breathing room to get the job done. Even if it is impossible to work out, you lose nothing by setting the possibility. There's always the possibility you will resell the property during the discount period to a cash buyer and then the importance of the discount will be measurable as money in your pocket.

Interest Only Until the First Is Paid

By negotiating an interest only payment to the seller until the existing first mortgage is paid, you can minimize the drain on the cash flow from debt service. This technique is especially helpful when the seller is asking a high price and you want to maximize the tax shelter aspects of the property.

There are, therefore, two major benefits to this technique: an increase in your cash flow because you are not paying off the principal balance of the purchase money mortgage; and, a more efficient use of the available tax deductions because the interest payment is fully deductible.

This technique is a sound way of maximizing your profit in any situation, but in some cases it is essential to the profitability of the acquisition. You are, in effect, asking the seller to defer payment of the equity represented by the purchase money mortgage. And from a time value standpoint, that is money in your pocket today and more valuable than it would have been if you had received it in the future.

When the cash flow is questionable this approach helps offset the risk. It's one more aid that can be combined with the other techniques to minimize your risk and maximize your profit.

Balloon Payments

Structuring private financing with well-timed balloon payments can often mean the difference between completing a transaction and letting it die from lack of ingenuity. A balloon payment is a lump sum principal payment that comes at the maturity of a note. But balloon payments can be placed at various points throughout a loan to provide an incentive for the seller to accept a smaller down payment or other terms you may want.

One clever application is the Christmas season balloon, which calls for an additional lump sum payment each year during the first part of December. The strategy here is to give the seller a Christmas incentive to offset other terms of the acquisition that are important to you.

Periodic balloon payments in addition to the regular amortization payments can often lower the amount of down payment required by the seller. Knowing that he will receive beneficially timed balloon payments can be more important than a large one-time down payment. The first part of April is another helpful date to receive cash because of income taxes.

The other benefit from balloon payments is that they can be used to structure an installment sale. Rather than lose the important benefits of installment reporting, it is much wiser to spread a down payment over a couple of years in the form of a balloon payment.

When you are acquiring real estate, balloon payments can help defer an immediate cash outlay for the down payment. But the way you time the payments will provide the incentive for the seller.

Sell with Option to Buy Back

If you're having difficulty getting a seller to part with his property, offer him an option to buy it back. This can be a solid form of protection for someone who thinks he may be selling too soon, and it's a small concession for you when the alternative is no transaction at all.

The terms of the buy-back option can be very flexible. You should build in a reasonable profit in case the seller does exercise the option. The danger here is that the seller has a marketable right in the option and may choose to sell the option itself to someone who wants to exercise it. To prevent this you can negotiate a clause that makes the option nontransferable.

This approach has been used successfully in joint ventures with options to buy partial ownership. In one case an investor retained an option to acquire a 25 percent ownership position in an office building developed on his land. The option had a five-year life and was eventually sold for a substantial profit when an insurance company bought the entire project.

There are several ways this technique can be worked into the specific requirements of any transaction. It's an aid to acquiring property when the seller wants to have his cake and eat it too. But it's also a financing tool for a seller who wants to raise money by selling now while still retaining the possibility of buying his property back later.

Reduce the Interest but Increase the Constant

When you are negotiating private financing the major objective is to retain as many benefits as possible, whether you are buying or selling. One way of structuring the benefits you want is to vary the components of the constant annual amortizing percentage which is applied to the loan balance. A portion of the constant percentage goes to interest and the remainder reduces the loan balance. For example, a loan with a $9\frac{1}{2}$ percent interest rate which amortizes over 30 years with equal monthly payments has a constant of 10.10%. This percentage represents $9\frac{1}{2}$% interest and .6% loan reduction.

This technique uses the constant to satisfy the seller's desire for rapid payoff. Instead of putting a due date toward the end of the loan you reduce the interest and increase the amount of constant—the total loan payment. The net effect is an increase in the speed with which the seller receives his total sales price.

It will also increase the amount of loan payment that he can allocate to lower capital gains tax rates. When you use this technique to acquire, you benefit by paying less interest and therefore less total dollars (interest plus principal) over the life of the mortgage. Of course you will have a slightly smaller interest deduction which may be of no consequence, depending on other shelter aspects of the transaction.

Reduce the Constant but Increase the Interest

Another method of using debt service payments to your advantage is to reduce the constant but increase the interest. If the seller wants long-term income, increase the interest rate and maintain a low portion of the loan payment for principal reduction. This will stretch out the term of the loan payoff and give the seller a large dollar amount of ordinary income from interest. It will also increase the total cost of the property acquisition, but your current net tax deduction will be larger due to the increased interest to debt ratio.

The point here is to meet the seller's requirements without destroying the profitability of the property. This approach allows the seller to maintain the size of his capital (loan principal) and receive income from it as interest over a longer period of time. As a trade-off for stretching out the amortization, the cash flow of the property is increased as a result of smaller debt service payment.

Sale Lease-back

A sale lease-back is one of the most effective real-estate acquisition methods. It is frequently used by large businesses but it can be equally beneficial for any size transaction when the seller is financially sound and wants to continue using the property.

This technique builds income into the transaction. Essentially, the seller agrees to sell and lease back at a rental rate based on the sales value of the property. This establishes a rate of return without the usual concern about finding tenants.

A sale lease-back is often used when an owner wishes to raise cash without losing use of the real estate. The objective in this application is to obtain capital for the business to finance expansion. If a corporation is in a sound growth industry, why tie up capital by owning real estate? The business will make more money by concentrating on its specialty rather than the ownership of real estate. Consequently the sale lease-back can often be viewed as a financing method from the seller's point-of-view.

Acquiring property that is leased back by the seller can give you quite an advantage. With a financially strong seller signing the lease, it's possible to obtain 100 percent financing. Of course, the details of sales price, interest rates, and lease terms play an important role in the profit you are able to structure.

Add the Interest to Principal

A property which does not have adequate cash flow to cover the debt service of a second mortgage is an opportunity for payment of interest only with no amortization of the second mortgage principal. In extreme cash flow problems, part of the interest not covered by income can be added to the loan principal. This is one temporary solution to the negative cash flow created by overfinancing or inadequate rental income.

This is a limited time measure designed to give you an opportunity to increase the income on the property. Not all property starts out making money, and if you're acquiring property that won't cover the debt service required by the second mortgage, this technique is a way to buy time. And really that's what you do. As the interest increases the loan principal compounds rapidly, raising the amount of indebtedness on the property. But in some cases it only takes a little time to turn property around.

This technique allows you to negotiate a loan that is designed to meet the seller's requirements and the limitations of the existing cash flow on the property. It provides time to set up your turnaround program and make the property productive.

The objective is to build the income up enough to amortize the loan principal with interest. Although this is a somewhat undesirable position to be in, there are benefits. The seller gets the added compounding value of interest paid on interest. It increases the total dollar return he will get for the property and compensates him for the delay.

Three-Year Interest Only Balloon

A three-year interest only payment followed by a balloon for the total amount of the mortgage can be a helpful way to structure the acquisition of vacant land. If you anticipate a resale within the three-year period, your return will be higher if you can minimize amortization of the debt.

The objective here is to resell the property prior to the balloon. The funds for payment of the balloon come from the new buyer's financing. In the event the property is not sold, you have ample time to locate financing to pay the balloon as it comes due. This is a logical opportunity to build in a request for a discount if you make the balloon payment early. It's a natural for an automatic discount.

The all cash payoff at the end of three years is the incentive for the seller to accept interest only. It may hit that middle ground between all cash at closing and a long payout that meets your needs and the seller's.

Subordination to Construction Financing

If you are ready to build but don't have the cash necessary to pay off the existing loan, subordination is one solution. The holder of the existing financing simply agrees to subordinate his security position to a new construction loan. When building is complete and permanent financing is established, the existing loan is paid in full. Consequently, there is a period of increased risk for the existing note holder because if there is a default the construction lender will have first claim to the property.

Also, if you're planning to acquire vacant land for development and want to maximize leverage, negotiate subordination of the seller's interest to construction financing as part of the purchase. This will allow you to build without paying off the land until construction is complete and the permanent financing is in force. This approach works to maximum benefit when combined with a mortgage-out strategy.

Subordination for Cash

If you own property that can be refinanced, ask the holder of the first mortgage to subordinate his mortgage to a new first mortgage. As an incentive, you might agree to pay an extra amount on your existing loan. With that unexpected cash incentive, the first mortgage holder may be willing to accept a secondary position, thus giving you the opportunity to pull out tax-free cash for acquisition of more real estate.

Subordination of a first lien position is normally associated with development, but it can also be a successful method of raising cash for acquisition. Vacant land that is encumbered and ready for development is the usual candidate for a subordination agreement, but it can be equally as effective when you want to raise acquisition capital, whether your property is improved or vacant land. The only requirement is that it can be refinanced.

The problem, though, is convincing the note holder to take a subordinate lien position. It is an increase in risk.

Therefore, to offset the increase in risk an additional cash payment is made. Ideally this payment will reduce the existing loan. In difficult situations, though, it may be necessary (and profitable) to pay an added cash bonus over and above the loan amount. It can be well worth paying a little extra when the end result is tax-free cash in your pocket. And, if the economics of the property support the new loan safely, the note holder will be in a better financial position than before.

Purchase Money Mortgage

This popular approach is often used when the seller wants installment reporting and/ or when institutional financing is not available. The seller deeds to the buyer, and the buyer gives a note secured by a mortgage to the seller. The seller consequently has a first mortgage position secured by the property he sold. In the event of default, the seller would foreclose. This is a private adaptation of standard institutional financing without the transfer of lump sum financing. The seller gets his money as the payments are made.

It is really a form of documentation, as are so many techniques. Often both buyer and seller know where they want to end up, and the only requirement is setting up the paperwork to get there. That's one reason why it's important to know the possible techniques; then you can explore alternatives with the seller during negotiation. It's the exploration process that touches the new alternatives that may be entirely acceptable to the seller. How many real estate transactions do you suppose have failed simply because the people involved didn't have access to the alternative that would get the job done? How many are stopped in their tracks because when the solution appeared they accepted someone's offhand remark of "impossible" or "that won't work"?

Real Estate Contract

Sometimes called a sales contract, land sales contract, or contract of sale, this approach to private financing provides a practical solution to the problem of foreclosure. The buyer literally contracts with the seller to purchase real estate. The real estate contract and the deed conveying title to the buyer are held in escrow until the terms of the contract are met, then the deed is recorded. A special deed is also placed in escrow deeding the property from the buyer back to the seller. This deed is recorded only if the buyer defaults under the terms of the contract and eliminates the lengthy foreclosure process. It's also final. There is no redemption.

Real estate contracts are usually set up as standard printed forms in states where they are commonly used. The terms and details of the document vary in different localities depending on state law.

The benefit of the real estate contract is the flexibility it provides for the buyer and seller to establish terms which meet their mutual objectives. It can be especially useful when you assume the existing mortgage and the seller accepts a down payment that doesn't cash out his equity. The real estate contract makes up the difference. Its face value is the seller's remaining equity. When the contract is paid, usually by monthly payments, the escrow agent (often a bank) releases the deed and the property is yours.

Second Mortgage or Second Trust Deed

When a buyer assumes an existing loan the seller will often be forced by reasonableness to carry back a portion of his equity on a second mortgage or trust deed. With this approach to private financing you get a deed to the property subject to the existing loan. Rather than sign a contract which must be performed, you sign a promissory note secured by a second mortgage.

In some states a trust deed is used instead of a mortgage. There are legal differences from state to state, but for our purposes the important factor is the negotiation possibilities of the documentation.

One element which any buyer should pay close attention to is the extent of personal liability possible in the event of default. As real estate prices explode beyond reasonable measures of value there are certain considerations that should be kept in mind when signing notes for real estate acquisition.

In the event the bottom drops out of the economy and you lose your real estate, what happens under the terms of the note and mortgage you sign? If you paid more for the property when you acquired it than it's worth under the depressed market condition in force when you lost it, there can be a negative consequence. If it can't be sold for enough to pay off the notes you signed, the mortgage holder can sue you for the deficiency—the difference between the market price and the amount you owe. If the court rules against you, a deficiency judgment is handed down which requires you to pay up. If you don't your other personal assets can be attached and sold. This is one good reason not to allow yourself to be caught up in excessive speculation—you can lose more than the property itself.

Any good real estate financing technique can be used imprudently, but don't let it happen to you. If you are acquiring property that has even the remotest possibility of ending up in trouble, insist on a limit to personal liability on the notes you sign.

Pledge, Collateralize, or Hypothecate

Using additional collateral is often a help in closing an acquisition, especially when the down payment is less than the seller feels is necessary for security against default. Insurance cash value, stocks, bonds, personal property, or other real estate all serve the purpose.

If the seller feels he needs a 20 percent down payment but you have only 10 percent, take a close look at other assets you own. Determine what the seller is trying to accomplish by requiring a 20 percent down payment. If he's just after security and can wait for his cash, hypothecating anything of value can provide it.

The key here is searching out what the seller wants. That's why it can be crucial for someone involved in the negotiations to thoroughly know what the seller wants to accomplish and what he really needs to accomplish it. It may very well be that his primary objective is to get out of management headaches, and a no down payment sale to an effective manager would be more satisfactory than 20 percent down by someone who will ruin the property and default on the mortgage.

Private Insurance Annuity

An income for life can often be more appealing to a seller than a sale. One solid way to provide income is to purchase an annuity from an insurance company that will continue for the life of the seller. The seller deeds the real estate to you free and clear and receives an income for life. The property is refinanced to generate the cash necessary to buy the annuity.

Another approach to acquisition by annuity is used between relatives. It has greater flexibility and does not involve the outright purchase of an annuity. An annuity agreement is used which establishes the payment terms. It simply states that payment for life will be provided as consideration for the property.

In this case, the seller relies only on the private agreement for future income. That's, of course, why it's generally more appropriate for use with relatives. Certainly there's no reason for this unfunded approach not to be used between individuals who are not related if the necessary trust is there.

The obvious benefit here is what you can do with free-and-clear income producing property if you don't have to borrow against it to purchase the annuity. It can serve as the basis for building a solid investment portfolio and provide the income to pay the annuity.

Purchase a Remainder Interest

In some situations the only way a seller will part with his or her property is if he or she can retain use of it during the balance of a lifetime. You can accomplish this by purchasing a remainder interest in the property and allowing the seller to retain a life estate interest. The seller gets all income from the property until death, plus the cash and notes you pay at closing.

This technique may be combined with a management agreement permitting you to operate the property to protect your interests. On the death of the seller, the entire fee interest automatically transfers to you.

Purchasing a remainder interest is an example of how a transaction can be closed even when the timing is not exactly right. It's a solution for what may seem an insurmountable barrier. It is also potentially very beneficial for the seller. The cash from a sale now may be much more useful than after death.

Since you're not receiving income during the balance of the seller's life, there is a certain price adjustment that can be made to compensate. This may be offset, though, by calculation of the property appreciation factor which may be necessary in calculating the remainder interest.

Walk the Mortgage

This technique has many applications. Walking the mortgage is a process of substituting different real estate as security for an existing mortgage. The mortgage is modified or rewritten so as to encumber different real estate. The objective is to free up property that can be easily refinanced. It is a technique that can provide significant future benefits if you negotiate it into the terms of property you're acquiring. Even if it isn't agreed to in advance by the seller, it's an excellent method of maximizing refinance proceeds if you can negotiate it later.

The significant factor is the flexibility walking the mortgage gives you. When you arrange to take a mortgage off you free up equity. Equity is acquisition power. This technique really hits home when you use it to refinance appreciated property.

In one case, an investor was able to walk a $45,000 mortgage from a four-plex to a large tract of vacant land. Although the land was solid, security banks wouldn't lend on it. But the individual who held the purchase money mortgage on the four-plex was happy to cooperate—especially when he received $1,000 incentive.

Reversing the Interest

By structuring an acquisition with separate notes that are due annually, you can place the high interest payments at the end of the amortization term rather than at the beginning. Negotiate the transaction so that each note is paid, plus accrued interest, at the end of every 12 months. For example, the first note bears one year's interest, the fifth bears five years' interest, and the twentieth bears 20 years' interest. Each year has a separate note. It may take 20 years of $10,000 notes to pay off the property. One mortgage is used to secure all the notes.

This technique intentionally places the burden of making large payments in the later years. It also gives you a larger deduction toward the end of the amortization term. The seller is able to defer ordinary income in the earlier years of the sale because the interest is reversed. This approach can be of benefit to someone who is retiring and anticipates being in a lower tax bracket as time passes. Consequently, it would be advantageous to take a greater portion of capital gains now and defer receipt of the higher-taxed interest income. However, be careful with this one. Compound interest grows fast.

This Year's Interest as Down Payment

The use of several years' prepaid interest as down payment has been eliminated from the beneficial tax techniques available to purchasers. This advanced deduction was a help with taxes and can still be used to some degree as a negotiating advantage when you are purchasing property at the beginning of the tax year.

If you are buying with virtually all paper and little cash, offer to pay the balance of the year's interest in advance in lieu of a cash down payment. This may give the seller the cash necessary to put his mind at ease. It will also increase his effective yield on the carryback paper. When used in conjunction with an interest-only mortgage, it results in acquisition with fully deductible dollars.

The most advantageous acquisition methods are those that do not require use of your own cash. When you can't quite reach this ideal objective, the next best approach is to maximize the deductibility of the cash you do put into the acquisition.

Often a down payment requirement is half need and half greed. If you can negotiate out the greed part and make the balance tax deductible interest you'll take a big step toward maximizing your profit.

The Bargain Sale

The bargain sale is a method of structuring complete deductibility and minimum taxable income during the initial years of ownership. With this approach, the seller agrees to reduce the sale price of the property in exchange for all of the net income for a specified period of time. The time period during which the seller retains income is based on the amount of price reduction. The price reduction is more than offset by the continuation of rental income flowing to the seller.

The seller or a third party manages the property, giving the seller a chance to earn more than was taken off the asking price. It is the potential of unspecified income that makes this technique pay off for the seller. The main advantage for the buyer is a large deduction and appreciation in anticipation of capital gain on resale.

When you acquire using a bargain sale structure immediate tax advantages are established. You make no equity down payment. Any cash paid to the seller at closing is structured as interest paid on the acquisition note to the seller. You receive no net income. The portion of the rent you do get is limited to the net operating expenses. Consequently, you acquire the property at a bargain price and set up a maximum tax deduction deal. The property depreciation and price reduction return as a second wave benefit when you sell at reduced capital gains rates in the future.

Furthermore, the deal is intentionally structured so the seller has a very good chance of receiving more for the property than under a conventional sale. The keys to the seller's added profit are management ability and the rental market potential during the time period he has the right to income.

Solid profit incentive is built into the transaction for everyone. This technique demonstrates as well as any that with cooperation and creative effort, maximum benefit can be structured for both sides, ensuring a winning situation for buyer and seller.

Diamonds Pledge or Cutting the Down Payment in Half

Diamonds of investment quality can be expected to appreciate. If you can find the right partner for your real estate deal, they can be bought at wholesale.

Instead of paying cash as a down payment, buy diamonds at wholesale and use them to secure a note for the down payment in an amount equal to the retail value of the diamonds. Then pay off the down payment note using the income from the property.

The diamonds used as note security are purchased at wholesale price—half the retail value and half the amount required for a down payment. The other advantage of this technique is that the diamonds may appreciate at a rate practically twice that of the interest on the note. If you negotiate an interest-only note with a due date in five years, the diamonds will have doubled in value and can be sold to pay the note. In this application your down payment is fully covered by diamond appreciation.

This is a high leverage technique that gives you the advantage of double asset appreciation. Your cash, which would normally go to the seller as the property down payment, is put to double use. It buys security for the down payment note, the diamonds remain your property (unless you default), and the appreciation is yours. Then the note acquires the real estate which also appreciates at a high rate. When you consider that your cash is depreciating with inflation, putting it to double use to acquire appreciating assets becomes even more profitable.

Lower the Interest and Increase the Price

This method decreases the ordinary income to the seller from interest but makes up the difference in capital gain from the sale. The seller's after-tax income is increased through the benefits of capital gains without causing him to sacrifice the total cash in his pocket.

If you don't mind losing an interest deduction, this technique can have an impact on your success when there's competition for property. The first effect is to get the seller's attention by offering more for the property. The second effect is to demonstrate how the low interest/high price adjustment will convert a large portion of the combined sales proceeds (interest and principal) to lower capital gains rates. The net after tax dollars will be greater for the seller but the same for you.

The key with this technique is to calculate the total dollars you would pay for the property at a certain high interest rate. Then calculate the total at a much lower rate. Add the difference to the seller's price. He pays a lower capital gains rate and gets more net after tax income even though the total dollars he receives is the same.

Although you lose an interest deduction, it may be a small price to pay when competition for property is rough and the alternative is not closing the deal.

Reduce the Price and Pay Points

If you prefer to increase the deductible portion of the transaction and the seller is carrying a note and mortgage, this technique can help.

Offer to reduce the sales price and offset the reduction by paying points. You will be able to write off the amount of the loan points over a short period of time, whereas a down payment, of course, is not deductible. If the seller will accept the ordinary income from the points, this method will reduce your after tax cost in the property.

This technique neither increases nor decreases the total dollars received or paid. It simply converts part of the total to a deduction for you. If you go in with this structure at the seller's asking price, there's the possibility that the reduction in price will hit what he was willing to accept anyway and the points in that case will be icing on the cake.

Management Fee for Specific Services

If the seller is to be involved in the management of the property after the sale, this technique can help reduce your net cost. Structure part of the offer as payment for management services.

This approach is another way of building a deductible payment into the acquisition. Management fees for the specific services performed by the seller after you acquire the property are deductible operating expenses to you.

If you're involved in a negotiation that appears to be headed toward free management provided by the seller, consider paying for it and reducing the purchase price. The total dollars received by the seller will be unchanged, but you will have an additional deduction. Furthermore, structuring the transaction this way will more accurately reflect the payments for what you receive. When you're paying out cash, always make sure you're not passing up a tax deduction that should be declared.

Acquiring Property from a Real Estate Corporation

Public corporations are required by the financial community to demonstrate earnings growth performance. This objective is practically impossible for a real estate corporation under accepted accounting standards. The problem is depreciation, which lowers reportable profits.

Although a public real estate corporation may have solid cash flow, property depreciation write-off tends to lower reported earnings for financial statement purposes. Consequently, the company appears to be in bad condition when it is in excellent shape. That is, earnings are lowered on paper but not in fact. It's a conceptual gap in standard accounting practice.

This technique is designed to help the corporation generate earnings while providing investment property for you. Approach the real estate company with an offer to buy 75 percent of a given property. Require the company to guarantee a 9 percent cash return on your investment before depreciation. If cash flow is generated above your guarantee, the company receives a 9 percent return on its 25 percent ownership interest. Any additional cash flow is split 50/50—not 75/25. You get a solid 9 percent return. The company generates capital for expansion and is able to report the gain from your acquisition as annual earnings. Furthermore, 75 percent of the depreciation is eliminated from the balance sheet while retaining 50 percent of the growth in cash flow. This technique is a natural for shopping centers that have high income growth.

Often the solution to finding real estate is mathematical. Although it may appear that nothing worth buying is for sale, a closer look at the needs of property owners can change the problem into your opportunity.

Applying the Multiparty Exchange as an Acquisition Technique

Structuring an exchange can be the solution to the problem of an owner who is reluctant to sell when discovering the impact of capital gains tax on the transaction.

Applying the benefits of exchanging as a help in an acquisition strategy is fundamental to the multiparty exchange. It is popular, in part, because it facilitates the acquisition of real estate that has a large profit that would be lost to taxes in an outright sale.

Although the details of exchanging are discussed throughout the first part of this book, its application as an acquisition technique should always be kept in mind. It is the tax-saving benefit to a real estate owner that makes exchanging the major solution to the tax problems of highly appreciated property. Conversely, exchanging is also the solution for the buyer who is confronted with an owner who refuses to sell because of the tax consequences. For the owner it is the only method of disposing of the property that is acceptable. Consequently, for the buyer it is the only method of acquiring the property that will work.

A strong desire to acquire a specific property is a major reason the multiparty exchange exists today. It is primarily an acquisition technique: A buyer wants to acquire a property that can't be sold because of the tax consequences; therefore, the owner finds other property, which the buyer acquires and exchanges for the owner's original property without the detrimental tax consequences. This is the most popular structure of the multiparty exchange, covered in detail in Chapter 3.

The application of the multiparty exchange as a solution to the tax problems encountered when trying to acquire real estate places it at the head of the list of techniques to use when you want to acquire a specific property.

18

Using a Lease
to Acquire and
Finance Real Estate

Land may be the backbone of real estate, but leasing is the muscle. Real estate starts with land and becomes a business with a lease. Land is a store of value. Leasing is a method of extracting the stored value.

It's the use of real estate that produces income. By definition, when you're working with the leasing process you're involved in the use of real estate for the production of income. From an investment standpoint, it is often the nature of the lease that establishes your profit potential and the management demands placed on your time.

Shopping centers have become sought-after investments largely due to the accepted practice of tying a lease to the gross sales of the tenant. A percentage lease ensures the center owner growing income as the tenant's business prospers. Often the tenant succeeds only because of the drawing power of the shopping center and profits far more than would be possible in a more isolated location.

Triple net or absolute net leases have demonstrated investment benefits of a different kind. If you're after management-free ownership they're the answer. Often used with the sale leaseback of single-use buildings, they provide reasonable returns without the problems of management.

Leasing is also a technique that can play an important role in your acquisition plans. It ties directly to financing as proof of income to service debt. In fact, when you look for acquisition financing and have a solid lease in hand you're practically in business.

Bond Lease

One of the most reliable, often-used methods to acquire real estate with a minimum of cash starts with the bond lease. This technique requires a tenant with a high credit rating who is willing to sign a long-term lease. The best candidates are national corporations with "A" ratings.

The basic process involves using the lease to secure your financing. Whether you're building a new building or buying an existing one, the commitment to lease is the first step. The lease is security for the financing and in effect guarantees repayment of the loan.

Usually, the lender requires that the term of the lease equal or exceed the time required to amortize the loan. This approach can also be used with smaller individual companies with good local credit ratings.

Using a bond lease to acquire real estate has an obvious and immediate benefit: you start with a reliable tenant. This fact opens the door to financing, and, when you have both good income and financing, you're well on the way to a profitable transaction. The key is putting all the components together so the net result is positive cash flow for you.

Lease-Condo

This technique is designed as an incentive to potential tenants for professional office space that is difficult to lease. It can form the basis for your acquisition of property no one else can deal with. The decision to buy real estate is easier when you see a way to make a profit that others have overlooked.

Offer current tenants and prospective new tenants space for a certain period of time, say four years. In your proposal agree to apply part of the lease payment as credit toward purchase of the space leased. Structure the lease so the tenant will have accumulated enough credit toward the down payment to make the purchase without additional cost.

This is an incentive for the tenant to set up business in a building that may not be in the most desirable location. It is a solution, also, for an owner who is having difficulty leasing. It is certainly better than having a building, that can't be sold as an investment, sit practically vacant.

There are certain important requirements that must be planned into the project. Conversion to condominium space has become widespread and a common practice in many areas so the mechanics are somewhat routine. Since you're dividing the ownership, you will need to have the individual spaces surveyed to establish legal descriptions. Individual financing will, of course, be necessary for each professional office.

Sandwich Lease

A sandwich lease is an excellent method of controlling property and generating investment income without capital. The key is to lease property that can be released at a higher rate. Your lease is then sandwiched between the owner and the new tenant, who pays a higher rent to you than you pay to the property owner.

You can use a number of methods to get the initial lease at a lower rate. If the market is depressed, maybe the owner would be happy to lease it at a rent less than you calculate the market will be after the slump turns to a recovery. If the property needs work, agree to upgrade it if the owner will give you a long-term lease at a low rate.

Negotiating the economics is the key, but in any event you should plan to include an option to purchase as part of the lease. This can be an important part of your strategy, especially if you turn the property around.

By signing your lease when the market in general is depressed and putting personal effort into upgrading the property, you may see a drastic increase in its value when rental conditions improve. Furthermore, when you release at a higher rate, the property value will automatically increase based on an income approach to appraisal. Its investment attractiveness will improve overnight and with an option to purchase at the previous value the profit will be yours.

Master Lease as Security for Development

A master lease is an overriding lease of a building (usually an office or shopping complex). It is used to guarantee a return to the owner in a sale-leaseback transaction, or, in some cases, to secure permanent financing. The developer of a project may underwrite sale of the project to a limited partnership and concurrently provide security for the long-term lender by establishing a master lease. The signatory to the master lease then covers his obligation by leasing to individual tenants at a profit.

In a way the master lease is an insurance policy against loss of rent. Its purpose is to establish a base return on investment for the owner and in some cases a guarantee for payment of debt service during the rent-up phase of a new development.

When you are acquiring property with a strong master lease signed by someone who knows what he's doing or a company with strong management and financial capabilities, it simply reduces your risk. It also increases your ability to obtain equity financing. Be careful, though. If the property itself is headed for trouble you may be forced to depend on the party signing the master lease. Of course, this is the purpose of the master lease— but when things don't work out as planned, even the strongest companies try to renegotiate or cancel.

Management Leaseback

This approach is often used in the sale of apartments to a limited partnership. A management company, which is more than likely a subsidiary of the company selling the limited partnership units, will lease the entire property after the sale. The limited partnership, therefore, has no concern over management, and the sales organization has a built-in aid. By arranging the leaseback concurrently with the offering, the investors know what their return will be and therefore will be more willing to invest.

This is an application of the master lease designed to meet the needs of investors who must be satisfied with both the professional management and projected return before committing their funds. It takes the risk down to a minimal level.

Real estate companies that specialize in limited partnership offerings are practically required to provide management for the property they sell. Often they have a separate corporation staffed by professional managers that handles this. A management leaseback actually transfers economic risk from the investors to the management company. The company is compensated for this risk by the income produced in excess of the leaseback obligation.

Consequently, negotiation of the master lease must take the normal management fee and the risk premium into consideration. The end result is more income for the company and less risk for the investors.

Lease Back the Vacancies

If you are acquiring property that has a high vacancy rate, ask the owner to lease the vacant units for a certain period of time to ensure your return. The seller only has to lease enough units to bring the cash flow up to a reasonable return. This approach avoids the extensive liability of a master lease-back and provides a method of reducing the seller's obligation as the vacant units are rented to new tenants.

Leasing back the vacancies is one of the many ways of working around apparent problems to structure a successful closing. If you are acquiring property with vacancies that exceed the risk you are willing to take, this technique may help.

Sellers who are tired of management and willing to work with you to solve their problems by helping you meet your objectives are often able to share risk to ensure a sale. If the transaction is on the borderline between problems and profit and you need that little incentive to go ahead, offsetting the vacancies can turn a questionable deal into a positive venture.

Lease Cash-out

If you are acquiring land that has potential for a lease, locate a tenant at the same time you make the purchase. Then take the lease to a lender as security in addition to the land itself and borrow the money to acquire the land. Income from the lease will offset the loan payments, and the land seller will cash out, possibly at a price favorable to you.

This is a technique that converts a potential passive land investment into a business opportunity. Anytime you can change the earnings performance of property concurrently with acquisition you tend to increase value. When you enter an acquisition that involves making raw land income-producing, you move considerably closer to a business proposition.

Arranging a lease for the land you want to buy is like creating the money you need to make the purchase. The future income represented by the lease has a present value. If that present value equals your purchase price, chances are you can acquire the land with no cash out of pocket.

The seller's cooperation will be essential and he has good reason to help out. When you finish putting the pieces together, the seller will cash out. As you proceed be sure to make the steps interdependent. Make the purchase contingent on financing and finalizing a land lease. Offer to cash out the seller only if every part of the transaction fits together as planned.

Land Sale Lease-back for Development

By selling and leasing back commercial land, you can often raise the cash necessary to complete development. Construction costs sometimes exceed the funds available for building. Consequently, a developer may have to sell part or all of the project land to raise development funds.

You may be able to raise sufficient cash by selling the parking area to an investor and leasing back. The land investor's interest would be subject to construction and permanent financing. You are able to add cash to cover construction and complete the project.

Selling property and leasing it back is a common financing technique. Applying this method to parking areas and freestanding portions of a shopping center such as automobile repair centers simplifies the requirements you must follow. In fact, if you anticipate the possibility of needing additional funds, try to hold back these somewhat separate land areas from your construction mortgage. This will keep you from having to negotiate a partial release if you have to structure a land sale lease-back later.

Package the Leases and Sell Out

This approach is designed to give you a rapid turnover of capital by packaging the entire project, including leases, financing, land, plans, and the construction contract. Virtually all of this is done on paper, with a minimum of out-of-pocket expenses. The cash comes when the package is sold to an investor at a profit. The cash outlay by the investor covers the real estate equity requirement and the equity you create by putting the package together. The investor gets a fully organized project and none of the headaches of putting it together. This approach is often used for establishing limited partnerships.

It takes skill and hard work to set up a successful shopping center or office building development. In the short run, getting solid tenants signed on leases is as valuable as land ownership is over the long pull. The value created by the leases is saleable. Selling a complete project package is a way of pulling out the value created by your efforts. It's a quick turnover of the capital invested to put the deal together without the wait normally associated with long-term real estate investment.

With the steady growth in requirements and bureaucratic regulations, the value (and of course the cost) of packaging a sound development project is increasing. As a business segment of the real estate industry, it has solid potential.

Lease When You Can't Buy

If you have spent time trying to acquire land, no doubt you have run into owners who refuse to sell but will lease. Although it is frustrating, the wisdom of their plan is apparent. Even in this situation there are advantages.

Leasing land eliminates the need for large amounts of front-end capital. Furthermore, if you plan to build and the landowner agrees to subordinate his interest to the financing you need, the possibility that you will be able to mortgage out is greatly increased. You will be able to put the deal together with less cash since you don't have to buy the land. By leasing land you gain control. What you do with that control will determine your profit. In that sense it's no different than outright ownership.

The extent of your long-term success with a land lease will depend to a large degree on what you are able to include and keep out of the original lease terms. Try to work in an option to buy. Work toward an option that can be exercised after a reasonable time period. In any event, push to get one in even if it's exercisable in 50 years or only after the death of the owner's last child.

It's crucial to avoid imprudent and short-sighted rent escalation clauses. Don't tie increases in rent to the consumer price index as it has proven to be very dangerous. If you have to include a provision for rent increases, and it would be unusual if you could avoid one, tie it to the long-term appreciation of the land and not the sporadic annual jumps in value that tend to be an appraiser's best guess. Keep in mind that you're renting the land, not offsetting the owner's loss in buying power due to inflation—his continued ownership of the land will do that, not your rental payments.

Lender Land Lease

This approach to financing often provides the incentive a lender needs to fund a project. The lender buys the land intended for development and leases it to the developer. Since the lender will be providing the first mortgage, there is not the fear of subordination that is common with landowners who are leasing. The lender (usually an insurance company) has full security, and the developer is in fact getting capital for the land acquisition from the lender in addition to long-term financing, thus reducing the need for equity capital.

This technique is practically a joint venture approach to a sale lease-back that eliminates the intervening step of acquiring the land. Instead you line up your lender and go into the project completely funded. The lender is really your backer and is investing in your ability to create a business out of vacant land.

From the standpoint of long-term investment, the lender has an advantageous position through ownership of appreciating land which also produces current lease income. From your standpoint the strategy is to package the project, mortgage out, and generate sheltered income.

Leased Land Pyramid

Buying land subject to the improvements and existing financing and then leasing it back to the seller is an increasingly popular investment medium. It is as good for small investors as it is for insurance companies. You can use leased land as a rapid estate-building tool by simply varying the capitalization rate.

For example, if you can buy land for $10,000 and lease it back to the seller based on a capitalization rate of 10 percent, your rental income is $1,000 per year. At this point you own the land and receive lease income on it. Then exchange the land tax-free based on a 5 percent capitalization rate. The $1,000 per year income has a value of $20,000 when capitalized at 5 percent ($1,000 ÷ 5 percent = $20,000). You double the value to $20,000 and increase your acquisition power overnight. It's a matter of negotiation. It's also a matter of risk evaluation.

This technique illustrates how you can build value into a general acquisition plan. There's a lot of truth to the statement that you make your money when you buy.

Sale Lease-back as an Investment Opportunity

The sale and lease-back of successful business real estate is an excellent source of investment real estate. Under the right conditions you can use this technique to bring property on the market.

Corporations often prefer to put their capital in the business for expansion rather than having it tied up in real estate which sustains current operations only. Every dollar of capital applied to the business serves to increase earnings, and having equity tied up in real estate can in some cases actually slow down corporate growth. In the more fortunate situations, earnings will grow as fast as capital permits the company to expand. Approaching companies that may not have thought of this possibility is one way to locate investment property when there doesn't seem to be anything worthwhile on the market. With the competition for investment real estate, techniques which embody an incentive for the seller can be invaluable.

The sale leaseback has a history of financing business expansion. From the standpoint of the company it is an investment-capital-generating technique. Traditionally, the larger national corporations have put it to effective use, but it works equally well with established and growing small businesses.

Sell at a Loss and Lease the Land

You can sometimes develop an opportunity by taking a look at the components of a particular real estate investment. For example, if the value of the improvements has dropped but the value of the land has increased, consider structuring the acquisition so the seller has a loss on the improvements but retains ownership of the land. There are solid benefits for both sides with this technique.

When you purchase improved real estate, you set up a depreciation schedule that requires allocation of value between land and improvements.

It is not uncommon for the land to appreciate and the improvements to depreciate during a given ownership period. The degree to which this occurs depends on the position of the property in the real estate cycle and general market conditions.

If the property you want has the right characteristics, here's a benefit you can offer the seller that may provide the needed incentive to close the deal. If the improvements are worth less than the seller's adjusted basis, buy them separately and lease the land. The seller will have a deductible loss on the sale and lease income from the land.

Work in an option to purchase the land after a certain date. You'll eventually get the land if you want, and in the meantime you'll be able to allocate the entire purchase price to depreciable improvements while deducting the lease payments.

Using a Lease to Gain Possession Before Closing

Leasing has many applications that go beyond the conventional association with space rental. It is a fundamental real estate tool that can help build a solid acquisition structure in various situations.

For example, if mortgage rates are killing the deal you're working on, consider escrowing the down payment and leasing the property until the money market eases. The seller will have a firm deal with cash in escrow to back it up plus lease income. You get use of the property now and time to arrange more satisfactory financing.

Leasing the property you want is a method of bridging the time gap that the reality of market conditions often presents. The gap may even be years long when you lease with an option to buy. Textbook investments are the exception to actual real estate practice. When you want possession is not necessarily when requirements of the transaction will permit possession.

This is clearly illustrated by the extended time demands of a multiparty exchange that often involves a lengthy process of finding suitable property to complete the transaction. If you want possession of the property as soon as possible but the owner must exchange for tax purposes, the delay can be prolonged while the search for exchange property is underway. There is a solution, though.

In addition to the standard exchange agreement, which will probably provide for several very necessary months to locate exchange property, arrange a separate lease so you can gain immediate possession. The rent should be based on fair market rates and run for a certain period with provisions to renew. It will allow you to have use of the property and still cooperate with the seller's objective of securing the tax benefits of an exchange.

19

Acquisition with Options

Options hold a special place in real estate acquisition. They are rights to purchase without the obligation to perform associated with a conventional purchase agreement. In some highly leveraged cases, an option increases in value at a much greater percentage rate than would be possible with an outright purchase of the underlying property. An option also carries an implicit time advantage.

In fact, when you buy an option you really buy the time you need to choose an action. If you choose not to acquire the property under option, it will expire at the agreed time with no consequence other than the forfeiture of its cost (if any) without benefit realized by you.

The time you buy with an option can be put to many and varied uses. It's standard operating procedure to obtain a few months' option on land to run soil tests and check out the title and municipal requirements before making an all-out commitment to commercial development.

Options are also a useful speculation method. If you see progress moving toward an overlooked parcel of land, a well-negotiated option can put you in the position to profit. It's timing your commitment that will make the difference. If you move too soon and the buyers haven't reached you before the option expires, you end up out of the money. Of course, who's going to wait. If you're really out to profit by reselling the option, you'll probably know the likely buyer even before you commit. In any event, options can take many forms and are adaptable to a number of different circumstances.

The basic option structure includes the price and terms for purchase of the property, the date, the right to transfer the option, and a provision allowing for extension of the option. Variations on this structure center around how the owner is compensated for granting the option, including the amount and timing of payment for the option. These negotiable terms can have a direct effect on your profit if you plan to resell the property or develop it. There's a worse effect if you can't obtain the option you need. That should not be a problem if you're serious about ultimately buying and willing to pay a fair price for the option.

Whether option costs should properly apply toward purchase or rest as separate payment for the time the property is off the market is negotiable. In fact, it depends on which side of the table you're sitting on. Certainly you want to negotiate the best deal possible for you.

Interest Option

An interest option is one of the easier methods of paying for an option. Although it is not quite as good for the seller as other option structures, it is a sound way to calculate option value.

With this approach, the option consideration is an amount equal to the savings account interest on the value of the property for the period of the option. The details vary with circumstance. In some cases the seller is paid only if the option is not exercised. If the option is exercised, the seller gets his price but no option consideration. Consequently, the option payment is compensation for loss of the sale and is made after the expiration date. If the option is exercised and the sale closes, there's no penalty to the seller (and no option payment) because he reached his ultimate objective—selling the property.

It makes sense to tie an option payment to the property value even if the interest rate is a negotiable item. The owner may prefer that the rate be tied to the prime lending rate or the consumer price index. In any event, there's considerable flexibility when you have an idea of the components that make sense in arriving at a logical amount.

For example, it may make sense to the owner if you also agree to pay the property taxes prorated over the option period. Although it may be a minor amount for a few months' option in light of the total sales price, the appeal to a seller can edge the negotiations in your favor.

Effort Option

Option structures are as flexible as the people negotiating them. Look at what you want to accomplish and you'll likely see an option method. An effort option stipulates that you will obtain preliminary development plans and all necessary municipal approval within the option period at your expense. If you don't exercise the option, the plans, engineering studies, and other documentation, including any lease commitments you've obtained, become the property of the seller.

Since the value of land is to a large degree determined by its use, this approach transfers a degree of uncertainty to the seller by allowing you to verify the property's suitability with no cost for the time needed to do it.

If the property proves to be unsuitable for development, all you've lost is the cost of investigation. The seller is not paid for the cost of discovering that his property is inappropriate for the use you intend.

Turning over the results of your effort is simply a way to negotiate option control. The paperwork developed on a certain parcel has value even if it's only to eliminate a proposed use as part of the search to find the highest and best use. This option approach reduces your cost and covers a portion of the risk when there's a chance a particular location is not practical for your project.

Letter of Credit Option

A letter of credit can eliminate the need for cash while meeting the seller's requirement for option security. With this technique you give the seller a letter of credit in the amount of the option consideration mutually agreed upon. If the option is not exercised, the seller collects on the letter of credit. If the option is exercised, the letter of credit is null and void.

The seller is fully protected in the event you don't complete the acquisition. You avoid the initial out-of-pocket cost of a standard option. With this approach there is no additional payment to the seller above the property cost. The letter of credit is more than anything a guarantee that you are earnest in your plan to complete the purchase.

The cost to you, assuming the purchase is completed as planned, will probably be no more than interest charged by the bank for issuing the letter of credit. From a negotiation standpoint, though, you gain the same advantage you would by paying cash when the option is signed.

An Automatic Rolling Option with First Right of Refusal

This technique illustrates how an option can be combined with other provisions of an acquisition to meet your specific project goals.

An automatic option occurs when exercising one option automatically establishes another option to acquire adjacent land. The owner grants subsequent options as you exercise the prior ones. When exercising your initial option, you automatically roll it over to adjacent land without an additional payment.

The consideration for each option is built into the purchase of the previous parcel. It may not be necessary to increase the purchase price to obtain the option. The cash from your initial purchase and the probability of additional sales can be enough incentive to satisfy the owner.

An added benefit to this approach is that although your legal option rolls only from one parcel to another at a time, there is a built-in first right of refusal to the entire tract which may include dozens of separate parcels. Consequently, you, in effect, tie up an entire project with only the expense of acquiring the parcels you need when you need them.

Continuing Option

A continuing option is set up by assigning the income from paper, which you own, to the owner of the property you are optioning. The property owner receives monthly income for a designated period, after which the option expires if not exercised.

This approach avoids a large up-front payment, and, depending on the terms, can provide the extended time necessary to sell the option for profit. It should be set up for a limited time with the right to renew for another period equal to the first.

The purpose is to build in continuity. First you establish an ongoing right by monthly option payments from the income-producing paper assigned to the property owner. The more he gets used to regular income, the less likely he will be to give it up. Second, you build in the right to renew or extend the option for a term equal to the original period. By providing for a continuing option, you build in profit potential when your objective is to speculate on the value of the property over an extended time period.

Increased Payment Option

This technique is designed to increase the option consideration in return for annual renewal. The initial agreement provides for increasing the payments to the seller if you choose to keep the option in force.

This is an incentive for the seller to grant a long-term option and allows you to tie up future appreciation early in the game. For example, you can structure the payments so the seller receives $1,000 the first year, $2,000 the second, $3,000 the third year, but $5,000 the fourth year and $8,000 the fifth. The longer you control the property the greater the payments to the seller.

It may also be appropriate to increase the purchase price as the option period progresses. If this requirement works into the deal, you may be able to offset it by applying part or all of the option payments to the purchase price. This can become a necessity toward the end of the option as payments increase faster.

Land Cost Option

Option consideration can be an excellent method for a seller to offset the costs of holding vacant land. With the right approach to negotiation, you can secure a relatively long-term option by simply paying the taxes on the property. If the owner knows he has this expense covered, and maybe a few other costs, negotiation of a long-term option can be smoother.

One of the drawbacks to investment in land that doesn't produce income is the cost of holding the property over a long time period. Unfortunately, many land buyers don't discover this until they experience it firsthand.

A property owner who has been hit with this realization is a likely candidate for negotiation of an option that will soften the cost impact he's lived with for years. It's the unexpected that hurts the worst. A new paving or municipal utility assessment has brought more than one parcel of land on the open market. If you size and time the option payment to cover the owner's cost, chances are you'll get his attention and have a good start toward acquiring the property.

Real Estate as Option Consideration

Deeding free-and-clear real estate or partial ownership shares can often be an effective option technique. This is a method of using the value of the land you have to acquire an option on additional real estate.

One of the best applications of this technique permits you to transfer value from lots that are far from areas being developed to property that is rapidly appreciating. The objective is to meet the basic requirement of sellers when granting options—to get a little extra consideration for giving you the right to purchase.

A subdivision of lots in a mountain area that never quite got the public acceptance necessary for success can be a source of solid option consideration. Offering an owner one lot for a year's option to buy property you believe will appreciate can, in effect, allow you to cash out of the mountain lots. Your option cost is essentially equal to the value of the lot. If you timed it right, you'll be able to sell the option for more than the cost of the lot and make a profit by this creative use of property that previously was thought to have little value.

20

Acquisition Techniques
for Special Deals

There are always a few special real estate acquisition techniques that stand out as especially useful over the years. They may involve institution financing that you might not normally consider unless the deal was too good to pass up. Or, they may involve methods of creating value by dividing property into smaller units that sell at a higher percentage value. A few of each of these techniques follow in this chapter.

In addition, there are techniques that will help protect your acquisitions and give you a slight edge if trouble develops.

Pledge Additional Real Estate as Security

If you are borrowing to make a down payment and the bank wants more than your signature, offer to pledge other real estate as security. The pledge is recorded encumbering the property and is released when the loan is repaid.

Financing Company Second Mortgage Loan

An increasingly popular source of loan money is from finance companies. They recognize the value of loaning on homes and are willing to loan money on the difference between your first mortgage and 80 percent of the appraised value.

This permits you to borrow on a portion of the equity you've built up and the appreciated value of your home. Home equity loans are also available from conventional banks. Care should be taken with this type of loan because the security is essential to keep—you need a place to live.

Discount Buy-Back: For When You Need Cash Immediately

If you need to raise cash in a hurry, consider selling your real estate at 50 percent of the market value, with an option to buy it back within three years for the actual market value on the day you sold it. Then, three years later, you buy the property back for a price based on the old value and either keep it or sell it at the appreciated value. Both the sales price today and the repurchase price three years later are below market value, yet everyone involved makes a profit. This approach requires that the property appreciate at a rate high enough to exceed the market value of three years ago.

Protect Level of Rental Income by Decreasing the Interest Rate as Vacancies Occur

If you are acquiring apartments or other rental property and are concerned about possible vacancies, this approach may solve the problem. A simple way to protect against a drop in rental income is to decrease the interest rate on the seller's carry-back loan if vacancies occur. Then, if the market improves and the vacancies are filled, increase the interest rate to the original amount. This will help protect your cash flow and transfer part of the risk back to the seller.

Lower Risk and Increase Profits by Subordinating Debt Service to Cash Flow

When you are acquiring distressed property that the owner really wants out of, you can lower your risk and increase your profit potential by arranging for the debt service on the seller's carry-back financing, to be paid only after you have received a certain amount of cash flow.

The amount over the agreed cash flow would apply to interest and principal on the seller's equity. If the property has unexpected expenses that cut into your profit, the seller would sacrifice debt service payments to protect your cash flow. The seller is, in effect, guaranteeing the profitability of the property by subordinating the debt service payments to your cash flow.

When Money Is a Problem, Buy with Paper but Cash Out the Seller

If you have no cash but the seller wants cash, raise the purchase price to offset a discount on the second mortgage. Assume the first mortgage and give the seller a second mortgage, which is then discounted and sold to get the cash needed for the down payment. The increase in the purchase price offsets the discount necessary to sell the second for cash.

Make an Installment Purchase

You can acquire property on an installment basis by arranging with the seller to pay a certain amount of cash into a special escrow account until the down payment amount is made. This approach involves setting up a special agreement that establishes a closing when the down payment amount is paid in full.

Minimize Your Risk by Making Price Contingent on Resale

If you are acquiring real estate for resale and the seller doesn't mind sharing the risk and the possibility of a higher profit, set a sliding scale for the purchase price that establishes a profit for you and a higher price for the seller if you succeed. The seller's trust in your ability to get a higher sales price can result in acquisition terms for you that are virtually without risk.

Protect Your Partnership Investment with a Buy-Sell Agreement

If you are acquiring property in partnership, be sure to establish a buy-sell agreement with the other partners. The agreement should cover the transfer of ownership and management in the event of the death of one of the partners. It should also set up a buy-out procedure if the partners can't get along in the decision-making process.

When You're Uncertain, Set Up a Buy-Back Agreement

If you are uneasy about the property you are acquiring, set up an agreement with the seller to buy the property back within a limited time period. For example, the agreement might require the seller to buy the property back within three months if you are dissatisfied for any reason.

Avoid Foreclosure by Entering into a Joint Venture with Notes

If an owner is in danger of losing his equity in vacant land because of an inability to make the payments, a joint venture may solve the problem. If the debt service payment is large, an acquisition in partnership by several individuals who are each easily capable of making their portion of the land payment is the first step. The seller's equity could then be purchased with several personal notes from the invididual partners to spread the risk.

Obtain a Discount in Exchange for a Large Cash Payment

If you are planning to pay off a privately held mortgage, don't overlook the possibility of acquiring additional equity which may be available for the asking. If you catch the mortgage-holder at the right time, she or he may gratefully give you a discount to receive a large and unexpected cash payment. Of course, this approach is a matter of negotiation and should not be requested in a manner that indicates that you will pay off the note even if the discount is not granted.

What to Do When a Note Is Due and There Is No Cash

What can you do when a note is due and there's no cash to make the payment? Try negotiating an extension, and, as an incentive, paying the note-holder a late charge.

If the lender is worried that you may not be able to pay the note at the end of the extension, offer additional security and an increase in the interest rate. The objective is to increase the benefits to the holder of the note as consideraton for an extension, or, if possible, a change in the terms of the note.

Maximize Leverage with Subordination to Construction Financing

If you're planning to acquire vacant land for development and want to maximize leverage, negotiate subordination of the seller's interest to construction financing.

This will allow you to build without paying off the land loan until construction is complete and the permanent financing is in place. This approach can work to maximum benefit when it is used with a mortgage-out strategy.

Reduce the Down Payment with a Broker Loan

If there is trouble in meeting the cash requirement for a down payment, the brokers involved may be a source of financing. This approach can be accomplished with the commissions or other funds the brokers may have available for a sound investment at a high interest rate. It can be especially attractive to brokers with high incomes who would benefit from a readily available investment with high income.

Refinance Property During Acquisition by Substituting Collateral While Preserving Installment Reporting

Refinancing property during acquisition can be a problem if the holder of the seller's original financing (the existing first mortgage) will not accept an early payoff because she wants to maintain installment reporting. The solution is to leave the note undisturbed but substitute different security.

A mortgage on different real estate or even a certificate of deposit could be used. This approach allows the property to be freed for the new financing, but the note remains untouched, protecting the original installment reporting for the note-holder (from whom the current seller originally bought the property).

Use an Inheritance Pledge to Facilitate Acquisition

If you have an inheritance that is established, it can be a help to you in acquiring real estate. Buy the real estate you want on a note secured by the inheritance. The holder of the note would get the first right to the proceeds at settlement of the estate. You get the real estate now, and the seller gets solid security.

Use an Irrevocable Trust as Security

If you have an irrevocable trust that is producing a very low return on equity that could be increased through real estate investment, you may be able to use it as security. The income from the trust could be pledged to secure a personal note or be diverted to actually amortize the note.

Put Off Making Large Payments, by Reversing the Interest

By structuring an acquisition with separate notes that are due annually, you can place the high interest payments at the end of the amortization term rather than at the beginning. One note is paid, plus accrued interest, at the end of each 12 months.

Consequently, the first note bears one year's interest, the fifth year's note bears five years' interest, and the twentieth bears 20 years' interest.

One mortgage is used to secure all the notes. This places the burden of making large payments in the later years. It also gives the purchaser a larger deduction toward the end of the amortization. The seller is able to defer ordinary income in the earlier years of the sale. However, be careful with this one. Compound interest grows fast.

When Mortgage Rate Is Too High, Escrow the Down Payment and Lease the Property

If mortgage rates are so high that they are killing a deal for you, consider escrowing the down payment and leasing the property until rates ease. The seller will have a firm deal with cash in escrow to back it up plus lease income. You get use of the property and a chance for cheaper mortgage money in the future.

Protect the Interest with a Noncompetition Agreement

Competition is a major factor in real estate investments. If you are acquiring property from a developer who might go into competition with you, consider requiring a noncompetition agreement.

The agreement should state that the seller will not build a competing project within, for example, a 3-mile radius of the property you are acquiring for a three-year period. In exchange for this agreement, the seller may require a fee, which could be offset by lowering the sales price.

Use an Anxious Seller as Co-signer

If the owner really wants out of a property, consider asking his aid as a co-signer on a short-term note for the down payment. If the property will pay off the loan, the seller has nothing to lose, but a sale to gain.

Lower the Loan Amount by Increasing the Interest

Market value of real estate is sometimes lower than the loan balances as a result of vandalism, fire, or market conditions. The key element to this solution is low interest on the original loans. If that is the case, you can negotiate a reduction in the outstanding loan amount, provided the monthly payments remain the same—both the same total amount of payments and the same loan payment amount. The owner of the loan will receive the same in gross income and total loan payments, but a greater percentage of the income from the debt service will be interest income. The benefit here is that the debt balance is reduced to a level that is more reasonable in relation to the reduced market value of the property.

Buy Paper at a Discount and Trade at Face Value

One of the best estate building techniques is to buy paper at a discount, and, with careful negotiation, use it as the down payment to acquire real estate. With this technique, you can pick up immediate profit while moving from a declining debt investment (paper) to an appreciating equity investment (real estate).

Assign the Payments—Don't Trade the Paper

Rather than conveying ownership of a note as down payment, establish an escrow agreement that assigns the payments from the note to the seller as security for a new note with identical terms.

The seller will receive the total income from the new note as consideration for the down payment. The original note remains intact and provides security for the transaction.

Always Try for a Release Clause to Lower Your Risk

If you are buying land, always try to negotiate the release of an appropriate percentage of the total as you reduce the loan principal. Releases often prove to be of special importance in determining the value of the property in the future. Release clauses allow you to avoid the necessity of paying off the entire debt balance before getting a development loan. If for some reason things turn for the worse, you will have part of the property free and clear if you have to default on the balance of the loan.

III

THE CASE LAW AND REVENUE
RULINGS OF EXCHANGING

The following brief presentation of the cases and rulings relating to exchanging is designed to provide a starting point for further reference. The problem in the past has been the lack of a one-source reference that brings together this varied body of information. The following is intended to correct that problem in a way that reflects the progress of certain themes as they evolved through the years.

Part III is divided into nine sections:

1. Recent Exchange Cases
2. Foundation Cases in Exchange Law
3. Business and Partnership Interests in Nontaxable Exchanges
4. Cases in Which the IRS Argued for an Exchange
5. The Foundation of Multiparty Exchanging
6. Successful Variations on Multiparty Exchanges
7. Cases That Expanded Application of the Multiparty Exchange
8. Multiparty Exchanges That Failed
9. Revenue Rulings on Exchanging

The following cases and revenue rulings are not only a valuable source of what is allowed and what should be avoided in practice, they are also an important source of money-making ideas.

Recent Exchange Cases

The following recent cases are arranged in alphabetical order for ease of reference. The one point that stands out in these cases is that you must avoid the right to the cash (generated from disposition of your property) that is used to purchase exchange property. The contractual right to, or unilateral control over, those funds triggers tax liability. Furthermore, these cases again demonstrate that the court continues to interpret section 1031 in favor of the taxpayer. You almost have to go out of your way to lose nontaxable treatment, and in a few of these cases that seems to be what happened.

Three cases deserve special mention because of their excellent insight into the heart of the nontaxable exchange. If you choose to go more deeply into the legal structures of a multiparty exchange, the full text of the Biggs, Barker, and Brauer cases are worth reading.

Please note also that the E. C. Lee case has opened the door for a "reverse exchange" wherein the taxpayer first acquires the replacement property and subsequently disposes of the original property. This strategy has possibilities when combined with the structure of a delayed exchange.

Joyce M. Allen, 43 TCM 1045 (1982)

A nontaxable exchange did not occur because the steps in the transaction were not interdependent. Two escrows were used that were not contingent on successful completion of each other.

A. L. Anderson, 49 TCM 1352 (1985)

A nontaxable exchange did not occur because the taxpayer sold property and two months later purchased other property. The transaction was a sale and subsequent purchase rather than an interdependent exchange.

Earlene T. Barker, 74 TC No. 42 (1980)

A multiparty exchange completed through a fourth party escrow arrangement did not prevent the taxpayer from offsetting all boot received by boot given. The escrow agreements were mutually interdependent and the taxpayer never had access to cash; consequently, the transaction met the requirements of Rev. Rul. 77–297, which outlines the procedure for a multiparty exchange.

Frederick W. Behrens, TCM 195 (1985)

The Tax Court held that a newly created debt could not be used to offset cash boot received in a two-way exchange of trucks. The Court held that there is no difference between created paper and existing loans assumed or taken "subject to."

G. S. Bezdjian, 53 TCM 368 (1987)

No exchange occurred when the taxpayers received property and subsequently sold their property. The substance of the transaction was a purchase followed by a sale.

Franklin B. Biggs, 69 TC 905 (1978)

Taxpayer completed a nontaxable exchange by acting as agent for buyer to arrange acquisition of exchange property. Exchange property was deeded to taxpayer through fourth party without title passing through buyer of taxpayer's property.

Joseph R. Bolker, 81 TC 782 (1983)

A nontaxable exchange occurred even though it was immediately preceded by a tax-free acquisition under Section 333. Here the tax-free transaction preceded rather than followed the nontaxable exchange under Section 1031 as in Magneson. Section 1031's holding for business or investment requirement is reciprocal, equally applicable to properties at both ends of an exchange. A 1031 exchange may be preceded or succeeded by a tax-free acquisition or transfer because the taxpayer does not cash in on the gain. (Note Rev. Rul. 75–292 and 77–337 for possible conflicts.)

Glenda Brauer, 74 TC 84 (1980)

A nontaxable exchange occurred through oral modification of the original sales agreement. Exchange property was deeded directly to taxpayer. The taxpayer did not have control over the funds in escrow due to the circumstances of the closing.

Dollie H. Click, 78 TC 225 (1982)

The court held that a nontaxable exchange did not occur when the taxpayer exchanged farmland for two residences, which she subsequently gave to her children. The exchange property was acquired for the purpose of giving it to her children rather than for investment purposes.

Antonio D'Onofrio, 47 TCM 29 (1983)

The taxpayer contended that the sale of his property was a mistake and he intended to make an exchange. The fact that the sale proceeds were later used to acquire property did not make the transaction an exchange. Although the taxpayer stated he intended to exchange, he did not act consistently with his stated intentions and consequently Section 1031 did not apply.

Phillip M. Garcia, 80 TC 491 (1983)

A nontaxable exchange occurred because the closing of a series of escrows were contingent and interdependent and no cash proceeds from the sale of the original property were actually or constructively received.

Stuart L. Gibson, 44 TCM 168 (1982)

The court held that the taxpayer did not show that proceeds from the transaction were restricted. Consequently, a sale and purchase occurred because the funds in the escrow account were available to the taxpayer. There was no agreement or escrow instructions that would cast the sale and purchase of the properties in the form of an exchange.

James Godine, Jr., 36 TCM 1595 (1977)

The taxpayer was denied the deduction of a loss because he completed a Section 1031 exchange. The taxpayer argued that he did not intend to exchange. The court held that intent was immaterial and an exchange was in fact done and what the taxpayer actually did not intend was the tax consequences of not being able to deduct a loss under Section 1031.

Carl E. Koch, 71 TC 543 (1978)

An exchange of fee for fee subject to a leasehold interest in excess of 30 years constitutes an exchange of "like-kind" property. Both the lessor and lessee have interests in the real property. The lessee has a leasehold interest which, if in excess of 30 years, is like in kind to real estate for purposes of Section 1031.

Land Dynamics, 37 TCM 1119 (1978)

A 1031 exchange did not occur because the taxpayer was a dealer and acquired the property for resale. The taxpayer did not prove its investor status in holding the property acquired by exchange.

E. C. Lee, 51 TCM 1438 (1986)

Nonrecognition was denied because the taxpayers did not demonstrate an interdependent exchange occurred when they acquired property and sold their original property several months later. Although the proceeds went to the sellers of the acquired property, that did not establish interdependency as part of an overall plan.

Norman J. Magneson, 81 TC 767 (1983)

The court held that a 1031 exchange occurred when the taxpayer exchanged property for a 10 percent interest in another property, then immediately contributed that property by a tax-free Section 741 transfer for a 10 percent interest in a partnership. The court ruled that holding property for tax-free contribution to a partnership is the same as holding it for investment.

C. W. Mars, 54 TCM 636 (1987)

This transaction did not qualify for nonrecognition because it was in the form of a sales agreement that was not amended to establish an exchange.

Byron Wayne Meadows, 42 TCM 611 (1981)

The transfer of sales proceeds to a separate escrow for purchase of replacement property did not meet the requirements of Section 1031.

Milbrew, Inc., 42 TCM 1467 (1981)

Taxpayers received a check which they endorsed over to another party for an interest in an apartment project. The transaction did not qualify under Section 1031 because the sellers received cash for their property.

Emsy H. Swaim, 45 AFTR 2d 80–1276 (1979)

Taxpayers liquidated their property and had free use of the funds with which they later purchased other land. A nontaxable exchange did not occur because the transactions were not interdependent.

Karl G. Von Muff, 46 TCM 1185 (1983)

The taxpayers sold their property and applied the proceeds toward acquisition of other property, contending it was a Section 1031 exchange. The court held that a sale for cash and reinvestment of the proceeds in a like kind property does not qualify as a nontaxable exchange.

Fred S. Wagensen, 74 TC 51 (1980)

A multiparty exchange of ranches qualified under Section 1031 even though the taxpayer conveyed it by gift after the exchange. The taxpayer held the ranch for a period of time after the exchange and continued to operate it as a ranch. The fact that he planned to eventually give it to his children did not change the fact that he held it for use in business and investment after the exchange.

R. G. Young, 49 TCM 1439 (1985)

Taxpayer sold land and reinvested the proceeds. The transaction did not qualify because there was not interdependency between the transactions.

Foundation Cases in Exchange Law

Detroit Egg Biscuit and Specialty Co. v. Commissioner 9 BTA 1365 (1928)

The court held that a sale rather than an exchange occurred when the taxpayer transferred its building for money and agreed in the contract to use the money to build a new factory. The taxpayer was feeling its way in this case—there was no guideline to follow as yet. It wasn't until 1975 that the IRS clarified the application of exchanging to this type of transaction (Revenue Ruling 75–291.)

E. R. Braley v. Commissioner 14 BTA 1153 (1929)

This case clarified the procedure for a two-party transaction. The court held that the exchange fell "squarely within the provisions" permitting the nontaxable exchange of real estate.

Loughborough Development Corp. v. Commissioner 29 BTA 95 (1933)

A nontaxable exchange occurred even though the taxpayer's charter gave it the power to act as a dealer. The court held that the property involved in the exchange was held for investment.

Burkard Investment Co. v. United States 100 F. 2d 642 (1938)

The taxpayer claimed a loss when the property it acquired by exchange had a fair market value less than its cost. The court held that the taxpayer was not a dealer and that the transaction was an exchange and the loss could not be deducted.

Regals Realty Co. v. Commissioner 127 F. 2d 931 (1942)

The court held that the property acquired by exchange and sold shortly thereafter was not held for investment and the exchange did not qualify under Section 1031. The court clarified that it is immaterial whether the acquired property is held "for investment" as distinguished from "productive use" provided it is like kind and not acquired for inventory or sale.

Commissioner of Internal Revenue v. Crichton 122 F. 2d 181 (1941)

The taxpayer exchanged an individual interest in minerals, which were real property under state law, for an undivided interest in improved land. The court held that the transaction was a nontaxable exchange of like kind property.

Coleman v. Commissioner 180 F. 2d 758 (1950)

The taxpayer was required to pay tax on $14,000 in cash received in an otherwise nontaxable exchange. The problem arose when a private mortgage holder refused to accept an early payoff, thus forcing payment of cash to the taxpayer to balance equities.

Olson O. Sayre v. United States of America 163 F. Supp 495 (1958)

The court held that the taxpayer properly allocated cash boot received in an exchange when he invested a portion of the cash in a new residence, thus limiting his taxable gain.

Ethel Black v. Commissioner 35 TC 90 (1960)

In 1955, the taxpayer exchanged land for residential property. She fixed it up, listed it for sale, and then sold it in 1956. The court held that the residential property was held primarily for sale and did not qualify under Section 1031.

Business and Partnership Interests in Nontaxable Exchanges

Norman A. Miller v. United States of America 63–2 USTC 9606 (1963)

The court held that the exchange of a 50 percent interest in a tavern for a 25 percent interest in an auto supply business was a nontaxable transaction under Section 1031. The real estate received in the exchange was considered taxable boot.

Emory K. Crenshaw v. United States of America 71–2 USTC 9698 (1971)

A series of step transactions involving the exchange of partnership interests were held to be taxable in the end result.

Rollin E. Meyer, Jr. v. Commissioner 58 TC 311 (1972)

A nontaxable exchange occurred when the taxpayer exchanged a general partnership interest in one California partnership for a general partnership interest in a California limited partnership where both partnerships were in the business of renting apartments.

Juhl Smith v. Commissioner 75, 153 P-H Memo TC

The court held that a sale occurred when the taxpayer received cash for an undivided half interest in land and later executed an exchange agreement.

Cases in Which the IRS Argued for an Exchange

Harr, Secretary of Banking of the Commonwealth of Pennsylvania v. MacLaughlin 15 F. Supp 1004 (1936)

The taxpayer was allowed to deduct a loss realized on property transferred by exchange. The IRS argued that since it was an exchange, the deduction of the loss should not occur. The property had been acquired by the taxpayer through foreclosure and was held for sale. The court agreed with the taxpayer and allowed deduction of the loss.

Century Electric Co. v. Commissioner 192 F. 2d 155 (1951)

The Court of Appeals held that a nontaxable exchange did occur when the taxpayer sold a foundry building and land to a college for cash and then leased back the property for 95 years. The taxpayer was not allowed to deduct a loss on the sale because the 95-year leasehold was considered like kind property.

Allegheny County Auto Mart, Inc. v. Commissioner 208 F. 2d 693 (1953)

The taxpayer contended that it had sustained a taxable loss on sale of certain real estate. But the Commissioner contended an exchange occurred (even though it looked like a sale) because the taxpayer concurrently acquired other realty from the purchaser of its original property. The court held that the transaction was a nontaxable exchange and a loss could not be claimed because the transfer was "part of a single inseparable deal."

Leslie Co. v. Commissioner 64 TC 23 (1968)

The taxpayer sold and leased back its new facility for 30 years, realizing a loss on the transaction. The IRS contended that a nontaxable exchange occurred because the leaseback was like kind property. The court disagreed and permitted the loss because the lease lacked capital value.

The Foundation of Multiparty Exchanging

Mercantile Trust Co. et al. v. Commissioner 32 BTA 82 (1935)

Mercantile Trust was the foundation for multiparty exchanging in the years to follow. It contained many elements that were refined in later exchanges, such as an alternative sale if the exchange didn't close and the netting of cash. This case launched the successful exchange of real estate involving cash and the acquisition of property for exchange purposes.

W. D. Haden Co. v. Commissioner 165 F. 2d 588 (1948)

This multiparty transaction established that exchange property can be deeded directly to the taxpayer without first deeding it to the party acquiring the taxpayer's property. The direct deeding in Haden was later affirmed in Revenue Ruling 57–244. The Haden case is important because the structure of multiparty exchanging was backed by the IRS. In this case, the taxpayer had attempted to claim a loss and the IRS argued for a nontaxable exchange and won.

James Alderson et al. v. Commissioner 317 F. 2d 790 (1963)

The taxpayer agreed to sell for cash. The agreement was later amended to require the purchaser to acquire other realty and exchange it in lieu of cash. The Court of Appeals held the transaction to be a nontaxable exchange, thus reversing a lower court decision.

Antone Borchard v. Commissioner 24 TCM 1643 (1965)

The court held that a nontaxable exchange occurred where the taxpayer signed an option to transfer his property in exchange for acceptable real estate or cash in the event exchange property wasn't located. Four separate properties were acquired contingent on the exchange and transferred to the taxpayer.

Successful Variations on Multiparty Exchanges

J. H. Baird Publishing Company v. Commissioner 39 TC 608 (1962)

The taxpayer deeded its business realty to a real estate agent in 1956 but retained use of it. The agent then sold the realty to a purchaser subject to the taxpayer's use and built a new building with part of the proceeds. The agent transferred the new building to the taxpayer in 1957. The court held that the transaction qualified as a nontaxable exchange.

Coastal Terminals, Inc. v. United States of America 320 F. 2d 333 (1963)

The taxpayer assigned its option to purchase terminal sites to an oil company, which acquired an existing terminal, built three new terminals, and then conveyed all four to the taxpayer in exchange for its deep-water terminal. The court held that a nontaxable exchange did occur.

Boise Cascade Corporation and Affiliated Corporations 74,315 P-H Memo TC (1974)

The taxpayer exchanged property with a subsidiary. The IRS contended that the subsidiary didn't have fee simple title because the taxpayer had an option to purchase. The court held that under local law an option didn't establish an interest in realty and the transaction qualified under Section 1031.

W. A. Mays v. District Director of Internal Revenue 246 F. Supp 375 (1965)

The court held that a nontaxable exchange occurred when the taxpayers exchanged a Texas ranch for a New Mexico ranch owned by a foundation, provided the foundation found a buyer for the Texas ranch. The foundation sold the Texas ranch to a family corporation in which the taxpayers owned a 40 percent interest.

Leslie Q. Coupe v. Commissioner 52 TC 394 (1969)

A multiparty exchange was upheld when the taxpayer transferred his farm for four parcels of real estate. The court held that the transaction fell within the provisions of Section 1031 even though the buyer refused to go into title and cooperate in the exchange.

Bruce Starker v. United States of America 35 AFTR 2d 75–1550 (1975)

The court held that a tax-free exchange occurred when the taxpayer transferred timber land under a contract that provided for the receipt of like kind property over a specified period in the future.

Front Street, Inc. v. Commissioner 65 TC 124 (1975)

Taxpayer owned an option on property that a buyer wanted. The buyer loaned the taxpayer money to exercise this option and then exchanged for the property. The court held that it was a valid nontaxable exchange.

Hubert Rutland 77,008 P-H Memo TC

An exchange under Section 1031 occurred rather than a sale and reinvestment of the proceeds. Although the final draft of the agreement omitted the possibility of an exchange, the parties agreed orally to work out an exchange and the exchange did in fact take place.

Multiparty Exchanges That Failed

Bloomington Coca-Cola Bottling Co. v. Commissioner 189 F. 2d 14 (1951)

In this transaction, the taxpayer contracted for a new plant and paid the contractor in part by conveying the old plant to him. The transfer of the old plant was held to be taxable.

Harry F. Estill v. Commissioner 19 TCM 334 (1960)

A sale rather than an exchange occurred when the taxpayer failed to convey a partial interest in a one-third ownership interest of a tract of land prior to sale of the tract.

John M. Rogers v. Commissioner 44 TC 126 (1965)

A sale rather than an exchange occurred when the taxpayer transferred optioned property after cash payment was received under the terms of the option. The taxpayer had the right to cash because the buyer of exchange property did not sign the exchange agreement.

June Pinson Carlton, et al. v. United States of America 385 F. 2d 238 (1967)

The taxpayer lost the advantages of Section 1031 by deviating from the original exchange agreement when the purchaser assigned its agreement to acquire the designated exchange property to the taxpayer and paid him the cash necessary to acquire same.

George M. Bernard et al. v. Commissioner 26 TCM 176 (1967)

The taxpayers acquired land with the intent to sell it to a third party concurrently with the execution of the exchange but actually sold it two weeks after closing. The court held that interdependence of the steps in the transaction did not exist and the property was held primarily for sale; therefore, Section 1031 did not apply.

Bernard Halpern v. United States of America 286 F. Supp 255 (1968)

This multiparty transaction was held to be taxable because the contract acquiring the exchange property was not a contingent part of the exchange nor did the buyer go into title.

Starker v. U.S., No. 76–81 5/13/77 USDC Ore.

The Court reversed its earlier finding in favor of the same taxpayer (Starker I 1975) and ruled against him in this case. It held that exchange for a promise was not reciprocal and simultaneous and the obligation of the other party amounted to a bankable asset.

Revenue Rulings

Revenue Ruling 55–77

Partition proceedings are held to constitute a nontaxable transaction.

Revenue Ruling 55–749

Where under state law water rights are real property rights, the exchange of perpetual water rights for a fee interest in land constitutes a nontaxable exchange.

Revenue Ruling 57–244

A three-way exchange with direct transfer of ownership constitutes a nontaxable transaction.

Revenue Ruling 57–365

Where a parent corporation causes one of its subsidiaries to exchange assets with another company, the real and personal property are considered property of like kind under Section 1031.

Revenue Ruling 57–469

The use of a sale and purchase agreement where state law does not permit an exchange by a guardian of a ward's property constitutes a nontaxable exchange in substance.

Revenue Ruling 59–229

An exchange of unencumbered farmlands, farm buildings, and unharvested crops for "like property" constitutes a nontaxable exchange within the meaning of Section 1031.

Revenue Ruling 61–119

Where a taxpayer sells old equipment used in his trade or business to a dealer and purchases new equipment of like kind from the dealer under circumstances that indicate that the sale and purchase are reciprocal and mutually dependent transactions, the sale and purchase constitute an exchange of property within the meaning of Section 1031 even though the sale and purchase are accomplished by separately executed contracts and are treated as unrelated transactions by the taxpayer and the dealer for recordkeeping purposes.

Revenue Ruling 65–155

A taxpayer who claims the benefits of Section 1031(a) and (b) may elect to use the installment method of reporting any cash payments provided the transaction otherwise qualifies as an installment sale under Section 453 of the Code.

Revenue Ruling 66–209

Where a corporation leases property and receives annual rents and fee interest in other than property from the lessee, the value of such other property is income to the corporation as an advance rental.

Revenue Ruling 68–36

The basis of two properties acquired in an exchange shall be the same as the basis in the exchanged property, and such basis shall be allocated between the two properties acquired according to their respective fair market values on the date of the exchange.

Revenue Ruling 68–186

The utilization of oil and gas properties and the treatment of equalization payments connected therewith are discussed. The exchange of working interests and equipment qualifies under Section 1031. The computation of basis is explained.

Revenue Ruling 68–331

An exchange of a leasehold interest in a producing oil lease extending to the exhaustion of the deposit for the fee interest in an improved ranch qualifies under Section 1031.

Revenue Ruling 68–363

The location of either property in an exchange is immaterial in determining the applicability of Section 1031.

Revenue Ruling 72–151

A multiple asset exchange requires that the underlying property be analyzed to establish basis.

Revenue Ruling 72–456

This ruling presents the proper treatment of brokerage commissions paid in an exchange.

Revenue Ruling 72–515

The exchange of unencumbered fee title to timberlands that differ in timber quality and quantity qualifies for nonrecognition of gain or loss under Section 1031.

Revenue Ruling 72–601

A son's exchange of a life estate to his father for a remainder interest does not qualify under Section 1031. The life estate received was not considered of like kind to a fee interest in real estate because the life expectancy of the father was less than 30 years.

Revenue Ruling 73–476

The exchange of an undivided interest as a tenant in common in three separate parcels for a 100 percent ownership of one parcel qualifies under Section 1031.

Revenue Ruling 74–7

The reconversion of a foreign country's currency into U.S. dollars is not a like kind exchange under Section 1031.

Revenue Ruling 75–291

An exchange of land and a factory used by a manufacturing corporation for land acquired and a factory constructed solely for exchange by an unrelated corporation qualifies under Section 1031.

Revenue Ruling 75–292

The transfer by an individual of land and building used in his trade or business to an unrelated corporation in exchange for land and an office building and, immediately thereafter, transfer of the land and office building to individual's newly created corporation, in a transaction that qualified under Section 351, doesn't qualify under Section 1031(a).

Revenue Ruling 76–301

Assignment of leasehold interest in a building for identical leasehold in a different location qualifies under Section 1031 even though the interests are in the same property.

Revenue Ruling 77–297

This ruling reaffirms the standard ABC multiparty exchange procedure when the taxpayer and buyer enter into an agreement to sell that also provides for an exchange.

Revenue Ruling 77–337

Individual's prearranged transfer of shopping center, received as only asset from liquidation of individual's wholly owned corporation and immediately exchanged for like kind property held by unrelated party, doesn't qualify for nonrecognition of gain or loss under Section 1031.

Revenue Ruling 78–4

The exchange of remainder interests qualifies for tax-free treatment under certain conditions.

Revenue Ruling 78–135

Gain or loss realized on an exchange of general partnership interests does not qualify for nonrecognition.

Revenue Ruling 79–44

The provisions of Section 1031 apply to the transfer of interests in real property held by tenants in common.

Appendix A

INTERNAL REVENUE CODE, SECTION 1031

Section 1031 of the Internal Revenue Code of 1986

Exchange of Property Held for Productive Use or Investment

Section 1031(a)

(A) Nonrecognition of Gain or Loss from Exchanges Solely in Kind.

(1) In General. No gain or loss shall be recognized on the exchange of property held for productive use in a trade or business, or for investment, if such property is exchanged solely for property of like kind which is to be held either for productive use in a trade or business or for investment.

(2) Exception. This subsection shall not apply to any exchange of—

(a) stock in trade or other property held primarily for sale,
(b) stocks, bonds, or notes,
(c) other securities or evidences of indebtedness or interest,
(d) interests in a partnership,
(e) certificates of trust or beneficial interests, or
(f) choses in action.

(3) Requirement That Property Be Identified and That Exchange Be Completed Not More Than 180 Days After Transfer of Exchanged Property. For purposes of this subsection, any property received by the taxpayer shall be treated as property which is not "like kind" property if—

(a) such property is not identified as property to be received in the exchange *on or before* the day which is 45 days after the date on which the taxpayer transfers the property relinquished in the exchange, or
(b) such property is received after the earlier of—

(i) the day which is 180 days after the date on which the taxpayer transfers the property relinquished in the exchange, or
(ii) the due date (determined with regard to extension) for the transferor's return of

the tax imposed by this chapter for the taxable year in which the transfer of the relinquished property occurs.

Section 1031(b)

(B) Gain from Exchanges Not Solely in Kind. If an exchange would be within the provisions of Subsection (a), of Section 1035(a), of Section 1036(a), or of Section 1037(a), if it were not for the fact that the property received in exchange consists not only of property permitted by such provisions to be received without the recognition of gain, but also of other property or money, then the gain, if any, to the recipient, shall be recognized, but in an amount not in excess of the sum of such money and the fair market value of such other property.

Section 1031(c)

(C) Loss from Exchanges Not Solely in Kind. If an exchange would be within the provisions of Subsection (a), of Section 1035(a), of Section 1036(a), or of Section 1037(a), if it were not for the fact that the property received in exchange consists not only of property permitted by such provisions to be received without the recognition of gain or loss, but also of other property or money, then no loss from the exchange shall be recognized.

Section 1031(d)

(D) Basis. If property was acquired on an exchange described in this Section, Section 1035(a), Section 1036(a), or Section 1037(a), then the basis shall be the same as that of the property exchanged, decreased in the amount of any money received by the taxpayer and increased in the amount of gain or decreased in the amount of loss to the taxpayer that was recognized on such exchange. If the property so acquired consisted in part of the type of property permitted by this Section, Section 1035(a), Section 1036(a), or Section 1037(a), to be received without the recognition of gain or loss, and in part of other property, the basis provided in this Subsection shall be allocated between the properties (other than money) received, and for the purpose of the allocation there shall be assigned to such other property an amount equivalent to its fair market value at the date of the exchange. For purposes of this Section, Section 1035(a), and Section 1036(a), where as part of the consideration to the taxpayer another party to the exchange assumed a liability of the taxpayer or acquired from the taxpayer property subject to a liability, such assumption or acquisition (in the amount of the liability) shall be considered as money received by the taxpayer on the exchange.

Section 1031(e)

(E) Exchanges of Livestock of Different Sexes. For purposes of this section, livestock of different sexes are not property of a like kind.

Appendix B

SAMPLE FORMS

EXCHANGE WORK SHEET

BALANCING EQUITIES

	Transferred	Received	Transferred	Received	Transferred	Received
1. Market Value						
2. Existing Loans						
3. New Loans						
4. Equity (L.1 less L.2 & 3)						
5. Cash Boot						
6. Other (Boot) Property						
7. Loan Proceeds						
8. Balance						

NETTING CASH

9. Cash Received (L.5 + L.7)
   Or (Paid) (L.5)

10. Commissions

11. Transaction Costs

12. Total Capitalized Costs
    (L.10 + L.11)

13. Net Cash Received
    Or (Paid) (L.9 less L.12)

EXCHANGE TAX TREATMENT

COMPUTING REALIZED GAIN

1. Market Value Of Qualifying Property Received _____
2. Market Value Of Other (Boot) Property Received _____
3. Cash Received _____
4. Liabilities on Property Transferred _____
5. Total Consideration Received (L.1+2+3+4) _____
6. Adjusted Basis Of Qualifying Property Transferred _____
7. Adjusted Basis Of Other (Boot) Property Transferred _____
8. Cash Paid _____
9. Liabilities on Property Received _____
10. Total (L.6+7+8+9) _____
11. Gain Or (Loss) Realized (L.5 less L.10) _____

DETERMINING BOOT RECEIVED

12. Liabilities on Property Transferred _____
13. Liabilities on Property Received _____
14. Relief From Liabilities (L.12 less L.13) _____
15. Market Value of Other (Boot) Property Transferred _____
16. Difference (L.14 less L.15) _____
17. Cash Received _____
18. Total (L.16+L.17) _____
19. Cash Paid _____
20. Difference (L.18 less L.19) _____
21. Market Value of Other (Boot) Property Received _____
22. Total Boot Received (L.20+L.21) _____

RECOGNIZED GAIN (L.11 or L.22 whichever is smaller)

Loss attributable to boot property transferred only (L.15 less L.7) (_____)

EXCHANGE BASIS COMPUTATION

TRANSFERRING BASIS

1. Adjusted Basis of Qualifying Property Transferred ⎯⎯⎯⎯

2. Adjusted Basis of Other (Boot) Property Transferred ⎯⎯⎯⎯

3. Cash Paid ⎯⎯⎯⎯

4. Liabilities On All Property Received ⎯⎯⎯⎯

5. Total (L1+2+3+4) ⎯⎯⎯⎯

6. Cash Received ⎯⎯⎯⎯

7. Liabilities on All Property Transferred ⎯⎯⎯⎯

8. Total (L.6+L.7) ⎯⎯⎯⎯

9. Difference (L.5 less L.8) ⎯⎯⎯⎯

10. Gain Recognized ⎯⎯⎯⎯

11. Total (L.9+L.10) ⎯⎯⎯⎯

12. Loss Recognized on Other (Boot) Property Transferred ⎯⎯⎯⎯

13. Basis of All Property Received (L.11 less L12) ⎯⎯⎯⎯

ALLOCATING BASIS

14. Basis of All Property Received (L.13) ⎯⎯⎯⎯

15. Market Value of Other (Boot) Property Received* ⎯⎯⎯⎯

16. Basis Allocated to Qualifying Property (L.14 less L.15) ⎯⎯⎯⎯

17. Market Value of Improvements on Qualifying Property ⎯⎯⎯⎯

18. Market Value of Qualifying Property Received ⎯⎯⎯⎯

19. Percentage Allocated to Improvements (L.17÷L.18) ⎯⎯⎯⎯

20. Basis Allocated to Improvements on Qualifying Property (L.19×L.16) ⎯⎯⎯⎯

*The basis of the boot property received is the same as its market
 value as indicated on line 15.

Appendix C

IRS FORMS FOR REPORTING AN EXCHANGE

Form 4797. Supplemental Schedule of Gains and Losses.

1987

Department of the Treasury
Internal Revenue Service

Instructions for Form 4797

Gains and Losses From Sales or Exchanges of Assets Used in a Trade or Business and Involuntary Conversions

(And Computation of Recapture Amounts Under Sections 179 and 280F)

(Section references are to the Internal Revenue Code unless otherwise noted.)

Paperwork Reduction Act Notice.—We ask for this information to carry out the Internal Revenue laws of the United States. We need it to ensure that taxpayers are complying with these laws and to allow us to figure and collect the right amount of tax. You are required to give us this information.

Changes You Should Note

● Losses from passive activities are subject to the passive loss rules. See the instructions under **Passive Loss Limitations.**

● The holding period for section 1231 property acquired after 12-31-87 is more than 1 year.

Purpose of Form

Form 4797 is used to report the following:

● The sale or exchange of trade or business property, depreciable and amortizable property, oil, gas, and geothermal property, and section 126 property.

● The involuntary conversion (other than casualty or theft) of trade or business property and capital assets held in connection with a trade or business or a transaction entered into for profit.

● Disposition of other noncapital assets.

● Recapture of section 179 deductions for partners and S corporation shareholders from property dispositions by partnerships and S corporations.

● The computation of recapture amounts under sections 179 and 280F when the business use of section 179 or 280F property drops to 50% or less.

Special Rules

Exchange of "Like-Kind" Property.— Report the exchange of "like-kind" property on Schedule D or on Form 4797, whichever applies. Report the exchange even though no gain or loss is recognized when you exchange business or investment property for property of "like-kind." For exceptions, get Publication 544.

If you use Form 4797 to report the exchange, identify on line 2, column (a), the property you disposed of. Enter the date you acquired it in column (b), and the date you exchanged it in column (c). Write "like-kind exchange" in column (d). Enter the depreciation allowed (or allowable) in column (e) and the cost or other basis in column (f). Enter zero in columns (g) and (h). (See section 1031.)

Involuntary Conversion of Property.— You may not have to pay tax on a gain from an involuntary or compulsory conversion of property. Get Publication 544 for more information.

Passive Loss Limitations.—If you are reporting a loss on an asset used in a passive activity, use **Form 8582,** Passive Activity Loss Limitations, to see how much of the loss is allowed before entering it on Form 4797. Gains from assets used in a passive activity should be reported on Form 4797 but should also be used on Form 8582 to offset losses, if any, from other passive activities.

At-Risk Rules.—If you are reporting a loss on an asset used in an activity to which the at-risk rules apply or any part of your interest in an activity for which you are not at risk, see the instructions for **Form 6198,** Computation of Deductible Loss From an Activity Described in Section 465(c). Also get **Publication 925,** Passive Activity and At-Risk Rules. Losses from passive activities are first subject to the at-risk rules and then the passive activity rules. When a loss from a passive activity becomes deductible under the at-risk rules, Form 8582 should then be used to figure how much is deductible under the passive loss rules.

Transfer of Appreciated Property to Political Organizations.—Treat a transfer of property to a political organization as a sale of property on the date of transfer if the property's fair market value when transferred is more than your adjusted basis. Apply the ordinary income or capital gains provisions as if a sale actually occurred. (See section 84.)

Allocation of Purchase Price.—If you acquire assets which constitute a trade or business, the buyer and the seller must allocate the total purchase price using the "residual method." Get **Publication 544,** Sales and Other Dispositions of Assets, for more information.

Form 1099-A, Information Return for Acquisition or Abandonment of Secured Property.—If you receive a Form 1099-A from your lender, you may have gain or loss to report because of the acquisition or abandonment. Get Publication 544 for more information.

Examples of Items Reportable on This Form—Where To Make First Entry

Below are common examples of items reportable on this form. Columns (b) and (c) show where to make the first entry on Form 4797. (a)	Held 6 months or less (1 year or less if acquired after 12-31-87) (b)	Held more than 6 months (more than 1 year if acquired after 12-31-87) (c)
1 Depreciable trade or business property:		
a Sold or exchanged at a gain	Part II	Part III (1245)
b Sold or exchanged at a loss	Part II	Part I
2 Depreciable residential rental property:		
a Sold or exchanged at a gain	Part II	Part III (1250)
b Sold or exchanged at a loss.	Part II	Part I
3 Cattle and horses used in a trade or business for draft, breeding, dairy, or sporting purposes:		
a Held for less than 24 months from acquisition date, sold at a gain or loss	Part II	Part II
b Held for 24 months or more from acquisition date:		
(1) Sold at a gain.	Not applicable	Part III (1245)
(2) Sold at a loss.	Not applicable	Part I
(3) Raised cattle and horses sold at a gain	Not applicable	Part I
4 Livestock other than cattle and horses used in a trade or business for draft, breeding, dairy, or sporting purposes:		
a Held less than 12 months from acquisition date, sold at a gain or loss	Part II	Part II
b Held for 12 or more months from acquisition date:		
(1) Sold at a gain.	Part II	Part III (1245)
(2) Sold at a loss.	Part II	Part I
(3) Raised livestock sold at a gain	Part II	Part I
5 Farm land held less than 10 years upon which soil, water, and/or land clearing expenses were deducted:		
a Sold at a gain	Part II	Part III (1252)
b Sold at a loss	Part II	Part I
6 Disposition of cost-sharing payments described in section 126.	Part III (1255)	Part III (1255)

10/27/87 page 746,421

Form 4797

Department of the Treasury
Internal Revenue Service

Gains and Losses From Sales or Exchanges of Assets Used in a Trade or Business and Involuntary Conversions
(And Computation of Recapture Amounts Under Sections 179 and 280F)
► Attach to your tax return. See Separate Instructions

OMB No. 1545-0184

1985

Name(s) as shown on return | Identifying number

Part I Sales or Exchanges of Property Used in a Trade or Business and Involuntary Conversions From Other Than Casualty and Theft—Property Held More Than 6 months (More Than 1 Year if Acquired Before 6/23/84)

Notes:
- Use Form 4684 to report involuntary conversions from casualty and theft.
- If you sold property that you claimed investment credit on, get Form 4255 to see if you are liable for recapture of the credit.
- File Form 6198 if you are reporting a loss and have amounts invested in the activity for which you are not at risk. (See instructions under "Special Rules.")

(a) Description of property	(b) Date acquired (mo., day, yr.)	(c) Date sold (mo., day, yr.)	(d) Gross sales price	(e) Depreciation allowed (or allowable) since acquisition	(f) Cost or other basis, plus improvements and expense of sale	(g) LOSS ((f) minus the sum of (d) and (e))	(h) GAIN ((d) plus (e) minus (f))
1							
APARTMENT COMPLEX	6-1-82	5-30-88	LiKe KiNd exchANge	68,000	119,500	∅	∅

2 Gain, if any, from Form 4684, Section B, line 21 . . . .

3 Section 1231 gain from installment sales from Form 6252, line 22 or 30 . . . .

4 Gain, if any, on line 31 from other than casualty and theft . . . .

5 Add lines 1 through 4 in column (g) and column (h) . . . .

6 Combine columns (g) and (h) of line 5. Enter gain or (loss) here, and on the appropriate line as follows (Partnerships see the instructions for your line references.): . . . .

   a If line 6 is zero or a loss, enter the amount on line 9 below and skip lines 7 and 8. (S corporations, enter the loss on Schedule K (Form 1120S), line 5.)

   b If line 6 is a gain, see the instructions under Part I, **Nonrecaptured Net Section 1231 Losses.**

   Note: If you had no prior year section 1231 losses and line 6 is a gain, enter the gain from line 6 as a long-term capital gain on Schedule D.

7 Nonrecaptured net section 1231 losses from prior years. (See instructions.) . . . .

8 Subtract line 7 from line 6. If zero or less, enter zero . . . .

   a If line 8 is zero, enter the amount from line 6 on line 10 below.

   b If line 8 is more than zero, enter the amount from line 7 on line 10 below, and enter the amount from line 8 as a long-term capital gain on Schedule D. See specific instructions for line 8b.

Part II Ordinary Gains and Losses

(a) Description of property	(b) Date acquired (mo., day, yr.)	(c) Date sold (mo., day, yr.)	(d) Gross sales price	(e) Depreciation allowed (or allowable) since acquisition	(f) Cost or other basis, plus improvements and expense of sale	(g) LOSS ((f) minus the sum of (d) and (e))	(h) GAIN ((d) plus (e) minus (f))

9 Loss, if any, from line 6 . . . .

10 Gain, if any, from line 6 or amount from line 7 if applicable . . . .

11 Gain, if any, from line 30, Part III . . . .

12 Net gain or (loss) from Form 4684, Section B, lines 13 and 20a . . . .

13 Ordinary gain from installment sales from Form 6252, line 21 or 29 (Applies only to sales before 6/7/84) . .

14 Recapture of section 179 deduction on property dispositions by partners and S corporation shareholders (see instructions) . . . .

15 Other ordinary gains and losses (include property held 6 months or less (1 year or less if acquired before 6/23/84)):

16 Add lines 9 through 15 in column (g) and column (h) . . . .

17 Combine columns (g) and (h) of line 16. Enter gain or (loss) here, and on the appropriate line as follows: . . . .

   a For all except individual returns: Enter the gain or (loss) from line 17, on the return being filed. See instructions for Part II for specific line references.

   b For individual returns:

   (1) If the loss on line 9 includes a loss from Form 4684, Section B, Part II, column (b)(ii), enter that part of the loss here and on line 19 of Schedule A (Form 1040). Identify as from "Form 4797, line 17b(1)"

   (2) Redetermine the gain or (loss) on line 17, excluding the loss (if any) on line 17b(1). Enter here and on Form 1040, line 15.

For Paperwork Reduction Act Notice, see page 1 of separate Instructions.

Form **4797** (1985)

10/85 page 746,425

Form 4797 (1985)

Part III Gain From Disposition of Property Under Sections 1245, 1250, 1252, 1254, 1255

Skip section 1252 on line 26 and in the instructions, if you did not dispose of farmland, or if a partnership files this form.

18	Description of sections 1245, 1250, 1252, 1254, and 1255 property:	Date acquired (mo., day, yr.)	Date sold (mo., day, yr.)
A			
B			
C			
D			

Relate lines 18A through 18D to these columns ▶ ▶ ▶ ▶	Property A	Property B	Property C	Property D
19 Gross sales price				
20 Cost or other basis plus expense of sale				
21 Depreciation (or depletion) allowed (or allowable)				
22 Adjusted basis, subtract line 21 from line 20				
23 Total gain, subtract line 22 from line 19				
24 If section 1245 property:				
a Depreciation allowed (or allowable) (see instructions)				
b Enter smaller of line 23 or 24a				
25 If section 1250 property: (If straight line depreciation used, enter zero on line 25g unless you are a corporation subject to section 291.)				
a Additional depreciation after 12/31/75				
b Applicable percentage times the smaller of line 23 or line 25a (see instructions)				
c Subtract line 25a from line 23. If line 23 is not more than line 25a, skip lines 25d and 25e				
d Additional depreciation after 12/31/69 and before 1/1/76				
e Applicable percentage times the smaller of line 25c or 25d (see instructions)				
f Section 291 amount (For corporations only.)				
g Add lines 25b, 25e, and 25f				
26 If section 1252 property:				
a Soil, water, and land clearing expenses				
b Line 26a times applicable percentage (see instructions)				
c Enter smaller of line 23 or 26b				
27 If section 1254 property:				
a Intangible drilling and development costs deducted after 12/31/75 (see instructions)				
b Enter smaller of line 23 or 27a				
28 If section 1255 property:				
a Applicable percentage of payments excluded from income under section 126 (see instructions)				
b Enter the smaller of line 23 or 28a				

Summary of Part III Gains (Complete property columns A through D through line 28b before going to line 29)

29 Total gains for all properties (add columns A through D, line 23)

30 Add columns A through D, lines 24b, 25g, 26c, 27b, and 28b. Enter here and in Part II, line 11

31 Subtract line 30 from line 29. Enter the portion from casualty and theft on Form 4684, Section B, line 15; enter the portion from other than casualty and theft on Form 4797, Part I, line 4.

Part IV Complete This Part Only If You Elect Out of the Installment Method And Report a Note or Other Obligation at Less Than Full Face Value

☐ Check here if you elect out of the installment method.

Enter the face amount of the note or other obligation ▶

Enter the percentage of valuation of the note or other obligation ▶

Part V Computation of Recapture Amounts Under Sections 179 and 280F When Business Use Drops to 50% or Less (See Instructions for Part V.)

	(a) Section 179	(b) Section 280F
1 Section 179 expense deduction or section 280F recovery deductions		
2 Depreciation (see instructions)		
3 Recapture amount. (Subtract line 2 from line 1.)		

Bibliography

1. James Alderson 317 F. 2d 790 (1963)
2. Allegheny County Auto Mart, Inc. 208 F. 2d 693 (1953)
3. J. H. Baird Publishing Company 39 TC 608 (1962)
4. George M. Bernard 26 TCM 176 (1967)
5. Ethel Black 35 TC 90 (1960)
6. Bloomington Coca-Cola Bottling Co. 189 F. 2d 14 (1951)
7. Antone Borchard 24 TCM 1643 (1965)
8. Boise Cascade Corporation 74, 315 P-H Memo TC (1974)
9. E. R. Braley 14 BTA 1153 (1929)
10. Burkard Investment Co. 100 F. 2d 642 (1938)
11. June Pinson Carlton 385 F. 2d 238 (1967)
12. Century Electric Company 192 F. 2d 155 (1951)
13. Coastal Terminals, Inc. 320 F. 2d 333 (1963)
14. Coleman 180 F. 2d 758 (1950)
15. Leslie Q. Coupe 52 TC 394 (1969)
16. Emory K. Crenshaw 71–2 USTC 9698 (1971)
17. Crichton 122 F. 2d 181 (1941)
18. Detroit Egg Biscuit and Specialty Co. 9 BTA 1365 (1928)
19. Harry F. Estill 19 TCM 334 (1960)
20. Front Street, Inc. 65 TC 124 (1975)
21. Gregory V. Helvering 35–1 USTC 9043 (1935)
22. Brooks Griffin 49 TC 253 (1967)
23. W. D. Haden Co. 165 F. 2d 588 (1948)
24. Bernard Halpern 286 F. Supp 255 (1968)
25. Harr v. Maclaughlin 15 F. Supp 1004 (1936)
26. Leslie Co. 64 TC 23 (1968)
27. Frederick R. Horne 5 TC 250 (1945)
28. Loughborough Development Corp. 29 BTA 95 (1933)

29. W. A. Mays 246 F. Supp 375 (1965)
30. Mercantile Trust Co. 32 BTA 82 (1935)
31. Rollin E. Meyer, Jr. 58 TC 311 (1972)
32. Norman A. Miller 63–2 USTC 9606 (1963)
33. North Shore Bus Co., Inc. 143 F. 2d 114 (1944)
34. Regals Realty Co. 127 F. 2d 931 (1942)
35. John M. Rogers 44 TC 126 (1965)
36. Olson O. Sayre 163 F. Supp 495 (1958)
37. Juhl Smith 75, 153 P-H Memo TC (1975)
38. Bruce Starker 35 AFTR 2d 75–1550 (1975)
39. Trenton Cotton Oil Co. 147 F. 2d 33 (1945)
40. Union Pacific Railroad Company 32 BTA 383 (1935)

Revenue Rulings

41. Revenue Ruling 55–77
42. Revenue Ruling 55–749
43. Revenue Ruling 57–244
44. Revenue Ruling 57–365
45. Revenue Ruling 57–469
46. Revenue Ruling 59–229
47. Revenue Ruling 61–119
48. Revenue Ruling 65–155
49. Revenue Ruling 66–209
50. Revenue Ruling 68–36
51. Revenue Ruling 68–186
52. Revenue Ruling 68–331
53. Revenue Ruling 68–363
54. Revenue Ruling 72–151
55. Revenue Ruling 72–456
56. Revenue Ruling 72–515
57. Revenue Ruling 72–601
58. Revenue Ruling 73–476
59. Revenue Ruling 74–7
60. Revenue Ruling 75–291
61. Revenue Ruling 75–292

Index

A

ABC exchange, 99, 148
ACB exchange, 99, 149, 163, 164
Addendum to Agreement, delayed exchanges, 189–91
Adjusted basis, 48
Advance payments deposit, as financing method, 227
Agents
  attorney-as-agent for buyer, 104–6
  taxpayer as buyer's agent, 103
James Alderson et al. v. Commissioner, 275
Allegheny County Auto Mart, Inc. v. Commissioner, 274
Allen, Joyce M., 270
Allocation trap, disqualification, 69–70
Amortization, long-term, as financing method, 230
Anderson, A. L., 270
Annuity, acquisition by, 242–43
Appreciation of property, increasing return-on-equity and, 145–46
Assignment and Agreement, delayed exchanges, 187–89
Assignments, of payments, 266
Assumption of mortgage, for no cash acquisition, 218, 219
Attorneys
  attorney-as-agent for buyer, 104–6
  power of attorney, 105–6
Automatic discount, as financing method, 236–37
Automatic rolling option, as acquisition method, 259

B

J.H. Baird Publishing Company v. Commission, 275
Balloon mortgage, as financing method, 231
Balloon payment
  Christmas season balloon, 237–38
  as financing method, 237–38
  three-year interest only, as financing method, 240
Bargain sale, as financing method, 244–45
Barker, Earlene T., 270
Basis, 48
  adjusted basis, 48

  allocating basis, 54
  determination of, 59, 62
  exchange basis computation, 142, 144
  increase in, 140–41
  land transferred to improved property, 141, 143
  reallocation of, 143
  transferring, rules for, 59, 62
Behrens, Frederick W., 270
George M. Bernard et al. v. Commissioner, 277
Bezdjian, G. S., 270
Biggs, Franklin B., 270
Ethel Black v. Commissioner, 274
Blanket mortgage, as financing method, 228–29
Bloomington Coca-Cola Bottling Co. v. Commissioner, 276
Boise Cascade Corporation and Affiliated Corporations, 276
Bolker, Joseph R., 270
Bond lease, as acquisition method, 249–50
Boot, 50
  equity balancing, 20
  forms of, 13, 50
  gain calculation and, 51, 54
  loss on property transferred, 54, 57
  mortgage boot, 13, 50
  offsetting mortgage relief with, 154–55
Antone Borchard v. Commissioner, 275
E.R. Braley v. Commissioner, 273
Brauer, Glenda, 271
Bridge loan, as financing method, 232
Broker loan
  financing source, 264
  for no cash acquisition, 220
Broker's fees, tax treatment, 68–69
Broker's role, two-party exchanges, 17
Builder's bailout, as financing method, 233–34
Bureau of Land Management, Forest Service exchanges, 159
Burkard Investment Co. v. United States, 273
Business exchange, 167–68
Buy-back agreement, 263
Buy-back option
  exchange with, 158
  as financing method, 238
Buy-sell agreement, partnerships, 263

C

June Pinson Carlton et al. v. United States of America, 277
Cash
  gain calculation and, 51
  taxable transactions, circumstances related to, 108
Cash and acquisition. (*See* Financing methods; no cash acquisition)
Cash take-out
  in exchange agreement, 82, 97
  exchange for, 149, 150
Century Electric co. v. Commissioner, 274
Certificate of deposit delivery, as financing method, 225–26
Christmas season balloon, 237–38
Click, Dollie H., 271
Closing credits, use of, for no cash acquisition, 210–11
Closing of exchange
  close of escrow, 124
  closing statements, 123–24
  exchange worksheet, 126, 129, 134
  multiparty exchanges, 125, 133
  title company and, 133
  title company documents, 127–28, 130–32, 135–37
  two-party exchanges, 124–25
Coastal Terminals, Inc. v. United States of America, 275
Coleman v. Commissioner, 273
Collateralizing
  collateral assignment, as financing method, 226
  collateral security agreements, for no cash acquisition, 216
  as financing method, 242
Commissioner of Internal Revenue v. Crichton, 273
Commissions
  broker split, 119–21
  as down payment, for no cash acquisition, 213
  fee agreements, 119
  fee versus percentage commission, 116, 119
  guidelines to getting paid, 114
Commitment letter, as financing method, 232
Compensating balances, as financing method, 227
Competition, noncompetition agreement, 265
Condominiums, lease-condo, 250
Consolidation of assets, advantages of, 148
Construction of building, for exchange, 170
Constructive receipt of cash, disqualification, 71
Contingent price sale, as financing method, 234
Continuing option, as acquisition method, 259
Corporations
  bond lease, 249–50
  real estate acquisition
    secured corporate note, 222
    stock issued for, 221

real estate corporations, acquisition from, 246–47
  sale lease-back, 254–55
Co-signers
  for no cash acquisition, 220
  seller as co-signer, 265
Leslie Q. Coupe v. Commissioner, 276
Credit certificate, for no cash acquisition, 221–22
Credit union loan, for no cash acquisition, 213
Emory K. Crenshaw v. United States of America, 274

D

D'Onofrio, Antonio, 271
Debt service
  exchange for lower debt service property, 146–47
  moratorium on, as financing method, 236
Deeds, transfer methods, 164
Delayed exchanges, 179–82
  Addendum to Agreement, 189–91
  Assignment and Agreement, 187–89
  designation letter, 186, 189
  documentation, 181, 189
  escrow, 183–85
  escrow agent, notification about property, 186–87
  escrow agreement, 183–85, 189
  exchange addendum, 181–82, 189
  new guidelines, 179–80
  property designation, 185–86
  purchase agreement, 187–89
  purchase offer, amending, 189–91
  reverse delayed exchange, 191–92
  structure of, 180
Designation letter, delayed exchanges, 186, 189
Detroit Egg Biscuit and Specialty Co. v. Commissioner, 273
Developers
  builder's bailout, 233–34
  land sale lease-back, 252–53
  mortgage out, 205–6
Diamonds pledge, as financing method, 245
Discounts
  automatic discount, 236–37
  buying paper at discount, 265–66
  discount buy-back, 262
  exchanged for cash, 263
Disqualification traps
  after the exchange, 70
  agreement, not signing, 70
  allocation trap, 69–70
  constructive receipt of cash, 71
  loan relief trap, 71
  written agreements, value of, 71
Documentation
  assignment of purchase agreement, 175
  closing statements, 123–24

delayed exchanges, 181, 189
written agreements, value of, 71
Down payment. (*See* No cash acquisitions)

E

Economic cycles, effect on real estate, 200–201
Effort equity, for no cash acquisition, 208–9
Effort option, as acquisition method, 258
18–month loan, as financing method, 231
Employees, executive incentive plan, 218–19
Employer influence, as financing method, 229
Equal partnership exchange, 166–67
Equity balancing
    with boot, 20
    flexible approach, 21–22
    like-kind exchanges, 156
    multiparty exchanges, 34
    multiple asset exchanges, 22–24
    refinancing, 37, 39, 42, 45
    two-party exchanges, 18
Equity-kicker, as financing method, 225
Equity profit, conserving, 3–4, 7–8
Escrow
    agreement in delayed exchanges, 183–85, 189
    close of escrow, 124
    converting sale to exchange, 176–78
    delayed exchanges, 183–85
    escrowing down payment, 265
    main concern during, 133
    multiparty exchanges, 39, 41
    refinancing through, 26–27
Harry F. Estill v. Commissioner, 277
Exchange addendum, delayed exchanges, 181–82,
    189
Exchange agreements
    attorney-as-agent for buyer, 104–6
    example agreements, 77–78, 80–81, 83–84, 87–96
    exchange worksheet, 86
    extension of agreement, 108–9
    as flexible tool, 73, 97, 110
    intent versus reality, 74–75
    multiparty agreements, 82–103
    option, use of, 104
    purposes of, 74
    sale viewed as exchange, 75
    taxpayer as agent for buyer, 103–4
    two-party agreements, 75–82
    when property not located, 106, 108
Exchange leaseback, applications, 158
Exchange methods
    acquiring property by loan, 169
    boot, 154–55
    business exchange, 167–68
    construction of building, for exchange, 170
    equal partnership exchange, 166–67
    exchange converted to sale, 161
    exchange leaseback, 158

exchange with buy-back option, 158
flight capital exchange, 160
Forest Service exchanges, 159
free and clear land, 159
General Services Administration exchanges, 160
increasing loan balance, 155–56
lease agreement, use of, 169–70
leasehold interests exchange, 165
like kind exchanges, 156
mineral rights exchange, 164–65
multiparty exchanges, 163–64, 166
negative cash flow, offsetting, 156–57
partial interests exchange, 167
personal notes, 153–54
real estate owned exchange, 157–58
recapture elimination, 160–61
reducing loan balance, 154
unowned property exchange, 168
water rights exchange, 165
Exchanges
    advantages of 6–7
        cash takeout, 149
        consolidation of assets, 148
        no cash exchange, 149
        personal benefits, 147, 150–51
        property acquired for future sale, 150
        return-on-equity increases, 143–47
        tax-savings, 140–43
    as business decision, 8–9
    delayed exchanges, 179–82
    equity profit, conserving, 3–4, 7–8
    logic of, 9–10
    multiparty exchanges, 29–46
    participants involved, 5–6
    Section 1031, Internal Revenue Code, 10–15
    steps in, 5
    tax-free exchanges, 12–15
    two-party exchanges, 17–27
Executive incentive plan, for no cash acquisition,
    218–19
Extension, exchange agreements, 108–9

F

Family loan, for no cash acquisition, 214
Farms, 70
    mineral rights exchange, 164–65
Financing companies
    loan as financing method, 232
    second mortgage loans, 261
Five year loan, as financing method, 231
Flexibility, importance of, 21–22, 27
Flight capital exchange, 160
Foreign property, flight capital exchange, 160
Forest Service exchanges, 159
Front Street, Inc., v. Commissioner, 276
Future income, for no cash acquisition, 222
Future profits, for no cash acquisition, 210

G

Gain, 48–50
  calculating when boot received, 51, 54
  calculating when cash received, 51
  realized gain, 48–49
  recognized gain, 48–49
Garcia, Phillip M., 271
General Services Administration exchanges, 160
Gibson, Stuart L., 271
Godine, James, Jr., 271

H

W.D. Haden Co. v. Commissioner, 275
Bernard Halpern v. United States of America, 277
Harr, Secretary of Banking of the Commonwealth of Pennsylvania v. McLaughlin, 274
"Held primarily for sale" trap, 12
Holding period, tax treatment, 68
Home equity capital, for acquisition, 207

I

Improvement costs, as financing method, 236
Increased payment option, as acquisition method, 259–60
Inheritance, note secured by, 264
Installment purchase, 262–63
  for no cash acquisition, 217–18
Institutional financing
  advance payments deposit, 227
  amortization, long-term, 230
  balloon mortgage, 231
  blanket mortgage, 228–29
  bridge loan, 232
  Certificate of deposit delivery, 225–26
  collateral assignment, 226
  commitment letter, 232
  compensating balances, 227
  18–month loan, 231
  employer influence, 229
  equity-kicker, 225
  finance company loan, 232
  five year loan, 231
  joint ventures 229–30
  letter of credit, 226–27
  negative pledge, 226
  open end mortgage, 224
  participation, 229
  repossessed property, 225
  sale buy-back, 224–25
  savings account transfer, 228
  seller banking at buyers bank, 228
  standby commitment, 230
  stock offering, purchase of, 230
  wraparound mortgage, 224
Insurance policy loan, for no cash acquisition, 220
Interest
  adding to principal, 239–40
  prepaid, as down payment, 244
  reversing interest, 244
Interest only payment, as financing method, 237
Interest option, as acquisition method, 258
Interest rates
  high, strategy for, 265
  lower rate/higher price, 245–46
  reduce constant/increase interest, 239
  reduce interest/increase constant, 238
Investment property, use of term, 11
Irrevocable trust, as security, 264

J

Joint ventures
  as financing method, 229–30
  with notes, 263

K

Koch, Carl E., 271

L

Land
  exchange leaseback, 158
  exchange strategy, 147
  free and clear, in exchange, 159
  land cost option, 260
  land sale leaseback, 252–53
  leased land pyramid, 254
  lender land lease, 254
  selling at loss/leasing land, 255
  transfer to improved property, 141, 143
Land Dynamics, 271
Land sale lease-back
  lease cash-out, 252–53
  for no cash acquisition, 217
Lease agreement, to provide possession before closing, 169–70
Lease-condo, as acquisition method, 250
Lease down payment, for no cash acquisition, 217
Leasehold interests exchange, 165
Leasing
  benefits of, 249
  bond lease, 249–50
  land sale leaseback, 252–53
  lease cash-out, 252
  lease-condo, 250
  leased land pyramid, 254
  lender land lease, 254
  management leaseback, 251
  master lease, 251
  packaging leases for sell out, 253
  possession before closing and, 255
  sale leaseback as investment opportunity, 254–55
  sandwich lease, 250–51
  selling at loss/leasing land, 255

success factors, 253
vacancies leaseback, 252
Lee, E. C., 272
Leslie Co. v. Commissioner, 275
Letter of credit, as financing method, 226–27 258–59
Liabilities
received and transferred, 57, 59
relief from, 57
tax treatment, 50
Liability, avoiding, multiparty exchanges, 36
Like-kind exchanges
equity balancing 156
tax-free, 12–13
Listing agreement
example agreement, 115–16, 117–18
exchange only listing, 114–15
fee agreements, 119
fee versus percentage commission, 116, 119
preprinted agreement, 116
Loan payments, variation based on occupancy, as
financing method, 235–36
Loan relief, 50
loan relief trap, 71
prevention, 59
Loans
for acquiring exchange property, 169
soft paper, 215
Loan value, exchange for, 146
Loughborough Development Corp. v. Commissioner,
273

M

Magneson, Norman J., 272
Management fees for services, as financing method,
246
Management leaseback, as acquisition method, 251
Mars, C. W., 272
Master lease, as acquisition method, 251
W. A. Mays v. District Director of Internal Revenue,
276
Meadows, Byron Wayne, 272
Memorandum of exchange, 71
Rollin E. Meyer, Jr., v. Commissioner, 274
Milbrew, Inc., 272
Norman A. Miller v. United States of America, 274
Mineral rights exchange, 164–65
Mortgage out, for no cash acquisition, 205–6
Mortgage relief
increasing loan on acquired property, 155–56
offsetting with boot, 154–55
paying down loan, 154
Mortgages. (*See* specific types)
Multiparty agreements
ABC exchange, 99
ACB exchange, 99
adaptation to transaction, 100–101

derived from two-party agreements, 85–86, 97
example agreements, 102, 107, 110–12
mapping exchange, 85–86
option, 101, 104
structure of, 99–100
uncooperative buyer and, 101
writing of, 101
Multiparty exchanges
ABC exchange, 99 148, 163
ACB exchange, 99 149, 163, 164
avoiding right to receive cash, 33–34
and buyer for property, 32
CBA multiple exchange, 42
closing exchange, 125, 133
delayed exchange, 179–82
derived from sale, 171–78
assigning purchase agreement, 174–75
documentation of assignment, 175
escrow instructions, 176–78
liability of buyer, 178
purchase agreement addendums, 172–74
steps in process, 175
transitional stage, 171–72
derived from two-party exchanges, 85–86, 97, 166
equity balancing, 34
refinancing, 37, 39, 42, 45
escrow, purchase out of, 39, 41
exchange worksheet, 35, 38, 40, 43–44
liability, avoiding, 36
methods for, 163–64, 166
offers/counteroffers, 32–33
principles of, 30–31
refinancing, 37, 42
reverse delayed exchange, 191–92
as solution to acquisition problems, 148
standard methods, 29–30
structure of, 41, 45
from taxpayer's viewpoint, 31
tax treatment 62, 65
title insurance, 36–37
title transfer, 33
and unowned property, 168
Multiple asset exchanges, 22–24
Multiple notes/one mortgage, for no cash
acquisition, 222
Multiple parcels, one transaction, 24

N

Negative cash flow, offsetting in exchange, 156–57
Negative pledge, as financing method, 226
Netting, 50–51
No cash acquisitions
assumption of mortgage, 218, 219
borrow against paper, 209
broker as lender, 220
closing credits, use of, 210–11
collateral security agreements, 216

No cash acquisitions (*cont.*)
 commission as down payment, 213
 corporate note, 222
 co-signer, 220
 creating paper, 207
 credit certificate, 221–22
 credit union loan, 213
 effort equity, 208–9
 executive incentive plan, 218–19
 family loan, 214
 first and second mortgages, use of, 215–16
 future income pledge, 222
 future profits, use of, 210
 home equity capital, 207
 installment down payment, 217–18
 insurance policy loan, 220
 land sale lease-back, 217
 lease down payment, 217
 mortgage out, 205–6
 multiple notes/one mortgage, 222
 note partnerships, 212
 performance second, 219–20
 private loan, 212–13
 professional services barter, 208
 real estate equity, 214
 rents, assignment of, 211
 repair partnerships, 211–12
 salary advance, 221
 second mortgage held by seller, 206
 seller pays buyer, 209–10
 signature loan, 221
 soft paper, 215
 stock issued from corporation, 221
 stock traded at purchase price, 221
 trust, borrowing against, 216–17
Noncompetition agreement, 265
Note partnerships, for no cash acquisition, 212

O

Occupancy, loan payments based on, 235–36
Offers/counteroffers, multiparty exchanges, 32–33
Offsetting, 50
 benefits, 57, 59
 calculations, 59
Open end mortgage, as financing method, 224
Options
 advantages/disadvantages of, 104
 automatic rolling option, 259
 benefits of, 257
 continuing option, 259
 effort option, 258
 exchange agreements, 104
 increased payment option, 259–60
 interest option, 258
 land cost option, 260
 letter of credit option, 258–59
 multiparty agreements, 101, 104
 real estate as option, 260
 structure of, 257
Overpaying the asking price, as financing method, 234

P

Packaging leases for sell out, lease cash-out, 253
Partial interests exchange, 167
Participation, as financing method, 229
Partnerships, buy-sell agreement, 263
Performance second, for no cash acquisition, 219–20
Personal benefits of exchange, 147, 150–51
Personal note
 creating paper, 207
 use of, 153–54
Points, paid by buyer, 246
Prepaid interest, as down payment, 244
Price reduction/payment of points, as financing method, 246
Private financing
 automatic discount, 236–37
 balloon payment, 237–38
  three-year interest only, 240
 bargain sale, 244–45
 builder's bailout, 233–34
 buy-back option, 238
 collateralizing, 242
 contingent price sale, 234
 debt service, moratorium on, 236
 diamonds pledge, 245
 improvement costs, as return of down payment, 236
 interest added to principal, 239–40
 interest only payment, 237
 loan payments, variation based on occupancy, 235–36
 lower interest/higher price, 245–46
 management fees for services, 246
 overpaying the asking price, 234
 prepaid interest as down payment, 244
 price reduction/payment of points, 246
 private insurance annuity, 242–43
 purchase money mortgage, 241
 real estate contract, 241
 real estate corporation acquisitions, 246–47
 reduce constant/increase interest, 239
 reduce interest/increase constant, 238
 remainder interest purchase, 243
 reversing interest, 244
 sale lease-back, 239
 second mortgage, 242
 seller as short-term lender, 235
 subordination
  for cash, 240–41
  to construction financing, 240
 trust deed, carry back, 242

walking the mortgage, 243–44
wraparound mortgage, 235
Private insurance annuity, as financing method, 242–43
Private loan, for no cash acquisition, 212–13
Productive use, use of term, 11
Professional services barter, for no cash acquisition, 208
Property designation, delayed exchanges, 185–86
Purchase agreement
  addendums, 172–74
  assignment of, 103, 74–75
  delayed exchanges, 187–89
  documentation of assignments, 175
  right to assignment, 174
Purchase money mortgage, as financing method, 141
Purchase offer
  amending, delayed exchanges, 189–91
  exchange agreement derived from, 76, 79
Pyramiding
  increasing return-on-equity and, 145
  leased land pyramid, 254
  process of, 145
  two-party exchanges, 20–21

R

Real estate
  scope of, 27
  usage categories, 10–11
Real estate acquisition
  no cash acquisitions, 205–22
  real estate cycles, 197–203
Real estate as option, acquisition method, 260
Real estate contract, as financing method, 141
Real estate corporation acquisitions, as financing method, 246–47
Real estate cycles, 197–203
  activity stages in, 203
  debt expansions in, 198–99
  economic cycles and, 200–201
  employment opportunity and, 197–98
  investor expectations and, 201
  1970s, 198
  1980s, 199–200
  speculative patterns, 201–2
  supply-demand factors, 197
  timing acquisitions, 202–3
Real estate equity, for no cash acquisition, 214
Real estate financing. (*See also* specific topics)
  institutional financing, 224–32
  leasing, 249–56
  options, 257–60
  private financing, 233–47
Real estate owned
  exchange of, 157–58
  repossessed property, 225

Realized gain, 48–49
Real property, definition, 12
Recapture
  avoiding, 65, 68
  elimination of, 160–61
Recognized gain, 48–49
Refinancing, 37, 42
  during acquisition, 264
  benefits of, 42, 45
  contingency in agreement, 109–10
  equity balancing, 37, 39, 42, 45
  home equity capital, 207–8
  multiparty exchanges, 37, 39, 42, 45
  seller holds second mortgage, 206
  through escrow, 26–27
Regals Realty Co. v. Commissioner, 273
Release clause, 266
Remainder interest purchase, as financing method, 243
Rents, assignment of, for no cash acquisition, 211
Repair partnerships, for no cash acquisition, 211–12
Repossessed property, acquisition of 157–58, 225
Residence, tax-free treatment, 11
Return-on-equity, increasing 143–47
  exchange for income property, 147
  exchange for loan value, 146
  lower debt service property, 146–47
  pyramiding, 145
  rapid appreciation and, 145–46
Revenue rulings, listing of, 277–80
Reverse delayed exchange, 191–92
  problems of, 191–92
Reverse exchanges, 270
Reversing interest, 264
  as financing method, 244
John M. Rogers v. Commissioner, 277
Rutland, Hubert, 276

S

Salary advance, for no cash acquisition, 221
Sale buy-back, as financing method, 224–25
Sale lease-back, as financing method, 239
Sale of property
  after exchange, 150
  exchange converted to sale, 161
  exchange derived from, 171–78
    assigning purchase agreement, 174–75
    documentation of assignment, 175
    escrow instructions, 176–78
    liability of buyer, 178
    purchase agreement addendums, 172–74
    steps in process, 175
    transitional stage, 171–72
Sales contract, as financing method, 241
Sandwich lease, as acquisition method, 250–51
Savings account transfer, as financing method, 228
Olson O. Sayre v. United States of America, 273

Second mortgage
    as financing method 215–216, 242 261
    held by seller, for no cash acquisition, 206
Section 1031. (*See also* Tax treatment)
    Appendix B, 283–84
    exception to gain/loss reporting, 48
    "held primarily for sale" trap, 12
    property of like-kind, 12–13
    property qualified under, 10–11
Section 1034
    allocation trap, 70
    sale of residence, tax-free, 10
Section 1245, property transfers, 65
Section 1250, recapture liability, 65
Seller as co-signer, 265
Seller pays buyer, for no cash acquisition, 209–10
Signature loan, for no cash acquisition, 221
Signatures, written agreements, 70
Juhl Smith v. Commissioner, 274
Soft paper, for no cash acquisition, 215
Speculative patterns, 201–2
Standby commitment, as financing method, 230
Bruce Starker v. United States of America, 276, 277
Stock
    issued from corporation, for no cash acquisition,
        221
    purchase of, as financing method, 230
    traded at purchase price, for no cash acquisition,
        221
Subordination
    for cash, 240–41
    to construction financing, 240
    construction financing and, 264
Swaim, Emsy H., 272
Sweat equity, 208–9, 236
Syndication of loan, participation, 229

T

Taxable transactions, circumstances related to, 108
Tax-free exchanges
    basis
        exchange basis computation, 142, 144
        increase in, 140–41
        land transferred to improved property, 141, 143
        reallocation of, 143
    like-kind property, 12–13
    long-range benefits, 140
    residence, 11
    structure of, 13–15
Tax Reform Act of 1986, effect on real estate, 201
Tax treatment
    basis, 48
        allocating basis, 54
        determination of, 59, 62
    boot, 50
    broker's fees, 68–69
    calculation examples, 52–53, 58, 60–61, 66

documentation, 71
exchange basis computation example, 55–56, 63–
    64, 67
gain, 48–50
    calculating when boot received, 51, 54
    calculating when cash received, 51
hidden disqualification traps, 69–71
holding period, 68
liabilities
    offsetting, 57, 59
    relief from liabilities, 57
loan relief, prevention, 59
lose on boot property transferred, 54, 57
to maximize benefits, 71–72
multiparty exchange, 62, 65
netting, 50–51
offsetting, 50
    benefits, 57, 59
    calculations, 59
recapture, avoiding, 65, 68
revenue rulings, listing of, 277–80
terminology, importance of, 47–48
transaction costs, 69
Title company
    and closing, 133
    documents of, 127–28, 130–32, 135–37
Title insurance, multiparty exchanges, 36–37
Title transfer, multiparty exchanges, 33
Transaction costs, tax treatment, 69
Trust, borrowing against, for no cash acquisition,
    216–17
Trust deed, carry back, as financing method, 242
Two-party agreements, 75–82
    basic elements, 75–76
    cash take-out in, 82, 97
    changing purchase offer to, 76, 79
    general phrasing, 76
    obligation to sell, inclusion of, 79, 82
    turned into multiple transaction, 85–86, 97
Two-party exchanges
    broker's role, 17
    closing exchange, 124–25
    equity balancing, 18
        flexible approach, 21–22
        multiple asset exchanges, 22–24
    free and clear property of equal value, 27–28
    hidden opportunities in, 27
    multiple parcels, one transaction, 24
    pyramiding, 20–21
    refinancing through escrow, 26–27
    restructuring deal, 18, 25
    turned into multiparty exchanges, 85–86, 97, 166
    unequal values balanced with boot, 20

U

Unowned property exchange, 168

V

Vacancies leaseback
  as acquisition method, 252
  lease cash-out, 252
Von Muff, Karl G., 272

W

Wagensen, Fred S., 272
Walking the mortgage, as financing method, 243–
  44

Water rights exchange, 165
Wraparound mortgage
  as financing method, 224, 235
  private, 235
Written agreements, value of, 71

Y

Young, R. G., 272